AMERICAN IMPERIALISM

in the Image of Peer Gynt:

Memoirs of a Professor-

Bureaucrat

Published with assistance from the Roger E. Joseph
Memorial Fund for greater understanding of public affairs,
a cause in which Roger Joseph believed

AMERICAN IMPERIALISM
In the Image of
Peer Gynt

★★★★★★★★★★★★★★★★★★★★★★★★

Memoirs of a Professor-
Bureaucrat

By

E. A. J. Johnson

> *"To the extent that we
> are all brothers in old Peer Gynt, Ibsen's
> image of the human condition takes its place
> as one of the invaluable reference points in
> mapping the present world."*
> Rolf Fjelde

UNIVERSITY OF MINNESOTA PRESS   MINNEAPOLIS

Published in Great Britain, India, and Pakistan by
the Oxford University Press, London, Bombay and
Karachi, and in Canada by the Copp Clark Publishing
Co. Limited, Toronto.

Library of Congress Catalog Card Number: 79-152300
ISBN 0-8166-0608-0

TO

MY SON

WITH

AFFECTION AND ADMIRATION

ACKNOWLEDGMENTS

BECAUSE memory often distorts reality, I have, wherever possible, had chapters of these memoirs read by people who partially at least shared my experiences. My sister Irma Robison detected some minor errors in my boyhood recollections, and for her corrections I offer my thanks. Esther Peterson Peel, who started in the first grade when I did in 1906 and was my classmate for the next twelve years, read chapter 3 on "The Village." Eleanor Poland, a graduate student at Radcliffe when I was at Harvard, very graciously reviewed chapter 5. That prolific Columbia professor Shepard Clough, who, as associate editor, helped me launch the *Journal of Economic History*, read and improved a portion of chapter 6. Three of my wartime associates, John W. Harriman, E. Ross Jenney, and John Enrietto, have read chapter 7, and their respective emendations have been most helpful. Jenney and Enrietto, who were with me in Norway, have made many suggestions for improving chapter 8. Colonel George Burr, my deputy when I served as director of the Korean Department of Commerce, proposed constructive revisions in chapters 10 and 11; so did Dr. Wilhelm Anderson, who headed our Korean National Economic Board and later became deputy chief of our ECA mission to Korea. I am deeply indebted to Burr and Anderson for their careful reading of these chapters and for their excellent suggestions. Victor Morgan, that versatile and conscientious civil servant who supervised our technical assistance program in Yugoslavia and later served his country in Laos, Egypt, Nepal, and Indonesia, examined chapter 15 and made helpful suggestions. Priscilla Mason graciously reviewed chapters 17 and 18, giving me the benefit of her long association with the School of Advanced International Studies. Ernest K. Lindley read my account of the Cosmos Club civil rights episode and offered me his wise counsel. Quite a number of people have shared with me their reactions to chapter 20 since these "Reflections on a Drop of Dew" were published in the 1969 summer number of the *SAIS Review* and were only slightly altered for inclusion in this volume. I am beholden to all these helpful critics as well as to Lisa Stevens for her translation of General Böhme's announcement of the surrender of the German forces in Norway, and to Professor Folke Dovring who made important improvements in chapter 2, correcting errors and misinterpretations concerning Swedish agrarian history, and who provided a transliteration of the runes on the Viking stone masoned into the tower of Landeryd church which I describe in that chapter. I am deeply indebted to the University of Minnesota Press for constructive and most helpful criticism.

But although I am most grateful to my colleagues, relatives, and friends for their efforts to improve my essays, I must very explicitly absolve them from any responsibility for my frank and sometimes bitter appraisals. After all, these are my memoirs.

E. A. J. Johnson

Barnaby Woods
Washington, D.C.
June 1970

CONTENTS

★★★★★★★★★★

CONTENTS

AMERICAN IMPERIALISM

in the Image of Peer Gynt:

Memoirs of a Professor-

Bureaucrat

1

THE BUTTON-MAKER'S MOLD

WHOSOEVER has read Ibsen's *Peer Gynt* must have found Peer's fruitless effort to dissuade the button-molder from casting his wizened little soul into a lead button the most poignant passage in that timeless human tragedy. For Peer felt he deserved something far more dramatic either as reward for his virtuous acts or as punishment for his sins. Smarting from the indignity of the button-molder's undisguised contempt, he protests:

> "But, listen, this is a rotten trick!
> I know I deserve a better shake —
> I'm not as bad as maybe you think —
> I've done lots of good on earth; to be frank,
> My offenses, at worst, have all been minor —
> I could never be called a major sinner."

To which the button-molder replies,

> "But, my friend, that precisely is your offense.
> You aren't a sinner in the larger sense;
> That's why you're let off the fiery griddle
> And go, like the rest, in the casting ladle." [1]

Why did these words wound Peer so sharply? Because in his heart he knew that he was mostly counterfeit, an opportunist who had cut corners, followed fashions, lived by making compromises, willingly accepting custom and habits "rather than making the painful struggle to realize himself in truth and freedom." [2] Lacking true integrity and basically short on

---

[1] Henrik Ibsen, *Peer Gynt: A Dramatic Poem*, a new translation with a foreword by Rolf Fjelde (New York: Signet Classics, New American Library, 1964), pp. 214–215.

[2] The quotations in this paragraph and the next are from ibid., Fjelde's foreword, pp. xv, xiii, xx, xxi, xxiii.

courage, Peer became one of the "windy exponents of the promise for the deed," a tragic "nonheroic hero" who lives, unfortunately, in all of us, and who has become "the pilot model of the hollow man of our own time rendered perplexed and anxious by problems of identity and direction."

Not that Peer had been troubled! His fault stemmed not from unsureness but from his impulsive overconfidence. As a boy, when no one invited him to a nearby fancy wedding, he went unbidden, and carried off the bride into the woods, far away from her intended husband. As a man, he made a fortune by selling both African slaves and sacerdotal artifacts thus turning "the essence of the human and the divine into commodities." Yet there was nothing devious about Peer Gynt; he found ample justification for his every decision, acted generously toward people, even toward those who deceived and cheated him: "This chronic liar whose life blows away like the desert wind, this clump of nothing," was "amazingly sincere." That was precisely the reason Peer could not understand why his virtuous acts did not merit some reward or, failing that, why his sins did not deserve punishment. In the end he simply ran away from the buttonmolder and sought refuge in the arms of Solveig, the poor blind girl he had earlier deserted, the only one who believed his ever-plausible words. He fled from the button-molder because he could not endure to have his ego "shrunk to scale."

As I look back over my graciously allotted three score and ten, viewing not just my own life but that of my life-stream fellows, I cannot escape the unpleasant conclusion that my generation has been peculiarly tainted with Gyntian weaknesses. Like Peer, who wandered all over the earth, "trying to discover what it is he ought to be or do," we have assumed that our presence, our actions, and our presumed good intentions would benefit mankind and earn us a claim on eternal praise and honor. Of course if it could be shown that we truly had sinned, as we would be prepared to deny, then it would be fair that we should be properly punished. Yet as we meet the button-molder, one by one, each of us, I fear, will face Peer Gynt's fate. Our shriveled little souls will go into the button-molder's casting ladle, and we shall be remembered in the same indifferent way that little, insignificant lead buttons are remembered because this is probably all we deserve. Where then did we fail? After all the promise, why such a pathetic achievement?

In a partial way this book tries to answer these questions, more in the international than in the domestic sphere. What a golden opportunity our country and my generation had to make life better for people in many parts of the world! Even though men who were policy-makers when we were boys glibly promised to "make the world safe for democracy," our generation must, I fear, take some responsibility for a worldwide erosion of political freedom, so evident year by year as political power is seized, in more and more countries, by military cliques. Yes, we must have contributed to this unhealthy situation. Surely we knew we were promising infinitely more to the poor, disadvantaged, and underdeveloped countries than we could possibly deliver. And did we not, rather deceitfully, pretend to be friends of both the exploiters and the exploited? Most of the foreign policies of our generation, our foreign aid, and our military-assistance programs have represented shameless compromises. Instead of formulating really consistent policies and trying to implement them courageously, like Peer Gynt we have always found it easier to go "roundabout." We have not dared to strike out for genuine novelty. We have been content with pretending to do something creative, smugly dressing up old, tired, ineffectual policies to make them appear different and modern.[3]

When we have so clearly demonstrated our creative capacity in science and technology, does it not seem odd that we are apparently incapable of directing more of our creative talents to governmental and diplomatic problems? I think it likely that the unexpected worldwide revolt of the younger generation is largely a manifestation of intense dissatisfaction with archaic politics and outmoded diplomacy, and represents a revulsion against the compromises that are regularly invoked to hide the mental bankruptcy of present-day policy-makers. Critical as I am, I would not make so categorical a statement as did one of our Nobel Prize winners, who, "in quiet desperation and disgust," concluded that our present "death-oriented" society is an inevitable outcome of the "terrible strain of idiots who govern the world."[4] I must assume that Dr. Szent-Gyorgyi used the word "idiot" in a figurative rather than in a psycho-semantic way, since it is hard to believe that all persons "who govern the world" are so deficient in mind as to be permanently incapable of rational thought or conduct. When I say that our policy-makers are "Gyntian," my adjective carries no pejorative implication whatever. It is an entirely forthright attempt to depict an endemic human weakness by the use of a term that is essentially descriptive in a psychological, anthropological, and moral sense.

In recounting my experiences, I shall try to show how these inherent shortcomings, not merely of our policy-makers but of all the men and

[3] Walter Lippmann ascribes the failure of American postwar foreign policy "to miscalculation, to misunderstanding our post-World War II position in the world. . . . The error lies in the illusion that the position occupied in the world by the United States at the end of the war was a permanent arrangement of power in the world. It wasn't." See Henry Brandon, "A Talk with Walter Lippmann, at 80, about This Minor Dark Age," *New York Times Magazine*, September 14, 1969, p. 25.

[4] See Robert Reinhold's account of his interview with Albert Szent-Gyorgyi, "Biologist Doubts Man's Survival," *New York Times*, February 20, 1970.

women charged with responsibility for carrying out policies as well, have compromised our good intentions. I shall try to describe with unvarnished candor the rather feckless way in which my generation shied away from challenges. For almost two decades I was engaged in military and governmental tasks in Europe and Asia. From the "grove of academe" for which, by conventional standards, I had been quite properly trained, I was catapulted by a war without bugles into an increasingly active role, only to find myself making big decisions, as most bureaucrats do, with far less caution and care than one normally employs in making small decisions. I have spent more of other people's money than I like to remember, and, although I am unsure of the attributable benefits, I am held quite blameless if there have been no useful results. But why, I might ask, just as Peer Gynt did, should I be criticized? Did I not follow patterns of action that others approved? Did I not work in well-designed organizations?

This may have been what was wrong: a naive confidence that organizations could make decisions that would be consistent, constructive, or socially and politically defensible. Every age has had approved methods for dealing with vexatious problems. Primitive societies performed strange rituals; the Greeks sought advice from Oracles, the medieval world prayed. In our age whenever we are confronted with problems we cannot solve as individuals, we form "committees." What strange fascination this Gyntian "roundabout" device has for us all! The word itself is innocent enough since by definition a committee is "a body of persons to whom some affair is committed." But the quaint assumption that lies behind the formation of a committee or the calling of a conference must be a pervading belief that the ignorance of individuals will, somehow, in a committee, in a conference, or in an organization produce collective wisdom.[5]

In many situations and quite a number of countries I have either witnessed or participated in this modern social ritual. Some of the organizations in which I served were huge, such as Supreme Headquarters Allied Expeditionary Forces about which a satirist opined that "never in the history of man have so few been governed by so many." Others, much smaller, seem to have been better attuned to the problems under their jurisdiction and more capable of finding solutions. The SHAEF mission to Norway, relatively small, rigorously trained, and unusually well staffed, could finish its work and close out its operations many months sooner than had been expected. Our aid mission to Yugoslavia, held to a "flex-

---

[5] The most irrational theory conceivable, said Plotinus, is that elements without intelligence should produce intelligence. For an analysis of this philosophical problem, see W. Macneile Dixon, *The Human Situation: The Gifford Lectures Delivered in the University of Glasgow, 1935–1937* (New York: Longmans, 1937), p. 352.

6

line" of twenty-two persons at Yugoslav insistence, stemming from their earlier disenchantment with large Russian missions, was also efficient because it was manageable. By contrast, the unwieldy Greek aid organization like Dante's wild beast seemed to grow hungrier the more it ate. It became larger and larger, more disorganized and less effective, until only drastic surgery could cure its chronic listlessness. There is something paradoxical in organizations. People create them presumably for their functional worth; and yet they often, without warning, proliferate into Frankensteinian monsters that can destroy the incentives, the loyalty, and the integrity of their human components. Just here we encounter a chief difficulty. The untidy, weakly integrated organizations through which we tried to devise and implement postwar policy allowed everyone to release his inherent Gyntian weakness, and in my typology of military-government officers, in chapter 11, I shall show how some of these frailties manifested themselves. A number of our overseas administrators, hurriedly moved from minor positions in trade unions or advertising agencies to very responsible overseas assignments, imagined themselves to be not only profound thinkers and great executives but superb diplomats. None of them, alas, even if they had read the play, would have understood Ibsen's ironical choice of a Cairo lunatic asylum as the place where Peer Gynt was acclaimed a king.

How did we get ourselves into this situation?

When World War I shattered our comfortable isolation and plunged us, intellectually, politically, and militarily unprepared, into a new role in international affairs, some Americans rather naively imagined that we could point the way to a world order that would be more just, more humane, and more democratic, whereas others thought we had better withdraw into the safer realm of isolation. As a consequence of these conflicting views, our interwar foreign policy was honeycombed with contradictions of which one illustration is classic. Sternly we demanded debt repayment from our wartime allies and thereby unwittingly approved their insistence on German reparations; yet by loaning the Germans money, for a wide variety of uses, we actually provided them with foreign exchange with which to pay reparations, thereby making it possible for our allies, for a time, to service their war debts. The outcome of this unplanned legerdemain was that when the stock market crash ended the flow of capital to Germany, the whole weird mechanism stopped working: the Germans defaulted on their loan obligations, and we discovered to our surprise that American investors in German securities had really financed the partial Allied war-debt payments the American treasury received. Even so, our interwar involvements were modest. The advent of World War II not only increased our commitments in international

7

affairs but brought a conviction that for the good of the world community we should assume widening military, political, and economic responsibilities. Those of us who found ourselves actors in this drama unwittingly became the executors of imprecise, changing, and often hastily improvised foreign policies.

My thoughtful and outspoken Cornell colleague Carl Becker sensed the new direction in foreign policy much sooner than the nescient architects of our diplomatic divagation. To him it was quite clear in the early forties that our country unavoidably would embark on some new variant of imperialism. There is no use dissembling, said Becker, with his characteristic honesty; we might just as well call it "imperialism" and "not be hypnotized or befuddled by words."[6] Yet despite Becker's warnings, no branch of our government made any conscious effort to explore the essential nature of the new "imperialism" into which we drifted with such unbelievable speed in the late forties and the fifties. Before any systematic policy planning occurred, we found ourselves with military advisory groups, military supply missions, economic aid missions, propaganda organizations, and covert intelligence agencies deployed on all the continents of this planet. No group of pundits had been masterminds who envisioned this global expansion of American influence. Some uncharted, unforeseen, ill-understood, centrifugal forces had resulted in an organizational sprawl — as unplanned as the widening suburbs of an exploding metropolis — that placed thousands of Americans in sensitive positions abroad, playing roles for which they were usually ill prepared technically and intellectually, carrying on their duties in unfamiliar cultural milieus where their all-too-evident ignorance produced a strange combination of fear and pity on the part of puzzled people in host countries.

How differently other "imperial" nations prepared their personnel for the roles they were expected to play! Look for a moment into the very candid autobiography of a dedicated British civil servant.[7] After serving in the British army in World War I and after graduating from Cambridge University, Victor Purcell wrote an examination that qualified him to become a "cadet" in Malaya. Since unrestricted Chinese immigration into that country was permitted, it had become clear that the Chinese would eventually become a majority "community" in Malaya. Consequently, of the ten cadets who arrived in Kuala Lumpur in May of 1921, five were selected to learn Chinese, the other five Malay.[8]

Purcell elected to study Chinese, a laborious yet for him a welcome

[6] Carl L. Becker, *How New Will the Better World Be? A Discussion of Post War Reconstruction* (New York: Knopf, 1944), p. 95.

[7] Victor Purcell, *The Memoirs of a Malayan Official* (London: Cassell, 1964).

[8] Ibid., pp. 89, 95.

opportunity: training that involved six months' instruction in Cantonese in Malaya and then, if he qualified, much longer instruction in China. Actually, in making his decision to concentrate on Chinese, Purcell automatically became a "specialist" on Chinese activities, and his whole career in Malaya would consequently be centered in the work of the "Chinese Protectorate." As a fledgling cadet, Purcell soon learned that British imperialism, a deadly serious business, called for most diligent application in the requisite preparatory training; "it demanded the industry of the Benedictine, the orthodoxy of the Dominican, the diplomacy of the Jesuit, and the silence of the Trappist on all controversial issues." [9] Having survived the initial catechism, not only in writing "characters" but in practicing "tones," [10] three cadets moved on to Canton for more exacting training. A two-and-a-half-year curriculum had been carefully developed for them so that these future imperial executives would have a sure capacity to read and speak Chinese, to check on the work of their Chinese assistants, and to translate documents accurately and clearly. The Dutch followed an even more rigorous policy; their civil servants could not occupy any post in their Chinese Secretariat until they had studied Chinese for seven years.

Language, though basic and indispensable, was by no means the only thing the British cadets had to learn. They were expected to acquire a thorough understanding of Chinese culture and a knowledge of the politics, the sociology, and the business practices of Chinese communities. All the strange customs and superstitions needed study, and the cadets were encouraged to explore every corner of the teeming city of Canton. But these activities were extracurricular, and were not formally covered in the exacting examinations given every six months in Hong Kong. Since Victor Purcell made good progress in South Chinese dialects, it was decided that he should proceed to Peking to acquire a working knowledge of Mandarin and to deepen his understanding of Chinese culture. When at long last his training tour had been completed and his final Chinese examination passed, Purcell was assigned to the Hong Kong government for three months to learn how its Education Department carried out the inspection and control of Chinese schools.[11] Only after three years of rigorous training, and testing by a succession of examinations, did the British government consider a brilliant Cambridge graduate prepared to take up his first minor post in Malaya.

When we contrast the shoddy, impulsive, indeed almost reckless way in

[9] Ibid., p. 99.
[10] How difficult this might be for a Westerner is evident when one learns that Mandarin has four tones but Cantonese has nine.
[11] *Memoirs of a Malayan Official*, p. 150.

which the United States approached its emergent "imperial" responsibility, we can appreciate how opportunistic and essentially amateurish American overseas activities have been. Despite efforts to extol American expertise and achievements,[12] we must admit, if we are at all honest with ourselves, that American "overseasmanship" (certainly one of the most bumptious words that I have ever encountered) has lacked planning, thoughtful direction, and, above all, proper preparation of the personnel entrusted with very important tasks. The risks enlarge far more than arithmetically as the numbers of overseas representatives increase. Consider the supervisory responsibility involved when the 331 Americans working abroad in military establishments in 1938 had become 23,426 in 1957.[13] Add to this group, in that year, the overseas employees of other United States agencies and the total reached 33,545 without counting any of the State Department personnel. It must also be remembered that unlike the 27,818 missionaries, the 23,418 employees of American business enterprises, and the 10,732 students and professors working abroad (in 1957), the overseas personnel of the departments of State, Commerce, Treasury, and Agriculture, the Central Intelligence Agency, and our inconstantly named foreign-aid organization [14] formally represented the American government abroad and were therefore the symbols of our new imperialism. So were their wives and their children, together with mothers, mothers-in-law, and other relatives who seized a golden opportunity to travel overseas at government expense and live, protected and insulated from "foreigners," in American-built compounds equipped with commissaries where American food and all other necessary American products were available so that there would be no "hardship" involved in foreign residence.

Oddly enough our new, modern, enlightened imperialism, inspired as it so often was by very good intentions, has nevertheless, in wholly unexpected ways, distressed and embittered people in many foreign countries and has seriously undermined the enviable reputation we had at the end of World War II. This does indeed seem strange since by the standards of British, Spanish, Dutch, French, or Portuguese imperialist practice we have consistently been "little sinners." None of our representatives abroad have tied "natives" to the breeches of cannon and blown them to bits.[15]

[12] *The Art of Overseasmanship*, ed. Harlan Cleveland and Gerard J. Mangone (Syracuse: Syracuse University Press, 1957).

[13] The figures are taken from ibid., pp. 14, 16, 18, 20, 22.

[14] Successively designated ECA, MSA, FOA, ICA, AID.

[15] As M. L. Cowan, deputy commissioner of Jullundar, did in 1872, to suppress a mild Sikh uprising in the Punjab: "In batches the Kookas were led to the mouths of cannon and blasted off. At 7 P.M., when the last batch of six men had been lashed to the guns, Cowan received an official order . . . to send the prisoners to trial . . . [but Cowan said] it would be impossible to stay the execution of the men

Unlike the Spanish conquistadors, about whom it was flippantly said, "First they fell on their knees and then on the aborigines," we have really tried to help people in poor and disadvantaged countries to improve and develop their economies. We have spent billions in this effort. Why have we become so suspected? And why have we so often been taken prisoner by politicians in the countries we have befriended? How was it possible for some of our "client" governments to become virtually our masters?

I cannot, I fear, answer all these vexing questions. I have, however, observed the impact of our hastily improvised foreign policies in Korea, Greece, Yugoslavia, and India; and in the seven chapters devoted to these countries I hope to present a very frank and candid picture of the problems that faced those of us who were expected to implement the wishes of Washington. The trouble was that the "wishes of Washington" always kept changing. Just when we had persuaded the Yugoslavs, after very difficult bargaining, that they simply would have to get along with 300,000 tons of imported American wheat, a Washington emissary arrived to inform us that we must prevail upon the Yugoslavs to accept at least a million tons because this was the minimum quota that the farm bloc insisted upon. Just how does one change direction so swiftly? And what credence will your diplomatic partners have in your veracity when you shift and veer so unpredictably? What effect will the intrusion of a single revision in an aid program have upon the total cluster of objectives that our government may have been striving to achieve?

This account of my modest involvement in foreign affairs is really not an autobiography in the conventional sense. It is rather a story of how I became a college professor (trained, fortunately, as an economic historian) and an account of how by chance I was plunged into a host of military and governmental activities. In Britain I helped plan the invasion of France and the liberation of Norway, where later I supervised the disposition of sequestrated German war matériel; while in Germany I was temporarily responsible for feeding more than three quarters of a million displaced persons. After I returned to the United States to reassume my academic duties, a series of chance events took me to Korea, where I became the third-ranking official in our military government, and when Korea became an independent country, I was importuned to head the Korea Program Division of the Economic Cooperation Administration in Washington. The Korean war brought me back to Korea where I witnessed the terrible

already tied to the guns; that such a proceeding would have the worst effect on the people around us; and so the last six rebels were blown away as had been the forty-three before them." When Cowan's superior officer heard of the action he had taken, he wrote, "My dear Cowan, I fully approve and confirm all you have done. You have acted admirably." Kushwant Singh, *The Sikhs* (London: Allen and Unwin, 1953), p. 95.

devastation caused by that unfortunate conflict. When the United Nations assumed responsibility for Korea's rehabilitation, I became economic adviser to our MSA mission chief in Greece, and after a brief sojourn there, I was assigned to Yugoslavia as deputy director of our aid program. In these several postings I had opportunities to see both the virtues and the serious shortcomings of our new "imperialism."

Three years in Italy and two periods of residence in India further widened my opportunities to appraise our American overseas activities. In dozens of contexts, then, I have observed the serious overcommitment of the United States abroad; the blunders of untrained, ill-trained, and often untrainable administrators; the unnecessary waste of foreign-aid funds; and the foolish parsimony, or lavish indulgence, of Washington bureaucrats. I have witnessed amazing dedication and devotion to duty by some of our American overseas personnel, shocking callousness and incompetence in others. In what might therefore be regarded as an auto-biographical odyssey, I shall try to evaluate some of the cultural factors that have molded American preconceptions and attitudes over the past half century, searching for reasons that may throw light on both our virtues and our intellectual and moral weaknesses. I shall, in short, attempt to explain why a generation of presumably well-equipped Americans have been singularly incapable of bringing to realization the hopes and aspirations not only of the American people but of large portions of the world community.

Behind this lies the very troublesome intellectual problem that Ibsen posed in *Peer Gynt*. Very succinctly stated it is just this: can one some-times do more good by being a "great sinner"? Becker had the courage to point out that the United States could not really help maintain peace and order in the postwar world "without resorting to power politics."[16] What we have had such trouble settling upon are the techniques we should employ to obtain really useful results by means of power. Just how, for example, can one discover the right mix of persuasion, benevolence, and force? We have never really faced up to the unpleasant and unpopular possibility that ultimate good might conceivably result from temporary authoritarian rule. Thus even though the British generally engaged in undisguised exploitation of their overseas dependent areas, they concur-rently made sizable investments in railways, schools, or hospitals that inured to the long-run good of Indians, Pakistanis, Nigerians, and Gha-nians. In much the same way, the Japanese effectively developed the min-eral, hydroelectric, and agrarian resources of the Korean peninsula at the same time that they ruthlessly relegated the Koreans to unskilled jobs in

[16] *How New Will the Better World Be?* p. 85.

order that all technical and managerial positions could be monopolized by the Japanese. This problem is not merely a historical one. When one considers the miracle of land reclamation in Israel that has made "the desert bloom like a rose," one can at least wonder whether the Israelis' neighbors should be protected so that they can perpetuate low levels of productivity and continue the waste of natural and human resources.

It may have been "immoral" for the Israelis to displace the Palestinian Arabs as it may well have been "wrong" for the Yugoslav socialists to sequestrate the properties of the ruling class they supplanted. The Yugoslav argument was that the old regime had failed to develop the country, and thereby had perpetuated poverty. Better to be a big sinner and do some good than to be a little sinner and accomplish nothing. With their penchant for storytelling the Yugoslavs recount how the late King Aleksandar appeared at the gates of heaven and demanded admittance. "Just wait there," said St. Peter, and Aleksandar waited, not very patiently. But when Marshal Tito arrived and was promptly admitted, the ex-king became furious. "How dare you keep me waiting while you admit that atheist," he shouted. "You forget that I was head of the Church." "Calm yourself," said St. Peter sternly. "When you were king no one went to church; but now, although Tito is only president, everybody goes to church."

Were we much too gentle in our dealings with Asian, African, and Latin-American governments? Did we try to play imperialist roles by aping the missionaries, and by assuming that countries that have always been despotic could quickly learn how to be democratic? Were we so fearful of committing great sins that we learned all manner of little sins from people so poor that petty corruption is ubiquitous?

> A sinner in the old flamboyant style
> One meets with nowadays hardly at all.
> There's more to sin than making a mess;
> A sin calls for vigor and seriousness.[17]

Were most of our blunders and mistakes the consequence of our abysmal ignorance of cultural patterns in the countries to which our military missions, our intelligence cadres, and our foreign-aid personnel were assigned? The first group of military government officers arriving in Korea in 1945 had been taught to speak a few words of Japanese; they soon discovered a strange coolness on the part of the Koreans, who found it incredible that their liberators should address them in the hated language of their oppressors. It is at least conceivable that a succession of such little sins may be one of the main reasons for a worldwide resentment of

[17] *Peer Gynt*, p. 215.

our strange new imperialism. Before our unfortunate Vietnam involvement we could scarcely be considered great sinners. Now a great moral issue confronts us as we wage, presumably for the good of future generations both American and Asian, a ruthless, cruel war. Would it, or would it not, have been much better for our policy-makers to have gone quietly into the casting ladle of oblivion as little sinners?

2

NEW HOPES IN A NEW LAND
★★★★★★★★★★★★★★★★★★★★★★★★★★★★★★

WHEN I try to stand outside of myself and look as objectively as I possibly can at my personality, I discover that I am a rather odd mixture of deep-rooted prejudices and impulses. There is a rebellious streak in my nature and I am easily incensed whenever I see people push other people around. Yet I'm not a very active crusader because I am much too individualistic to join movements or causes. I have many friends and I may appear to be a gregarious person; but this is largely a façade since I am almost pathologically lonely. Instead of participating in games or any other form of collective activity, I work alone. I am morbidly industrious, and very critical of people who are not equally diligent. I discipline myself ruthlessly, and hence I can meet any situation, however difficult, with quiet composure. There is little doubt that I am intellectually quite snobbish, a strange form of vanity when in all honesty I know that I do not have an exceptional mind. Yet for all these peculiarities and idiosyncrasies, despite my industry, earnestness, and discipline, I am a rather happy person largely, I suspect, because I am so incurably romantic, venturesome to the point of recklessness, and always able to find beauty and poetry where others fail to notice anything unusual. These facets of my personality, which obviously color my views of the world in which we live, are, I believe, the consequences of my Swedish ancestry and of the informal education I received in a midwestern Swedish-American boyhood home. In order to explain myself, I must therefore describe in some detail the reasons why my parents came to the United States, the kind of people they were, and the training, guidance, and inspiration that their children received from them.

Both my parents were born in Östergötland, a lush agricultural province in south-central Sweden that glistens with clear, limpid, interlinked lakes which reflect, in their clear water, the dark green pine forests on their shores. In deciding to leave their native villages, my father and my mother joined an outward flow of ambitious young Swedish men and women, a migration that had begun in the 1840's and grew to such proportions by the 1880's that in this short span over a half million able-bodied Swedes, in the full vigor of their youth,[1] had come to the United States. So massive and so swift was the outmigration that in some Swedish rural districts from a third to half of the inhabitants migrated.

In such a large and persisting population movement it is hard to particularize the motives that led so many people to leave their ancestral homes.[2] Yet when I recall the accounts of life in Sweden that I heard as a boy, not merely from my own parents but from dozens of relatives, friends, and neighbors of Swedish origin, I think it fair to say that these migrating young people simply refused to remain economic prisoners of the Swedish ruling classes, the landlords, clergy, and burghers. They rebelled by the simple, albeit hazardous act of migration.[3]

On my father's side, two children out of four came to America; on my mother's side, four out of eight migrated. Thus in both families 50 percent of one generation left Sweden, all before they had reached their twenty-first birthdays. They left the country of their birth with high hopes but undoubtedly with a sadness that came from a realization that they might never again see their parents or their other relatives and friends who remained in Sweden. What did they seek? Vilhelm Moberg, in his inimitable way, has given this answer:

There were two worlds — nature's world and the Bible's world, this world and the coming world. But *this* world was again divided into two parts: an old and a new. . . . [The Old World] was frail, worn-out, and full of years. Its people were worn-out, decrepit, old and weak and finished. In their ancient villages time stood still; in their old moss-grown cottages nothing happened which had not happened before; the children obeyed their parents and imitated them, and did the same thing again which their parents had done before them. . . .

But far away, on the other side of the globe, there was a New World, recently discovered, recently settled. The New World was young and fresh,

---

[1] The majority of the migrants were in the 18–35 age group. Their departure not only deprived Sweden of their productive capacity but saddled the country of their birth with an aging population.

[2] In an excellent study Florence Edith Janson has shown the wide range of motives that led Swedish people to emigrate. See her *The Background of Swedish Immigration, 1840–1930* (Chicago: University of Chicago Press, 1931), especially pp. 108–116, and chapters 5 and 6. For the emigration figures see the appendix, table II, p. 499.

[3] For vivid details, see Donald S. Connery, *The Scandinavians* (New York: Simon and Schuster, 1966), pp. 352–353.

and full of splendor and riches beyond imagination. And those who emigrated and settled there were young and swift and nimble people whose whole lives lay ahead of them. The New World was populated by the most daring and the most intelligent people from the Old World: by those who had left their lords and masters behind them. It was populated by all those who wanted to be free, who did not want to serve under masters. To the New World all those emigrated who at home were poor and oppressed, all those who were harassed and suffering, the destitute and those full of sorrow, the hunted ones and those full of despair.[4]

The dream did not always materialize into a haven of joy. To some "green Swedes" life proved so difficult that, like my uncle Karl, they returned to Sweden. The great majority, however, adapted themselves to a new environment. They could do so because they were young, energetic, and pleased with any improvement over the economic situation from which they fled. Three-fourths of the immigrants were single; most of them came from peasant homes where they were accustomed to hard work and inured to very modest standards of living. Work was what they wanted first of all, but for most Swedish immigrants the ultimate hope and ambition was to become independent farmers, self-employed craftsmen, or businessmen. High wages and cheap land constituted the lures that brought Swedes to the midwestern and west-coast states, while the prospects of employment in machine shops, furniture factories, and shipyards account for the Swedish migration to New York, Massachusetts, Pennsylvania, and Michigan.[5] But the greatest number sought a rural life where a nearness to nature satisfied the basic romanticism of the Swedish soul.

My father was born in 1868 in Rystad Parish, a peaceful farming community within sound of the bells of a handsome Romanesque parish church. His father (born in 1839) had been in the Swedish army long enough to entitle him to a cottage together with a small parcel of land.[6] I saw this cottage, my father's birthplace, in 1928 when I first visited Rystad. Like most of the Swedish country cottages it was built of square-hewn timber, planked up and down, battened, and painted red with white trim: a simple, sturdy house. My father's mother, Maja Lena Månsdotter, came from a parish across the lake (Roxen) from Rystad, a community called Stjärnorp. She was born in 1832 and died in 1883 when my father was fifteen years old. He felt estranged when my grandfather married again and soon thereafter left the Rystad cottage to earn his own living.

[4] Vilhelm Moberg, *The Emigrants* (New York: Simon and Schuster, 1951), pp. 47–48.

[5] For figures on the distribution of the Swedish population, see *Swedes in America, 1638–1938*, ed. Adolph B. Benson and Naboth Hedin (New Haven, Conn.: Yale University Press, 1938), p. 82.

[6] The soldier was ordinarily housed by the parish and occupied a respectable status. See Janson, *Background of Swedish Immigration*, p. 61.

17

I suspect it was his mother's death (he always spoke of her with deep affection) as well as the unpromising prospects in a semifeudal Swedish rural society that made him dream of travel to a land where he could begin a new life. Since as a boy of about sixteen, with only a few years of parish school education, he could earn but little as a farm helper, it took several years before he could save enough for his passage. Moreover he had to learn where to go — to northwestern Illinois where people from the Rystad area had already migrated.[7] I am not quite certain but I think he left Sweden in 1888. I know that he was naturalized in Rock Island, Illinois, on April 1, 1895. Like most Swedish immigrants who came to Illinois he found employment as a "hired man" on a farm, although he worked in a Moline lumber mill during winter months.

He had known my mother in Sweden, and they met again in Illinois. She was born in 1869 in Sörby, which lies about eight miles from Rystad. There is a wistful beauty in this part of Östergötland. Dark forests crowd in on the arable fields, forests that in my mother's girlhood were allegedly inhabited by ghosts and trolls, so that little girls dreaded nocturnal journeys. Landeryd Parish Church, where my mother was baptized and confirmed, has a romantic charm since into its tower a runestone has been masoned, indicating that the hill on which the church stands very likely had once been a pagan ceremonial place. The Landeryd runestone is of exceptional historical interest. After having served for centuries as a threshold for the church door, thereby presumably indicating how the Christian Church had triumphed over pagan memorials, it was built into the church tower in the early eighteenth century when the church was reconstructed. What makes this runestone so unusual is the glimpse it gives us of the Viking age. A transliteration of the runes succinctly tells a dramatic story: "Väring erected this stone for his brother Tjälve, the fighter, who was with Knut." Since the style of the runestone clearly indicates that it belongs to the period circa 1000 A.D., there can be little doubt that the Knut whom Tjälve served was none other than Denmark's Knut the Great, known in English history as King Canute, who invaded Britain in 1015 and became king of England (and of Denmark and Norway as well). For his assault on England, Knut recruited "a host" of soldiers of fortune from many parts of Scandinavia, and Tjälve from Sörby was evidently one of these. Since villages such as Sörby were mostly composed of kinship groups, Tjälve may have been one of my

[7] As early as 1842 a few emigrants had left southeastern Östergötland for Wisconsin, but after the Jansonist (communal) settlement at Bishop Hill, Illinois, in the late 1840's, was publicized, a stream of emigrants from Östergötland went to Bishop Hill, Rock Island, Moline, Andover, Swedona, Galesburg. All these places are within twenty miles of Orion where my parents bought a farm.

Viking ancestors.[8] He must have been a great warrior to have deserved a runestone to commemorate his deeds. "In those days of incessant warfare, the life of a warrior," as Du Chaillu has said, "was a magnificent drama from beginning to the end; his death the closing of a great career; and his entrance into Valhalla the reward for a life of bravery."[9]

Sörby was only one of many village communities that belonged to a large estate called Sturefors; it consisted of four farmsteads, three on the west side of the road, one on the east side. The four farmhouses are identical — long, solid-wood structures,[10] painted, like my father's birthplace, red with white trim. When I first visited Sörby, on midsummer's day in 1928, a maypole that had been raised seven weeks earlier was still standing with its ribbons fluttering in front of my mother's childhood home, and reminded me of the stories I heard as a child about the May Day festivals.

My mother's father was not one of the four legal tenants of Sörby, but rather one of the *statare*, the almost landless hired workers, who lived with their families in crowded rooms on the upper floors of the farmhouses and eked out a precarious living. I have never been able to find out why my grandfather did not come into possession of a landholding or at least become a craftsman, and I have always suspected that he was an embittered person who considered that he had been cheated out of a landholding. At any rate, he remained a casual farm laborer who drank to excess, as did so many discouraged Swedish peasants in the nineteenth century. His wife was a most diligent, hardworking woman, but even her constant efforts to add to my grandfather's entirely inadequate earnings could not keep up with the food and clothing needs of their brood of eight children. Consequently, as was the custom in that cruel, impoverished society, my mother and her brothers and sisters were turned over to farm families at tender ages and expected to earn their board and lodging by their labor.[11] I recall the bitterness with which my mother spoke of

[8] For information about the Landeryd runestone see *Sveriges Runinskrifter*, vol. 2 (Stockholm, 1918), pp. 109–111, and Martin Sjöbeck, *Östergötland Färdvägar och Vandringsstigar utgående från Statsbanorna* (Stockholm, 1929), p. 64. For accounts of Knut's exploits recorded in Norse Sagas, see Paul B. Du Chaillu, *The Viking Age: The Early History, Manners, and Customs of the Ancestors of the English-Speaking Nations* (New York, 1889), vol. II, pp. 486–498.

[9] Du Chaillu, *The Viking Age*, vol. II, p. 431.

[10] I remember going up to the second story of Östgården (the east court) in 1928, and hearing my second cousin, the legal tenant, say, after he warned us to duck our heads, "If the damn fools had only laid on another tier of timber when they were building this house, we wouldn't have to do this, but as it is we have been doing it for more than a hundred years."

[11] Memories of childhood hardships, by immigrants who had experienced similar assignments, are vividly recounted in Janson's *Background of Swedish Immigration*, pp. 108–116.

some of her erstwhile foster parents and, conversely, the gratitude and affection she had for others.

The whole system of rural organization was shamefully exploitative. Tenant farmers paid their rents in money, in produce, and in labor services; hence all the villages belonging to Sturefors had to send milkmaids to the manorial stables, and these hapless children, such as my mother, came twice a day walking miles from their homes. Both boys and girls also did field work for the elegant estate; and tenant farmers, in addition to their rents (in money, produce, or labor service), were required to give out of every ten sheaves of grain one sheaf for support of the minister, the crown, and local poor relief. Although Sörby was only about ten miles from the handsome cathedral city of Linköping, the rigid separation between town and country made it very difficult for country young people to find employment in the city. Normally, then, there was only one means of escape: migration to the "new world," and this became the dream of young persons in every Swedish village community. Yet there were no agronomic reasons why the peasantry of Östergötland should have been poor, and the twentieth century clearly proved that Sweden had adequate resources which could have made possible a satisfactory standard of living for all.[12] What was lacking in the nineteenth century was a willingness by the ruling classes to share resources, to open up reasonably equal opportunities, and, above all, to plan for the common welfare.

My mother's brother Karl was the first of the family to seek his fortune in the United States. He, in turn, persuaded his brother Franz to join him, and the two then financed the travel of Charlotta Johannah (my mother) and her younger sister Albertina in 1889. Because of her long household apprenticeship, my mother had no difficulty in finding employment. She worked for English-speaking families, the Coffees, the Burnses, and the Bothwells. I remember her saying that she was miserably unhappy at first and each Sunday she would rearrange the few possessions in her trunk counting the days until she would have saved enough money for the return trip. Then, miracle of miracles, after about a year she suddenly discovered that she liked the "new world," and she gave up any plans to return to Sweden. She and my father were married in Rock Island on March 1, 1894, and after carrying on farming operations on rented farms for two years they moved to a sixty-acre farm they had purchased a quarter mile from Orion, a village in Henry County about fifteen miles southeast

---

[12] Traditionally in Sweden landless people had been allowed to carve out homesteads from unused ("virgin") land. By the middle of the nineteenth century, however, the wilderness land had been engrossed or otherwise taken up so that allodial rights no longer had any meaning. In Östergötland, for example, instead of increasing, the number of peasant "freeholds" steadily decreased in the nineteenth century. See ibid., pp. 46–47 and 54–55.

of the joined cities of Moline and Rock Island. This is where I was born in 1900, and here all five of the Johnson children, Ruth, Theophile, Irma, Edgar, and Dorothy, grew up.

For the most part my father was not a very shrewd businessman, and he was, I fear, often outwitted by cattle buyers or horse traders. He did, however, make one transaction that stood him in good stead. The Orion farm, which had been carved out of the prairie in 1837, cost him $2800 (a sum fully paid by 1899, which, I think, testified to the extraordinary industry of my parents). In 1906 when the C. B. & Q. Railway found that it needed additional land in order to relocate tracks, my father sold seventeen acres to the railway for $3000, which meant that he more than recovered his initial investment and still had forty-three acres debt free. It was this transaction that made it possible for him to build a new house and make improvements in the farm buildings.

My father was a prodigious worker; indeed it is hard for me to describe his energy, persistence, and strength. Nor was it an impulsive type of activity — rather, a steady, rhythmic, vital force revealed itself in the carrying out of his daily tasks. Rising at five in the morning (earlier in peak-load work periods) he would kindle the fire in the kitchen stove before he began his morning chores: milking, grooming the horses, caring for hogs and calves. Then after breakfast he would go, with his horses (who were so dear to him) and his wagon or his implements, to the fields or elsewhere in the community to undertake one of the many tasks for which he was hired because he was so skillful a teamster and so dependable an artisan on construction or grading work. He was frequently importuned to plow gardens, unload lumber, brick, or sand, bring coal from a nearby mine, help move a traveling tent show or chautauqua.

His rigorous self-discipline made him rather a hard taskmaster. He expected a boy to do a man's work, and I fear he lacked the rare knack my mother had of making work zestful and self-rewarding. He never, however, restricted our activities, as did my aunt Albertina's husband, Will Kran, who hated to see me come for a visit because he knew I would be dulling his tools and using up his lumber and nails. My father held quite the opposite view; he was glad to see us learn to be carpenters or masons, trappers or hunters, and the many artisan skills I possess were largely learned from him.

He was a very thorough craftsman. When he built fences, as he did for the boundary of every field, the "hedge" fence posts were peeled and set a full three feet in the ground; the corners were braced so well that when the woven or barbed wire was stretched the tension was comparable to that of piano strings. He did many things that I look back on with admiration. Not only could he repair harness and do good carpenter work, but he was a competent cobbler who resoled our shoes. He was wonderfully self-reliant and needed no outside stimulus. In contrast to so many of his fellow Swedes who avidly joined lodges or fraternal organizations, my father preferred to be individualistic. He belonged to no organization whatever, and prided himself on his consistent independence. I suspect he carried this too far because he might well have benefited from closer association with farm groups that were trying to change the pattern of agriculture.

Not that he was an inefficient or unprogressive farmer; quite the contrary. His crop yields were consistently high, and he was exceptionally skillful at pasture management, fertilizing and mowing his meadows so that the grass would be thick and nutritious. Indeed it was for this reason that we could keep a relatively large dairy herd on what was really a small farm. But although my father was willing to plant new crops (such as alfalfa) when he could clearly see the benefits, he was rather stubborn about making changes on any experimental basis. My older brother, for example, wanted to weigh the milk from each cow and keep performance records, but to my father this was all nonsense; one should be able to tell a good milker from a poor one without all that fuss!

He took great pride in his farm. On rainy days many farmers went to the village and spent hours talking with neighbors in the grocery store, the hardware store, the barbershop, or the livery stable. But not my father; those were the days when I had to turn the grindstone a long wearisome time while he sharpened his scythes, his hedge knife, and his brush cutter. Then off he would go in his rubber boots to cut weeds in the fence rows, trim the Osage orange hedges, or dig out sour docks in the oats or the clover. His excellent farm practices converted a fair farm into a truly exceptional one, and this was attested after his death when the highest acre yield of corn in the state of Illinois was achieved on one of the hillside fields whose fertility he had built up.

With all his work and his penchant for excellence in the performance of his tasks, he had little time for reading. But he regularly read a weekly Swedish newspaper, scanned the daily Moline newspaper, and leafed through one or two farm magazines. After he retired he read widely, all of Sandburg's *Lincoln*, for example, and a great many other books. He read my *American Economic Thought in the Seventeenth Century* and commented on it with shrewdness and insight. He often astonished me by his knowledge of plants, trees, and natural history. I think as children we were tardy in learning to appreciate that he had a rather sharp mind. But politics held no interest for him; in this regard he seemed to fear that one party would mismanage things as badly as another.

I am certain that I learned my disdain for weakness from him. He could bear pain without complaint, whether from an accident (of which there are always many on a farm) or from the disease that finally took his life. Yet for all that, he was gentle and wonderfully kind. Before we had a motor car we would sometimes go to parties by horse and buggy. We never asked him to harness and hitch up the horse; it went without saying that he would! And no matter how late it was when we returned, he would be waiting to unhitch the horse and stable him.

I often wish he had not changed his name, after he came to the United States, from Klaes August Stedt to Gust C. Johnson; and I am not certain just why he did so. Nor do I see why if he preferred the patronymic, he did not form it accurately since it properly should have been Jonasson (his father's name being Jonas Petter Stedt). But some quirk led him to despise the name his father had earned as a soldier (Stedt), which his brother and half-brother retained, and we thereby lost an identity with one facet of our Swedish heritage. The prevailing philosophy of a "new start" may have had something to do with it. Like most of the nineteenth-century Swedish-Americans he was intensely patriotic toward his adopted country [13] and I sensed this especially when I traveled with him in Sweden, forty years after his migration, because he was very critical of many Swedish customs and practices. Nevertheless, there was evidence of a tender love for his native land that he could not conceal; and this affection for the charming and beautiful country from which we stem has been transmitted to me.

My mother was as energetic as my father, and showed a remarkable mastery of large and small domestic, educational, and planning tasks. Trained in nearly self-sufficient Swedish farmsteads, she could do everything: cook the wonderful, rich, traditional foods; sew and repair clothes for men, boys, women, and girls; and make quilts and curtains. That she could prepare three meals a day for seven people and yet find time to make cheese, preserve foods (she always canned at least 400 quarts of fruits and vegetables each year), make soap, and care for several hundred chickens and ducks testifies to her boundless energy.

Planning improvements was her real joy. The new house, built in 1907, needed a lawn, shrubs, and a kitchen garden. I marvel at the things we presently had: apple, peach, pear, plum, cherry, and walnut trees; raspberries, gooseberries, blackberries, currants, strawberries, grapes, rhu-

[13] "The Swedes, more than any other [immigrant] group, became naturalized as soon as it was legally possible for them to do so, and practically 100% of them became citizens of their adopted country." Benson and Hedin, eds., *Swedes in America*, p. 87. The reason for this readiness of immigrant Swedes to acquire American citizenship becomes understandable when one considers that as late as 1887 only 6 percent of the people in Sweden had the right to vote. Janson, *Background of Swedish Immigration*, p. 292.

barb, horseradish plants; flowers of all kinds. It was my mother who suggested that I buy a hive of bees, thereby launching me on a boyhood avocation that financed many of my college expenses. It was she who suggested that we build an ice pond thereby adding another source of income for the family. Since I had an older brother who served as my father's main helper, I, in turn, became my mother's chief helper. I built the chicken coops, planted and cultivated the kitchen garden, picked the fruit, cared for the lawns and hedges. In this role I could observe my mother's restless mind visualizing the next step in our material progress. Running water in the house was a first achievement, then a central heating plant, electric lights, and presently an icebox to obviate the backbreaking task of hanging food and milk down a well to keep it cool.

Although it was fun to work for my mother, she — like my father — was a stern taskmaster. Life was ordered. Children were to come directly home from school without loitering. Chores were to be performed faithfully. At the same time she was constantly watchful over our health and comfort. How many injured hands and feet did she bandage? How often did she come, despite her weariness, to console us in illness? I remember, too, the cold winter mornings when she had hot bricks ready to put in the buggy before I drove my sister to the country school where she taught.

My mother is remembered by her children for her loving concern not only for our immediate well-being but for our intellectual and social development. She constantly identified herself with our schoolwork. I recall an incident when my eldest sister, Ruth Elizabeth, entered high school and began a course in zoology. We were moving some farm buildings at that time and I remember how my mother came with a baking-powder can and gave me instructions to capture every kind of insect I saw. A bit of cyanide in the can quickly turned a live insect into a "specimen" that could be mounted on a cork. We worked like beavers in school to justify her confidence in us. I can see her now listening to us while we recited our "declamations," and hear her pointing out the weak spots and making us stress the key passages.[14] Fortunately we were bright enough to keep at the head of our classes despite the frequency of our absences occasioned by household or farm duties. I think the relative ease with which I was able to acquit myself in grammar and high school led to my snobbish attitude toward my fellow students.

[14] We all profited from her sense of the dramatic and this is why I have established a public-speaking prize in her memory. The first annual award of the Charlotta Johannah Johnson Prize was made in 1969, the hundredth anniversary of my mother's birth, at the graduation exercises of the Orion High School. Was it only a coincidence that the judges gave the award to a Swedish-American girl from Andover, that place, now only a small village, that had been such a beacon light of opportunity for immigrants from Östergötland?

One reason why my mother came to like America was that here she found a new religious freedom. While in Sweden she had rebelled against the league of the established Lutheran church with the landed aristocracy and city burghers, and had come to dislike the mighty organ in the huge stone cathedral in Linköping; it was in the "free church" chapel that she had found solace. This rebellion against orthodoxy was intensified in Illinois. Although all of her children were baptized in the Lutheran church, they were presently sent to the Methodist Sunday School, and in 1920 both my father and mother joined that church. She was, of course, bitterly criticized for her apostasy but she had a decided independence of mind and I can remember her standing her ground in doctrinal disagreements. For her the Methodist church was something of a compromise; what she sought was some simple exposition of ethical principles and her most cherished book was a copy of Dwight Moody's *Gems of Truth and Beauty*. And how she loved to sing the great hymns! I can recall coming home from school as a small boy and hearing her. By the open window my mother would be sewing new shirts for my brother or myself and singing in her lovely voice, "Skall vi mötas bortom floden?" (Shall We Meet beyond the River?) or some other familiar hymn.

My mother attributed much of her suffering as a child to her father's intemperance and gambling. She was therefore an ardent prohibitionist and a sharp critic of her party-loving younger sister Albertina. But recreation was not forbidden. We had croquet sets and we played tennis. Our first musical instrument, a reed organ, was replaced with a piano, on which my sister Irma proved to be our most proficient performer. We were encouraged to take part in school and church activities, and my mother was ever ready to bake pies or prepare other food for school parties. We would sometimes go on fishing trips and quite often we would go in the carriage to visit relatives. Later, after my brother and I purchased a secondhand Ford, we could travel more easily, and once we had one car it soon became our mother's dream that we should have a really nice automobile. It turned out to be a Reo, sturdy but a bit clumsy (which made changing tires on dusty roads and inflating them up to seventy pounds by means of a hand pump little fun). A birthday meant a feast and six presents. Christmas was a long-planned happy event with a Christmas tree lighted by real flaming candles while we sang the beautiful old Swedish Christmas hymn "Var hälsad, sköna morgonstund." My father had a fine tenor voice and my mother's voice was a rich, vibrant mezzo-soprano.

In our home there was, then, play and fun, but no drinking or dancing or "card-playing." (However, my mother loved to play "Somerset," and never seemed to realize that it was really just a card game which had other symbols for hearts, clubs, diamonds, spades, knaves, kings, and queens. And she was devilishly sly and crafty as a player and delighted in sweeping the board with a well-played trump card.)

If my mother had any fault it was an excess of intensity. Perhaps the most unfortunate heritage she received from her Sörby background was a strange sense of guilt. Thus when my brother, a very talented and almost brilliant boy, became temporarily ill and had to be briefly hospitalized, she was convinced that it was her fault, divine retribution visited upon her for some peccadillo; and none of our protests could dissuade her. Her emotions ran so deep that her reactions were always strong. But momentary pique, anger, or dismay would swiftly be suppressed by compassion. As I think back on my boyhood, I feel that her dominant characteristic was her sense of justice; thus I recall the day she told our neighbor that "it wasn't fair" for him to prevent her children from taking the short-cut to school over his pasture. How could our little feet possibly hurt the grass? And so well did she argue the case that this difficult and usually irascible man said, "Tell Gust to make a little gate here so the children won't need to climb the fence." Despite some troubles such as my brother's illness, our home was a happy one, largely, I believe, because my mother imparted to us a sense of obligation to each other, not by orders but by subtle suggestions, and mostly by her own example.

Since both my father and my mother had worked, three and four years respectively, for English-speaking families before they were married, they had already somewhat modified their Swedish way of life. Even so, I grew up in an essentially Swedish home, although progressively, as my older brother and my two older sisters went to school, more and more English words became typical in our conversation, and gradually American customs began to supersede Swedish conventions. We adapted more rapidly in dress than in food, rather fortunately, I think, because of the excellence of so many of the traditional Swedish dishes. At Christmas, for example, we always had *risgrynsgröt*, the delicious sweet rice porridge.[15] Even more ambrosial was *ostkaka*, made of fresh curds and sugar, and served with fruit sauce usually made from lingonberries. Of the more plebeian foods we ate herring, which we ordered from a Swedish purveyor in Chicago, and which, like the lingonberries, came in firkins. For the most part, however, we lived on our own produce: potatoes, carrots, parsnips, and beets were the main root crops, while a variety of summer vegetables came from the kitchen garden as did fruits from our orchard.

Like all farm families we butchered a pig from time to time, but I suspect the Swedish families made fuller use of everything edible than their American neighbors. The hams and shoulders were merely layered in

[15] Since rice could not be grown in Sweden, it was regarded as a luxury food, appropriate for the most important festivals.

26

large thirty-gallon jars and covered with salt brine, but almost everything else required much more specialized preparation. The head, for example, was boiled in order to extract all the gelatine for headcheese; the entrails were scoured to receive the sausage mixed with ground raw potatoes, and these "potato sausages," in turn, were immersed in salt brine in twenty-gallon jars. Even the carefully collected blood was stirred into wheaten dough, and it blackened the plump round loaves. This bread, fortified by the nutrient blood, was then sliced and dried in the coal-stove oven, after which the rusklike pieces were stored in snow-white flour sacks. All through the cold, blustery Illinois winters, this black bread provided our main breakfast food. Pieces of the dried bread would be steamed until soft, and then a thick white cream sauce would be served as a covering gravy. With this, salt pork or potato sausages were normally eaten, but fried eggs or fried rabbit constituted typical variations.

Swedes are instinctively gregarious even though they have, throughout their history, lived mostly in dispersed dwellings. Indeed this circumstantial isolation, on farms, on fishing boats, or in forest employments, seems to have intensified the need for occasional feasts, banquets, or other forms of collective collation. Among the immigrant families these events became extremely important, large family dinners for ten to twenty people or more. At such an event, called a *kalas* in my boyhood, a great display of most delectable food was customary. Days of preparation were required to bake the saffron- and cardamom-flavored bread, to prepare the blended meats and mashed potatoes that would be molded into the delicious meatballs (*köttbullar*), to make *ostkaka*, to say nothing of pulverizing the spinach for the creamy *spenat* purée, roasting the chickens or ducks, preparing the dozen or more dishes of vegetables, preserves, and pickles, and baking not one but several cakes. This competitive form of hospitality, derived from peasant pride not only in the variety of food but in culinary skill, brought well-deserved distinction to a capable hostess even though it involved a tremendous amount of work and worry.

In a sense every conjugal Swedish immigrant family belonged to a larger extended family, not necessarily a kinship group, but a grouping determined by the circumstances and vicissitudes of migration. My mother, her sister, and her brothers, for example, had been given initial hospitality by a family that had migrated from a neighboring Swedish village, and we therefore belonged to their family grouping. In the same way I recall how, one by one, distant relatives or friends of my mother would arrive and stay with us until they found employment. After they were more or less settled they still, in a rather indefinable way, seemed to belong to our family. If they were unmarried they would appear from time to time and stay a few days almost as if it was their right to do so. I recall one of these characters very vividly for two reasons. He had looked for gold in Alaska where he found very little gold but millions of mosquitoes, which he described with great feeling. The second reason I remember him is that he didn't dare to bring his bottle of aquavit into our house, because he was well aware of my mother's aversion to strong liquor; so he would hide it in a hedge before he reached our house. But my mother loved "Klondike Charley" despite his weaknesses and he was welcomed sincerely whenever he came. Closer relatives, to be sure, had a kinship claim to hospitality. I recall that we were just finishing supper one night when someone knocked on our door. A complete stranger told us that he was my mother's nephew who had just arrived from Sweden. Not even a letter had been sent to forewarn us.

After the big family dinners the ladies would help the hostess clear the table and wash the dishes while the men and boys would stroll about looking at the crops and inspecting the calves, litters of recently farrowed pigs, or other livestock. Sometimes they might disport themselves by pitching horseshoes, but generally they talked about their farm problems. Our scale of operations, even though we rented fifty-seven acres of land, thereby using a total of one hundred acres, was somewhat smaller than that of our neighbors and relatives, and, as a consequence, our methods tended to be more labor intensive. We owned no hay loader, for example, which meant that all hay had to be pitched onto the hayrack. We had no corn elevator, and the brutally hard work of shoveling corn into cribs was something I rather painfully remember. Actually we had only four farm machines: a grain binder, a hay mower, a corn planter, and a cream separator. We did have a dump rake but no side-delivery rake or hay tedder, an end-gate grain seeder but no grain drill. We had no manure spreader before 1917, and no windmill until 1920. Since we had no silo, a large amount of work was involved in shocking corn to provide winter fodder for our dairy herd. For all these reasons the man-hours invested in our farm produce was consistently high.

A workaday life of this kind called for discipline for each member of the family. Yet for us no compulsion was needed since our whole family seemed animated by the hope of steady economic progress. Each had his or her assigned tasks. Thus as far back as I can remember, which means to the time when I was perhaps five years old, it was my responsibility to keep the woodbox filled and to gather corncobs to produce the very hot coals needed when my mother baked bread, cookies, and pies, or prepared oven dishes.[16] All the cream from our cows was converted into my

[16] There is a family story about me that confirms this recollection. My mother lay down to rest one evening and I, then the youngest child, came and lay down beside her. "Let's close our eyes," my mother said, "and tell each other what we

28

mother's famous butter and we children had to churn it all in the morning before we went to school. Then there was water to be carried from the well, almost a quarter of a mile away, to wash the butter again and again. The girls had their equally exacting tasks: washing, ironing, cleaning, mending; they also had the unpleasant duty of filling the kerosene lamps and washing the sooty lamp chimneys. I recall too when I was very little, perhaps five, we all sat each night and sewed rags into continuous strips which we rolled into large balls so the village weaver could make us a new rag carpet.

We worked with a will, all of us, finding by experience the tasks that we could do best. My sister Irma, for example, could not only handle horses but build a neat load of hay, and my younger sister Dorothy drove the ice wagon when she was eleven years old, leaving me free to ride from house to house on the tail-gate step poised to cut the proper-sized blocks of ice for the scores of iceboxes I filled. Our heavy work peaks, of course, came at planting and harvesting time, particularly the latter, and my brother and I could count on missing school completely for at least three weeks at corn-husking time. These were the days when we rose at four in the morning in order to be in the fields before sunrise. And those were the nights when we put glycerin on our cracked and scarred fingers and soaked our aching wrists in hot water tinctured with carbolic acid. It took some effort to stay at the head of our school classes when the urgencies of farm work made so many absences necessary.

During summers, as a boy of eight, nine, or ten years, I had one task that I really liked. Since we could spare, from arable uses, only about fifteen acres of "bottom land" along the creek for permanent pasture, our comparatively large dairy herd kept this stinted area close-cropped. One of my tasks, from June until September, when no more urgent work interfered, was to "herd" our cows on the highway, allowing them to graze on the fine stands of blue grass and sweet clover that grew between the roadway and the boundary fences which would otherwise be wasted.[17] Because I had to drive the cattle over a railroad grade-crossing, I had to be ever watchful and alert, and since the hungry animals would drift along in search of more succulent forage, I could not carry a book with me and read, as I would very much have liked to do. Instead I spent these summer hours observing clouds, birds, flowers, bees, and trees, all the while day-

see." Then she told me about a romantic picture that swam before her eyes. "Now what do you see?" she asked. "All I can see," I answered, "are three corncobs." This happened in the "old house," which means that I must have been about five years old.

[17] Undoubtedly to my parents it seemed entirely proper that I should do this since traditionally in Sweden boys were expected to act as herdsmen or shepherds. For more about child labor in Sweden, see Janson, *Background of Swedish Immigration*, pp. 110–115.

dreaming. What could have been a monotonous chore became an intellectual and emotional adventure.

Part real, part imaginary, this experience lingers in my memory. I can still see the wild roses that grew on the banks of the road even as I can hear the bees humming in the sweet clover. My interest in bees and beekeeping began on these summer afternoons when I was about nine or ten years old. I would catch a bee in my bare hand so I could see just how the golden wads of pollen had been packed on its legs, knowing full well that if I did not pinch or bruise it I need have no fear of being stung. I noted the contrasts between the bark of the wild cherry trees (we called them "chokecherries") and that of all the other trees. I remember so well the corner of the "Westerlund forty" that had never been plowed but was still matted by a heavy growth of prairie grass. Here stood a few aspen trees whose silvery leaves glistened when the wind shook their branches as it rippled through the prairie grass. And here was the only place I knew where the shooting stars grew, pushing up their tender shafts through the dense tangle of grass roots.

In my daydreams I could never decide what I wanted to be. Sometimes, probably because of some book I had just read about the Canadian wilderness, I imagined myself a great hunter and trapper. When that mood passed, I might dream of being a great singer, for, joy of joys, I always sang at my work as my mother did. I constantly visualized myself as a great traveler, an ambition that has indeed been realized. I don't recall thinking that I would become a great scholar or a great artist although I did imagine that I could be a great architect and even a great poet. When I revisit this mile of road where I herded cattle during my boyhood, the terrain seems distressingly unromantic; the hills, which I thought quite steep, have now such easy grades, and the fields seem so regular, much too level, and monotonous. But that wasn't the landscape I saw with the wide eyes of a boy. Surely there could be no more beautiful tree anywhere in the world than the single hawthorn that grew in our neighbor's pasture.

> That is the land of lost content,
> I see it shining plain,
> The happy highways where I went
> And cannot come again.[18]

In a Swedish-American home there were seldom any books, because overworked farmers and housewives had little time to read. In our home

[18] From "Into My Heart an Air That Kills," from *A Shropshire Lad* (authorized edition), from *The Collected Poems of A. E. Housman.* Copyright 1939, 1940, © 1959 by Holt, Rinehart and Winston, Inc. Copyright © 1967, 1968 by Robert E. Symons. Reprinted by permission of Holt, Rinehart and Winston, Inc., and The Society of Authors as the literary representative of the Estate of A. E. Housman.

in my early years, except for the books we children brought home from school, or from the township library, I recall only three. One, a zoology book in Swedish, had become pretty badly tattered by the time I could read because three older children had already used it. Another book, about the Holy Land, *Med penna och kamera i heliga landet,* though not very exciting, had the virtue that it probably led me to read John Lawson Stoddard's *Lectures* at school.[19] The third book, which my father thought we ought to have and therefore bought from a house-to-house salesman, proved to be our greatest joy. Its flamboyant title, *Good Times at Home,* did not exaggerate its potential since it included "Seven Instructive Books in One Volume." In Book I we found poems "chronologically arranged from Shakespeare to the present time." Book II, entitled "The Model Reciter and Speaker," proved invaluable with its "narrative," "pathetic," "humorous," "moral," and "patriotic" selections. Next came a "book" on "Games, Amusements and Sports," followed by one on "The Songs We Love to Sing." Book V was particularly useful in attuning us to American customs since in this "Home Book of Etiquette" we found all the instruction needed to give us social graces. But for me, Book VI held the greatest fascination; it had for a title "Wonderful and Remarkable Things and Facts," and it dealt with history, religion, politics, and anthropology as well as "marvelous facts about small creatures." Finally, in Book VII was found an account of "distinguished people," their "anecdotes" and their achievements. I am forever grateful that my father bought us this book. More than anything else it eased our transition from one cultural milieu to another.[20]

I grew up in a zestful atmosphere, rigorously disciplined to be sure, but, as I have said, we accepted discipline willingly. I realized this very clearly when I worked on a neighbor's farm the summer I was fifteen years old. I got up at four o'clock each morning, helped milk seven cows, and then fed about a hundred hogs while the farmer took the milk in a "spring wagon" two miles to the railway station in time for it to go to Moline on the 7:32 train. Then after we had washed out-of-doors, in cold well-water, we had a breakfast of fried potatoes and fried eggs before we went to the fields to "plow" (cultivate) corn. I found no joy in this daily drill; all the compensation that came from a joint participation in a family development

---

[19] Stoddard traveled widely and made a reputation as a lecturer on travel subjects. Ten volumes of *John L. Stoddard's Lectures* were published in 1897–98, and five additional volumes appeared in 1901.

[20] Stimulated by this book, I found ways of beginning my own library. I sold subscriptions to *McCall's* magazine in order to acquire eight small volumes called *Masterpieces of the World's Best Literature,* and then I purchased for cash a book that completely fascinated me, *Langstroth on the Hive and Honey Bee.* I still have these nine books that were for me so intellectually exciting. I also have *Good Times at Home,* woefully worn but still complete.

effort was missing. At home it must have been the "new hopes" that made the difference, not merely hopes of gain or profit but of self-fulfillment. But I am entirely certain that my parents' "hopes" were for us much more than for themselves.

They both lie sleeping in Western Cemetery now, just two miles from the scene of their relentless labor. My oldest sister and my brother, both of whom died in their thirties, are buried there also. Great fleecy, cumulous clouds, like the ones I watched when I herded our cattle, float over the burial plot almost every day, and whenever I think of this I recall Edgar Lee Masters's lines

> Clouds, like convoys on infinite missions,
> Bound for infinite harbors
> Float over the length of this land.
> And in the centuries to come
> The rocks and trees of this land will turn,
> These fields and hills will turn
> Under unending convoys of clouds.

This land, rich and fertile, this "tender land," as Aaron Copland has called the nearby land in Iowa, had for the Swedish immigrants virtues that modern people who speed through the Middle West on wide interstate highways cannot possibly understand. For this land epitomized the freedom that people born to hardship found in a "new" world. These fields were not merely meadows or areas of rock-free soil where oats, corn, or wheat could be planted. The immigrant found something spiritually satisfying in

> This land of the free ordinance,
> This land made free for the free
> By the patriarchs.

May it be that the thoughts the newcomers could not themselves express have been written for each of them in these lines:

> O Earth that looks into space,
> As a man in sleep looks up,
> And is voiceless, at peace,
> Divining the secret —
> I shall know the secret
> When I go down into this land
> Of the great Northwest! [21]

[21] *Starved Rock* (New York: Macmillan, 1919, 1947), pp. 126–127.

3

THE VILLAGE
★★★★★★★★★★★★★

LIKE millions of my fellow countrymen, I was born in a small rural community. My birthplace lay on the outskirts of the village of Orion, in Henry County, Illinois. The little world I first knew was therefore inhabited by farmers, village tradesmen and artisans, together with a few professional people: the three doctors, the dentist, the three clergymen, the two bankers, and the school principal. Some social stratification existed, based more on a family's length of residence in the community than on wealth, literacy, or political influence. Cultural conflicts could not be avoided, but fortunately exclusive groups were few, and although latecomers tended to form separate social enclaves, these divisions were constantly being eroded as interrelations among the several groups became more and more common. The early settlers had been almost all farmers of English, Welsh, or Scotch-Irish extraction. By stages these pioneers had moved westward, southwestward, or northward up the Mississippi from its confluence with the Ohio. A very interesting blending of people, traditions, and customs resulted, and the very names of the early arrivals indicate the geographic pattern of their travel routes. Chases and Stearnses, for example, were true New Englanders; Pearces and Keels from Pennsylvania, Lloyds, Loves, and Fergusons from Ohio, though also northerners, had somewhat different roots; while Sayreses, Wrights, and Worthingtons traced their families back to Virginia via Kentucky. To this community a few Irish had attached themselves, some as farmers but more typically as artisans or railway section men, and only gradually did Bambricks, O'Learys, and Kelihers intermarry with children of the first settlers. The Irish were always a small minority, too small to have their own local Catholic church, and it was probably their feeling of being

33

outnumbered that caused some of them to show animosity toward the ever-increasing Swedish-American group, sizable enough to have the largest village church where for more than thirty years the long sermons were preached in Swedish.

Cultural conflicts, whose cutting edges would often be sharp, reflected not merely an antipathy between ethnic groups. The established Swedes looked down on the "Green Swedes," although to their everlasting credit there were a few early Swedish settlers who stood ready to find jobs for the recent immigrants or loan them money until they had a chance to fit into the local work force. Yet for all the overtones of social difference, which led Swedish-American children to feel ashamed of their parents and thereby robbed most of them of a linguistic heritage, a tolerable measure of equality existed between the ethnic groups and between the early and later arrivals. In a community where there were many Swansons, Carlsons, Petersons, Gustafsons, Larsons, and Andersons, nicknames were more useful than surnames for certain and prompt identification. Some of these nicknames were occupational ("Wagon-Box" Anderson), others descriptive ("Nig" Swanson or "Big" Dahl). But it was not only the patronymic Swedes who had colorful nicknames. Our postmaster who had some reputation as a hunter was always spoken of as "Coony" Wilson, and his brother, a livestock buyer, was called "Hog" Wilson; "Morning, Hog," my father would say quite naturally when he telephoned to ascertain when Ed Wilson was next shipping hogs. All these democratic designations led to a rather relaxed social atmosphere, and this no doubt helped meld old and new, native and foreign, richer and poorer elements into a community. But nicknames can be pejorative as well as descriptive, and many children were wounded by their schoolmates who taunted them with their fathers' overly descriptive nicknames.

As I look back on my boyhood in this village community of some six or seven hundred people, I often wonder whether I was lucky or unlucky. My parents could have chosen to live in Moline, Rockford, or any of the other Illinois cities to which Swedish immigrants were attracted by employment opportunities in implement factories or machine shops. Or, since they decided on farming as a way of life, they might have bought a farm not on the edge of a village but five, six, or seven miles from any settlement. What would have been my situation then? Instead of attending a four-room village school, with as many teachers, I would have gone to a "district" school where one hapless and almost entirely untrained teacher would be trying vainly to teach all basic subjects for all eight grades. From this tragic educational experience I was at least saved, even though the Orion school left much to be desired. Yet its inadequacy ought not be attributed to the teachers, for they were, I believe, quite dedicated to their tasks. The trouble stemmed from the parsimony of the school board whose penuriousness in turn was compelled by the modest tax revenues available; and these insufficient appropriations for the school really reflected the inefficiency of the local village economy. Because incomes were small, local government officials in every village, township, and county were under the strongest pressure to keep taxes low. From these compulsions not only education but public health suffered, as did fire protection, highways, public utilities, and cultural amenities.

It seems remarkable how well the Orion teachers, faced as they were with inadequate school funds, performed their duties; moreover, it was a liberal rather than a vocational education that they stressed. One of my second-grade books is still fresh in my memory: an "Art and Literature" reader with illustrations of paintings by Sir Joshua Reynolds, Sir Edwin Landseer, and Rosa Bonheur, among others; with interesting stories about artists and writers; and with short poems by Longfellow and Helen Hunt Jackson. This single book made an indelible impression on me; I recall seeing the "Blue Boy" in London in 1929 and found it was precisely as I thought it would be because I had known just how it looked ever since I was seven years old. Perhaps it was because our educational resources were so meager that we made such thorough use of them. *Grimm's Fairy Tales* and Stoddard's *Lectures* were the only reference books I remember in the room that seated the third, fourth, and fifth grades, and I presume this is why I read every word of these books. There were, to be sure, a limited number of books in the township library. They could be counted in the hundreds rather than the thousands, but I suspect that these well-worn books provided enough of a self-educational supplement to make the skeletal school system tolerably adequate. The real educational pinch came in high school. Until 1914 the only high school teacher was the school principal who was responsible for a three-year curriculum covering Latin, history, mathematics, English, and science. Fortunately when I entered high school, in the autumn of 1914, there were two teachers; the school principal taught mathematics and science, and a very conscientious young lady was responsible for Latin, English, and history. Two years later a third teacher was hired when civics and German, as I recall, were added to the curriculum.

Small classes made it possible for our teachers to give personal attention to some of their more eager pupils. In my high school class, for example, there were only eighteen students, and when I recall that three of us were allowed to go beyond second-year Latin (Caesar) to third-year (Cicero) and then two of us to fourth-year Latin (Vergil), I realize that for some students a small, poorly financed high school provided almost the equivalent of tutorial instruction. But there were, at the same time, serious weaknesses. An incompetent mathematics teacher blunted my interest in that essential subject and seriously handicapped my career as an economist; while totally inadequate, indeed almost nonexistent, laboratory facilities made our scientific training thin and superficial. Yet for all these obvious shortcomings there was something about the school that galvanized our interests and whetted our intellectual curiosity. I marvel at the ornithological observations I made in my zoology notebook, the herbarium of wildflowers I prepared for our botany course, my complete scansion of Vergil's *Aeneid*, the model of Caesar's bridge over the Rhine that I built, the Latin quotations that are indelibly graven on my mind, and the German poems that I recall today as readily as passages from Emerson's *Essays*. There must have been something in the school system that inspired the members of a family of first-generation Americans. My eldest sister was valedictorian of her class, my brother (despite his serious illness) salutatorian of his class, my next sister valedictorian of her class, and I had the same honor when I graduated, while my youngest sister, although fractionally outpaced by two other Swedish-Americans, had a four-year scholastic average of 96 percent.

Time, to be sure, mellows our memories, and hence I may perhaps be overstating my indebtedness to a penny-pinching village community. Aside from a single leather-padded "horse" over which boys could leap-frog, our school had no recreational facilities whatever; drinking water from a nearby (uninspected) well was carried in by the janitor and poured into stone jars equipped with spigots. The steam-heating system was noisy and most inefficient, and the only fire escape consisted of a single canvas chute. The village itself had no water or sewage system, and two cisterns provided the only water reserves for the (volunteer) fire department. Children drank from a tin cup chained to the village well near the post office, and this no doubt had much to do with the unfailing succession of infectious diseases that seldom missed a household. Without running water or sewers, each family had to make its own "sanitary" arrangements, which for the great majority of homes consisted of small buildings with crescents or stars as typical gable or door embellishments. Little or no supervision was thought necessary over the careless disposal of waste products at the local slaughterhouse, and there was, as far as I know, no inspection of the local dairy or the restaurant. Many villagers kept chickens and a pig or two in their back yard, some had cows, and before the advent of automobiles most people had a horse. Everyone knew that flies spread diseases, but with stables, manure piles, and pigpens so well distributed, flypaper, fly traps, fly sprays, and window screens could not cope with this ever-present public-health hazard.

Why was not an artesian well drilled and a water system built? If that had been done, a sewage system could have been the next essential public improvement. Once again the trouble was the pressure for low taxes, an insistence that stemmed from the very modest levels of family incomes. Yet during the period of my boyhood (1906–18) there were no serious "depressions"; indeed by late-nineteenth-century standards this was a rather satisfactory chapter in American economic annals. Despite all the fulmination against trusts, railway monopolies, and "robber barons," the basic reason for low incomes in midwestern rural communities really lay in the village structure of the economy and the faulty organization of space. Consider what the situation actually was in Orion around the year 1910. The village had a population of about seven hundred people and this nucleus served as a trade and marketing center for a compass of farmland with a radius of no more than six or seven miles. In this hinterland seven or eight hundred farm people lived, making the total potential customers for the village enterprises not more than fifteen hundred persons. Yet no fewer than eighty-one petty business enterprises tried to survive on this wholly inadequate market demand. The dirt roads had heavy layers of dust in the summer and then sticky mud from the September equinoctial rains to the end of April when the "gumbo prairies" finally began to dry out; under either condition the speed of buggies and wagons was reduced to less than three miles an hour, thus imposing rather rigid spatial limits on the village trade and banking areas. Consequently until roads improved so that the speed of transport could be increased, as they were when the Model T Ford came into general use, there was little chance of expanding the typical market area that an Illinois village served. Meantime in most uneconomical ways these little markets had come to be divided among redundant enterprises.

How could the three Orion grocery stores hope to obtain a volume of business that would provide their owners with adequate income? How much could the local candy shop net in profits? How often would one of the two implement dealers sell a manure spreader or a corn planter? When the total trade area had only about 1500 men, women, and children, what net earnings could each of the three doctors expect? How could a photographer, a newspaper publisher, a millinery store, or a jewelry store generate enough business to ensure a profitable reward for invested capital and for technical and managerial labor? Nor did any real competition exist between the superfluous firms that could bring any important benefits to consumers. Because their volume of business was so small, both of the two drugstore proprietors charged high prices, a duopolistic situation where neither firm dared to lower prices for fear of spoiling the market. The two lumberyards followed the same "live and let live" high-price policy, yet they could scarcely make a decent income. For lack of enough business for two livery stables, most of their horses stood idle. The three barbers, the dentist, and the proprietor of the shoe store were also idle most of the time, and they overcame the tedium of waiting for occasional customers by pitching horseshoes on the main street of the village where the Methodist preacher, the harness-maker, or an implement dealer could help make up the changing foursomes. The two blacksmith shops were probably related in some tolerably sensible way to the horses that needed to be shod, the wagons to be repaired, and the plowshares to be reforged or sharpened. But there was by no means full employment for the three building contractors, the three painting and decorating firms, the tinsmith, the well-driller, the teamster, the hack driver, or the carpet weaver. The two livestock shippers must have had very modest profits, and whereas the poultry-dressing plant with its group of rowdy "chicken pickers" seemed busy enough in winter it encountered business doldrums all through the summer months. The undertaker, who also sold furniture, had a none-too-profitable monopoly as did the printer, the butcher, the tailor, and the baker. There simply wasn't enough spending power to justify so many enterprises, and none of them had a scale of operations that would meet even the most minimum standards of managerial efficiency.

The advent of the automobile, which began to lengthen market radii even before "hard roads" made it possible to stretch them much more, ultimately released most rural communities from these unhappy spatial limitations. Gradually and experientially larger market centers serving far larger hinterlands emerged, albeit with wasteful duplicatory investments as each village aspired to become the business center for areas with market radii of twenty-five or thirty miles. The advantages of these larger zones stemmed from the familiar geometric fact that areas of circles increase by the square of their diameters. If a Model T Ford traveling at fifteen miles an hour could range five times as far afield as a horse and buggy traveling at three miles an hour, the potential trade area of a market center might be twenty-five times as great as it had been in the horse and buggy age. But the lengthenings of market radii, which were destined to transform the American countryside and create what Karl Fox and Brian J. L. Berry have called "functional economic areas,"[1] had scarcely begun during my days in Orion, so that until World War I vast stretches of the American countryside still suffered from minuscule markets and from an almost grotesque oversupply of petty enterprises.

Low business income meant not only low profits (or none at all) but low

[1] Fox, "Agricultural Policy in an Urban Society," paper presented at the annual meeting of the American Agricultural Economics Association, August 19, 1968; Berry, *Metropolitan Area Definition: A Re-evaluation of Concept and Statistical Practice*, U.S. Department of Commerce, Bureau of the Census, Working Paper 28, June 1968.

wages for the relatively few village wage earners; and the low level of local wages played into the hands of the railroads which needed only to pay the going local wages to their section men. Calvin Hoover has vividly described the situation in another small Illinois town about fifty miles from Orion.[2] His father worked on the railroad ten hours a day, six days a week for a paltry wage of $55 a month; and from the time he himself was thirteen years old the future dean of Duke University's Graduate School worked during the summer at the backbreaking job of a section hand at even lower wages; his father, after all, was a foreman!

How then did the families in the community of Orion maintain any tolerably decent standards of living? First of all they raised most of their food in their kitchen gardens, and they stored away in basements potatoes, squash, onions, and apples for the winter. They canned peaches, plums, strawberries, raspberries, gooseberries, applesauce, and cherries; they put down cucumbers in salt brine, and they canned beans, tomatoes, peas, beets, and corn. Many villagers, as I said, kept chickens; some had a pig or two and a cow. My parents had an advantage because we had a farm — forty-three acres plus some fifty-seven areas of rented land. Our family income was therefore a little more flexible. Yet we were dependent on the village population for the sale of our butter, one of our important cash crops. Although we had the only local ice business, after our competition gave up trying to share the petty market, I am by no means certain that the cash income compensated us for the vast amount of work involved: the discomfort of cutting and "putting up" ice in the winter, and the brutally hard work of delivering it to the customers in the summer. I can speak with some sureness about these trials since I was the iceman.

On a farm, although a small one, we, of course, had our own supply of milk, cream, eggs, poultry, and pork. These standard items my brother and I supplemented by scores of rabbits, squirrels, doves, and quail. Moreover, I knew where every wild apple tree, plum tree, and raspberry bush grew, where every currant bush was in the Osage orange hedges, and I regularly made the rounds of fence rows in the spring to find the succulent spears of wild asparagus. From the time I was fourteen I kept bees; by the time I finished high school my apiary consisted of twenty-four modern hives, and I was by far the most knowledgeable bee-keeper in the community, whose advice was sought by my elders. Thriftiness was approved in a low-income economy; hence it was no disgrace to pick up bright black coal that had fallen off the long trains of gondola cars that thundered north on the C. B. & Q. Railroad from the southern Illinois coal fields to the bunkers in Minneapolis and St. Paul. Our problem as

[2] See his most interesting *Memoirs of Capitalism, Communism, and Nazism* (Durham, N.C.: Duke University Press, 1965), chapter 1.

young people was how to obtain some personal cash income, and to this end we trapped muskrats and skunks and seized every opportunity for occasional employment. At the age of eleven, twelve, and thirteen, I regularly acted as a water boy for harvesters at threshing time, and once a year I earned a little money when the village oiled the streets, a dirty, unpleasant job in the days when the oil was spread on the dusty streets with hand sprinklers. We sometimes could get jobs unloading sand or bricks at the local lumberyards, but the trouble, of course, was that there were more boys looking for work than there were jobs to go around.

This employment deficit permeated the whole village economy mainly because the small enterprises catering to such minuscule markets simply could not expand. Moreover, their owners themselves provided the necessary manpower so that very rarely did local enterprises have any hired employees. The tinsmith and plumber had an assistant, as did the printer; and the baker, the dry-goods store, and one of the grocery stores each had a hired clerk. But neither lumberyard employed any full-time workers. A little seasonal work was provided at the chicken-dressing plant and on our ice pond when we filled the icehouse, and occasionally there might be a need for extra manpower at harvest time. One of our high school principals, for example, usually succeeded in getting work "pitching bundles" during the threshing season; he deserved the job, for he was a very efficient worker. Because of this very scant demand for village wage earners, most farm boys who hoped to do something other than farm work really had only two options. They could seek employment in nearby cities, such as Moline, Rock Island, Galesburg, or Peoria; or they could try to set up still another petty enterprise in the village where they were already known and where none of the strangeness of city life would be encountered. Year after year, these hopefuls would attempt to make a living in villages already overcrowded with small business ventures. The automobile created the only really new demand for manpower that emerged during my boyhood by developing a limited number of openings in the villages for garage mechanics and operators of filling stations, and a few new opportunities for automobile dealers. The total of these new jobs, however, was very modest; in Orion, as I recall, fewer than a dozen people found employment in the two garages, while "gasoline pumps" were not yet "filling stations" that could provide full-time employment.

Despite these endemic constraints, most farm boys hesitated to migrate to cities even though nationally the gradual townward drift, reflected in the census figures, showed a steady advance of urban over rural population. Occasionally an Orion farm boy would become a switch-engine locomotive engineer in Galesburg or a machine operator in a Moline implement factory. But until the automobile age made commuting fifteen or twenty miles possible, the village structure persisted, with all its limitations on productivity, employment, and income. Meantime there was another peculiarity of the villages which contributed to their economic sluggishness. A very large fraction of the village population consisted of retired farmers who had very modest needs for clothing, furniture, or even food, since they were all accomplished gardeners. The typical rural villages contrasted rather sharply, therefore, with modern suburban village communities where recent family formations generate a strong demand for house furnishings and where a swarm of young children expect their parents to buy them a wide range of clothes, toys, bicycles, television sets, and a host of other conveniences and status symbols, factors that markedly contribute to business briskness.

Because Illinois villages in the 1910–15 era were economically unprogressive, it should not be assumed that they were necessarily monotonous or culturally barren places. Their spatial isolation, which railroads had never relieved, compelled people to find their own amusements and develop local cultural amenities. Orion had its choral society to which almost everyone who could sing belonged; it had a band, whose members provided not only their own instruments but their own uniforms, and later it also had a small orchestra. A number of lodges — Masons, Odd Fellows, Modern Woodmen — were well populated although I knew little about their activities since my father, intense individualist that he was, belonged to none. Patriotic events were dutifully celebrated; on "Decoration Day," ceremonies in the "Opera House" were followed by hayrack rides to the cemetery where, under the watchful eyes of the living Civil War veterans, we decorated the graves of those members of the Grand Army of the Republic from our little village who had fallen in a tragic war. The Fourth of July brought a long-awaited parade, sporting events, picnics, and a band concert in the village park. But although almost every Illinois village had a fairly similar pattern of cultural and civic activities, Orion had something unique: it had the Jessie Colton Theatrical Company.

A very talented actress, Jessie Colton, by some inexplicable vicissitude, had found her way from Broadway triumphs to a far less glamorous life in this Illinois village. Thrice married she had talented children by each of her husbands. Her eldest daughter, Lottie Pearce, rivaled the dramatic talents of her son and daughter by another marriage, Isaac and Philena Chapel; these older children somewhat overshadowed her two youngest children, George and Bertha Richardson. Her third husband, Bert Richardson, son of one of our two blacksmiths, had some way or other brought Jessie Colton to our village. Jessie's daughter Lottie then married Bert Richardson's brother Ralph, and when Lottie and Ralph had a charming

41

daughter, Rosalie, the Jessie Colton Company was so far as I remember complete except for one or two hired actors. Jessie's family included no fewer than nine actors, well distributed in age from Jessie herself, who was probably the oldest, down to Rosalie who could play Little Eva in *Uncle Tom's Cabin* or break the hearts of her audience when she sang "Ireland must be Heaven for my mother came from there!"

The Jessie Colton Company gave its plays — and they ranged from *East Lynn* to *Hamlet* — in their own tent, playing a four- or five-day stand in more than a score of villages. Tent, chairs, trunks, and scenery moved by hired wagons from village to village but Orion was the alpha and omega of the annual peregrinations, which meant that we had both an opening and a closing set of plays each summer and then, as a special bonus, we had Jessie Colton with us throughout the rest of the year! She and her husband coached our high school plays, and she trained some of us in dramatics and public speaking. A wonderful, zestful teacher, Jessie Colton taught me how to stand, gesture, complete my gestures, how to project my voice so that every corner of an auditorium could hear, how to find precisely the right words to emphasize, and, above all, how to speak with clarity, sonority, and oral richness. I owe much to Jessie Colton, and each time I revisit Orion I pay my respects at her grave. She and Bert and her daughter Philena are buried in Western Cemetery only a few steps from where my parents, my eldest sister, and my only brother lie. Quite fittingly on Jessie and Bert's tombstone there is engraved "Life's Drama Has Ended; the Curtain Has Fallen."

The more devout church members, whether Lutheran, Methodist, or Baptist, had some reservations about the Jessie Colton troupe. "Show people" were often thought immoral, and Jessie's three marriages seemed a bit excessive. One ought not be too critical, however, of the clergymen and the churches. In their somewhat circumscribed ways they fulfilled many quasi-educational and social functions, however much they emphasized dogma, since each brand of Christianity seemed very certain that its tenets were the right ones. In the Methodist Sunday School to which my mother sent us after she withdrew from the Lutheran church, we learned to sing the dull, banal hymns of Reverend Johnson Oatman set to music by E. O. Excell. Years later the talented daughter of the Reverend Johnson Oatman was my next-door neighbor in Norman, Oklahoma, but I never had the temerity or the rudeness to tell her how stale and vapid I thought her father's hymns were. In Orion most people belonged to some church although there were quite a few who ignored this accepted hallmark of respectability. One really had little choice; either you accepted the mores of the churchgoers or you automatically allied yourself with the indifferent or the scornful. No great intellectual harm resulted from church affiliation even though the mental capacity and the range of knowledge of the ill-paid clergymen scarcely qualified them for their didactic duties. One learned precious little from the rhetorical sermons of partially literate preachers, or from untrained Sunday School teachers.

Fortunately the school, the township library, the countryside, and the unsuspecting village artisans provided me with better educational opportunities. Of the school and the library I have already spoken. Concurrently the countryside and the artisan shops provided some of my rich educational experiences. Like Thoreau who said he had "travelled a good deal in Concord," I knew the flora and fauna of the area within walking distance of our home with considerable accuracy. Trees, shrubs, flowers came to be systematically organized in my cognitive faculties; birds, insects, and animals were equally well recognized. I knew where the yellow-billed cuckoo nested, and where the shooting stars, bluebells, and dog-tooth violets were to be found. Of geology I learned little because the land on the edge of the prairie had too few outcrops. Even less knowledge of anthropology could be acquired, though I did succeed in finding about a dozen Indian arrowheads which I mounted and which I still possess among my many collections. Some of my most valuable educational experiences, however, were obtained from my repeated visits to the artisan shops in the village. When I delivered the *Chicago American* to a couple dozen readers who seemed to prefer that wretched newspaper, I would loiter all too long, I fear, watching the blacksmiths shape pieces of wrought-iron craftsmanship on their anvils. Sir William Petty, I learned much later, haunted the artisan shops in Romsey when he was a boy in Hampshire. The cabinetmakers possessed skills that I thoroughly envied, and I observed their methods carefully so that I could try to emulate their precise techniques. I watched the roofers, the plasterers, the masons, and was fascinated by the skill of the cigar-maker who could cut freehand a wrapper which would envelop the "filler" perfectly.

The outbreak of war in 1914 had no immediate effect on our little community although horse buyers soon appeared looking for animals suitable for pulling French or British artillery caissons. By the end of 1916, however, the effect of the increased volume of international trade which the neutrality period produced could be felt; the prices of grain, pork, and lard had risen almost 50 percent over the 1914 levels, and this upward surge in farm prices had led to an increase in the price of farmland. Once the United States entered the war, a much larger number of economic changes came in swift succession. By the time of the Armistice, in November 1918, prices had risen another 50 percent, and local labor shortages had developed following the withdrawal of manpower for the armed forces and the recruitment of labor by the Rock Island arsenal and factories busily engaged in war production in Moline, Rock Island, Davenport, and Peoria. Wages rose, farm incomes increased markedly, more people purchased automobiles, and farmers borrowed money to buy more land or to invest in more and better farm machinery. But this burst of unfamiliar prosperity, which led to a very unwise overvaluation of farmland, ended far more abruptly than it had begun, and after a short postwar boom our unreconstructed rural community was plunged into a long and unhappy depression.

It was during this short-lived evanescent period of prosperity that I left my natal community. From the time I entered high school I had my sights fixed on a college education, however unusual higher education had been for Orion boys. It was, of course, easier to go on to the university after 1916 since by that time our high school was fully accredited. Before then, very seldom did an Orion boy go to college, and when he did, he usually enrolled at nearby Knox ("Good Old Siwash") in Galesburg or Augustana (a Lutheran college and theological seminary) in Rock Island. I believe I was the second Orion High School graduate to enter the state university. This transition from high school to college was made rather easy in 1918 because most colleges and universities became an integral part of the war effort. In order to train officer personnel, all upper classmen and all entering students in the participating universities and colleges were urged to accept induction into the Students Army Training Corps (SATC), and the overwhelming majority did. In doing so, they became members of the armed forces but their military duties occupied only a portion of their time, thus allowing them to continue their college studies while their suitability for more intensive military training at officers' training camps was being determined. Full of hope, excitement, and not a little apprehension, I set out for Urbana in early October 1918, traveling, as we all did in those days, by train. When the C. R. I. & P. local train left the Orion station for Peoria, where I would change trains, I sensed that I would never again be a part of the village community where I had been born and nurtured.

4

LEARNING AND LABOR
★★★★★★★★★★★★★★★★★★★★★★★

THE University of Illinois was in a state of very evident confusion the day
I descended from the dusty Big Four Railroad car that had brought me
from Peoria. The military authorities had failed to complete the housing
project for the expected three thousand student-soldiers even though they
had engaged the services of almost every carpenter in Champaign County.
What they had planned to do, and ultimately succeeded in doing, was to
put a second floor in the university armory, a building so huge that it
covered an area two city blocks long and almost a block wide. A forest
of 10 by 10 uprights presently supported miles of joists so that an upper-
floor room could accommodate three thousand cots; while the first-floor
area, with its thousands of posts and angle braces, would serve as an
equally colossal cafeteria. All this construction — plus the building of
washrooms and toilets outside the armory and the addition of a massive
kitchen ell where steam cookers, grills, and ovens capable of preparing
nine thousand meals a day were installed — took more time than expected.
Meantime the student-soldiers had arrived, and to tide over the emergency hasty temporary arrangements had to be concluded with owners of
rooming houses, irate because the huge dormitory would deprive them of
their usual lodgers, with fraternities, and with private householders.

The university authorities found themselves in an equally frustrating
situation. The War Department had been woefully tardy in deciding precisely what courses should be offered in all participating colleges and universities. More than that, in order to speed up the training of second
lieutenants ("ninety-day wonders") all the colleges and universities with
SATC units had to adopt a trimester system. This called for drastic changes
in courses, personnel, budgets, and facilities. As I recall, only two required

45

courses, "War Issues" and French, finally had to be shoehorned into every student-soldier's program; for the rest we had little or no guidance other than a five- or ten-minute vetting of our programs by so-called faculty advisers. No one asked me anything about my academic plans or interests, or attempted to ascertain my aptitudes. As a result I found myself registered for a cluster of courses that included chemistry, a subject for which I had, to say the least, little enthusiasm.

We finally moved into our huge bedroom, where neatly made cots stretched almost to the horizon, and here we lived a strange life. At five forty-five when "first call" reverberated through the arcuated trusses that supported the roof far above our heads, sergeants and corporals made hasty bed checks to see that all their charges promptly put on their woolly uniforms, rough shoes, and ill-fitting leggings. Then with a great clatter the three thousand hurried down the wide, cleated ramps and out into the morning darkness to their appointed places to stand reveille, a formality followed by a none-too-pleasant fifteen minutes of setting-up exercises. After this was over, we all rushed back up the ramps, grabbed our toilet kits, and dashed to the washrooms so that we might finish our ablutions quickly enough to have a reasonably unhurried breakfast. At seven o'clock we marched to the drill field where for the next three and a half hours the shavetail company commanders, fresh out of officers' training camps, and their newly selected noncommissioned officers drilled their squads and platoons. I can still hear the cacophony of some 375 corporals, 60 sergeants, and 15 company commanders barking out their orders!

How well did this combination of university study and military training work? Most upperclassmen adapted themselves reasonably well, but for first-year students the adjustment proved so difficult that a great many did not return once they received their army discharges in December 1918. I suspect that those of us who stayed on had fallen into rather bad academic habits. With no place to study other than an overcrowded library or the noisy three-thousand-cot bedroom, one abandoned any hope of excellence; the problem was how to survive. My own situation proved particularly complicated because I had to absent myself for about a fortnight for a trip to the United States Military Academy at West Point. While a senior in high school I had written our congressman asking for a June 1918 appointment to the Military Academy but in that effort I was unsuccessful. Quite unexpectedly, however, I received an appointment in early October because a special class of cadets had been authorized. I arrived at the academy the day after the Armistice, an event which rather took the glamour off a prospective military career. Consequently, when a week later laboratory tests showed that I had symptoms of nephritis,

I was not wholly unhappy to be physically rejected. Back I went to the university handicapped by unwritten themes and unperformed chemical experiments. Nevertheless I passed all my subjects even though I had been improperly registered, by my casual "adviser," for nineteen hours of coursework.

As time went on I became more and more disenchanted with the university. I had no complaint about military training under the required two-year Reserve Officers Training Program; I needed the calisthenics so exactly required, and I benefited from the posture improvement that came from close-order drill. But I had expected more faculty guidance, and I was wholly unprepared for the utterly impersonal character of mass education. I found, moreover, that the College of Arts and Sciences had become largely a service center for the ever-expanding professional schools. Economics, for example, had been moved en bloc into the College of Commerce. From the days when I read Stoddard's *Lectures* I had dreamed of foreign travel or residence; for that reason I was attracted to the "prefabricated" curriculum on foreign trade in the College of Commerce. When I went to see the dean of arts and sciences to obtain permission to transfer, he merely signed my transfer without even asking why I was making this change in academic plans. It proved to be not a wise decision. The prescribed program of studies, specifying the "right" courses for each semester, presumably would give one the proper training for some overseas business career. But later on I discovered it had given me a very thin and superficial education. Fortunately the foreign-trade program had fewer technical subjects than the other commerce programs and laid relatively more emphasis on courses in history, government, and international law. Another virtue was the annual language requirement, and I wisely opted to stay with a single language thereby acquiring a tolerably satisfactory command of French.

Aside from entomology and elective courses in public speaking, both of which stirred my enthusiasm, I found little intellectual stimulus in my classwork for the first three years at Illinois. Assembly-line teaching techniques characterized practically all my courses. For "lectures" we thronged into a large auditorium where an effort was made to baptize us in droves into the mysteries of general economics, money and banking, and corporation finance. Sandwiched in between lectures were the "section meetings," presided over by none-too-competent graduate-student instructors. For each of these large courses a prescribed textbook supplemented by a bulky book of readings [1] constituted the complete instruc-

[1] I recall that in elementary economics, for which Ely's *Outlines of Economics* was the text, the readings had been compiled by Marshall, Wright, and Field; similarly Scott's *Money and Banking* was supplemented by a massive book of read-

tional literature. We read no monographs except in one instance where Arthur Stone Dewing's systematic analysis of *Financial Policy of Corporations* had been selected as a textbook. That book I read with eager enthusiasm, and it proved to be an interesting coincidence that its scholarly author was to be one of my most rigorous examiners when I presented myself for my oral qualifying examination for the Harvard Ph.D. degree.

Most dissatisfying were the technical and completely descriptive courses that no commerce student could avoid, dreadfully tedious exercises in accounting and required courses in business English and in a presumed discipline alliteratively called "business organization and operation." Because of my contempt for these superficial subjects, taught by pompous pretenders, I nearly failed to get passing marks in these required courses. Business law, foreign trade, and personnel administration proved to be only a little more challenging. Since I had accelerated my study program by following, each semester, the practice, unwittingly approved during my first term, of carrying more than the normal number of credit hours, my senior year consisted of a single semester, and fortunately this small fraction of my undergraduate education proved to be rich and memorable. With Nathan Weston, a first-class teacher and scholar, I had a course in economic theory in which we read the whole of Alfred Marshall's *Principles of Economics*.[2] Meantime with James Garner I explored problems of international law, and with E. B. Greene, who soon thereafter moved to Columbia University, I studied colonial history, reading original documents and a number of excellent monographs. I therefore had one semester out of the equivalent of seven (the university returned to the semester system after the war) that could be called genuinely educational.

At Illinois in my day the "technical high school" idea had largely undermined the European concept of a "university." Everyone was apparently in training for some more or less routine career. In the rooming house where I lived three students were registered in commerce, two in architecture, four in engineering, two in agriculture. Although we talked a good deal, we never discussed philosophical, political, or any essentially intellectual issues. What became of my housemates I don't know; like the vast majority of Illinois graduates they no doubt fitted into their planned professional activities and spent their lives as business executives, accountants, architects, farm-organization bureaucrats, journalists, or engineers. Only two or three members of my class seem to have attained any academic distinction. One, Donald Erb, became president of the University

ings; and in economic history Bogart's text together with *Readings* by Bogart and Thompson provided the entire intellectual menu.

[2] Two years later when I began my graduate work at Harvard I was among the very few who had had a systematic course based on Marshall.

48

of Oregon. But Erb did what I did; he went on to Harvard for graduate study.

If the promise of the first word of the University of Illinois motto, "Learning and Labor," did not materialize to my complete satisfaction, I surely received full benefit from the second. Although tuition was free for residents of the state of Illinois, and as a high school senior I won a statewide essay competition that gave me a scholarship prize of $150, I had to work regularly to keep myself in college. A student who worked his way needed large reserves of energy. One's food could, of course, be best obtained by waiting on tables at a fraternity house. Room rent, books, clothes, travel at vacation time, and incidental expenses called for cash earnings. Odd jobs could be found for Saturdays through the university Employment Office doing such things as beating rugs or cleaning silver. I fired a furnace one winter, and during a spring term I cared for the university golf course, a doubly trying job because of the long walk to the golf course and the very hard work of mowing the greens with a heavy, multiple-geared machine. The fairways were mowed by horse-drawn rotary mowers but it was my responsibility to see that the sand-boxes and water pails were always filled. Wooden tees had not yet been invented, and hence every golfer had to make a neat sand-column tee out of wet sand. Fortunately my Orion apiary helped finance my college expenses. I shipped many hundreds of pounds of honey to Champaign, selling it at near-retail prices to fraternity-house dining-room stewards. Even so, I lived in a very exacting workaday world, rising early and studying late. Precious little time for recreation remained, and very little money could be spared for theaters, concerts, or other amusements.[3] I turned, therefore, to free activities in Le Cercle Français and at nearby churches, and of course, to the university lectures and free concerts.

At one of the church functions during my freshman year I was paired off with a dark-haired girl, deeply serious but extremely quick-witted and possessed of a winsome and gentle disposition. I learned later that she had been graduated at the head of her class in a quite large southern Illinois high school with the highest grades that had ever been earned. The more I saw of her the more I came to respect her judgment and her clear intelligence. It was a joy to spend a few fleeting hours with her on Sunday afternoons and by the end of the year we were devoted to one another. Fortunately I did not need to spend money to impress her since she was as penniless as I, earning her way by serving as a nearly full-time baby-sitter for a faculty family. We wrote to one another during the next summer

---

[3] I find, however, that I did attend recitals by Paul Althouse and Arthur Shattuck, concerts by the Cincinnati and St. Louis Symphony orchestras, and one opera, *Carmen*.

vacation and happily renewed our association when our sophomore year began. The better I came to know her the more did her character, her mind, and her lovely disposition impress me. She returned from Christmas vacation two days before I did and became quite suddenly very ill; when I returned she was in the Isolation Hospital with pneumonia, much too ill to receive any visitors. Daily I went to make inquiry, but each day the news became more discouraging. Because of my dining-room duties I had to go early to the hospital, where, since her room was on the ground floor, I could look in through the window and listen fearfully to her troubled breathing. One morning when I stole up to the window of her room I realized all was lost; the lights were on and her bed was empty. It was St. Valentine's day.

I had high school friends who had died, and as a boy I twice served as a pallbearer; but the death of my college sweetheart profoundly saddened and to some extent embittered me. It was sheer nonsense to say, as the churchgoers did, that her death was God's will, and from the time of this intense sadness I became increasingly cynical toward formal religion. Actually the change in outlook was not a sharp one, for I had long shared the theism of Wordsworth and Thomas Moore. A year before this tragedy, I had written in my "Memory Book" one of Moore's quatrains:

> The turf shall be my fragrant shrine;
> My temple, Lord! that Arch of thine;
> My censer's breath the mountain airs,
> And silent thoughts my only prayers.

I went to her funeral. By arrangement with her parents, her letters to me and mine to her were to be buried with her. How indescribably lovely she looked in her coffin holding the thick bundle of our letters tight against her breast! Whenever I think of her, Wordsworth's lines, occasioned by a similar loss, always come to mind:

> She lived unknown, and few could know
>   When Lucy ceased to be;
> But she is in her grave, and, oh,
>   The difference to me!

In an effort to divert my mind from my despondent moods, I tried, despite my work and my heavy academic program, to find time for new activities. I helped direct a French play; with a fellow student I raised queen bees for the department of entomology; and when a cavalry ROTC unit was organized and some hundred or more remounts arrived I spent as much time as I could spare from my work and my studies in improving my horsemanship. As a boy I had had a riding horse, but I knew nothing about the art of equitation. Fortunately we had at Illinois a superb teacher in Captain (later Major General) Robert Grow. Since I planned to enter the advanced ROTC program in my junior year, I arranged to attend the cadet training program during the summer following my sophomore year at Fort Oglethorpe, Georgia. This six-week tour of duty gave me an opportunity to see a part of the country about which northern boys had read so much and yet really knew very little. The charm of the magnolia-shaded homes and the apparent kindness of all the people I met made the rigidly enforced racial segregation seem incongruous. The training program gave me a chance to demonstrate I could do things as well as or better than my fellow cadets, not only in horsemanship but in a wide range of duties. In our training we had a sense of adventure: we swam our horses across rivers, took them down steep slides; we engaged in maneuvers in the hills, valleys, and forests of the Chickamauga reservation; and we made a long road march over the mountains to the Catoosa rifle range where we tethered our horses and bivouacked. I apparently did well in the program, for in the autumn I was commissioned in the Cadet Corps and given charge of one of the newly formed cavalry-unit troops.

In the ROTC I discovered that I had certain leadership qualities not hitherto given an outlet. Because in some way I succeeded in eliciting the full cooperation of the members of my troop, we easily won the individual prizes and the unit cup at the first gymkhana;[4] and G Troop had the honor of leading the parade at the annual military day celebration, one of the really big university events. By the second semester of my junior year, when the cavalry regiment had grown to twelve troops, I was promoted to cadet major with responsibility for a squadron of four troops. Since we had enough horses to mount only one troop at the time, I had no opportunity then to drill a squadron, but I did have that exhilarating experience the next summer at Fort Ethan Allen, Vermont. Meantime we arranged another gymkhana, and this time I ran off with far more than my share of prizes[5] by placing in the high jump, winning the Roman race (standing astride two horses), and taking second place in the steeplechase.

Without any exaggeration I think I can say that my ROTC activities proved to be my most stimulating educational experience at Illinois, not because of the inherent importance of the subject matter but because of the disciplinary and organizational benefits derived. I discovered that the army officers detailed to our cavalry ROTC unit were far better teachers

[4] The *Daily Illini* account said "Two thousand people watched troop G carry off the winner's cup at the first cavalry gymkhana . . . Capt. E. J. Johnson, in addition to receiving the loving cup for his troop, won the blue ribbon in the last event, form equitation."

[5] Once again the *Daily Illini* recorded that "Major E. J. Johnson '22 . . . carried off the honors . . . bringing the Cavalry Cup to Troop A to which he was attached for the day."

than most of my university instructors. In the classroom or on the drill field I soon discovered that I could not succeed unless I made the most methodical preparation for each task. I learned how to show city-born boys that horses responded to the confidence that a rider exhibited, that galloping in a muddy field could be sport, that map reading could readily be taught, and above all that criticism is willingly accepted if mixed whenever possible with praise and commendation. That I succeeded as a cadet officer is attested by the recommendation for a commission in the regular army made by a very respected cavalry colonel on my camp certificate the next summer at Fort Ethan Allen, where I served as one of the two senior cadet officers with responsibility over some 400 cadets from Culver, Norwich, the universities of Massachusetts, Illinois, and Georgia, and a number of other schools. Actually I was offered a commission a half year later, but I had concluded that although I could undoubtedly acquit myself creditably in the army, as a career it offered inadequate opportunity for what I hoped to do: teach, travel, and write.

During my one-semester fourth undergraduate year, I was the senior cadet officer of the University of Illinois cavalry regiment with the rank of cadet lieutenant colonel. Because I now received a modest government stipend (as I had the preceding year) I could reduce the amount of my outside work and devote more attention to the studies that, at long last, I found challenging. The only discouraging aspect of this autumn semester stemmed from the bleak prospects of future employment now that my so-called education as an undergraduate was ending, for a short postwar boom had been succeeded by a severe nationwide business depression. By regularly importuning the dean's office, I learned that an Illinois graduate of some years past who served as head of the research and planning department of a chain of Milwaukee department stores wished to interview any candidates who might be interested in joining his staff. I rushed off posthaste to Milwaukee and found John Ball an extremely interesting person. Trained as an engineer, he tried, much in the spirit of Herbert Hoover, to apply engineering methods to a range of business problems. He convinced me that I could learn things about economics in his practical laboratory that I could never discover in books. Although the pay was strictly Ricardian, specifically twenty dollars a week, I took the job partly because the prospect intrigued me but mostly because I received no other offer.

After completing all requirements for a B.S. degree in January 1922 and after having been commissioned a second lieutenant in the Cavalry Reserve, I left the University of Illinois for a month's vacation in Burlington, Vermont, as the guest of a family whose lovely daughter I had met at a University of Vermont concert the preceding summer. That pleasant

February vacation, when heavy snowfalls made snowshoe expeditions in the beautiful Vermont countryside delightful events, passed all too soon. March 1 found me in Milwaukee. I engaged a room in a lodging house within easy walking distance of John Ball's office where I shared an outer room with a secretary, a draftsman, and four recent college graduates, each as warily hopeful as I. Because it was primarily an industrial city, Milwaukee was suffering badly from the postwar depression. More than that, the Volstead Act had put all the breweries out of operation, and their specialized properties could not be utilized by other industries without very extensive expenditures for conversion. The metal-working light-manufacturing industries operated at a fraction of capacity, and the heavy industries faced an even more unpromising prospect. A pervasive grim-ness, a depressing drabness, and the often-seen slow parades of bitter picket-line guardians that strikers posted around factories, lofts, and retail shops further added to the unpleasant social atmosphere. With heavy unemployment throughout the city, retail sales had fallen, and one main objective of John Ball's organization in Schuster's three department stores was to find ways of reducing costs and increasing sales. Accordingly we were given tasks to test our imagination. I feel confident that I fully earned my weekly pittance during the five months that I wrestled with Schuster's problems. I found, for example, that more than twenty separate depart-ments or components of the 3rd Street store were sending out laundry, and that by consolidating the entire volume of business and negotiating an over-all contract the cost could be reduced more than a third. In solving this problem I visited at least a dozen laundries and saw still more of the seamy side of an industrial city. Next I arranged a consolidated contract for gift boxes, and here the savings turned out to be even greater than in the case of the laundry because pasteboard-box manufacturing costs are greatly affected by the volume of purchases.

Mr. Ball had, himself, very greatly reduced the cost of store deliveries by ingenious mechanical devices installed in central wrapping and pack-ing rooms which made it possible to segregate the parcels for each section of the city swiftly, easily, and with little waste of time or energy. As he observed the workings of his classifying device, the great variation be-tween deliveries destined for the various parts of the city convinced him that the money currently spent for newspaper advertising had little or no effect in certain sections of the city. In his opinion, a systematic study was therefore needed to ascertain where the demand weaknesses were in a spatial sense, since only after this had been done could useful research be initiated to discover the causes for the differential response to the store's advertising and promotion outlays. He therefore had huge sectional maps of Milwaukee prepared showing every existing residence or apartment house. All delivery records over a period of time were to be analyzed and colored pins used to record the data spatially. This elaborate analysis, which had just been begun when I left the organization, should have revealed very vividly the areas where there were some ethnic groups and families with certain income levels that did not respond in the expected way to newspaper or other traditional types of advertising.

However interesting all this was, our little group of researchers and planners found it difficult to envisage any great future for ourselves in a retail organization since it seemed most probable that research and planning would remain, as they then were, an interesting but nevertheless essentially marginal component. Having reached this conclusion quite promptly, I set about finding an alternative type of employment. Since my last semester in college had greatly re-whetted my somewhat suppressed intellectual interests, I decided to try to obtain an instructorship in a college or university where I could teach and study.

The tactics of our research and planning department gave me clues on how to proceed. First it was clearly necessary to survey the collegiate scene to find schools where instructors with only a bachelor's degree were listed on the faculty rosters. The Milwaukee Public Library had almost a complete set of college catalogues and I spent many nights perusing them. Systematically I isolated the possibilities and then proceeded to address letters of inquiry to department chairmen. My gracious former professor Nathan Weston agreed to write letters on my behalf whenever I got a nibble, and as a result of this procedure I received a year's appointment as an instructor in economics beginning in the autumn of 1922 at the University of Oklahoma. A new School of Business had been authorized there, and the dean was somewhat attracted to my preparation at Illinois and my presumed practical experience in Milwaukee. However ill prepared I was, I at least now had a teaching position; and on the assumption that I could succeed in my new duties, my Vermont fiancée and I decided to marry in August.

My few months in Milwaukee proved educational in an entirely unplanned way. My landlord introduced me to his neighbor Victor Berger, that remarkably intelligent and courageous socialist who did so much to make Milwaukee a progressive city and who was one of the leaders of an imaginative group of social reformers that included such talented people as Lillian Steichen, her brother Edward Steichen, and her husband, Carl Sandburg. A few hours with Berger revealed the extraordinary range of his mind, the catholicity of his interests, and the pervading humanity of his motives. Another quite different experience had perhaps a more far-reaching effect on my life. By sheer chance I was invited to join the choir of All Saints Episcopal Cathedral, a very fortunate event since I received ten dollars for each Sunday, thereby increasing my meager weekly income by 50 percent. All Saints, very "high church" and formal, had a scholarly and most gracious dean who regularly invited some of us to his pleasant rooms at Armitage House after the evening service. What wonderful talk we had as we nibbled at candied fruit, smoked, and ate creamy rich chocolates. Here I found the kind of exciting conversation I had hoped to find at the university. Out of these sessions came a decision to make a night hike to Nashotah Seminary some twenty miles from Milwaukee. We set out rather late, rode the streetcar to the end of the line, and then took to the road. Alternately we talked, sang, or kept silent to listen to the soft night noises. It must have been four thirty in the morning when we arrived at the seminary, but the professor of church history, Father Gavin, already was at work since he followed a strict medieval regimen, rising at four. A perfectly charming gentleman who obviously loved a disciplined life, and therefore did all his reading and his writing standing at a waist-high lectern, he delighted us with his contagious enthusiasm.

Quite unwittingly that morning Father Gavin shaped the pattern of my life. We were discussing my appointment at the University of Oklahoma and I needed his advice about where I might best begin my graduate work after a year of teaching. I told him of my disappointment with Illinois and that I would very much welcome his counsel since I had attended no other university. "There is only one place for you to go," said Father Gavin; "you must go to Harvard." Years later after I had received my Ph.D. from Harvard and was teaching at Cornell, Father Gavin, then professor of church history at the General Theological Seminary, came to Ithaca to preach at the university chapel. For the only time in my six years at Cornell I went to Sage Chapel. I was sorely tempted to go up after the service and tell him that he had very profoundly influenced my education, but I wisely decided to leave the chapel as anonymously as I had come. No words that I could possibly have used could have expressed my indebtedness.

My marriage to Virginia Gravelle in Burlington, Vermont, in early August of 1922, began my long and happy companionship with someone who could, because of her innate kindness, cope with my all-too-often petulant personality. After a wedding trip by car through the Adirondacks, along Lake George, down the Hudson, and on to Philadelphia, we went by train to Niagara Falls and from there to Battle Creek, Michigan, where I had very neatly arranged for a two-week tour of military duty with the 14th Cavalry. Then after a brief visit with my family in Illinois we left for our first year's adventure in Oklahoma.

Only when we are plunged into responsibility can we discover the talents we have! With no teaching experience other than that which the

ROTC program had provided, I was able to pretend, to large University of Oklahoma classes, that I knew a great deal about economic principles, business law, business policy, and even office management, for that also fell to my lot to expound. The unsuspecting students were, of course, woefully cheated, whereas I benefited enormously from the compulsion of systematic preparation for every dreaded hour. One must, to be sure, serve one's academic apprenticeship somewhere, and it may have been fortunate that I could do so where my students were so mercifully uncritical. Moreover the tolerant attitude of my colleagues and the gracious hospitality of the entire university community made our life in Oklahoma not only happy but genuinely stimulating. I found time, despite the long, nocturnal preparations I had to make for each day's classes, to take part in a French play, to help teach equitation on Saturdays, and to go duck hunting (at four A.M. in order to be back home in time to dress for a daily eight o'clock class). We were overwhelmed with invitations to social events, which in our modest circumstances we could not very well repay. All in all, my first year of college teaching confirmed my earlier assumption that an academic life would be self-rewarding.

Oklahoma in 1922 exhibited all the vitality, freshness, and confidence of the American frontier. Everywhere one sensed that feeling of "becoming" that my future Cornell colleague Carl Becker so vividly described in his inimitable essay on "Kansas." Moreover everyone, whether taxi driver, lawyer, realtor, or doctor, felt that he had had some role in this developmental process. "I hauled the stone for that there law building," said a taxi driver who drove us to a fraternity dance we were to chaperone, while a garage man with great pride told me that his sister had already become an "assistant professor" in the university. The irrepressible confidence of my associates surprised me and completely baffled my New England-born wife. "I plan to write plays that will be produced on Broadway," said my dear friend Lynn Riggs, then an instructor in English. That is precisely what he did, and I recall how proud we were to have known him when some years later we saw *Green Grow the Lilacs* on Broadway, the play which became the basic libretto for the fabulously successful *Oklahoma*. My colleague Joseph Benton, who, like Riggs and myself, was then an instructor (in music), was just as sure that he would someday sing in the Metropolitan Opera. Years later I visited him in his dressing rooms at the "Met" and reminded him of his prophecy.

Confidence ought not be confused with arrogance, for whereas arrogance is too often merely a manifestation of vanity, confidence reflects a measured appraisal of what one conceivably can accomplish if he has the courage to set goals and the perseverance to take the action necessary to attain them. Although I lacked neither ambition nor resolution, I nevertheless benefited richly from the contagious confidence that the whole atmosphere of Oklahoma radiated. Yet however pleasant my first year of teaching at Oklahoma proved to be, I realized all too well that my advancement in this exacting profession would be unlikely if I did not undertake graduate study at the earliest possible time. To be sure, names of instructors with only bachelor's degrees were liberally sprinkled on the faculty list in the university catalogue, not only in the department of economics but in many other departments: French, German, Spanish, sociology, and political science. Indeed the chairman of the political science department had no other degree than his Harvard A.B., and everyone knew he had gone to Cambridge because of his fabled skill on the football field. And although I felt both flattered and delighted to be a member of the University of Oklahoma faculty, I already had the optimism to dream that someday I might be associated with a university where the preparation, the ability, and the scholarly attitude of the student population might be somewhat better than at a state university where graduates of any high school, however mediocre, could almost automatically be admitted.

It did not take much insight to perceive that the University of Oklahoma, as a newer and less well staffed institution, suffered even more than the University of Illinois from the same encroachment of the "technical high school" idea. Not that the training of geologists, engineers, lawyers, or business executives was an unworthy educational purpose, for in a state fairly recently settled an urgent need for "high-level manpower" obviously existed. Yet somewhere within the educational system something other than this vocational emphasis was needed if a genuine intellectual center worthy of the "university" tradition was to develop and flourish. A small cadre of scholars, disinterestedly concerned with the pursuit of knowledge, had been attracted, but they constantly had to resist the proposals of the more "practical" professors whose programs of study and whose demands for enlarged appropriations made a strong appeal to even more "practical" members of the Board of Regents. The Oklahoma defenders of cultural and humanistic values deserve the highest praise for their refusal to compromise. Dean Frederick Holmberg not only built up the School of Music on the Norman campus but founded a symphony orchestra in Oklahoma City; in the fine arts, Oscar Brousse Jacobson, himself a capable painter, attracted talented people to his department. Good scholars were also to be found in the departments of zoology, botany, physics, and mathematics, and after my time, the University of Oklahoma Press brought national attention to Stanley Vestal and Paul Sears, who played seminal roles as defenders of the liberal and fine arts.

When I had definitely decided to begin my graduate work I asked for an appointment with the president to ascertain whether I might be granted a leave of absence so that I would be certain to have some teaching post to which I could return. He had made inquiries about my teaching and very graciously assured me that I could return after a year's leave of absence. He then asked me where I planned to study and when I said "Harvard," he surprised me by saying, "I wouldn't go there if I were you. What I want here is a faculty with Ph.D. degrees. If you go to Harvard you may or may not obtain a degree; in fact some of our faculty members have been there four or five years and no one knows when, if ever, they will receive their degrees. Why not go to a school where you can be certain to obtain a Ph.D. in three years?" I thanked the president for his advice and left his office with a very uneasy feeling. On an impulse I stopped in to see the vice-president, a crusty old academic frontiersman who had been an original member of the Oklahoma faculty. When I asked his advice about whether I should go to Harvard, he replied in his usually salty way: "I've seen them come and go for a long time. What do they tell me about their graduate work? 'When I was at Iowa,' one says, 'Iowa had the best physics department.' 'When I went to Texas,' another says, 'Texas had the best zoology department.' Or another confesses that although Wisconsin may have slipped a little, 'when I was there it had the best sociology department.' " Then the vice-president looked at me rather slyly and said, "But I've noticed that when they take their Ph.D. degrees at Harvard, they never apologize."

A month later, in a $125 Ford with a "hoopie" body, my wife and I started out over unpaved roads for Cambridge, Massachusetts. It had been a rewarding year for both of us, for me as a teacher, for my young wife as a student. Both of us had been charmed by the vigor of a rapidly developing frontier community, by the color and variety of a state where Indians, cowhands, and true pioneers were still very much in evidence. Clearly Oklahoma had a very promising future not only economically, but intellectually, if the inner core of the university could be protected and strengthened.

5

THE LUSTER OF THE IVY
★★★★★★★★★★★★★★★★★★★★★★★★★★

WHEREAS I had taken French every semester at Illinois, I had given no attention to German since high school days. In order to overcome this linguistic deficiency, I hurried to Cambridge for a concentrated summer school course in German under a gifted teacher. Before the fall term began I had passed the comprehensive German examination so that, with my certified French, I was admitted to full candidacy for the master's degree. All I now had to do was to acquit myself creditably in my courses in economics. When I saw my fellow students for the first time, at the initial meeting of Professor F. W. Taussig's course in economic theory, I felt hopelessly inadequate in the presence of such a glitter of Phi Beta Kappa keys. But I soon sensed that almost all the first-year graduate students, however well schooled, were as apprehensive as I. When four of us organized an evening study seminar, we thought we had embarked on something unique only to discover that there were probably a dozen similar groups that kept wives hidden away while hopeful young scholars disputatiously aired their opinions about stubborn analytical problems. An endemic sense of intellectual inferiority put everyone on his mettle, and although our Harvard professors richly stimulated our thinking, the graduate students actually set the standards. Because I was so fearful that I would not be able to hold my own against Princeton, Yale, Amherst, McGill, and Swarthmore graduates with outstanding academic records, I worked ten hours a day seven days of the week except for a three-hour respite on Saturdays.

That my fellow students were really formidable competitors has been amply demonstrated by their subsequent careers. Edward Mason, Talcott Parsons, Edward Chamberlin, Seymour Harris, and Overton Taylor became distinguished Harvard professors. Frank Whitson Fetter, Richard Overton, and Harold Williamson brought academic prestige to Northwestern University. Samuel S. Stratton was chosen president of Middlebury College; Donald Erb, as noted earlier, president of the University of Oregon. Milton Heath, Christopher Roberts, and Earl J. Hamilton at North Carolina and Duke universities greatly increased our knowledge of economic history. Paul O'Leary served not only as chairman of the economics department at Cornell but as dean of the School of Business and Public Administration. Donald Gilbert became provost of the University of Rochester. Eleanor Dulles demonstrated her ability in a distinguished governmental career, while Howard Ellis at the University of California proved his versatility by his very able writings on a wide variety of subjects. Harry Dexter White and Lauchlin Currie occupied critically important governmental posts in the New Deal era, while Gardner Means made his reputation by his brilliant analysis of the modern corporation. John W. Harriman became a Dartmouth professor, a government official, and an economic analyst who exhibited unusual imagination. Philip Wernette, after serving as president of the University of New Mexico, demonstrated his ability as a professor at the University of Michigan. Theodore Yntema, who gave wise counsel to the Committee on Economic Development when he was a professor at the University of Chicago, became vice-president of the Ford Motor Company. Bernard Haley not only distinguished himself as a professor at Stanford, as Theodore Kreps also did, but served for many years as editor of the *American Economic Review*.

Almost without exception the ninety graduate students in economics in my day at Harvard represented high ability, intense interest in their studies, and an intellectual dedication that would be hard to surpass. Every one of them was destined to play some important role. As a member of the Canadian foreign service, Norman Robertson served as ambassador to the United States and as high commissioner in the United Kingdom. Paul Ellsworth, who became a professor of economics at Wisconsin, was entrusted with a succession of overseas governmental assignments. James Shoemaker had lived several years in Asia before he came to Harvard; he brought his expertise to the Board of Economic Warfare and later occupied a key position in our military government in Korea, after which he became vice-president of the Bank of Hawaii and more recently vice-president of the University of Alaska. Melvin de Chazeau repeatedly filled important advisory roles for the government in addition to his academic duties at Virginia, Chicago, and Cornell. With students of such promise, the Cambridge atmosphere literally crackled with the escaping intellectual energy.

During my first year at Harvard I had courses with F. W. Taussig, C. J.

Bullock, Allyn Young, and John H. Williams. Because it was the last year that Frederick Jackson Turner would give his "History of the West," I felt I had to find the time to audit this famous course; and because of my growing interest in economic history I also attended Abbott P. Usher's lectures. How wonderfully stimulating all these great teachers were even though their methods and techniques were totally dissimilar. Taussig relied on a dialectic so effective that his students would leave the classroom in wrangling clusters, and so animated were the disagreements that at some class meetings Taussig's role was mainly to umpire the still on-going spirited debate. From the vantage point of modern economics, the subject matter of Taussig's "Ec 11" seems woefully unreal and old-fashioned, but one must remember that in 1923 such concepts as imperfect or monopolistic competition had not been formulated, and national accounts were not used as analytical devices because the distinction between micro and macro economics had not yet been clarified. We groped our way through the disharmonies that existed among those writers to whom Taussig directed our attention: David Ricardo, J. S. Mill, Henry George, Francis Amasa Walker, Eugen von Böhm-Bawerk, J. B. Clark, and Alfred Marshall. But although the literature now seems not merely "classical" but often archaic, the rigor and precision with which we were expected to defend a point of view by accurate analysis proved to be a permanent benefit we received from this remarkable teacher.

Professor Bullock's didactic techniques differed completely from Taussig's. By his blistering sarcasm leveled at careless thinkers, living or dead, he attempted to make us searchingly critical of everything we read or heard. In his course on the history of economic thought we learned why the "classics" deserved that appellation. An inordinate amount of time seemingly was devoted to Aristotle but the emphasis was more methodological than substantive. We didn't just "read" *The Nicomachean Ethics* or *The Politics*, we searched and sieved them for meaning, as we did with Plato's *Republic* and *Laws*. In the same hypercritical way we were introduced to Machiavelli's *Prince*, John Hales's *Discourse*, the collected works of Sir William Petty, and Adam Smith's *Theory of Moral Sentiments*. Meantime we were expected to cover secondary literature in English, French, and German. Among the general books I recall reading were Onken's *Geschichte der National Öconomie*, Gide and Rist's *Histoire des Doctrines Économiques*, and Ingram's *History of Political Economy*. Only a few of us who had the privilege of writing theses under his direction really came to appreciate the infinite kindness that Bullock's cynical mask concealed.

Taussig conducted his large class as a seminar in which everyone was not merely expected but virtually compelled to participate; by contrast neither Bullock nor Allyn Young asked for or even seemed to welcome student comment. I think Bullock's attitude stemmed from his innate shyness. In Young's case it had, I believe, quite a different cause; his preoccupation with his subject was so intense that he did not want any interruption in his close-knit chain of thought. Undoubtedly the most gifted of all my Harvard teachers, Young seemed to make no formal preparation whatever; at the appointed hour he dropped into his chair, surveyed his audience with his blue eyes, then inclined his head toward the desk and began to talk. By watching his restless hands, the hunching of his shoulders, or the knitting of his brows, one could almost measure the cerebral intensity that produced the impeccable logic of these extraordinary extempore performances. The beneficiaries more of his current thinking than the recipients of any systematic analysis of money and banking, we were both tremendously impressed and baffled, since it became very difficult to weave his talks into an integrated set of classroom notes. He was equally unsystematic about giving us bibliographic guidance — the only two books that he insisted we read for his money and banking course were R. G. Hawtrey's *Currency and Credit* and Keynes's *Tract on Monetary Reform* — and hence we largely had to make up our own reading lists.

Like Young, John H. Williams had the capacity for long analytical discourses. In his treatment of international trade he took rather sharp issue with the essentially Ricardian doctrines that still formed the basis of economic analysis in this difficult area, and this disagreement called for very precise analysis. Williams, who before he had turned his attention to economics had taught English at Brown University, was a magnificently lucid speaker. Unlike the fluent Williams, Abbott Payson Usher had difficulty in lecturing. Crowded with qualifications, his sentences were both too long and too loose, a forensic handicap that led all too many Harvard graduate students to neglect hearing one of the most thoughtful, profound, and seminal minds that Harvard had to offer.[1] In contrast to Usher's involved and sometimes pleonastic exposition, Frederick Jackson Turner's course had all the qualities of a theatrical performance. Illustrating his finished lectures with very helpful slides, maps, and blackboard diagrams, he vividly unfolded the story of the moving frontier. Genial, friendly, and gracious, Turner would always be surrounded by a bevy of inquiring students after each of his lectures.

With such fascinating teachers, and with such challenging fellow stu-

[1] Many years later, as a past president of the Economic History Association, I had the honor to pay formal tribute to Usher's memory and to his contributions to economic history. See the foreword to *Journal of Economic History*, vol. XXV, no. 4 (December 1965).

dents, my exciting first year at Harvard contrasted so sharply with my undergraduate years that I felt I had been badly cheated at Illinois, particularly when I realized that not only the Harvard graduate students but undergraduates as well were tasting this heady Cambridge vintage. I knew that I simply had to continue my graduate work at Harvard beyond the A.M. degree; the problem was how to finance it. Since I had borrowed all the money needed for my first year, my immediate responsibility would be to repay this debt; and when the University of Oklahoma offered me an assistant professorship, after I had received my Harvard A.M., I gladly accepted the position but on the condition that I would not be required to teach any business-school subjects. This request was granted, and during the next two years I taught economic history, corporation finance, labor problems, and international trade, learning a great deal about these subjects in the process. Before returning to Oklahoma, however, I made a short trip abroad, the first of fifty ocean crossings.

From Charles Poletti, one of the two Harvard College seniors who had been allowed to take Taussig's graduate course, I learned that there were ways whereby one could work his way across the Atlantic. Accordingly in June of 1923, I left Boston for Liverpool as one of about a score of young men who served as feeders and waterers of some 625 Canadian Hereford steers. After a pleasant and instructive fortnight in London,[2] I signed the ship's articles and made the return voyage as a second-class fireman, which really meant that I spent nine days painting the walls of the engine room. Once back in the States, after a tour of duty with the 14th Cavalry at Fort Custer, I returned with my wife to Norman, Oklahoma. During the next two years, I carried out a rigorous study program and undertook some outside teaching in Oklahoma City so that I could repay my debts. I drove myself much too hard. As a result, signs of pulmonary trouble developed, and just after I had the great good fortune to be appointed an instructor at Harvard, which would make it financially possible for me to complete my work for the Ph.D. degree, I found it necessary to spend a summer in bed in a tent on my family's farm in Illinois. Fortunately my recovery was rapid, and in September of 1926 my wife and I joyously returned to Cambridge.

I have had so many happy years that it is difficult to assign priorities. But the next three busy years at Harvard certainly must be counted among the most rewarding. As an instructor I taught three sections of

[2] When in the letters I wrote to my wife from London I reread my detailed and graphic descriptions of the museums and libraries I visited, I can sense again the great excitement that my first foreign travel produced. My memories of the Tower of London are therefore more vivid than my recollections of Luxor and the Valley of the Kings even though my visit to the Tower occurred almost fifty years ago and my trip to Luxor only six years ago.

"Ec A," the introductory course generally taken by Harvard sophomores. At the same time, like most instructors, assistant professors, and some more senior faculty members, I served as a "tutor" in the division of history, government, and economics. In this capacity I met with my assigned "tutees" (I believe I had six, seven, or eight) individually, supervised their reading, and assigned papers for them to write. Paul Sweezy was one of my tutees and I recall that he wrote several good papers dealing with British economic history. Meantime in the Ec A classes, which averaged about eighteen students, we instructors did our best to involve every student in the discussions at each meeting. All of us met once a week with Professor Harold H. Burbank, who had over-all charge of the course, and at these sessions we tried to agree on the points of emphasis for the coming week. This closely supervised instruction contrasted with the almost anarchic freedom I had had, despite my inexperience, at Oklahoma, and I soon learned to my chagrin that the tactics I had employed in Norman, Oklahoma, did not suit the situation in Cambridge, Massachusetts.

In Oklahoma one's reputation as a defender of standards depended on the fearlessness with which one failed or otherwise penalized lazy, indifferent, or incompetent students. Priding myself on my "standards," I had a high percentage of low grades and even some failures when I turned in my first grades at Harvard, and I was not a little embarrassed when Professor Burbank pointed out that if my grades properly measured the comprehension that my students had of elementary economics there must be something wrong with my teaching methods. "These students are well prepared," he said; "they have been carefully selected. It is our task to make certain that they perform as their records show they can perform." I had completely failed to appreciate the difference between the two student samples, and although Professor Burbank's remarks both shocked and hurt me he did not need to admonish me again. I made certain that each student comprehended the economic theory we were analyzing as fully as his ability would permit, and presently I discovered a prodigious amount of unsuspected talent. One of my Ec A students, J. J. Rorimer, became so deeply interested in the interrelation between economic progress and artistic development that at his request I met evenings with him to explore this topic. The more I saw of this able young man the more certain I became that he would make a name for himself.[3]

[3] As curator of the Cloisters in Fort Tyron Park he showed a rare combination of taste and judgment. I saw him during the war when, with the arts and monuments section of the European civil-affairs operation, he was busily engaged in recovering artistic treasures the Germans had carried off. Later he became director of the Metropolitan Museum in New York, and it was he in 1961 who made the $2,300,000 bid for the Rembrandt painting "Aristotle Contemplating the Bust of Homer."

My growing interest in the history of economic thought and my decision to attempt an evaluation of the growth of American economic thinking in the seventeenth century made it necessary for me to do further work in colonial history, the study of which I had begun under E. B. Greene at Illinois. Now I had the good fortune to work under Samuel Eliot Morison, that remarkable scholar and superb stylist. Outwardly cold, distant, and forbidding, Morison was actually kindness itself. He recommended my first-semester seminar paper, "Some Evidence of Mercantilism in the Massachusetts Bay," to the *New England Quarterly*, and that journal published it in July 1928. This, my first published article, was soon followed by "Economic Ideas of John Winthrop," a reworking of my second-semester seminar paper. It also appeared in the *New England Quarterly* (April 1930) and was described in rather flattering detail in a long editorial in the *Boston Herald*.[4] But Professor Morison did even more for me. He asked me to write three articles for the *Dictionary of American Biography*,[5] and in order to squeeze all the essential historical data into a rigidly limited space I learned how to delete every dispensable word. Later on when I was asked to write articles for the *Encyclopaedia of the Social Sciences* I knew how to compress and condense and yet maintain felicity of style. For many invaluable lessons I am indebted to that artful and elegant master of English prose, Professor Morison.

To complete my complement of courses, I did further work with Allyn Young and studied economic history with Edwin F. Gay thereby learning to know that stimulating man with whom I would be very closely associated in the 1940's when a group of us not only founded the *Journal of Economic History* but planned the research undertaken by the Council on Research in Economic History that a foundation grant of a quarter million dollars made possible. Gay drove his graduate students energetically, and by this tactic stimulated them to produce a series of very solid and lasting monographs. Yet he himself wrote very little, although what he did write has stood the test of time and of searching criticism.[6] My intended research, however, fell more properly in Bullock's field of competence, and with many fears and misgivings I decided to ask whether he would be willing to supervise my dissertation. To establish my credentials I told him I had already published an article dealing with

[4] An abbreviated version of this article appears in *Issues in American Economic History*, ed. Gerald D. Nash (Boston: Heath, 1964), pp. 8–12.

[5] On Jonathan Amory, Elisha Cooke, and Thomas Cushing.

[6] Herbert Heaton has described in detail Gay's methodical preparation for his academic career which involved fourteen years of study in Germany, Switzerland, and Britain. His letters from Europe record his self-criticism and his fear that he could never achieve the degree of perfection that he thought graduate teaching required. See Heaton's "The Making of an Economic Historian," in the *Journal of Economic History*, Supplement to vol. XI (1949), pp. 1–18.

aspects of the subject I planned to explore. He asked who had read my article before it was published. I said that Professor Morison and Professor Gay had both read it, and that I would like to have him read it. "No," he said rather scornfully; "if those two great scholars have read it, I don't want to see it. One an 'Oxford professor' who now thinks American history must be rewritten; the other a great newspaper editor."[7] In view of this sarcasm, my prospects of enlisting his aid seemed rather hopeless, but to my surprise Bullock said, "Go to the library, get a copy of Bradford's *History of Plymouth Plantation*, and note down every economic idea you can find in that book; then come back and show me your notes." He explained precisely how he wanted my notes prepared. Excerpts were to be copied in the mid-portion of 5 by 8 note cards while on the upper parts of the cards the excerpts were to be summarized succinctly. Fortunately I had already read Bradford's *History* with care, and in less than a week I came back with a sizable pack of notes. Bullock read each excerpt aloud, and each summary, commenting critically, or approvingly, about my paraphrases. I had passed muster; and this session, which lasted over two hours, inaugurated a long series of similar conferences during which he verified hundreds of my notes. Our meetings took place in the late afternoon at Professor Bullock's house, and since I knew that he had already put in a full day at his office I often felt that I was imposing mercilessly; but nothing I could say would change the procedure. When I began to write my chapters, Bullock insisted on reading my handscript; consequently when my dissertation was finished he not only had seen all the raw data and approved my plan of work, but had read every word of my final text. When I consider the fidelity with which Professor Bullock supervised my work, I pity the present-day swarm of graduate students who seldom are able to see their so-called thesis directors and who may even finish writing their theses before they receive any criticism.

Before I began my dissertation I had, of course, taken my oral qualifying examinations. At Harvard in the 1920's this was a dreadful ordeal since one's whole career largely depended on a single performance before five examiners. If a candidate failed, that usually was the end of the road, although I recall two cases where very brilliant candidates were allowed to come up again. Lack of preparation in an "outside field" brought one of these talented young men to grief, while overconfidence caused the other extremely able candidate to eat humble pie. I had made careful preparation, and just before my examination, in early October of

[7] Morison had been Harold V. Harmsworth Professor of American History at Oxford from 1922 to 1925. After World War I, Gay became editor of the *New York Post*, and it was when that venture failed that he returned to Harvard.

1927, my wife and I had the use of a cottage on Swan Lake, near Searsport, Maine. Here in the serenity of a New England September I reviewed my notes and read a number of important monographs. The "Boston Boat" was still operating between the Penobscot and Boston so one could board the boat in Belfast and wake up the next morning as it was docking in Boston. These simple joys, alas, have been destroyed by automotive "technological progress." My examination came two days after our return from Maine, and I remember that my wife and I walked down to the Charles River just before the critical hour and from a book of verses I read "The Dying Gladiator" not knowing whether puckishly or prophetically. F. W. Taussig, Allyn Young, Abbott Usher, Samuel Morison, and Arthur Stone Dewing grilled me in turn on economic theory, money and banking, economic history, American colonial history, and corporation finance. After I had been excused I waited in deepest suspense, and when Taussig came to tell me I had passed I had a feeling of joy that I experienced only one other time in my life, when I completed my first solo airplane flight.[8]

Thanks to Professor Bullock's help and guidance I made such swift progress on my thesis that I felt I could afford a two-month respite during the summer of 1928 to accompany my father on a trip to Scandinavia. I considered this extremely important since it would be my father's only return visit to his native land and would give me an excellent opportunity to meet Swedish relatives and learn firsthand about my ethnic and cultural roots. My father offered to pay for my ticket but I persuaded him to travel outbound on a freighter. From my experience in 1924, I had learned that there were even better ways of crossing the ocean than shipping as a cattleman or joining a ship's crew. By signing a ship's articles and by paying a very modest daily sum, one could travel as a passenger. On this voyage to Europe, for example, my father and I each paid four dollars a day and for that we had our meals with the ship's officers and comfortable places to sleep.[9] We had a splendid crossing; I had brought important books to read and in a deck chair over the wheelhouse I had all the comforts of a private yacht.

Our ship, the *West Harcuvar*, sailed direct from Boston to Hamburg with a mixed cargo of grain, manufactured goods, and eighty-nine mules. That a market for these weary-looking, overage animals existed in Germany showed how severely all animal herds had been drawn down during the period of hyper-inflation, and indicated how long it takes to build up a domestic supply of draft power even in a nation with a sizable agri-

[8] On the day of my fortieth birthday I began flying lessons to prove to myself that I was still alert, resilient, and venturesome.

[9] My father had the steward's cabin; I slept in the hospital room.

cultural sector. Yet there could be little doubt that German recovery was in motion, and the confidence one sensed in a vibrant city such as Hamburg made one realize that Germany would soon again be a leading European power. None of the depression psychology that pervaded Liverpool and London in 1924, and that I was to encounter again when I spent 1929–30 in Britain, cropped out in my discussions with German businessmen. My impressions, however, stemmed only from observations in Hamburg where we spent a few days. We discovered that if we bought our return passage (from Oslo) in Hamburg, we could have free second-class rail and water tickets from Hamburg to Oslo via Copenhagen and Stockholm. My father therefore purchased cabin-class steamship tickets on the *Frederick the VIII* for our trip from Oslo to New York and off we went to Sweden by way of Copenhagen.

Immigrants' children hear so much about the "old country" that one would think they would know what to expect when they actually visit their parents' native land. For me it was wholly otherwise. Far more beautiful than I had ever dreamed, all of Scandinavia delighted and thrilled me.[10] Why as a small boy had I been ashamed of being a Swede when all this was my heritage? To be sure the Sweden I saw differed markedly from that which my parents had known. To travel by chauffeur-driven car from Linköping to the parish church where my father was baptized and confirmed could scarcely compare with walking these six miles, as my father did as a boy. The Swedish aristocracy had built charming country estates such as Sturefors, which my father and I visited, but I could not easily forgive the hardships, the fatigue, and the actual suffering that their splendor had imposed on my peasant ancestors who paid labor services to both the nobility and the clergy.

Gracious, generous, gentle relatives overwhelmed us with kindness. When we woke in the morning our shoes had been shined; if we went off on excursions we would return to find our shirts, underwear, and socks freshly laundered. Wherever we visited we encountered the traditional seven collations,[11] all unbelievably delicious. But for me the richest joys came from seeing the scenes of my parents' childhood, the houses in

[10] In a letter to my wife written on June 23, 1928, the day I arrived in the cathedral and market town that both my parents had known in their youth, I wrote, "I have spent the last five hours trying to overcome my astonishment. All my life I have had nebulous conceptions of Sweden and of Linköping but never had I once dreamed of finding a veritable fairyland . . . In the botanical gardens we encountered a profusion of lilacs such as I have never seen, growing on little trees rather than bushes with clusters a foot long and in colors I never dreamed could exist, white and lavender, of course, but also crimson, purplish-blue, dozens of shades."

[11] Coffee and cakes on rising followed an hour later by breakfast; then morning coffee with pastry, luncheon, afternoon coffee, dinner, and, finally, late refreshments.

which they lived, the churches where they were baptized and confirmed, the places where they worked, the dark forests they may have feared, the lovely skies where cumulous clouds always drift and beneath which they dreamed their dreams.

After an unhurried visit to all our relatives in the Linköping area, my father and I spent a fortnight with my father's brother on an island in Lake Mälaren outside of Stockholm. This gave me time to explore the museums and libraries in that fascinating city. From Stockholm we traveled north to Uppsala, and then to the lovely lakes and hills of Dalecarlia. By chance, at Leksand, I encountered Gustav Cassell, the distinguished Swedish economist whom I had met when he visited at Harvard. One other happy event occurred: my father and I had tea with Selma Lagerlöf at her country home in Sunne, Värmland. Then we proceeded to Oslo where after seeing the Viking ships, some of Edvard Munch's inimitable paintings, and Vigeland's impressive if not always beautiful statues in Frogner Park, we sailed on the *Frederick the VIII* to New York. It would be seventeen years before I would return to Oslo, and then under very different circumstances.

I finished writing my thesis in the autumn of 1928, a 260-page essay which I published four years later almost without change.[12] After I had passed my final oral examination, I was asked whether I could fill a part-time position at the Massachusetts Institute of Technology. Since it meant an additional $1000 to add to the inadequate $2500 salary that I received from Harvard, I readily agreed. The penny-pinching days, at long last, had ended.[13] Now we could go to the Boston Symphony Orchestra concerts, hear Rachmaninoff, Chaliapin, and Rosa Ponselle, even go to the theater to see *Cyrano de Bergerac*. Still more good fortune came our way; in the spring of 1929 I was awarded a $3000 Social Science Research Fellowship to make possible a year's study of British economic changes parallel to the American survey I had just completed.

We decided to sail from Quebec so that we might visit my wife's relatives. Her paternal ancestor arrived in Quebec from Dinan, Brittany, in 1641, while a maternal ancestor, Abraham Martin, gave his name to the

[12] *American Economic Thought in the Seventeenth Century* (London: P. S. King, 1932). Since all the unbound sheets were destroyed when German fire bombs ignited the publisher's warehouse during the early part of World War II, the book was out of print until 1961 when Russell and Russell brought out a reprint.

[13] When I became an instructor at Harvard, in 1926, my salary was $2000. We paid $65 a month for the rent of a one-room apartment. This left $1220 to cover food, clothing, insurance, books, medical and dental costs, and all other expenses for a twelvemonth, something that called for rather careful budgeting. I recall one night on our way home from a shopping expedition in the Blackstone fruit and vegetable market (where bargains could be obtained late on Sunday nights), I asked my wife what she would like to have and she replied, "I'd like to have just one dime."

"Plains of Abraham." As poor relatives we basked in the luxury of her uncle's large home across the river in Levis and the even greater elegance of her cousin's house in Quebec opposite Wolfe's monument, and enjoyed the copious and faultlessly served meals at the Garrison Club. The crossing on the *Empress of Scotland*, redeemed from its roughness by the delightfulness of Canadian, Australian, English, and American fellow passengers, gave us a sense of well-deserved freedom from overwork and tension. When we reached London I could profit from my brief visit there in 1924 and avoid the drab "bed and breakfast" lodgings in Bloomsbury, where most unsuspecting Americans go, and find instead a delightful flat in Kensington with a balcony overlooking Edwardes Square. The great Foxwell Collection of early English economic literature, which the Worshipful Company of Goldsmith had purchased, was housed in the Imperial Institute, near enough to Edwardes Square so I could walk to my work. Since I planned to be in London only until the beginning of Michaelmas Term at Oxford, I worked hard five days a week, leaving two days for our systematic exploration of the vast historical, cultural, and artistic resources of London. Meantime the more I probed into the so-called mercantilist literature, the more convinced I became that it had been very partially understood and, as a consequence, very imperfectly interpreted. A new book on this complex subject had to be written, and sooner or later I would do it. For the nonce my task was to gather the materials.

In Oxford we lived in a pleasant pension frequented largely by parents with children in the nearby Dragon School. This gave us an opportunity to meet many very interesting and knowledgeable people. Evening conversation ranged from the problems of India to the history of architecture; it was always full of surprises, for we Americans have been prone to neglect something that was quite wonderful in British culture, the art of conversation, something that has now, alas, been almost destroyed by cheap and tawdry television programs. But in 1929–30, conversation was still a real British accomplishment. We had the good fortune of meeting a large number of Rhodes Scholars and through them British undergraduates and a few dons. Borrowing a friend's car we visited lovely Cotswold villages, as well as Stratford, Worcester, Tewksbury, Gloucester, and Banbury. Fortunately we did this in October, for when the November and December fogs enveloped the upper Thames valley one could scarcely see across an Oxford street. With no lights in the Bodleian library, I could only work from ten to three, so with time on my hands at the pension, I began to translate a book on American economic thought written by Ernest Teilhac, a professor at the University of Poitiers.[14] So persistently

[14] My translation was published in 1936 under the title *Pioneers of American*

did I apply myself to this task that I had a full text ready for Professor Teilhac to verify when we visited Poitiers in January 1930.

In exchange for covering the rather expensive British automobile insurance premium, we were given the use of an English Ford roadster by an American student in Christ Church College for a six-week Continental tour. We crossed the channel to Boulogne-sur-Mer and proceeded to Paris by way of Amiens. After a week in Montmartre, during which time we not only visited the museums but went to the opera, we drove to the valley of the Loire where we meandered from one chateau to another: Amboise, Blois, Chaumont, Chambord, Chenonceaux, Loches. Then we drove south to Poitiers where we stayed a week as guests of Professor Teilhac while he and I vetted my translation of his book.

When once again we took to the road our route went south through Gascony to Toulouse, and to the frowning walled city of Carcassonne. At Montpellier we visited with Patrick Geddes at the Collège des Écrivains, after which we explored the Roman buildings at Nîmes and stood on the famous bridge at Avignon. In a rather foolish attempt to go from Nice to Geneva by the *routes des Alpes* in mid-winter, we encountered so much snow that we were forced to return and follow the all-weather route up the Rhone. Yet everything thrilled us, scenery, food, wines, architecture. It was bitterly cold in an open car crossing the Bernese Oberland from Vevey, on Lake Geneva, to Lucerne, by way of Gstaad and Interlaken; but youth can ignore hardship by transmuting it into adventure. From Lucerne our route took us to Basel and Strasbourg, then down the Rhine to Karlsruhe, Heidelberg, Wiesbaden, Bonn, and Krefeld, entering the Netherlands at Arnhem. Despite the raw, gloomy winter weather, the Dutch landscape, with the windmills that now, alas, have almost all disappeared, the barges, moved with such a prodigal use of human labor, and the ubiquitous bridges, fascinated us. We stayed in a native hotel on the Zuider Zee in Amsterdam and walked one frigid morning to the Rijks Museum to see the Rembrandts, Frans Halses, and Brueghels. A succession of short jaunts took us to Leyden, The Hague, Delft, Antwerp, Brussels, Waterloo, Ghent, and Bruges, revealing in a very vivid way that great town-building chapter in Flemish history that Pirenne has so dramatically described.[15] Very reluctantly we drove on to Dunkirk and Calais, vowing that we would return to the Continent, a promise we were fortunately able to keep more amply than we could then have imagined.

Posting back to Oxford to gather up our luggage we now moved to Cambridge, and from the moment we saw the colleges, the "backs," and

Economic Thought in the Nineteenth Century by the Macmillan Company; it was reprinted in 1967 by Russell and Russell.

[15] Perhaps best in his *Belgian Democracy, Its Early History* (Manchester, 1915).

the lovely rural setting, we fell in love with Cambridge and Cambridge-shire.[16] Grantchester, within walking distance of our Garden House Hotel, still keeps, I am happy to say, its simple rustic charm; while Ely, that lovely fenland cathedral, is another of the many comely spots in an un-spoiled landscape. Cambridge proved equally pleasing in its academic hospitality. I was passed on from one "high table" to another. The bursar of Trinity invited me to his college so I could meet Dennis Robertson. At King's, where I was Keynes's guest, I met Sir John Clapham and A. C. Pigou. C. R. Fay invited me to Christ's, where I was surprised that no one rose when a toast to the king was proposed, but it seems that Edward VI once told the dons they needn't rise and ever since they have followed his injunction. My high-table invitations came not merely from economists but from anthropologists. With time on her hands my wife had volun-teered to help the curator of the Australian collection (who lived in our hotel) catalogue his artifacts. As a consequence, I met the scholars at the Museum of Ethnology, and they invited me to dine at Trinity Hall, Queens', and a number of other colleges.

I worked very hard at Cambridge not only at collecting material in the university library but in the preparation of an article that Keynes accepted for publication in *Economic History* and which later became chapter 13 of my *Predecessors of Adam Smith*.[17] Life proved so pleasant in Cam-bridge that I was reluctant to leave even though I needed to make impor-tant archival searches in the British Museum and in the Public Records Office. I had no immediate plans until one morning, while I was having breakfast at the Garden House Hotel, a telegram was brought to me offering me an associate professorship at the George Washington Univer-sity at twice the salary I had received at Harvard. The prospect of carrying on research at the Library of Congress intrigued me even though George Washington University had but limited attraction. Rather recklessly I accepted the offer, and we hurried to London so that I could complete my archival work before embarking on my new duties in Washington. What I actually encountered at George Washington University did not in any way coincide with my expectations.

[16] So much that we felt duty bound to let our son sample Cambridge life. I there-fore arranged for him to spend a year at Sidney Sussex College after he had taken his M.A. at Johns Hopkins in 1957.

[17] Published by Prentice-Hall and P. S. King in 1937; reprinted by Augustus M. Kelley in 1960 and again in 1965.

6

THE GROVE OF ACADEME
★★★★★★★★★★★★★★★★★★★★★★★★★★★★

GEORGE WASHINGTON UNIVERSITY had an odd and uneven assortment of students. The "day" students seemed to be, for the most part, young people who had not been able to enter better schools or whose parents insisted they should go to college in their home city. The "night" students divided into two easily recognizable categories: the truly ambitious and the sleepy ones who hoped that by mere presence they could ultimately acquire rather than "earn" a college degree. Among the graduate students, however, were to be found a few really talented young people. Finding didactic norms that would, in some tolerable way, suit such a variegated and dissimilar student population posed a continuing problem for faculty members. I might possibly have adjusted myself to this awkward situation if there had been other compensating satisfactions. But I discovered to my distress not merely that I would be expected to teach fourteen hours a week but that my classes were distributed morning, afternoon, and evening throughout five days a week; and since everything had been programmed long in advance of my arrival nothing could be done to change things, which made it quite impossible to find blocks of time for research. Worst of all a variety of presidential paternalism pervaded the institution so that department chairmen could make virtually no decisions without the express approval of the president.

I had been given charge of the large introductory course in elementary economics and this involved lecturing twice a week not to one large class but to two, since every "general" course for day students had to be repeated for the night students. Quiz sections for day students had been distributed over the week during morning and afternoon hours, and for night students every evening of the week. A single assistant and I were expected to meet all these sessions. In addition to this large course, I had been assigned a junior-senior course on labor problems, about which I knew little or nothing, and a graduate seminar on the history of economic thought which I very much enjoyed. Since my chances of doing research at the Library of Congress proved all but hopeless, I felt both trapped and victimized. More than that, I could see little future for a school so ill financed that most of its income came from student fees. With few exceptions, the faculty lacked scholarly sparkle,[1] and hence the whole environment seemed dull and listless. I decided to complete the college year dutifully and move elsewhere. By early spring I had two attractive offers, one as Taft Professor at the University of Cincinnati, the other as an assistant professor at Cornell.

It is almost unbelievable how perverse and shortsighted some college administrators can be. Because very few George Washington professors received invitations from other institutions, President Marvin apparently could not believe that I had any bona fide offers. Consequently when out of courtesy I called on him to tell him that unless more flexible arrangements could be made so that I could resume my research I could not remain at George Washington, he coldly said, "If you have such fine offers you should accept them"; to which I replied, "I most certainly shall." I learned, within an hour, that immediately after I left his office the president telephoned the dean warning him not to make any promises to me about a lighter or more concentrated teaching load since he was very certain I had no offers to go elsewhere. The episode recalls Sydney Smith's witty remark when he heard two irate women in London shouting at each other from their windows on opposite sides of the street. "They will never agree," said Smith, "for they are arguing from different premises." President Marvin's unwarranted skepticism illustrates the dilemma of many so-called institutions of higher learning. Not only do weak schools attract poor professors but they are often headed by even more marginal presidents and administrators, who attempt to compensate for their short-comings by pomposity and overconfidence. Marvin, for example, embarrassed the faculty by his misuse of the English language, but no one dared correct his errors. Students would snicker when he castigated "swādo (pseudo) scientists," and even women's club listeners would titter when he confused *demur* and *demure*.

The tragedy of the Washington situation in higher education still continues. Unlike the capital cities of Europe, or of Asia for that matter,

---

[1] Outstanding exceptions were Samuel Flagg Bemis who became Sterling Professor at Yale, and R. E. Gibson who later was the distinguished director of the Johns Hopkins Applied Physics Laboratory. Truman Michaelson in anthropology and W. C. Johnstone, Jr., in political science were two other able scholars.

Washington has no distinguished national university to compare with the great institutions in London, Paris, Berlin, Vienna, Tokyo, Madrid, Rome, Copenhagen, or even Delhi. Yet in Washington the resources for a great unified educational institution exist, just as they did in London and Toronto where imaginative educational statesmen consolidated a number of colleges and schools into two great universities. Toronto showed that Protestant and Catholic schools could be conjoined, while London demonstrated that not only colleges could be knit together but institutions, conservatories, and even provincial colleges could be integrated and greatly strengthened in the process. Had there seemed to be any prospect of such a program of unification in Washington, I would willingly have stayed to help the cause, but with college heads as stubborn, unimaginative, or sectarian as those in control of the Washington schools in 1930 the outlook seemed hopeless and events since then have, unfortunately, confirmed my pessimism because the outlook is fully as bleak today. It was therefore without any sense of guilt that I moved to Cornell in the autumn of 1931 after an almost wasted year at George Washington University.

What a contrast I found in Ithaca! An atmosphere of genuine intellectual inquiry pervaded the whole institution because in each department one found a group of scholars. In economics a number of young men had been recruited from excellent graduate schools: Royal Montgomery from Chicago, Frank Southard from California, Paul O'Leary from Cornell, and myself from Harvard. Two able, somewhat older men, Harold Reed and Paul Homan, already had established reputations. In economics Cornell has long had a rather unusual tradition: young men have made their mark in scholarship there and then gone on to other universities; and hence the list of economists who at one time or another taught at Cornell is an impressive one that includes Thorstein Veblen, Frank A. Fetter, Edwin Kemmerer, Allyn Young, Abbott Usher, Sumner Slichter, and many others. I found the history, philosophy, and government departments staffed with excellent scholars, and the cross-fertilization between the social sciences at Cornell not only proved stimulating but made possible an interchange of ideas that prevented the narrow disciplinary specialization that so often contracts mental horizons. My greatest help came from that remarkable group of historians who taught at Cornell when I was there: Carl Becker, Max Laistner, Carl Stephenson, Preserved Smith, superb scholars and felicitous writers, worthy successors to George Lincoln Burr, Nathaniel Schmidt, and Charles H. Hull, all of whom, though retired, still made the rounds of our open-door offices in Goldwin Smith Hall.

This sharing of views constituted perhaps my richest experience at Cornell. Almost to a man we were writing. George Sabine was at work on his classic history of political thought, Montgomery was collaborating with Millis of Chicago on their three-volume analysis of American labor, Homan with two associates was writing on the Puerto Rican sugar industry, Carl Stephenson finished his splendid work on *Medieval History* in 1935, the year before I published *Some Origins of the Modern Economic World*, which he very kindly read and criticized in manuscript. In the government department Robert Cushman, George E. G. Catlin, and Herbert Briggs added their contributions to the stream of monographs, articles, and texts. The secret of this exemplary scholastic productivity lay, of course, in the careful selection of promising scholars for all faculty appointments, relatively light teaching loads, good library facilities, and, as I have already emphasized, the stimulation of associates.

For me this interdisciplinary interchange was especially enriched by a rather exclusive organization to which I was elected, one that bore the innocuous name of "The Circle." It came into being when a professor of botany and a musicologist decided that a small group ought to be formed to meet together about once a month and share their intellectual explorations. The two founders thereupon chose two others, a historian and a psychologist. The four agreed upon four more to be invited (myself, a philosopher, a political scientist, and another historian). Then the eight of us chose eight others, making a total of sixteen. Meeting once a month for the (eight-month) academic year would require each member to report to "The Circle" once every two years. These sessions produced some excellent papers and wonderful discussions. I remember how Carl Becker delighted us with his witty, yet profound, paper on "Form and Substance in Literary Discourse." My own contribution was published in 1938 in the *International Journal of Ethics*, an essay on "Just Price in an Unjust World."

During my six years at Cornell I published four books.[2] One of these, to be sure, was my doctoral dissertation, and another, my translation of Teilhac's book, had been largely, though not entirely, completed in England. My really important book, *Predecessors of Adam Smith*, which involved a tremendous amount of work, was, except for the chapter that Keynes had published as an article in *Economic History*, all written at Cornell. In the hope of obtaining criticism about my interpretations, I published several chapters of this book as articles in learned society

[2] *American Economic Thought in the Seventeenth Century* (London: P. S. King, 1932); *Some Origins of the Modern Economic World* (New York: Macmillan, 1936); *Pioneers of American Economic Thought in the Nineteenth Century* by Ernest Teilhac, translated from the French by E. A. J. Johnson (New York: Macmillan, 1936); *Predecessors of Adam Smith: The Growth of British Economic Thought* (New York: Prentice-Hall, 1937; and London: P. S. King, 1937).

76

journals,[3] a technique that I recommend to young scholars. This carefully prepared study has stood the test of time; reprinted for a second time, it is, I am told, required reading for Ph.D. candidates in most important graduate schools. The Cornell setting proved ideal for this painstaking kind of scholarship, and I have acknowledged in the preface to the *Predecessors* my indebtedness to a number of my former Cornell colleagues. But although the *Predecessors* proved to be my most important book at this stage of my career, I concurrently wrote a small book, *Some Origins of the Modern Economic World*, that unexpectedly became the foundation, albeit with successive improvements, of two other books that have been widely used in American colleges and universities.[4] Meantime, at Professor Taussig's request, I prepared a critique [5] of the ambitious fifteen-volume *Encyclopaedia of the Social Sciences*, for which I had written three articles.[6] A large number of book reviews constituted another part of my output during my six years at Cornell, reviews that appeared in quite a variety of learned society journals.[7] I had used my opportunity for research and writing well, and as I look back on my years at Cornell I sometimes feel that what was said about one of my English worthies, Nehemiah Grew, might equally have applied to me: "Those who knew him best have often said that they believ'd he has the least mis-spent time to answer for of any they ever observed."[8]

Despite this intense application — which during the three years I lived within walking distance of the campus brought me to my office not six

[3] Chapter 7 on Nehemiah Grew (based on a manuscript I found in the Lansdowne papers in the British Museum) first appeared in the *American Economic Review* (vol. XXI, September 1931, pp. 463–480); chapter 9 on David Hume was published in the *Revue d'histoire économique et sociale* (vol. XIX, 1931, pp. 225–243); chapter 15 was reprinted from the article I prepared for the *Journal of Political Economy* (vol. XL, December 1932, pp. 750–770); chapter 14 is a revision of an article I published in the *Quarterly Journal of Economics* (vol. XLVI, August 1932, pp. 698–719); chapter 3 on Gerard de Malynes came out first in the *American Economic Review* (vol. XXIII, September 1933, pp. 441–455); while as has already been mentioned, chapter 13 first appeared in *Economic History* (vol. II, January 1931, pp. 234–253).

[4] *The Origins and Development of the American Economy*, with Herman Krooss (New York: Prentice-Hall, 1953); and *The American Economy: Its Origins, Development and Transformation*, with Herman Krooss (New York: Prentice-Hall, 1960).

[5] Published in the *Quarterly Journal of Economics*, vol. L (February 1936), pp. 355–366.

[6] These were biographical accounts of John Rae, Gerard de Malynes, and Edward Misselden.

[7] E.g., the *Journal of Political Economy*, the *American Economic Review*, the *Philosophical Review*, the *Annals of the American Academy of Political and Social Science*, the *Journal of the American Statistical Association*, the *Journal of Modern History*, and the *American Historical Review*.

[8] Rev. John Shower, *Enock's Translation*.

but seven days a week — I found splinters of time for quite a range of other activities. I learned the art of wine making, an accomplishment which only unique circumstance could have made possible. With the Volstead Act still on the statute books, however weakly enforced, the grapes of the Finger Lakes region proved an irresistible temptation to hundreds of amateur wine-makers. I joined a group of such tyros the autumn I arrived in Ithaca, but since my associates insisted on trying to prove that potable wine could be made out of Concord grapes, a thesis that has yet to be demonstrated, I withdrew from that pleasant fellowship,[9] and formed my own small syndicate, meantime apprenticing myself to Giorgio di Grassi, a descendant of the Berberini family of Italy, who demonstrated his versatility not only as a cataloguer of foreign books in the Cornell Library but as a masterful wine-maker. Under his tutelage I learned how to ferment the local Clinton, Isabelle, Catawba, Delaware, and Agawam grapes and then how to blend the juices before the "fining" processes began. He taught me how to make excellent still wines and, by mixing the juice of Delaware grapes with that of Clinton or Isabelle, a superb sparkling wine as well. My associates Professors Arthur Whitaker (history) and Gustav Cunningham (philosophy) and I would hire a truck, drive over to the vineyards on Lake Seneca, and come back with a ton of grapes. My cellar became our *cave* where the "must" barrels stood and where the various-sized barrels and casks lay in a solemn row ready to receive the precious juice once the initial fermentation had been completed. As I recall, we had space for 262 gallons of wine, and these casks, so precious before the repeal of the Volstead Act, may still be resting in the wine cellar I built in our Greek temple house in Dryden, New York. Obviously there was no point in moving this equipment to New York when I left Cornell in 1937 since after good wines came on the market once again the short-lived home industry had contracted more rapidly than it had expanded. Yet this experience deepened my admiration for the great skill of wine-makers throughout the world. When, in 1945, I was taken to see the famous wine cellars of Johannisberg Schloss, which convert the grapes from the fifty-three-acre vineyard that belonged to Charlemagne long before it became the property of Prince Metternich, I discovered that the way di Grassi had taught me to make wine duplicated precisely the method the cellar masters still use at Johannisberg.

Other diversions that my wife and I enjoyed while I taught at Cornell were the auction sales of random varieties of time-seasoned commodities rather inaccurately called "antiques." By the 1930's New England had been combed bare of such items, and the supplying area had moved west

[9] Which included that witty and talented raconteur Morris Bishop whose "Limericks before Lear" had delighted the readers of the *New Yorker*.

some two or three hundred miles, where country auctions might include some fairly good furniture, marked pewter, glass, and Staffordshire china. While I was writing my book on the seventeenth century at Harvard, my wife and I had seized every possible opportunity to visit colonial houses. Out of this came an interest in early pine, maple, and cherry furniture; in the household effects of the colonial period; and in a wide range of other so-called antiques. When we discovered that frequent auctions were held in Cortland, and at other places within easy driving distance of Ithaca, we joined the eager band of hopefuls who looked for treasures at bargain prices. Of course we found precious few treasures, and lack of money made it impossible for us to purchase highboys or any of the larger pieces of furniture, but since the depression had sharply reduced the "carriage-trade" demand for collectibles, many of the things we were able to afford proved to be excellent investments. We have, for example, a Sheraton chest of drawers for which we paid thirty-four dollars in 1932 and which would bring ten times that amount today. We thoroughly enjoyed the antique auctions, the farm auctions, and the pleasant and useful contacts we made with dealers from dozens of towns and villages in upper New York State. We were able to build up a good collection of pewter and a truly unusual assemblage of Canova china,[10] and to acquire a few excellent pieces of furniture.

Our son was born in Ithaca in December 1933, and I recall that the following February there were nineteen days when the temperature did not come up to zero Fahrenheit. We lived at that time on the upper gorge of Fall Creek where we could look out through a picture window on the cascades below. But in the winter of 1933–34 our water line froze and our house, standing on a rock shelf of the gorge, could only be kept warm by stoking the furnace every half hour and by constantly feeding wood into the fireplace. Dreading another such winter we regretfully left this house, located so idyllically within easy walking distance of the campus, and purchased a house of Greek temple type in the village of Dryden, twelve miles from Ithaca. It had been the childhood home of Jennie McGraw Fiske, one of the early benefactors of Cornell. We restored this house faithfully to its early nineteenth-century beauty, removing porches added in the 1890's and refurbishing the original graceful recessed porch with Ionic

[10] Earthenware made by a number of Staffordshire potters (T. Mayer, Enoch Wood, G. Phillips, R & J Clews) commemorating the work of Antonio Canova, who had carved a statue of George Washington for the state of North Carolina. My wife and I began collecting Enoch Wood's "Washington Statue" plates, platters, and tureens but when these were priced beyond our reach we shifted to the "Canova" patterns of other English potters. After almost forty years of collecting we now have about a hundred pieces in dazzling color contrasts. Julia D. Sophronia Snow has written an excellent article on "Canova Commemorated on Staffordshire" in *The Magazine Antiques*, October 1932, pp. 143–145.

columns from a house built about the same time as ours. Our house became something of an architectural showpiece after we had restored it, and we had a stream of visitors.[11] In Dryden once again, however, I discovered the sociological limitations of a village. Moreover, I had neglected to take account of what effects automobiles and hard roads had produced since the time I had myself lived on the edge of an Illinois village. In the case of Dryden, the village had been stripped of its best talent, leaving the less energetic, less able, and least adventurous. With a fair-sized city ten miles to the east and another twelve miles to the west, only a few local establishments could survive: a garage of sorts, a hardware store, a combined grocery and meat market, a coal and wood yard, and a lumber and building-material yard. Only a few of the many services that had once existed remained: an undertaker, a tinsmith, and a painter-paperhanger. More saddening than the economic contraction, for that, as I have explained in a recently published book,[12] might actually increase regional productivity, was the distressingly low level of education and intelligence. A scourge of undulant fever, undoubtedly attributable to an uninspected milk supply, was accepted as something inevitable. When a new well urgently needed to be drilled to ensure an adequate water supply, a search for proper location was made with water witches, and only after money had been wasted on three dry holes would the village leaders agree to ask advice from a Cornell geologist. On the map Dryden lay only twelve miles from Ithaca but intellectually it seemed to be a thousand miles distant.

Wine making, however pleasurable, and antique collecting, agreeable as it can be, could not, unfortunately, compensate for some of the limitations of Cornell's location. Ithaca was inconvenient to reach by rail, and, in my day, there were no air connections; as a result theater companies and orchestras seldom came.[13] To compensate for this lack, my wife and I tried to spend a week in New York, Boston, or Washington at vacation periods, and in the summer we attended the whole series of Boston Symphony Orchestra concerts in Stockbridge, Massachusetts. One other serious shortcoming of the Ithaca region was the lack of sunshine since the Finger Lakes area receives less than half the "maximum-possible sunshine" that even gloomy Boston does, something in the neighborhood of

[11] I wrote a short article describing in some detail the architecture and the history of this lovely and most satisfying structure which we called "Anthemion House." See "Echoes of Hellas in Tompkins County," in *The Jeffersonian*, vol. V, no. 12 (December 1934), pp. 10–11.

[12] *The Organization of Space in Developing Countries* (Cambridge, Mass.: Harvard University Press, 1970).

[13] The Boston Symphony Orchestra came once a year, as did the Detroit Symphony. The only play by a visiting company that I recall seeing was Eugene O'Neill's *Mourning Becomes Electra*.

23 percent. The dreary, murky climate leads both to physical ailments — colds, sinus trouble — and to psychological strains — morbidity and hypertension. Some people become irascible, super-sensitive, or downright irritable; they are climatological victims in a region of great natural beauty. It was when I began to appreciate this physical peculiarity of the Ithaca area that I came to understand why so many great scholars had not stayed on indefinitely at Cornell. After six years, when a suitable offer to go elsewhere came, my wife and I were ready to leave, even though for my professional purposes Cornell had been wonderfully beneficent.

Actually there were a number of other reasons which made it seem wise to accept an offer to teach in the graduate schools of New York University. The depression had made promotions at Cornell all but impossible. Actually we had all received a 10 percent salary cut, and some assistant professors (there were no associate professors), eager for tenure, accepted full professorships at less than the salaries they had received before the 10 percent reduction. New York University offered me an initial 30 percent increase and then two years later gave me another 15 percent increase. In the days of low professors' salaries the promise of even a 30 percent increase had strong attraction. I realized, of course, that in a sense I would be leaving the "grove of academe," and to this "opportunity cost" I gave very serious consideration. There were things, however, that I could do far better in New York than in Ithaca. Much against the advice of some of my punctilious Cornell colleagues who considered any commercial venture inappropriate for true scholars (presumably they should be essentially monastic in their habits) I had agreed to edit a series of textbooks for Prentice-Hall, Inc., an aggressive publishing firm that had been very successful with business books, and with various tax services, but, until about 1940, had not been able to make much progress in the social sciences. After consulting colleagues with less doctrinaire or rigid views than the fearful ones, men whose judgment I respected, including eminent scholars such as Carl Becker and George Sabine, I decided to sign up with Prentice-Hall. It proved to be one of the wisest decisions of my life. In doing so mercenary objectives were not my exclusive concern.

I had noted in my teaching experience that relatively few outstanding scholars had written textbooks [14] and that all too many textbooks in use failed to incorporate the findings of recent research. In my own teaching I had tried to downgrade the importance of any single textbook, and had devised tactics that would make it necessary for students to read widely,[15]

[14] Some had: for example, Taussig, Ely, and Dewing.

[15] In my course in economic history at Cornell I required each student to pay a fee similar to a laboratory fee commonly charged in science courses. From the pro-

but I recognized that mass education would inescapably require textbooks. I made it quite plain, however, to the chairman of the board (Charles Gerstenberg) and the president (Richard Ettinger) of Prentice-Hall that I wanted to experiment with textbooks much nearer to current monographs, written, for the most part, by young scholars more likely to be abreast of new developments than the septuagenarians who so often had been plodding away at the manuscripts of their already outdated textbooks for decades. If I were to find young scholars to write the new-type textbooks, advise them how to attune their books to all possible market outlets, and help them relate their books to modern trends in undergraduate instruction, I needed to be near to the Prentice-Hall offices during the formative years of my series so I could consult all the firm's college travelers, the editorial staff, the advertising department, and the sales office. I intended to make a systematic search for the best possible authors, plan a series of books that would cover all the major courses customarily offered, and do all this swiftly enough so that an investment of about five years of my career would give me a measure of economic security.[16] For the most part I succeeded in realizing these ambitions. Altogether thirty-three books appeared in my Prentice-Hall Economic Series, among which were a number of firsts. Thus Albert L. Meyers's *Elements of Modern Economics* was the first textbook that incorporated the theory of monopolistic competition, Theodore Morgan's *Introduction to Economics* the first to use national accounting as an analytical device, and *Economic Analysis and Public Policy* by Mary Jean Bowman and Lee Bach the first to appraise in depth the economics of the firm. Within a few years most of the volumes in my series had become leading textbooks; Eric Roll's *History of Economic Thought*, James A. Estey's *Business Cycles*, Joel Dean's *Managerial Economics*, and Herman Krooss's *American Economic Development* are only a few examples. Meantime some monographic studies in the series, such as Arthur Marget's *Theory of Prices* and Dudley Dillard's *The Economics of John Maynard Keynes*, very greatly enhanced the reputation of Prentice-Hall.

My compensation consisted of a royalty based on the receipts from the sales of books in my series. It started with a modest $105.21 for fiscal year 1937, but had increased tenfold by 1942. The war, which sharply contracted the college population for about four years, flattened the earn-

ceeds of these fees duplicate copies of many books were purchased for the library and thereby a sizable number of books rather than any single book became the required reading corpus.

[16] Before teachers' pension plans had been established, and before any governmental social-security payments had been authorized, many an emeritus professor faced real hardship during his retirement. I recall a very distinguished Cornell colleague who eked out his declining years in genteel poverty.

ings curve, but beginning in 1946 an upturn occurred which brought my 1947 royalties to $7685.16. From then onward I have had an unbroken sizable royalty income all of which could be invested in appreciating securities. It should be remembered, however, that I "earned" this outside income by patient and persistent work, reading and rejecting three, four, or five times the number of manuscripts that I accepted. Moreover it should also be noted that I brought well over four million dollars of new business to Prentice-Hall at a time when a 300-page book sold for $2.75. Although Prentice-Hall was sharply criticized by competitors who found it difficult to keep pace with its aggressive policies, I found no reason for complaint whatever. To be sure Messrs. Gerstenberg and Ettinger were hard-boiled businessmen, as they needed to be in the book business where sentimentality has often brought disaster. But I found that although they expected careful market analysis to be made before a manuscript was accepted for publication, they were always prepared to take reasonable risks. Thus in 1940 when I read three essays on the economics of war by an author wholly unknown to me, I hurried over to Mr. Ettinger's office asking permission to invite the author of these penetrating essays to prepare a one-semester text on "The Economics of War." "How many courses are there on this subject?" Mr. Ettinger asked. "There are no courses," I replied. "We will publish a book that will create the courses." It proved to be as I had predicted. We brought out Horst Mendershausen's book in the late summer of 1941 and before the next college year was over so many courses on the economics of war had sprouted up that six competing textbooks were published in 1942. But by then we were ready with a revised edition, which came out in 1943, and once again we swept the market. By that time, however, I was in uniform.

Before I entered the army (July 1943), another genuinely exciting event had occurred: without vanity I think I can say that I played an inceptive role in the creation of a new learned society. For some time among economic historians, whether trained in history or economics departments, there had been a feeling that no organic unity existed among them similar to that in other disciplines. In 1939, moving spirits in both the American Historical Association and the American Economic Association gathered economic historians together, and it was agreed that a joint effort should be made to create a separate learned society. All these founders[17] realized, however, that there would be no permanence, no central focus, not much membership attraction to a new society unless it published a journal, and

[17] Among whom should be mentioned for their particularly seminal roles Francis F. Gay and Arthur H. Cole of Harvard; Ann Bezanson and Joseph Willitts of the University of Pennsylvania; Harold Innis of Toronto; Herbert Heaton of Minnesota; Earl J. Hamilton of Duke; Edward Kirkland of Bowdoin; and Frederic C. Lane of Johns Hopkins.

for reasons beyond my knowing they chose me as the editor of the yet-un-born journal and Shepard Clough of Columbia as the associate editor. Apparently the founders assumed that because I was an economist and Clough a historian we represented the two primary approaches to economic history; because we were both in New York we could easily collaborate; and since we both had demonstrated that we were productive scholars we would not seriously disgrace the emergent guild.

With some misgivings Clough and I accepted our election, although within a week we began to doubt whether we should have been so easily flattered. When we sought advice from a former editor of the *American Historical Review*, he explained that it would be quite impossible for us to launch a new journal without an assurance of generous subvention. We had nothing, absolutely nothing, but our courage and audacity: no office, no secretary, no publisher, no articles, no books to review, no printer, and almost no money since fewer than a hundred people had agreed to become members of the proposed new society and then only on the condition that a semiannual journal would requite them for their three-dollar annual membership fee. I have never quite understood why Clough and I were so recklessly optimistic; apparently the very challenge intrigued us. I blush when I recall what we did. Clough begged his Columbia colleagues to join the association as I did mine; we literally compelled our graduate students to take "student membership" at reduced rates, and we virtually gave membership quotas to all the founding fathers. Meantime I persuaded the provost of New York University that it would be such an honor for New York University Press to publish the new *Journal of Economic History* that he should make the editorial facilities of the Press available to us gratis. Once I had his acquiescence, I went to the dean of the School of Commerce and obtained an office and one day's secretarial assistance each week. Next I enlisted the help of one of my most talented graduate students, the wife of a New York University professor, who became our invaluable assistant editor. The problem of finding a printer I solved by conspiring with my brother-in-law, who was in charge of the job-printing department of the Burlington Free Press, to obtain off-peak printing rates. His role was to convince his employer in Vermont that the *Journal* could be set at slack times. All kinds of difficulties arose, however, because when the *Journal* copy had been assembled, New York University Press, unaware of my shameless misrepresentation, wanted almost immediate composition.

Meantime Clough and I had to find authors who were writing articles or would agree to do so. We combed the country, and by good fortune found enough articles for an initial issue of the *Journal*. Getting books to review from wary, depression-bitten publishers proved a tough job; moreover once we had obtained books we had to find competent reviewers and convince them that we had to have their reviews within an unreasonably short time. We adopted a very precise editorial procedure. After both Clough and I had approved an article for publication we then edited it for substance and structure, never changing a word but appending dozens of pink tabs suggesting changes. Then Winifred Carroll would edit the manuscript for grammatical corrections and for literary felicity. We followed the very same procedure in editing the book reviews.[18] Our meticulous editorial work delighted some of our authors, puzzled some, annoyed others, and irritated a few. But our names appeared on the masthead, and as long as Clough and I edited the *Journal* these rigid editorial practices obtained.

Sixteen weeks from the date Clough and I were notified that we had been chosen to edit the new publication the first number of the *Journal of Economic History* was presented to each of the officers of the Economic History Association. Library subscriptions for the *Journal* now increased our strained and precarious bank balance, and a few book publishers agreed to buy advertising space in future issues. The second issue came out on the announced publication date and by careful budgeting our accounts were just barely in the black. When the first annual meeting of the association was held at Princeton I found the papers presented so uniformly excellent that I raised enough money from a score of the more prosperous members of the association to finance the publication of a supplemental issue to volume I of the *Journal*. To commemorate in perpetuity the title of President Gay's address at this the first meeting of the association, I called the supplemental issue of the *Journal* "The Tasks of Economic History," a designation which has ever since been used for the papers presented at the annual meetings of the association.

Although my deep involvement with the *Journal* for the next three years very seriously reduced my research and writing, I did manage to bring out one book,[19] I wrote a large number of book reviews, and I ghost-wrote portions of a book for a corporation vice-president. Yet I feel that my work in launching the *Journal* proved far more important than any one book or even any pair of books I might have written in the time I spent on my editorial and promotional tasks. The *Journal* has now passed its thirti-

---

[18] For reviews we set up certain guidelines that we urged reviewers to follow. Our thought was that a review should point out what an author had tried to do, evaluate whether this task justified the effort, and then appraise whether the author's purposes had been achieved. We asked for very frank, unvarnished, genuinely critical reviews. Sometimes we got what we hoped for.

[19] *An Economic History of Modern England* (New York: Nelson, 1939). This book, which I wrote at the request of Raymond Leslie Buell, was to be part of a collaborative work on Western Europe. Unfortunately Buell's other authors failed to deliver their manuscripts and I therefore had to publish my part separately.

eth anniversary, and when I look over the articles that have been published in it during these thirty years I cannot help experiencing a sense of pride. Admittedly Clough and I edited the *Journal* for only three years, and our six successors have all left their scholarly imprint on the other volumes. But Clough and I founded the *Journal*, and in doing so we ensured that the association would live and grow. If ever I have a tombstone, which I very much doubt, my executors could properly inscribe on it: "Creator and First Editor of the *Journal of Economic History.*" Unlike many tombstone inscriptions, this one would be true!

Whereas my busy and rewarding professional activities in New York were entirely agreeable, my wife and I soon discovered that living in the city had serious disadvantages, particularly since we had a young son who needed clean air and adequate recreational facilities. We made a number of experiments, living one spring in Pound Ridge and one year in Bronxville, but we finally decided to buy an eighteenth-century house in Stockbridge, Massachusetts, a lovely New England town we had come to know well by reason of our repeated attendance at the Boston Symphony Orchestra concerts there. This proved an ideal solution for our several purposes. Since I rearranged my classes so that all met on the first three days of the week, I could go by train to New York on Sunday night and return to Stockbridge on Wednesday afternoon, thus having the benefits of both city and country. Meantime my family could live in a delightful place and we could all of us have the Tanglewood concerts, the Stockbridge Playhouse summer theater, and a number of other cultural activities, all within a ten-mile driving range. This rather idyllic life, which gave me four days out of each week during the academic year plus four summer months in the country, was to be abruptly ended by the war. After Pearl Harbor I knew that it would be only a matter of time before I discovered some niche in the armed services that I could fill. It took some searching to find such a place, but I succeeded much better than I could ever have expected.

7

WAR WITHOUT BUGLES

★★★★★★★★★★★★★★★★★★★★★★★★★

WHEN the War Department decided to mechanize the cavalry, in the thirties, I lost interest in my reserve commission even though I had been promoted to first lieutenant in 1926 and to captain in 1931. "Cavalry" without horses had no appeal, and since I made no effort whatever to obtain a "certificate of capacity" entitling me to promotion to the next grade, my captain's commission expired in 1936. Consequently when the war came I had to be recommissioned in order to enter the army, and this meant that I had to find some type of duty that would require the qualifications I had to offer. I toyed with an offer — not a very definite one — in military intelligence, and I went to Washington for an interview about prospects in motor transport. Not until the civil-affairs cadres were being formed, however, did I find any type of service for which I seemed reasonably well suited; but once my *vita* had been seen, my military experience had been noted,[1] and I had been interviewed, a commission with the rank of major was offered me in the early summer of 1943. I began my civil-affairs training in August in the Provost Marshal General's School at Fort Custer, Michigan.[2]

[1] During the time I held reserve commissions between 1922 and 1936 I had been quite dutiful in accepting active duty and participating in reserve organizations. I served two tours of duty with the 14th Cavalry at Fort Custer, Michigan; three with the 3rd Cavalry at Fort Ethan Allen, Vermont; and one with the 5th Cavalry at Fort Clark, Texas.

[2] Fort Custer, which I had known in 1922 and 1924 as a cavalry tent camp, had by 1943 become a veritable city of two-story barracks buildings, all equally bleak, smoky, and crowded. No one, I suspect, will look back on our weeks there with any nostalgia. "Cadet life all over again," I wrote to my wife on August 28, 1943, "with meticulous regulations for the arrangement of books, clothing and other items." The average age of my classmates seemed to be about forty: lawyers, engineers, accountants, professors (only three), social workers, geologists, administrators, and bankers.

87

A well-publicized school of military government had been initially established at Charlottesville, Virginia, but when a large-scale invasion of the Continent appeared more and more imminent in 1943, it seemed prudent for the army to create several similar training centers. Accordingly, after the hundred and fifty officers in "Class IV" finished their hurried and superficial training at Fort Custer, in September 1943, they were divided into two contingents, seventy-five men assigned to the new Civil Affairs Training School (CATS) at Harvard, the other seventy-five to a corresponding new organization at Yale. It suited me very well to find myself in the Yale component since although I had often visited New Haven I had never spent any time there. Moreover I had a number of very good friends on the Yale faculty, one of whom promptly arranged for me to have a study for my private use in Berkeley College. Since I knew I would soon be going overseas, I brought my wife and my son to New Haven so that we might be together as long as possible. Once again friends helped us, and soon we had a snug apartment on Prospect Street and my son was entered in the nearby Foote School.

My stay in New Haven, however, proved to be very brief: before a month had elapsed I had been picked as one of the first two officers to be sent abroad from the Yale CATS unit. Yet even from my brief taste of the training that Yale offered, I found it of excellent quality, well planned and equally well implemented. The lectures on German politics and history by Arnold Wolfers, Cecil Driver, and Whitney Griswold were insightful and yet explicit enough to be well suited to the needs of a group of future civil-affairs officers with widely differing professional training; while John Allison's lectures on France reflected his innate artistry as much as his scholarship. Since we were presumably being trained for the Franco-German area, heavy emphasis was necessarily laid on language instruction. We messed at the Fence Club, and here also we held our seminars, our tactical exercises, and a range of other instructional meetings. But for me all this interesting experience abruptly ended when I received orders to report to Fort Hamilton, the designated "staging" center for officers scheduled for assignment to the European theater of operations.[3]

On a wild, cold November night we boarded the *Queen Elizabeth* and began an ocean crossing to Greenock, Scotland, in a fashion so bizarre that it now seems almost unbelievable. Built to accommodate two thousand passengers, the *Elizabeth* on this voyage probably carried from twelve to sixteen thousand.[4] Long after, when my wife learned that I

[3] The "movement orders" which I received applied to twenty-seven officers from the School of Military Government at Charlottesville, two each from Civil Affairs Training schools at Harvard, Yale, and Pittsburgh, one from CATS-Western Reserve, plus four officers from more specialized military organizations.

[4] I recall the figure to be sixteen thousand but when I inquired of Wood Gray, an

WAR WITHOUT BUGLES ★

had crossed on a luxury liner, she said she was "green with envy," to which I replied (July 15, 1945): "This time you really have no reason to be envious. We were racked up like stock-fish, with six majors in a cabin built for one passenger. The bunks were in two tiers of three, so that the bottom man was about four inches off the floor and the top man about twelve inches from the ceiling. There were but two meals a day and in order to feed all passengers the serving process was continuous. From 4:00 A.M. until 9:00 P.M. the loudspeaker instructed numbered 'groups' to 'form their lines.' I had a reasonable schedule with my first meal 8:30–9:00 A.M., the second 4:30–5:00 P.M. No, wartime travel is not the same as peacetime travel. We had our Thanksgiving dinner on the *Elizabeth* but as I recall we had ham, not turkey."

In our "officers' lounge" all furniture had been removed, so that everyone perforce sat on the floor and, in gypsylike fashion, dozens of groups played cards or chess. Since enlisted men slept alternately on the blacked-out decks one night and in hammocks inside the ship the next night, in the morning the decks resembled stables, as the heat of a long row of bodies converted moist sea air into a steaming mist. To avoid being a target for lurking enemy submarines, the ship constantly zigzagged, so that every few minutes it would roll sharply, making it very difficult for us to walk about in the daytime or to sleep at night. We seem to have wandered all over the Atlantic, from cold arctic to semitropical waters. But thanks to radar, the ship's speed, the disagreeable zigzagging, and truly superb seamanship, we arrived safely in the Firth of Clyde and anchored one raw late-November morning near Greenock.

It took all day to disembark the multitude and our group was not lightered ashore until about four o'clock in the afternoon. We boarded railway carriages at dockside and within minutes were on our way to Lichfield Barracks which we learned would be our receiving depot; here we arrived about midnight and were shown to quarters. Routed out of bed next morning for prolonged setting-up exercises at four thirty, we found ourselves, after a hasty breakfast, engaged in censoring soldiers' letters, a task that makes anyone with a conscience experience a most distasteful sense of uncleanness. About eleven o'clock we were given a break so that we could listen to a carping harangue by the American commanding officer, a disgruntled, none-too-successful professional soldier,

army historian, who also made that weird voyage, he estimated a much lower figure, pointing out that because the *Queen Mary* on one voyage had almost keeled over, the passenger maximum was reduced downward toward twelve thousand. This figure was confirmed by my fellow voyager John Harriman (who once sat beside me in Taussig's course at Harvard), who discussed the matter with a Commodore Marr when Harriman again crossed the Atlantic on the *Elizabeth* in 1967.

who ran Lichfield Barracks in such a tyrannical way[5] that he ultimately faced a court-martial. Fortunately our stay in this unwelcome atmosphere proved brief: within a day the necessary paper work had been completed and we entrained for London. At the billeting office, we had a wide choice of quarters, and my old Harvard friend Major John Harriman and I elected to stay at a South Kensington hotel in that part of London I knew best. Next morning we reported to the unit to which we had been assigned, momentarily rather vain about the honor that had seemingly been conferred on us since presumably our little group of thirty-eight officers had been selected from a roster of about five thousand civil-affairs officers then in training. For what urgent duty had we been hurried overseas so precipitately?

We learned that COSSAC, the mysterious letters on the cards that had been stealthily given us on shipboard, meant that we were assigned to the chief of staff of the (yet unnamed) supreme allied commander, and that our task, in conjunction with British opposite numbers, was to plan the civil-affairs part of "Operation Overlord," the imminent cross-channel assault. Presumably this planning echelon included a full spectrum of the specialists needed to envisage a comprehensive plan for the administration of liberated (or conquered) territory; at any rate our group contained persons assumed to be capable of dealing with problems of rationing, price control, public safety, finance, transportation, housing, electric-energy production and distribution, trade and industry, communications, public health, and agriculture. Our ranks therefore included economists, engineers, doctors, geographers, geologists, police officers, and quite a number of other specialists. The big question was whether such a group of civilian experts could collectively produce some kind of plan or a cluster of plans that could cope with the confusion and chaos that might actually be encountered in liberated or conquered areas.

Much more reliance seemingly was placed on the presumed potency of organization than upon any basic principles. Each section, whether it be police, trade and industry, public health, finance, or electric power, therefore proceeded to make its separate plan and little provision seemed to

---

[5] Although our group consisted of captains, majors, and lieutenant colonels, at Lichfield we were treated as if we were raw recruits. But at least two members of our group refused to be intimidated. Because our toilet and bathing facilities were very crowded, Lt. Col. Axel Oxholm and Major Chauncey Snow found an adjacent set of facilities which they proceeded to use. Presently a very angry lieutenant arrived informing them that the commanding officer forbade any officers in transit to use unassigned toilet facilities. "Oh my poor boy," Lieutenant Colonel Oxholm said to the lieutenant, "What have they done to you here? You worked so hard to get your commission and what is your reward? Those heartless, cruel men have made you a shit-house inspector! It just isn't right, and you should refuse to do their dirty work." The abashed lieutenant disappeared without saying a word.

90

have been made for knitting these disparate plans into some agreed-upon operational sequence. Consequently we found ourselves becoming increasingly compartmentalized, an unfortunate tendency that the insistence on secrecy accentuated. Forbidden to visit libraries or to consult with banks, business enterprises, or research agencies, we tried to flog out our respective problems in the semimonastic confines of our rabbit-warren offices in Cadogan Square, aided only by such documents as came to us through military channels. Those of us who had been accustomed to individual research were able to adapt ourselves to these constraints, and although we fretted and often felt frustrated, we plugged along and did our best. Many very able experts, on the other hand, could not make the necessary adjustment; to them all this "planning" was just so much boondoggling, and many of these malcontents who could not obtain transfers to organizations where they could be more active sat in the seats of the scornful and ridiculed what the rest of us dutifully tried to do.

The gloomy winter of 1943–44, made exceptionally depressing by the rigorously enforced London blackout, did little to buoy our spirits. We left our billets in darkness, and groped our way to Cadogan Square back of Harrods. Yet it was rather amazing how quickly we grew accustomed to the blackout. One learned streets and sidewalks, the knack of estimating distance from houses, steps, curbings. Shadows came to have definite meaning so that one learned how to move straight ahead to one's objective. "Torches" were permitted, if shaded, but everyone was expected to avoid using them. In dingy Victorian five-story houses that had been clumsily joined together by breaking open connections on one floor or another, we spent our days in ill-heated rooms equipped only with deal tables, folding chairs, files, and blackout curtains. Every section reflected "combined operations" so that each American was paired by an English, Scottish, Australian, Canadian, or South African opposite number. For the most part, the arrangement led to quite amicable cooperation although occasionally frictions arose. In my section the only disagreement concerned the ventilation of our little room where six officers spent their wearisome days. The British wore heavy underwear and thick, woolly battle jackets, and hence they wanted the windows wide open even on the rawest day. The Americans, accustomed to well-heated offices, had lighter clothing and were usually chilled to the bone. The battle continued throughout our three months of coexistence, and about all we Americans could do was to come early and close the windows, hoping that our British counterparts would for a time at least ignore what they called "stuffiness."

As I look back on COSSAC, I think a good deal of useful analysis and helpful planning resulted even though in a sense we were expected to make bricks without straw. My task, which was to work out a generally applicable rationing and price-control program, proved extremely difficult without access to any libraries or archives. After I had exhausted the little source material available (such as a very general description of the extremely complicated German Food Estate) I had to resort to pure speculation. I therefore prepared among other things a rigorously reasoned paper that I called "The Pure Theory of Rationing." This blessed document, which I wrote to save myself from utter boredom, was reproduced and circulated widely. Wherever I went on the Continent in 1944 and 1945 someone would be sure to ask, "Have you seen this paper?" "Oh yes," I would reply, "I saw that quite some time ago." We overplanned, in the sense that every expert tended to concern himself with little details appropriate for his specialty, yet we underplanned because wholly inadequate coordination and integration occurred. Yet COSSAC planned and prepared the way for SHAEF (Supreme Headquarters Allied Expeditionary Forces). Our work at COSSAC during December 1943 and January and February of 1944 was very hush-hush and for very good reasons. The plan for the division of Germany into British, American, and Russian spheres was indeed "top secret" when I first learned about it on December 1, 1943. A month later I knew where the Allied landings would be made, information I never once dreamed of mentioning to other officers, even to my COSSAC associates. I could have learned the date of the planned assault, information I preferred not to have.

The next stage in civil-affairs planning overcame many of the shortcomings of COSSAC. In March 1944, about five thousand future civil-affairs officers were brought to the European theater and "pooled" with the COSSAC group in one of the more modern British military installations, at Shrivenham, some ninety miles west of London. Here "missions" to be dispatched to each of the liberated countries were formed, as well as a large "German country unit" for occupational tasks in German conquered areas. Each of these organizations had to build up a suitable table of organization, and each had to staff all the personnel slots with the appropriate experts. Since I had the good fortune at that time to be attached to Supreme Headquarters, I had nothing to do with these organizational problems until in mid-April 1944, when I joined the "SHAEF Mission to Norway." I did, however, journey to Shrivenham once a week during March and April, lecturing each Saturday and Sunday on economic problems to the emergent country missions. My main duty at that time, however, was to prepare over-all plans for employment policies to be followed in liberated areas by all Allied military organizations that would require local manpower. In the absence of some guidelines, uncontrolled competition for local labor pools, or for more limited special skills, could very easily inflate wage rates to such an extent that serious disruptive effects on local and regional economies might result. But if the controlled wages were to be effective as incentives, and yet reasonably fair in relation to prices, as much data as possible on probable living costs had to be obtained. On this problem I worked in cooperation with our London embassy, OSS, all relevant military organizations, and the British Ministry of Economic Warfare.

Life in London, from the time I arrived in late November 1943 to the time when I moved to Edinburgh in early August 1944, was never dull since the threat of serious enemy action steadily increased. During December 1943 and January 1944 enemy aircraft would occasionally be picked up by the searchlights that constantly searched the heavens. Beams from many searchlights would converge and then the rocket launchers in Hyde Park would go into action spewing out great flashes of lemon-colored flames as they released their projectiles. Hundreds of barrage balloons held up taut cables to snag low-flying aircraft, forcing the raiding planes to fly so high that their bombing accuracy proved unsatisfactory. The Germans, therefore, resorted to fire bombs that could be sowed indiscriminately or sometimes used huge flares to help make possible some degree of precision bombing. It was an eerie sight when a series of huge global flares, the color of the lady's-slipper blossoms one finds in New England forests, would float slowly downward in a laddered sequence completely illuminating the skyline so that a following wing of swift-flying planes could pick their targets between the barrage-balloon cables. These random sorties were followed in February 1944 by much more concentrated bombing for about ten nights, a period generally called the "little blitz." [6]

In June of 1944, however, something quite different occurred which in a less-disciplined nation than Britain might have had totally demoralizing effects. On Tuesday night, June 13, 1944, low-flying aircraft were heard over London, planes that seemed to ignore the risks of being snagged by balloon cables. Three days later Herbert Morrison, the home secretary, gave out a statement explaining that the apparently fearless German raiders were actually "pilotless airplanes," and assured Britons that vigorous countermeasures would be taken against "this much-vaunted new weapon." [7] It took some time, unfortunately, to perfect these countermeasures. The first impulse was to shoot down the V-1s — called "doodle-

[6] The headlines in the *Evening News* for Saturday, February 19, 1944, proudly announced "Big Barrage Foils Bid to Burn London. 60 Raiders Cross Coast. Heaviest [Raid] since Blitz." The text of the article began: "The Luftwaffe failed early today in their greatest bid since the big raids of 1940–41 to set London ablaze." During these raids jagged parts of fragmentation bombs fired at the invading planes would rain down on the London streets. I have a collection of these lethal pieces of metal that I picked up in front of my hotel during the "little blitz."

[7] *Evening Standard*, June 16, 1944.

bugs" by the Americans, "buzz-bombs" by the British — but on Sunday, June 18, when one was fired on, it plunged into a military chapel where its ton of high explosives detonated, killing more than a hundred worshiping British soldiers. It became apparent that if the V-1s were to be attacked, as they later were by fighter planes, the "kills" would have to be attempted before the flying bombs reached densely populated areas. It also came to be realized that the London balloon cables, which had forced piloted planes to fly high, offered no protection against V-1s. Quite the reverse; the forest of balloon cables served as trip wires, deflecting the flying bombs and causing them to plunge down and detonate their explosive charges in the city whereas if left alone many of the V-1s might have overflown the city. Very hastily the winches wound up their cables, and all the balloons that had floated over London for more than three years were brought down and deflated. As swiftly as possible the balloons were used to establish a barrage on the channel coast. Even so the ten weeks that followed the first V-1 attacks proved to be exceedingly unpleasant.

From launching sites on a long Continental arc, the V-1s were angled in on London. Day and night they came, and in a ten-week period at least fifty unloaded their lethal and destructive charges within a half-mile radius of the hotel where I lived in South Kensington.[8] At first we took shelter, at our Princess Gardens offices, whenever we heard a "doodle-bug" approaching; but we soon found this to be quite foolish since most of the V-1s either were overflying our buildings or were well to the right or the left. We therefore posted a lookout on the roof of our row of buildings, providing him with an old-fashioned school bell. Only when a V-1 seemed to be headed directly our way did he clang the bell, whereupon we would take our chosen places near an inside wall, sitting with our arms folded and our heads down until the danger had passed. We grew rather hardened, I fear, in our attitudes. Thus when we walked across Hyde Park to our Grosvenor House mess,[9] we would pause when a V-1 came in sight, watch its flight, and note the number of seconds from the time the motor cut off to the time a mushroom cloud of smoke and dust indicated that a building had been demolished. "Well, it's down," someone might say; "at least that one didn't hit us!" But it had probably killed or mutilated quite a number of people.

[8] In a letter to my wife, dated June 20, 1944, I wrote, "I have seen dozens [of V-1s] both day and night and heard hundreds. They are a very real menace especially on foggy or rainy nights. Six hits during the last twenty-four hours within a quarter mile of where I live." The German attempt to hit the Battersea Electric Plant probably explained the heavy concentration of V-1s in the Kensington area.

[9] The basement skating rink had been converted into a cafeteria that seated a thousand officers. Someone called this vast operation "Willow Run," a delightfully descriptive term that everyone soon used.

The British quickly adapted their home-guard operations to meet this new emergency, and I had the greatest admiration for the quiet and efficient way in which rescue operations and fire prevention were conducted. Whereas the V-2s, which fell in Britain a few months later, were rockets that traveled through ballistic curves, and therefore came down almost vertically so that their blast force was exerted upward in an inverted conical pattern, the V-1s came flying in at an elevation of about twelve hundred to fifteen hundred feet. Consequently when the motors cut off, the bomb load would glide down; detonation would occur on impact, and the blast force of some two thousand pounds of high explosives would be exerted almost parallel to the earth's surface.[10] The vacuum created by the explosion would cause windows to bulge out and fragmentize so that often a veritable snowstorm of flying glass would swirl over fairly large areas.[11] If a V-1 plowed into a building, then the explosive charge might be so placed that the whole structure would disintegrate into a mass of tangled timbers and smoking plaster.

How did the British cope with these situations? If the "hit" was of the latter type, this was the normal sequence of the well-planned and skillfully phased operations: First an inspector would arrive who would assess the situation and begin sending radio instructions, calling sweeping machines or fire engines if necessary. Soon an ambulance would appear bringing a doctor who would engage a nearby room which he could quickly convert into an emergency hospital. Presently public-utility personnel arrived who cut off gas mains and tested water hydrants. Then the "light rescue" crews, dressed in pale blue clothes, would appear. Shod with tennis slippers, these lightweight, lithe, athletic men would gingerly climb onto the pile of wreckage that once had been a building, looking for persons who could be seen or heard. Any injured they extricated would be helped out and led to the surgery. Then almost by prearranged schedule the "heavy rescue" crews in dark blue clothes would come lumbering down the street with their mobile cranes. Soon they would anchor their cables, and the cranes would gently lift up beams and planks so that the light rescue crews could penetrate deeper into the jackstraw mass of timbers, staircases, and floors. The whole operation was splendidly con-

[10] I recall reading in a British newspaper that in Clapham, a section of London with small houses, a single V-1 destroyed or damaged about seventy-five houses.

[11] A British friend of mine whose face was horribly lacerated by such glass particles still suffers from this painful experience more than twenty-five years after the unhappy event which occurred when a V-1 struck the top story of a building that housed the Ministry of Economic Warfare. I had interviewed an official of that ministry on that top floor less than a half an hour before the explosion. Once the British realized the glass blizzard problem, they gave first priority to street-sweeping machines. Until these precautions were taken, hospital wards were filled with doctors and nurses with lacerated hands who had slipped on the minute glass particles.

ceived, thoroughly integrated, and successful in saving thousands of lives. Even so the casualties were very high. It has been estimated that of the almost half million persons killed by enemy action in London during the war, about one-third of the deaths occurred in the ten-week period when the V-1s rained in. After a huge barrage-balloon barrier was raised on the south coast of England, fewer "doodle-bugs" reached their target, and once the Allied forces on the Continent captured the launching sites, the danger ended. But while it lasted it took a ghastly toll.

For me the memorable day was Monday, July 3, 1944. The V-1s had been pouring in so steadily for two weeks that I had had very little sleep.[12] I arranged therefore to spend Saturday night, Sunday, and Sunday night with an English family in Sonning, near Reading, bringing our authorized "hospitality rations." Refreshed by this peaceful interlude, I returned to London early on Monday morning to find, first of all, that a V-1 had landed near enough to my hotel to break all the glass in my bedroom and bring down the ceiling plaster. Two blocks away, quite near our offices, another hit had completely destroyed a five-story building that housed the Czechoslovak embassy and this blast had broken all the glass in our Princess Garden offices. While I was contemplating this jumbled situation the telephone rang. It was one of our four enlisted men calling from a hospital informing me that a V-1 had struck their billet at Sloane Square. He thought that a great many of our soldiers had been killed, and that the wounded men might be found in any of the area hospitals.[13] I went in search of our enlisted men and succeeded in finding them. One had both his legs and both his arms broken, another had severe contusions, a third had serious head injuries; the sergeant who had telephoned me had tumbled down when the outer wall of the building collapsed, falling on an oil can in such a way that the spout pierced his hand. It was a rather rough morning. We all breathed easier when the severity of the V-1 attack began to taper off.

Shortly after the Normandy invasion the mission to France crossed the channel, soon followed by the missions to Belgium, Luxembourg, and the Netherlands. Meantime Supreme Headquarters moved to Versailles. Although I had been slated to be the senior rationing and price-control officer in the German country unit, I felt so displeased with the announced Washington policy for German occupation that when Colonel Graeme Howard, deputy chief of the SHAEF mission to Norway, asked me to be-

---

[12] We slept in our clothes, keeping our helmets within easy reach.

[13] Lt. Col. E. Ross Jenney, M.D., one of my closest army friends, wrote after he had read the original draft of this chapter, "In the V-1 explosion in our E.M. [enlisted men] quarters, one of our sergeants was killed. The next morning, English residents in and near Princess Gardens sent flowers with one of the most moving notes I've ever read."

come head of the economics branch of that mission I gladly accepted. This was why: In our COSSAC planning we had estimated, as best we could, the imported quantities of food, fuel, clothing, and other items that would be minimally necessary to prevent destitution, disease, and political unrest in liberated areas. When we proposed similar provision for uncovered enemy territory, the Washington answer was the notorious directive "J.C.S. 1067," which forbade us to make any provision whatever for Germany, the presumption apparently being that the entire nation ought to be isolated like a colony of lepers, walled off from the world, and left to subsist as best it could. The stupidity of this kind of thinking overlooked among other things the fact that there would be perhaps as many as a million displaced persons within the political boundaries of Germany, and I dreaded the responsibility of caring for these hungry hordes unless supplies could be programmed in advance. Yet by the irony of fate, after we had neatly discharged our responsibilities in Norway, it became temporarily my task, as acting chief of supply control in Germany, to supervise the feeding of hundreds of thousands of displaced persons, finding the resources as best I could. It had been the fear of just that contingency which led me to join the mission to Norway in the late spring of 1944.

For the Norway operation we assembled a carefully selected group of officers, many of whom were Norwegian-Americans. Since the British, when they attempted west-coast landings, had been thrown out of Norway in 1940, it was agreed at Supreme Headquarters that "Operation Apostle" (the liberation of Norway) although a "combined operation" would be mainly a British show. Those of us who were chosen for the mission therefore served under General Sir Andrew A. F. N. Thorne, K.C.B., C.M.G., D.S.O., who became the senior commander of Allied Land Forces Norway.[14] We became part of his staff in a Civil Affairs Organization headed by Brigadier Percy Hansen, V.C., D.S.O., M.C. What a joy it was to work under such gracious, cultured, and distinguished officers. General Thorne and Brigadier Hansen were both Etonians, cultured gentlemen who had profound respect for the professionally competent Americans selected for the Norway mission. The whole operation was planned in closest consultation with the Norwegian government in exile, and, since the Norwegians were lodged in Kingston House, we needed only to cross a narrow street to confer with our Norwegian counterparts during the time our mission had quarters in Princess Gardens.

Once the fundamentals of our liberation, disarmament, and civilian-relief plans had been sketched out and agreed upon with the Norwegians,

[14] General Thorne had been aide-de-camp to King George VI and warden of Windsor Castle. During the early years of the war he was the senior officer in charge of the defense of south England.

our mission moved to Edinburgh where Scottish Command became the nucleus of the several task forces that would ultimately move to Norway. Here during the autumn of 1944 and the following winter we revised our operational plans again and again. We had to do so because as the military situation on the Continent became more fluid the situation that confronted us kept changing. Thus in late October 1944, when the Germans, under heavy pressure from the Russians, withdrew from the most northerly province of Norway (Finnmark) destroying every house, haystack, barn, and boat in their retreat, we were faced with the nearly impossible task of getting some relief supplies to the homeless Norwegians in this remote region. This involved the shipment of small-bulk, high-calorie foods and the most essential and compact of other supplies, goods that could be sent on the "Murmansk run" of ships swift enough to evade the scores of German submarines that could put out from the bomb-proof pens in Bergen and Trondheim.[15]

Although we began these relief operations with high hopes we soon ran into serious difficulties. As the Germans retreated, the Russians moved into the uncovered areas. Two questions therefore arose: would the Russians allow us to conduct relief operations in territory they controlled; and would SHAEF permit us to send supplies into territory not under Allied control? The answer to both of these questions we found to be negative. First SHAEF forbade us to send any more supplies until agreement had been reached with the Russians regarding the entry and disposition of civil-affairs supplies in Russian-controlled territory. When such agreement could not be reached, the relief of Finnmark had to be entrusted to the Norwegian government in exile, who were even less capable

[15] Since the Russians were dependent on essential military supplies that could only be delivered to their northern forces by the Murmansk run, the shipping space that could be allocated for civil-affairs supplies for the Norwegians in Finnmark was perforce very limited. To cope with this problem I worked out a differential supply table which assigned space priorities. If only twenty-five tons could be taken, for example, the types and amounts of highest priority commodities were specified. As the permissible tonnage increased, additional goods were added as were greater quantities of certain already-chosen commodities. The senior commander, General Thorne, was very pleased with my solution to this troublesome problem.

In reviewing records that I have been able to consult, I find that by January 27, 1945, we had shipped 5183 tons of relief supplies to Finnmark, of which 3515 tons represented our civil-affairs supplies, while the other 1668 tons had been procured by the royal Norwegian government. To indicate how our 3515 tons had to be fitted into Murmansk-run ships, it is interesting to note that only 45 tons could be accommodated in the first shipment (October 28, 1944), 145 tons in the second (November 26, 1944), 1287 in the third (December 28, 1944), and 2038 in the fourth (January 25, 1945). The first shipment consisted entirely of sugar, salt, and coffee. The second brought canned meat, evaporated milk, margarine, biscuits, blankets, clothing, soap, and medical supplies. Only when more space was allocated for the third and fourth shipments could kerosene, diesel oil, petrol, and a few trucks be included along with additional amounts of the first essentials.

than we would have been in obtaining shipping space or ensuring proper distribution of relief supplies to the Finnmark people. Although we continued to help the Norwegians plan shipments to northern Norway, we were most unhappy that SHAEF would not allow us to risk sending some of our programmed supplies to Finnmark even though the Russians would not have allowed us to supervise their distribution.

Fortunately, except for this emergency, we had time enough for systematic and careful preparation, which, for civil-affairs operations, involved both macro and micro planning. The macro planning, for the entire country, was the responsibility of the SHAEF mission to Norway working in the closest possible cooperation with the Norwegian government in exile. Agreement had to be reached about the types and amounts of relief and rehabilitation supplies we proposed to bring in because, with characteristic pride, the Norwegians insisted on paying for all programmed civil-affairs imports. Our commodity specialists and their Norwegian consultants therefore calculated, for example, the proper amounts of coal needed and the various tonnages and types of petroleum fuels required for the many specialized types of Norwegian fishing boats. Specification of the exact kinds, grades, and gauges of cordage for fishing gear proved to be a very complex task, but fortunately I had a fisheries officer, Major Rasmus Monge, who had the requisite experience to cope with this problem. Agricultural supplies such as fertilizers and pesticides could be fairly easily programmed, but tractors, tools, and agricultural-processing equipment involved problems not merely of selection but of procurement from British or American factories all overcommitted with war contracts. Electrical equipment turned out to be another complex programming problem, particularly when it involved "package plants" that were wanted for Spitsbergen in order to reactivate mining operations there. Consumer goods for the most part could be specified without great difficulty, particularly such commodities as coffee, lard, sugar, and bread grains. We did encounter real difficulty in arranging for an adequate quantity of fats, and we had to persuade the Norwegians to accept certain unfamiliar articles of diet, such as peanut oil or peanut butter. Sizes and varieties of children's shoes, dresses, and suits called for patient computations especially in view of the climatological differences in a maritime country more than two thousand miles in length. Medical supplies involved not merely the selection of the right kinds of pharmaceuticals but the collection of a great deal of information concerning needed hospital and laboratory equipment, data that had to be gathered through Swedish intelligence sources.

The micro planning was both complementary to the macro planning and different. Our liberation plan involved sending six highly trained but small civil-affairs detachments to Oslo, Stavanger, Bergen, Trondheim,

Tromsö, and Kirkenes.[16] Their planning task was to ascertain the precise needs of these key places so that there could be the swiftest possible restoration of normal peacetime activities. The detachments studied their respective areas with meticulous care, sieving all available information and keeping their data current by skillfully arranged espionage. An industry officer, for example, in the Stavanger detachment would be familiar with all the mills, canneries, factories, shops, tanneries, and other productive enterprises. He would know where warehouses, lumberyards, or marine installations were located; and he would have a complete dossier of dependable *jössings* (patriots) to contact on arrival at his assigned post. The specific raw materials, fuels, and other supplies needed had to be carefully calculated; indeed much of the macro planning was based on such local computations, not all to be sure, since many of the supplies for interior communities had to be roughly estimated.

Civil-affairs responsibility was not by any means confined to supply and rehabilitation activities. Public safety, public health, finance, and the control, care, and repatriation of refugees and displaced persons also called for imaginative if somewhat less precise planning. All our activities had to be properly interrelated with the responsibilities of the military task forces, whose major duties would be the disarmament of enemy forces, maintenance of public order, repatriation of prisoners of war, disposal of weapons, ammunition, or other kinds of military supplies, and restoration of the legitimate Norwegian government. In order to ensure that all our civil-affairs preparations would be properly interlocked with both Allied and Norwegian military plans, we held, at Edinburgh, a comprehensive "exercise" during which we explained in great detail to the British army, navy, and RAF commanders and their staffs (which included a number of Americans), to the Norwegian government in exile, to the Norwegian army, navy, and air force commanders, and to the Norwegian district military commanders the basic elements in our civil-affairs preparations. This five-day "course," designated "Exercise Percy" (for Brigadier Percy H. Hansen), had been very carefully planned. Crown Prince Olav attended every session, as did the five Norwegian ministers nominated by their government to accompany the Allied force, while all other Norwegian ministries were also represented. A full digest of the exercise with summaries of the lectures was later printed by Scottish Command, complete with appropriate organization charts. I gave two of the lectures, one on "Economic Rehabilitation,"[17] the other on "Rationing"; officers

---

[16] As it turned out, the military situation in the province of Finnmark and lack of Russian cooperation made it impossible to send a civil-affairs detachment to Kirkenes.

[17] I pointed out how a properly planned economic rehabilitation could (a) end relief, not perpetuate it, (b) shift the Norwegian economy back to a free, purposeful

in my Economics Branch described our proposals for agriculture, fisheries, forestry, transportation, public utilities, and labor. Spokesmen for the detachments outlined how their work would be coordinated with that of the SHAEF mission to Norway and with the activities of the Norwegian (military) district commanders.[18]

I prepared for these "Exercise Percy" lectures with considerable trepidation and on the eve of the course, on August 12, 1944, I wrote to my wife: "Although I have been bombed and fly-bombed, I have never been as frightened as I am now. Tomorrow I must speak before a galaxy of generals, brigadiers, government officials, and a touch of royalty. It's all like a meeting of the American Economic Association, fully that formidable, except that instead of discussing abstract research topics I must define and defend a very definite program. What I have to say is loaded with dynamite, and the whole tone of the 'Exercise' has thus far been so distressingly polite that I fear I am going to detonate a terrific explosion."

I must have done well on August 13, 1944, because the next day I could write joyfully, "Ever since yesterday I have been overwhelmed with gracious remarks. Four [Norwegian] cabinet ministers came up immediately to tell me how much they appreciated my lecture; then came to congratulate me our commanding general, two foreign generals, and our foremost celebrity, H.R.H. Crown Prince Olav. Today my lecture was referred to at least a dozen times, and fifty or sixty people have spoken to me about my address. All in all I feel quite content. But virtue instead of being its own reward is once again its own punishment. Today I have been asked to speak on Thursday next to another command on a new subject, a task which will involve considerable preparation. . . . If things go as planned, we may be the most fortunate group of civil-affairs officers. We won't be mayors of bombed-out towns and villages; we are already the counselors of the mighty."

In order to be quite sure that the activities of the several detachments would be properly interrelated with the tasks of the SHAEF mission to Norway and with the responsibilities of the Allied and Norwegian military forces, a field exercise was held from November 12 to November 16, 1944. In this exercise, very appropriately called RUFFIT, the several detachments were deployed in "hutments" scattered within fifty miles of Edinburgh. All possible situations that might arise were simulated, from wandering bands of refugees to military insurrections. The ability of the detachments to carry out orders from the mission, their resourcefulness

civilian basis, (c) make goods more abundant, (d) make the best use of factories, foundries, mines, and farms, (e) hasten the transition from a German-controlled economy to a democratic and economically efficient scheme of things. *Exercise Percy, Digest* (Edinburgh, April 1945), chapter 16.

[18] Ibid., chapter 7.

in dealing with unexpected situations, and their reliability in integrating their local activities with Norwegian civilian and military organizations and with a comprehensive national civil-affairs program were carefully evaluated by disguised judges. This exercise, conducted in atrocious weather, did for the detachments what "Exercise Percy" had done for the headquarters staff of Scottish Command and for the SHAEF mission to Norway. I described "Exercise RUFFIT" in a November 14 letter to my wife: "Great sheets of rain are slashing against our windows. For three days now it has rained. We are extremely conscious of it inasmuch as we have been holding training exercises. Fortunately our detachments, even though they are scattered over the [Scottish] countryside, are in 'hutments' that have watertight roofs and which also have stoves. But for this elaborate training exercise we couldn't have gotten worse weather. Gusts of wind drive the rain into sheets of water that crash against buildings and vehicles. I have been lucky today because it was my day to stay in a comfortable office. Yesterday it rained, but gently, so I really enjoyed my travel from one site to another in a jeep. But today it must have been really miserable for those who had to move about. . . . As usual I have been fortunate; I have not had to go out into the field and live several days in a Nissen hut; instead I rove about and observe, returning at night to the comfort of my excellent, aristocratic hotel."

Since several other missions had already gone into action on the Continent, it seemed wise for us to detail as many officers as possible on temporary duty with those organizations so that our officers might have the benefit of actual operating experience. Accordingly I served a tour of duty with the mission to France in the winter of 1944,[19] and other officers in our Norway organization had similar field experience in France, Belgium, and Holland. The Battle of the Bulge had delayed the deployment of the huge German country unit, which remained outside of London at Bushy Park demonstrating, long before its annunciation, the reality of Parkinson's Law.[20] Our problem at Edinburgh centered around the maintenance

[19] Although one might think that three weeks in Paris would be a pleasant experience, I don't think I have ever been so uncomfortable. The luxury hotels where I stayed, the Crillon, Meurice, and Gallia, had no heat whatever, and after two months of frigid weather were unbelievably cold. At the Gallia we had hot water one day each week and hence a hot bath on that day was a memorable event.

[20] Major Herbert P. Woodward, with whom I served at COSSAC, ironically explained to me that the German country unit was so busy that he couldn't believe it could ever give up its work to move to Germany. "Everyone arrives promptly in the morning," said Major Woodward, "and begins working on documents in his 'In'-box. Daily conferences are scheduled at which careful minutes are kept, new ideas are proposed, outlined, and circulated, so that the organization generates a huge flow of documents that keeps a host of typists, clerks, and messengers busy. We are completely self-contained; we never need to go to Germany; we can go on here, fully employed, forever!"

102

of morale while we waited for the time of our departure for Norway, and we did our best to use our time constructively and effectively. A number of our officers became very impatient, unfortunately, and we lost some talent by transfers. For the most part, however, our cadres remained intact, and when the time came for us to go our units were prepared for the tasks for which we had trained and planned so carefully.[21]

In order to maintain liaison with the Norwegian government in exile and with dozens of London-based organizations, we kept a small office in London, and it became my duty to alternate between Edinburgh and London, in a three-week cycle. A check of my military file shows that I made at least nine such trips between Edinburgh and London, tiresome and unpleasant journeys in cold, crowded trains. But there were some compensations, since, despite the war, London did have symphony concerts and theaters. I recall going to a concert in Albert Hall the evening of the day when I was promoted to lieutenant colonel; and I shall never forget Ralph Richardson's superb acting in *Peer Gynt* at the Old Vic. We did, fortunately, have a few cultural events in Edinburgh as well: a small but well-balanced symphony gave concerts at Usher Hall, and the Sadler's Wells Ballet came once while I was in the Scottish capital. But by the winter of 1944 we were really growing impatient although, largely because of the Battle of the Bulge, we had several months yet to wait for our zero hour. When it came we were ready.

On November 29, 1944, I had been in Britain a full year, and hence it seemed appropriate to take stock of the learning process I had experienced. In cossac days, 190 British and American officers were cooped up in dark little rooms trying to puzzle out answers to hypothetical problems. The whole shape of things was vague and uncertain. A year later those of us who had demonstrated a capacity for staff duties were in fairly responsible positions. Not only had the ideas we developed, discussed, and screened been converted into policy directives, but many had been adopted as the basis of operations. Because I was among the first Americans to come to the emergent SHAEF planning echelons, I had the opportunity to work in a number of organizations in a direct or advisory capacity and

---

[21] Whereas many SHAEF missions became almost unmanageably large, the civil-affairs personnel roster for Norway was scaled down to the smallest possible number. The mission consisted of 46 officers (23 British, 23 American) with an OR/EM (OR = other ranks, EM = enlisted men) complement of 90. The detachments included 79 officers (46 British, 33 American), assisted by 137 OR/EM of whom 121 were British. Thus the entire civil-affairs roster consisted of 125 officers and 227 OR/EM (clerks, drivers, cooks, storemen, and general duty men). See Brigadier P. H. Hansen in *Exercise Percy*, chapter 2.

A majority of our officers spoke a second language: 28 spoke Norwegian, 10 Swedish, 6 Danish, 1 Finnish, 19 German, 12 French, 4 Italian, 1 Russian, and 1 Spanish. Ibid., p. 3.

had therefore been able to see the process whereby plans gradually metamorphosed into operating principles and policies. In COSSAC, we were not allowed to go outside our own organization except through very restricted channels. This irked us no end at the time, since there was so much information we needed and wanted. Yet these restrictions proved very wise for if there had been none a throng of ill-oriented people would have been fluttering around everywhere, leading to inevitable security risks. In the fullness of time, when we had learned our proper roles, we extended our range, so that by the end of 1944 we had access to all manner of governmental, research, and military agencies. We now knew how to use our intelligence sources; moreover we had learned how to operate amicably with our British associates and our Allied counterparts.

As the dimensions of our problems became clearer, we could concentrate on the most essential tasks although the completion of one part of our planning edifice always revealed other aspects that demanded attention; "when you work out one item," I wrote to my wife after Exercise Percy, "it merely opens up a dozen other things that must be planned." Fortunately my duties were always challenging. Things had to be settled, flogged out in conferences, written up succinctly yet forcefully, defended, and modified wherever necessary. I profited so much from my daily association with my British associates, and they helped sharpen my methods. Progressively I learned techniques and skills, and when I had clearly demonstrated my capacity to operate as a staff officer, General Thorne called on me to prepare drafts for him. Since of the twenty-three Americans who had been "seconded" to Scottish Command I was the only one who had lived in England before the war and had studied at Oxford and Cambridge, I had a definite advantage over my fellow Americans in a British unit.[22] I could write and speak English as well as American, and, best of all, I thoroughly enjoyed the whole atmosphere provided by my polite, quick-witted, and talented British associates. I knew I had made the grade when both my brigadier and the commanding general began calling me by my first name.[23]

[22] Operating under British regulations, messing on British food.

[23] This is not a trivial matter. Nigel Nicolson explains in some detail the advice his father gave him on this delicate point of British etiquette. See Harold Nicolson, *Diaries and Letters, 1930–1939*, ed. Nigel Nicolson (London: Collins, 1966), p. 26.

8

LEVE KONGEN, LEVE KONGEN

★★★★★★★★★★★★★★★★★★★★★★★★★★★★★★★★★★

IN PLANNING the liberation of Norway it was assumed that one of three military or diplomatic developments would precede the entry of Allied forces into the long-occupied country: a thinning out and a reduction in strength of German forces; a definite withdrawal of German occupying troops; or an armistice involving the surrender of all enemy forces in Norway. Any of these conditions might occur with or without damaging ("scorching" in military parlance) the Norwegian economy and could take place in winter or summer. The worst situation would be "winter scorched," the best "summer unscorched"; and we actually got both. In the northern provinces the Germans withdrew during winter weather, and ruthlessly scorched the economy of Finnmark. In south Norway all German forces surrendered, and there the fortunate outcome was, with only very minor exceptions, summer unscorched. But up to the moment the first Lancaster bomber of the liberating Allied task force actually landed at Gardermoen airfield, no one could be entirely certain that the Germans in Norway were surrendering or that the economy would be undamaged. By a stroke of luck I arrived in Norway on that Lancaster bomber which brought the advance party of the 1st (British) Airborne Division, and I was therefore the first American officer [1] to reach the country whose liberation had so long been the object of our planning.

In war things seldom go precisely as planned. In the event of a German

---

[1] An Oslo newspaper, *Aftenposten*, for May 22, 1945 (p. 2), carried my picture under the heading "Den første amerikaner som kom" with this gracious explanation (my translation): "The first American to arrive in Oslo after the [German] surrender was Colonel Edgar Johnson. He is one of the men we must thank for the food and other imported supplies that are arriving so promptly. Before the war he was a professor of economics. He is of Swedish ancestry and has always been a friend of the Nordic countries."

surrender that would include the forces in Norway it had been intended that General Frans Böhme, the German commanding general, would be ordered to send surrender delegates to Edinburgh in a white airplane. These delegates, who would include experts on a specified number of technical matters such as mine fields, military matériel, personnel, and installations, would be temporarily incarcerated in Edinburgh for inter-rogation. Meantime, a Disarmament Commission from the Allied Joint Force would go directly to Norway in the same white airplane that had brought the surrender delegates to Edinburgh. Concurrently a task force consisting of the 1st (British) Airborne Division would be dispatched to Norway as the first echelon of a combined British and American occupy-ing force. But things did not work out this way. The penetration of Gen-eral Bernard Montgomery's 21st Army Group into Schleswig-Holstein, the collapse of the German defenses of Berlin under tremendous Russian pressure, and the decision of Admiral Karl Dönitz to sue for peace led to such competition for communications that General Thorne's Edinburgh headquarters found it almost impossible to ascertain whether the Norway forces were included in the surrender overtures.[2] General Thorne there-fore decided to send in his airborne task force and let the battle-scarred veterans of Arnhem ascertain whether the Germans in Norway were ac-tually surrendering. Very hurriedly on May 7 a small group of civil-affairs officers and a somewhat larger number of British officers from other sec-tions of Scottish Command, plus a few Norwegians, were dispatched to airfields from which advance parties and "first lifts" of "Operation Dooms-day" would depart for Oslo and Stavanger.[3] I remember traveling by train the night of May 7 and spending the night of May 8 in a mushroom shed somewhere in Essex, near Braintree. For the next day my military file provides this information:

LIST OF PERSONNEL ATTACHED TO 1ST AIRBORNE DIVISION
FOR OPERATION DOOMSDAY

Oslo Advance Party	Aircraft No. 7	Earls Colne Airfield
	Take Off 10:00 hrs., 9 May	
Col. Hagle	Col. Mossfeldt	Maj. MacRoberts
Lt. Col. Roll	Capt. Evang	Lt. Col. Johnson

Early in the morning of May 9 this advance party left the mushroom shed and was driven in a lorry to a bomber airdrome. Since we didn't know

[2] There had been many persistent intimations that even if Berlin were lost the Germans might try to hold one "fortress" around Berchtesgaden, another in Norway.

[3] Out of the 125 officers in the civil-affairs section of Scottish Command only 9 were initially selected to fly to Norway with the 1st Airborne Division. The rest were to travel from Edinburgh by water transport although as urgent needs for personnel emerged a number more did go by air.

what to expect in Norway, we were equipped with chutes, and with our packs and weapons we looked rather overladen. We took off not at ten A.M. as scheduled, but at one o'clock.[4] Although one could see little from a Lancaster bomber, I did manage to notice that we followed the east coast of England for the better part of an hour before we turned right, crossing the North Sea in about an hour and a half. We reached the Norwegian coast just above Kristiansand and then followed the Oslo fjord. We circled over Oslo, then went forty-four kilometers further to Gardermoen airport.

Who were the six officers chosen for this first task-force plane? Each had a discrete mission. Colonel John Thoralf Hagle, a Norwegian officer, was the personal representative of H.R.H. Crown Prince Olav, charged with all manner of confidential tasks. Mr. Roll, who had a simulated military rank, had instructions to take possession of the Oslo broadcasting center by one means or another. Colonel Burger Frederik Motzfeldt (Mossfeldt) represented the Norwegian air force that had been trained in the United Kingdom; his task was to make arrangements for the transfer of this force to Norway. Captain Vilhelm Andreas Evang (Norwegian) and Major Walter Diak McRoberts (British) were counterintelligence officers who needed to make the earliest possible contact with the leaders of the Norwegian resistance. My task was to make logistic arrangements for the incoming civil-affairs personnel and to deal, on behalf of General Thorne, with any urgent and immediate civil-affairs problems. With these latter tasks I was soon almost overwhelmed.

Contrary to our fears, we had no difficulty in landing on the completely empty runway of Gardermoen airport.[5] Our pilot taxied the bomber fairly

[4] But whereas we took off on May 9, the personnel for the "first lifts," scheduled for departure on May 10, had to cool their heels for several days, as I shall presently explain.

[5] Unknown to us was General Böhme's announcement of the German surrender published on May 8, 1945, in German, in the *Deutsche Zeitung in Norwegen*. The full translated text of that announcement follows:

To THE SOLDIERS IN NORWAY

The Supreme Commander of the 20th Army and Commander of the German Armed Forces in Norway, General of Mountain Troops, Böhme, addressed his soldiers as follows:
Soldiers!
As the Supreme Commander of the 20th Army and Commander of the German Armed Forces in Norway, I am addressing you in this most difficult hour of our people. After six years of heroic battle against a world of enemies the war has now come to an end. In his address to the German people the Foreign Minister, Count von Schwerin-Krosigk, has announced the unconditional surrender of the German Armed Forces in all zones of combat.
I know that all of you join me in deep feelings of pain and sorrow. But as soldiers we must not succumb, in this serious hour, to feelings of indifference, sullen inactivity, or even despair. Even though our mission to protect the occupied areas of Norway has come to an end, our task has not been fulfilled. We have to accept the

near the main hangars; our eighteen soldiers quickly dropped out and set up a ring of machine guns around our aircraft; we had arrived in Norway. Our counterintelligence officers then walked over to the rigidly correct Luftwaffe officers standing near the hangar. They asked that vehicles be made available to take us to Oslo. Compliance was almost immediate; the German license plates were removed, British and Norwegian flags were unfurled, and, leaving only a few "Red Devils" to guard the plane, we set off for Oslo. The news of our arrival must have spread very swiftly since by the time we reached the outskirts of Norway's capital city, crowds of cheering, flag-waving Norwegian men, women, and children lined the road. It was a triumphant procession. We went directly to the Bristol Hotel in Oslo, which then served as a billet for senior German officers. The billeting officer was instructed to have single rooms ready for each of us in ten minutes. We found, somewhat to our surprise, that the fourteen members of the Disarmament Commission from Scottish Command had already arrived at the Bristol Hotel. Their plane had flown direct from Edinburgh on May 8 to an airfield near to the city (Fornebu) and consequently the commission had reached the hotel almost a day before we did.[6] All of which proved very fortunate since now I had a senior

harsh conditions imposed on us by the enemy with the clear understanding that this is the only way to avoid further bloodshed and the senseless destruction of our country.

Soldiers!

For five years you have held the Norwegian territory and have done your duty as true German men.

At this moment when fate has decided against us, you will maintain the same firm comradeship and unity that have welded us together in six years of battle and bloodshed.

In carrying out this order — the most difficult ever issued to you — you must show once more the same strict discipline and unconditional obedience that distinguished your performance throughout this war.

Keep up your courage and respectability and demonstrate by your bearing and appearance that you have been the soldiers of a people whose history and unique excellence in this war have filled each of us with the greatest pride.

This war has been an epic poem of the German people, unequaled in the history of other peoples. It is our duty to keep the German soldier's shield of honor unsullied and free. It is our hope that from now on we shall deal with men on the other side who respect the soldier's honor, and we expect that the Norwegian people will show the German soldier the same discipline that he has always maintained vis-à-vis the Norwegian people.

Soldiers!

Our love for the German people and our belief in its immortality will always remain unchanged.

[6] Between the time our group (picturesquely called "the heralds") left Edinburgh and the time the advance party enplaned on May 9, General Thorne must have received information about the inclusion of the German troops in Norway in the general surrender. At any rate, he dispatched the Disarmament Commission before the German surrender delegates arrived in Edinburgh.

officer, Brigadier R. Hilton, with whom I could consult and coordinate my work.

Because the German surrender created a vacuum, the Norwegian resistance, the *hjemme fronten* (home front), had already assumed some governmental functions. First of all, these very capable persons released hundreds of Norwegian political prisoners that the Quisling-Terboven government had incarcerated, and at the time of our arrival they were busily engaged in rounding up those opportunistic Norwegians who either had been real quislings or had aided and abetted the Germans [7] and their Norwegian henchmen. Very appropriately, all such captured persons were locked up in the same prisons that had housed the patriotic Norwegians and were subjected to the exact prison rules that the Terboven government[8] had prescribed. The resistance designated certain persons to provide liaison with the incoming British and American personnel, and within an hour of my arrival I had made contact with a Mr. Nansen (a nephew of Fridtjof Nansen, the famous explorer) and an extremely competent Dr. Christophersen.

It was lucky that I had, for very soon after my arrival at the Bristol Hotel I had a stream of visitors, and without the advice and help of these two Norwegians I would have been unable to cope with the importunities of my visitors. The mayor of Oslo, sent to me by Brigadier Hilton, told me the whole public transport system of Oslo would grind to a halt within twenty-four hours unless gasoline and other petroleum products could be obtained at once from the German-controlled tank farms. I sent for the appropriate German officer and instructed him to release the necessary petroleum. Meantime the director of the state railways was waiting to see me. He also needed fuel, both coal and wood blocks. A French consular officer wanted advice about repatriating some fifteen hundred Frenchmen who had been brought to Norway by the Germans. All through the night my visitors came. Meantime, I could hear enough shooting in the city to realize that members of the Norwegian home front were using whatever force they found necessary to advance their liberating activities.

[7] Our civil-affairs police section estimated that by May 23, 1945, about thirty-two hundred Oslo quislings were being held in prison pending trials. This would suggest that the national total might have been more than twice this number.

[8] Although Vidkun Quisling proclaimed himself the head of the Norwegian government on the day of the German invasion (April 9, 1940), he was apparently unable to find a sufficient number of persons willing to serve in a government that he would lead; and quite soon Josef Terboven, a German from Essen, was appointed *Reichskommissar* for occupied Norwegian territories, on April 24, 1940. Quisling served as leader of the Nasjonal Samling (the Quisling neo-Fascist party) until February 1, 1942, when he was formally installed as "minister president" with rather dubious powers since Terboven remained the Führer's representative in Norway.

When morning came I expected my fellow officers would soon arrive as scheduled on the first lift of the task force. Airborne troops were also to arrive that day. What happened was that the 186 aircraft that took off from airfields scattered all along the east coast of England from Kent to Lincolnshire encountered a wild storm over the North Sea, and at least five aircraft were lost. One crashed in south Sweden, another just a short distance from Gardermoen airport, and three fell into the North Sea, one of which carried an air vice marshal, one of our joint commanders. Except for one plane, which miraculously landed at Gardermoen, the aircraft returned to England, and our little group of six — the advance party — and the fourteen officers of the Disarmament Commission continued to mess with German officers on German rations, realizing all too well that our safety depended more on the fidelity with which the Germans would observe the armistice than upon our capacity for self-defense although we were, of course, heavily armed. Two more days passed before the weather cleared, but on the following day a steady drone of aircraft told us that the entire 1st Airborne Division was coming. The arrival of Colonel Eric Summers, our chief staff officer; Lt. Col. John Enrietto, our legal officer; Lt. Col. E. Ross Jenney, our public-health officer; Major Paul Fredrickson, my (Norwegian-American) labor officer; and my indispensable sergeant, Eric Stern, relieved me of an infinite number of worries and responsibilities. Next day we moved out of the Bristol Hotel into offices vacated by the Wehrmacht, the Disarmament Commission having by then ordered the Germans to move all their personnel at least ten kilometers from Oslo.

To take over the actual rooms from which the Germans had, with humorless severity, controlled the Norwegian people for five years was an emotional experience for all of us chiefly because we became so painfully aware of the omnipresent evidence of cultural schizophrenia. Each quickly vacated office still contained, over each desk, a picture of Hitler and, on each desk, a large number of rubber stamps for authenticating all manner of documents and, almost without fail, a vase of flowers — these items testifying to the German devotion to authority, *ordnung*, and beauty. Sergeant Stern, of German Jewish extraction, was not at all impressed; he dashed from office to office grabbing the many different likenesses of Hitler, throwing them on the floor and stamping his combat boot through the glass of each framed picture. But although the departure of the Germans provided us with offices, we no longer had German rations, and since we would not consider consuming any of the all-too-scarce Norwegian food supplies, we had to depend on airlifted "iron" rations until our own commissary supplies could arrive by boat. It became unbelievably tedious to look forward, three times a day, to hard biscuits, corned beef, and tea, never anything else. One discouraged wit said it reminded him of a "wayside pulpit" he once saw in a churchyard on which was printed "Jesus Christ, the same yesterday, today, and tomorrow!" Gastronomically the month or more that we lived on air-dropped British rations seemed endless,[9] and tempers markedly improved when our commissary supplies finally arrived.

We did not, however, suffer from lack of something to drink. In Edinburgh our officers had worried about whether we would be able to obtain the customary (British) liquor ration when we reached Norway, and careful arrangements were therefore made to ensure proper supplies. Had we known what a gigantic stock of wines, champagne, and liqueurs the Germans had built up in Norway, we need not have wasted time on assuring ourselves the very modest British whiskey and gin rations. When during the first fortnight about 600,000 bottles of wine and champagne were seized in a Drammen warehouse we reveled in our good fortune. This first "liberation" was soon followed by the discovery of another cache of about 1,250,000 bottles at Lillehammer together with barrels of wine and casks of liqueurs. Col. Orville Baldwin, our G-4 (supply officer), estimated that altogether we took possession of the equivalent of 19,000,000 bottles of alcoholic beverages. We therefore allowed each of the 14,000 British, the 5000 Americans, and the 2500 Norwegians in uniform to purchase, at their option, the following "full weekly ration": two bottles of champagne, two bottles of French brandy, two bottles of red wine, two bottles of white wine, one bottle of *Verschnit* (a type of German gin), and either one bottle of Benedictine or one bottle of Cointreau.[10] Most of the Americans could afford to buy their full ration and were therefore able to provide very desirable "hospitality rations" to their Norwegian friends. The British, with much lower army salaries, bought usually only a fraction of what they were allotted, and the Norwegians also had to pick and choose. Even so, in the six-month period that the Allied troops stayed in Norway, something in excess of a million dollars had accumulated in the liquor fund.

Although many of my associates thought the sequestrated liquors should have been given away, I took a very different attitude and in this

[9] "We are still on bully beef and biscuits," I wrote to my wife on June 10, "and it's getting damned monotonous as I start a second month, for whereas we are served in excellent hotel style, it's disheartening to start each day with corned beef, bitter tea, jam, and hard biscuits."

[10] On a trip I made to Scottish Command headquarters at Edinburgh I landed at Turnhouse airport where I cleared customs. When asked if I had anything to declare, I replied quite truthfully, "Only my weekly liquor ration." The unsuspecting customs officer promptly cleared me, and the precious ten bottles I brought to British friends were very, very much appreciated in a war economy which allocated only one bottle a month to registered persons and where black-market whiskey cost about twenty-five dollars a bottle.

111

I had the support of our legal officer, Lieutenant Colonel Enrietto. My worriment centered around a possible demand for restitution of property carried out of France by the Germans, particularly when the Norwegians were instituting restitution claims. Since one of my main responsibilities came to be overseeing the rational disposal of enemy war matériel, I argued that in order to protect Allied Land Forces Norway against any possible claims, we would be well advised to sell all confiscated liquor at estimated (winery) cost prices, holding the money in escrow so that if the French did demand restitution we would be prepared to meet it. But the French made no demands on us,[11] and as the liquor fund grew larger, week by week, all manner of proposals were made for the use of the money. Scholarships for Norwegian students who might study at British or American universities seemed a sensible and appropriate proposal. But since there was no certainty that restitution claims might not someday be made, I convinced General Thorne that the liquor proceeds should be paid, in direct proportion to the British, American, and Norwegian troop liquor expenditures, into the British Exchequer, the American Treasury, and Norges Bank. As I recall, about $350,000 from the liquor fund was actually paid into the United States Treasury, a transaction about which Lieutenant Colonel Enrietto and I have always felt very proud.

Once the hectic first days [12] had passed, and once our full complement of civil-affairs personnel had arrived, we settled down as best we could to our respective preplanned duties. There proved to be many tasks, however, which we had not anticipated or whose difficulty we had underestimated. We had not expected, for example, that the total number of displaced persons would be so large,[13] or that the uncovering and disposal of German-owned or -controlled property would be so huge and so complicated a task. There was, fortunately, less urgency about the disposal of most German-controlled property than about the care and repatriation

[11] Which might suggest that the Germans had probably purchased the wine, champagne, and brandy with their occupation currency.

[12] It would take many pages to describe these "hectic" first days. "To have gone into the streets last night [May 9]," I wrote to my wife, "would have been foolhardy. I would have been literally mobbed by hysterically happy people." Letter from Oslo dated May 14 but written in snippets May 9, 10, 11, 12, and 13.

[13] Although much of the intelligence we obtained through clandestine sources in 1944 and 1945 proved fairly accurate, consistently the personnel data were greatly underestimated. Thus whereas about 30,000 Russian prisoners of war were presumed to be in Norway the actual number was nearer to 83,000. In addition, some 4000 Yugoslavs and more than 20,000 Poles brought the P.O.W. figure well over 100,000. In addition at least 105,000 non-German Wehrmacht personnel, Belgian, Dutch, Danish, Czech, Italian, and Russian civilian workers, had been brought to Norway. In addition to these foreigners, some 5000 to 6000 Norwegian political prisoners were "displaced" as were thousands of other Norwegian workers who had been relocated by the German "Labor Service" of the *Reichskommissariat*.

of displaced persons, although some of the supplies we uncovered were perishable and many things were urgently needed for the feeding and clothing of prisoners of war. Repatriation priorities had to be decided upon, and I find that as early as May 16 we realized that the most urgent problem concerned the Russian P.O.W.'s, some 75,000 of whom were bursting out of the 400 work camps located mainly on Norway's west coast.[14] But repatriating all of the 83,000 Russians proved to be a complex and difficult task.

The first trainloads of Russians left Norway on June 13, 1945, from Trondheim, Narvik, and Oslo. Miserably clad as they came out of the German work camps, they marched, as I saw them do in Oslo, in ragged clothes, some only in their underwear, singing their sad songs. Arrangements had been made with the Swedish government, on May 28, 1945, for the evacuation of most of the Russian P.O.W.'s on Swedish trains to Swedish ports on the Baltic. From the northern section of Norway, however, evacuation seemed easier by way of Murmansk, and accordingly a first convoy left Tromsö on June 22. My records indicate that by June 29 at least half of the Russians had been repatriated, about 6600 by sea, and about 37,000 by rail. On July 3, when we received 9000 of the 40,000 reconditioned British battle-dress uniforms we had been allotted to reclothe some of the ragged Russians, we estimated that all the ex-prisoners might be evacuated by July 12. A fortnight later only 1253 Russians remained, and these undernourished, sick, or invalided persons were evacuated on two trips by a hospital ship to Murmansk.

In an article published in 1968, twenty-three years after the event, a fellow officer in Norway, Lt. Col. E. Ross Jenney, M.D., whose responsibility it was to gather up the last remnants of the Russian ex-prisoners of war and take them to Murmansk, has graphically recalled this touching experience.[15] The fashionable prewar cruise ship *Stella Polaris* had been hurriedly converted into a hospital ship, entrusted to a Norwegian captain and crew, and staffed with British doctors, nurses, and attendants. Lieutenant Colonel Jenney, the only American aboard, was in charge of the evacuation. From Bergen, where *Stella Polaris* had been tied up during the war, the floating hospital proceeded beyond Tromsö to Kvesmenes, a tiny settlement at the mouth of the Lyngenfjord. Waiting to be embarked were the surviving Russian ex-prisoners of one of the most shameful of the many German atrocities. During the autumn of 1944 the Russian offensive in the north pushed the Germans out of Finland and across the

[14] During our first couple of weeks in Oslo, Russians who had been released from P.O.W. cages or Oslo work camps wandered about the city like lost souls saluting every member of the British or American forces whether private or brigadier.

[15] E. Ross Jenney, "Mission to Murmansk," *Medical Opinion Review*, vol. IV, no. 10 (October 1968), pp. 142–157.

bleak landscape of Norway's most northerly province (Finnmark). By December the Germans had retreated to the Lyngenfjord, and here in the middle of winter a defensive system, "the Lyngen Line," was built from the Finnish frontier to the fjord. Some eight thousand Russian prisoners were set to work building an aerial tramway to lift cement, lumber, steel, guns, and supplies to the crest of a high plateau where other prisoners were used to build elaborate defensive works. Until April of 1945 the work went on, with prisoners toiling as virtual slaves until they were unable "to lift a log or swing a pick." Those incapable of further work were shot, and hence the upper work compounds became, in effect, extermination centers.

Before he was ordered to gather up the survivors of this horrible and grisly operation, Lieutenant Colonel Jenney had been present when 143 complete autopsies were performed to confirm stories the surviving Russians had told about what had happened to their comrades. After examining the exhumed bodies, the pathologists listed as the causes of death extreme emaciation, multiple fractures, bullet wounds, internal hemorrhage caused by clubbing, scurvy, pneumonia, starvation, frostbite, and gangrene. There was even evidence of cannibalism. The survivors, many so ill they had to be hoisted on board by the winches of the *Stella Polaris* in wooden crates, had told the war crimes investigators some weeks earlier just where the mass graves could be located. Thus in one grave they said 104 bodies could be found, and when the Germans, who were ordered to exhume the bodies, removed the boulders and the transplanted birch trees that had camouflaged the grave site, the 104 still-frozen bodies that lay there corroborated the Russian testimony. Yet those who had escaped from German brutality were met with no sympathy when the *Stella Polaris* reached Murmansk, tying up at a dock crowded with lend-lease supplies ranging from Sherman tanks to Wisconsin cheese. To the Russian military authorities, apparently, every soldier who had surrendered was considered culpable, and to the distress of the Allied doctors and nurses, who had cared for the weak and the ill so tenderly, even the stretcher cases were forced to march from the dock. "Herded away, each staggering group was stripped of all clothing and pitiful possessions and marched naked far into the interior of a dismal and seemingly endless shed. I never saw them again"; thus, Lieutenant Colonel Jenney ends his account of this pathetic, albeit well-intended, rescue operation.[16]

While first priority had been accorded to the Russians,[17] very soon we succeeded in repatriating most of the other P.O.W.'s and non-German

[16] Ibid., p. 157.
[17] Not even the French, numbering about fifteen hundred, were allowed to leave until the Russian evacuation was well under way.

displaced persons. My records indicate that we had evacuated 3800 Danes by May 22, 35 Dutch sailors on May 30, 50 Britons on June 9, and over 1000 French, Dutch, and Belgian civilians on June 28. A number of Yugoslavs were moved from Tromsö to Trondheim on July 2, while 1400 French P.O.W.'s left Tromsö for Dieppe on July 15. In all cases there were lots of complications concerning negotiations, transport, and documentation. But with the Polish P.O.W.'s and D.P.'s we encountered another type of difficulty. A Russian delegation, headed by a General Ratov, had arrived on June 1, 1945, to supervise the repatriation of Russian P.O.W.'s. To the consternation of General Thorne and his staff, on July 19, General Ratov demanded freedom to visit all Polish P.O.W. camps since he believed certain "disputed persons" might have taken refuge there. Because of the political situation some of the P.O.W.'s understandably did not want to return to Poland, and were asking permission to join the Polish refugees in the United Kingdom. It was therefore decided that the officers of General Ratov's "Repatriation Commission" would not be allowed to visit the Polish camps unless accompanied by British and American officers. Although some Russian officers nevertheless did enter Polish camps clandestinely at night, the issue was gradually resolved after September 11 when Polish representatives arrived to screen their nationals, segregating those who did from those who did not wish to return to Poland. Meantime while the thousands of non-Norwegian displaced persons moved out of Norway, Norwegian refugees returned. The largest number came from Sweden, about 30,000; they began arriving in late May, as did others who had escaped to the United Kingdom.

The repatriation of German soldiers, who numbered over 365,000, was not our (civil-affairs) responsibility although we were inescapably affected by the presence in Norway of this large group of persons during most of the time that we were performing our varied tasks. There were several reasons why the repatriation of German soldiers had to be delayed. Many of them were needed to clear mine fields; [18] dump unusable ammunition into the ocean; [19] clean, oil, and inventory all weapons since these could be usable in the continuing war with Japan; and to load the ships [20]

[18] On June 11, 1945, I made a trip to Bergen with Major General Robert E. Urquhart on a Sunderland flying boat. When we touched down in the Bergenfjord and taxied to the landing pier the noise that greeted us must have equaled the decibels of a full-scale battle. The Germans had been put to work unearthing and detonating the thousands upon thousands of land mines that they had earlier placed to protect the slopes of the fjord from Allied landing parties. The cannonading sounds continued during the twenty-four hours we were in Bergen.

[19] A very dangerous operation which unfortunately led to many casualties.

[20] In the afternoon of August 17 I had had a conference with the Norwegian foreign minister, Trygve Lie, in his office on the fourth floor of Radhuset (Government House). When I was in the elevator going down to the ground floor a power-

that would transport weapons, ammunition, and other matériel out of Norway. A second reason for the delay was the priorities on billeting and transport facilities accorded to the Russian, Polish, and other P.O.W.'s and to displaced persons from Allied countries. Still a third factor interfered with a prompter German evacuation: the lack of P.O.W. cages [21] in Germany and the inability of the occupying forces to absorb the surrendered personnel from Norway. For these several reasons repatriation limped along, and the target established on June 12 for a weekly evacuation of 25,000 could not be met; two weeks later only 17,000 Germans had left Norway. Shipping became another bottleneck, and Swedish ships had to be co-opted to speed the process. Another complication arose from the delicate question of how many surrendered Germans should be repatriated to the Russian occupied zone, an evacuation operation that was hampered not only by political factors and lack of transport facilities, but by the probability that no port in the Russian zone would be free of mines in much less than two months' time.

Pending their repatriation the surrendered German military personnel kept rather correctly to their encampments. Meantime all German non-military nationals were registered and moved into concentration camps, except those who had collaborated with the Norwegian resistance. Once transport and reception facilities were assured, the evacuation of all Germans could finally proceed. The first trainload through Sweden left Oslo on August 1. A month later about half of the surrendered soldiers (approximately 180,000) had been evacuated. Many were still at work dumping ammunition [22] but gradually the unwelcome visitors departed; 205,000 had been evacuated by September 8; 232,000 by September 22; 247,000 by the end of September. Aside from a few retained for closing-out operations, virtually all Germans had been evacuated by mid-October.

Bringing in relief or rehabilitation supplies and allocating sequestrated enemy property constituted the major tasks of the Supply and Economics Branch [23] of our Civil Affairs Organization. It would be both difficult and

ful swish of air flung open the elevator doors at the third floor. The elevator stopped until the (out-swinging) doors again closed. When I reached the street level, people were all looking toward the waterfront. I later learned that one of thirty-two German soldiers engaged in loading an ammunition ship had dropped a bomb into a whole hatch of bombs. The entire mass of ammo exploded, completely wrecking the ship and killing many Germans. It was the blast-force vacuum that had opened the elevator doors.

[21] In my travels in Germany in November 1945, I saw how large and how crowded were the P.O.W. cages, wherein thousands of green-clad Germans formed milling hordes of constantly moving men seeking both exercise and warmth during those bleak, overcast, dreary days.

[22] My records indicate that about twenty thousand were still needed for this work in Tromsö as late as September 4.

[23] I was head of the Economics Branch of Allied Land Forces Norway and deputy

tedious to itemize the many supplies that we programmed, "called forward," and actually had delivered into Norwegian ports. Beginning with the coffee we brought by navy destroyers into all the major ports within a few days after liberation for morale-building purposes,[24] the list includes a wide variety of consumer and producer goods. The most important single item was coal: for locomotive fuel, for firing the few, but important, thermal electric plants, and for producing gas. The task of programming and bidding for our share of coal from the SHAEF coal-allocating committee became so specialized that two of our officers had the bringing in of the necessary hydro-carbons as their primary responsibility. Diesel oil for the brisling fishing fleet and for the herring fleet going to Icelandic waters was critically important; moreover the timing of the arrival of the fuel would determine whether a normal catch would be likely. Our supply ships began to arrive in Tromsö, Trondheim, Bergen, Stavanger, Kristiansand, and Oslo during the latter part of May, bringing petroleum and salt for the fishing industries, wheat, coal, medical supplies, and miscellaneous food products. While we were still in London, we had organized a "Four-Party Supply Committee" so that the royal Norwegian government, the SHAEF mission to Norway, and all British and United States civil agencies [25] could coordinate their programming, "calling forward," and shipment of supplies, thus obviating duplicating procurement and ensuring that ships would be fully loaded.

I was in charge of the secretariat of this committee and as I review the elaborate minutes, I am more than ever impressed with the thoroughness of our supply planning. At the second meeting of the Four-Party Committee (London, February 22, 1945), I pointed out that our task was to

head of the Supply Branch, an interlocking that proved not only wise but almost mandatory since the most efficient use of resources, whatever the origin, had to be our main goal.

[24] I proudly made an announcement shortly after my arrival that shipments of coffee would soon come to Oslo, Stavanger, Bergen, Trondheim, Tromsö, and Narvik, and this news was headlined in all Norwegian newspapers. When the coffee arrived, the general rejoicing and the overflowing gratitude we had anticipated did not materialize. Several days after the coffee had gone into distribution we received a cable regretfully informing us that all the coffee shipped to Norway had been accidentally contaminated by proximity to caster beans and warning us not to use it. Only profuse apology could overcome this unhappy miscarriage of our good intentions.

[25] Leafing through the minutes of the committee, I find that representatives of the British ministries of War Transport, Food, Production, and Supply and of the United States Foreign Economic Administration and War Shipping Administration attended our sessions, as did representatives from the United Nations Relief and Rehabilitation Agency. Officers from the British and American embassies were, of course, always in attendance, as were spokesmen for all the appropriate Norwegian ministries (e.g., Supply, Foreign Affairs, Social Welfare, Shipping, Commerce, Agriculture).

117

coordinate the "military" responsibility of the Civil Affairs Organization with the "political and humanitarian" responsibilities of the civil agencies and with the "constitutional" responsibility of the Norwegian government. I went on to say that "a practical programme should merge these responsibilities so that an adequate stream of supplies would be provided whereunder the military would provide the initial supplies needed to prevent the spread of disease and unrest whereas the civilian agencies would arrange for other items that would properly articulate supplies to needs and tide over the period before Norwegian direct purchases can be brought forward from abroad." Actually we effected a better coordination than I had foreseen, so that increments of supply from all three sources often were brought in on the same ship.

Not that the supply situation satisfied us or the Norwegians. By June 15 when we had expected 116,000 tons of petroleum products, so urgently needed, particularly for the fishing fleets, we had received only 17,961 tons, less than 16 percent. Captured enemy stocks helped ease the emergency somewhat, but we discovered all too often that at SHAEF our needs were generally considered far less important than those of France, Holland, Belgium, or Italy. A worldwide diffusion of Norwegian purchases, and utilization of shipping from a large number of countries,[26] helped overcome some of these bureaucratic blocks to our good intentions. But we nevertheless had a fuel crisis in Tromsö in mid-June which delayed the proper seasonal deployment of the Norwegian fishing fleet and the whaling ships from that port. To add to our troubles, when we had received only 84,000 tons of coal out of the 153,000 tons allocated for July, we had to release sizable tonnages intended for Norwegian industrial purposes to bunker the ships that were repatriating surrendered German soldiers.

Sometimes when we had worked hard to locate supplies, the Norwegians, to our distress, elected not to accept them. I recall how happy I felt when we received an allocation (July 18, 1945) of 804 tons of coffee and 1750 tons of evaporated milk. Before we called these items forward we needed a concurrence from the Ministry of Supply. The coffee was readily accepted but not the milk. When I pointed out that the Norwegian schoolchildren, who had lived on from 1200 to 1500 calories, needed the milk, the supply minister explained that his government could not pamper the people by leading them to believe that anything they needed could

[26] Wheat, rye, pulses, molasses, meat, butter, lard, and sugar had been purchased in Sweden; wheat, sugar, eggs, pork, butter in Denmark; wheat, meat, maize, leather, wool in the Argentine; coffee, lard, sunflower oil, cotton, flax, blankets, cotton yarn, cotton sheeting in other South American countries; wheat in Canada; sugar, syrup, chemicals, phosphates, tinplate, and salt in the United Kingdom; lead and bitumen in Mexico; salt in Tunisia and Spain. This widely diffused procurement took pressure off the Allied supply boards.

be imported. "We must produce our own milk," he said, "and save our foreign exchange for things we can't produce." Fortunately I had more agreeable news for the minister of supply a few hours later. Information came that the S.S. *Montevideo* from the United States was passing through the Orkneys carrying 2182 tons of sugar, 189 tons of blankets, 3 tons of medical supplies, 492 tons of coffee, and 4494 tons of wheat.

Because the Germans had taken possession of thousands of Norwegian horses, very understandably Norwegian farmers wanted to repossess them in order to carry on their springtime farming operations. In much the same way the Singer Sewing Machine Company sought to regain control over some two hundred sewing machines that had been leased to the Germans. Within ten days after my arrival in Oslo the demands for enemy-owned or enemy-controlled property kept growing more and more insistent. The minutes of my brigadier's staff meeting for May 24 record that I therefore proposed that an enemy-property disposal committee be created, one on which appropriate military units and suitable Norwegian agencies would be represented. At regular and frequent meetings of such a body, I said, "many cases could be disposed of during a short sitting, and all the parties involved would be able to make their needs known." My suggestion was acted upon with alacrity. A Control Memorandum dated May 24 established a "Joint-Force War Disposal Committee" with authority to dispose of "all war matériel in Norway." The chairman would represent and speak for the commander of Allied Land Forces Norway, while other members would represent, respectively, the British navy (the flag officer, Norway), the royal air force, the Norwegian military forces, the royal Norwegian government (mainly the Ministry of Supply), Q/G-4 (the combined British and American Army Supply Branch), and CA/G-5 (the British-American Civil Affairs Organization). Subcommittees of the Joint-Force Disposal Committee were then authorized for the several "zones" of the country, using procedures identical with those of the parent committee. All commodities not required by the army, navy, or air force were to be released to the Civil Affairs Organization on bulk receipt, and it then became our responsibility to release such supplies to the appropriate Norwegian governmental authorities and to obtain from them precise and accurate receipts.

Suggest something in a military staff organization and you are almost certain to find yourself loaded down with another task. Over-all responsibility for the disposal committee promptly became mine, but fortunately the system worked splendidly. The military forces, whether British, American, or Norwegian, who uncovered enemy property notified my office of their findings, itemizing or estimating the quantities as accurately as possible. On the basis of this telephoned or courier-delivered data, the daily

119

agenda would be prepared. Each morning the committee would meet and as the items to be allocated were read off the members of the committee would advance their claims to the property in question. Thus, if Q/G-4 thought a carload of plywood was needed for erecting barracks for troops, this priority would override the desire of the Norwegians. Little by little, however, "operational needs" came to be well understood, and disagreement seldom occurred. The great bulk of property was turned over to the Norwegian government, forming a most welcome addition to the inadequate relief and rehabilitation supplies that were imported.

The variety of commodities our committee released can be sampled from data for the first fortnight of our operations. During that period (May 26–June 9) we turned over to the Norwegian government the following items for the indicated uses: 500 tons of coal for the brisling fishing boats, 150 tons of coal for fish canneries, 900 tons of coal for the herring fishers and the seal hunters, 100 tons of petrol to maintain transport services in Oslo (this was the allocation I made my first weird night in Oslo), 500 tons of diesel oil for the brisling fishing fleet, 3000 tons of fuel oil for industrial purposes, 2000 tons of diesel oil for reserve stocks for fishing boats, 832 tons of potatoes for the Oslo area together with 1750 tons of herrings, 2100 tons of fish (herring and fish are always separate categories in the Scandinavian countries), 20 tons of sauerkraut, and 59 tons of cocoa beans. The industrial materials we allocated during that first fortnight included 60 tons of tin, 40 tons of raw rubber, 80 tons of tungsten, 6968 tons of pyrites, 535 tons of iron ore, 252 tons of graphite, 150 tons of salt, 20 tons of charcoal, 16 tons of concrete pipe, 82 tons of bricks, 15 tons of cement, 630 tons of smelting flux, and 65 tons of lumber. We also disposed of 1100 tons of hay, 35 tons of straw, 300 kilos of oats, and 725 tons of fish meal. In addition to the foregoing items, we turned over to the Norwegians 32,000 canning tins, all the food supplies left by the Germans at the Akers Hospital, and the hospital and maternity supplies at Hurdal. We released some road-repair machinery, a sizable quantity of printing equipment, and a large number of boilers and boiler tubes to the state railways. Although weapons and ammunition were usually reserved for "operational purposes," we did hand over to the Norwegians 55 seal-hunting rifles with 93,000 rounds of ammunition.

The 20,000 tons of enemy property we allocated during the first fortnight represented only the beginning of a huge operation. As the Germans were repatriated, our troops reported an increasing volume of supplies in dumps, depots, warehouses, stockpiles, tank farms, or freight cars and ships. I have no records to indicate all the property our committee allocated but it might well have been in excess of a million tons. Nor does avoirdupois weight give a proper index of the committee's activities. I find that by July 27, 1945, a month after the establishment of our disposal committee, over three hundred releases of enemy goods had been made to the Norwegian Ministry of Supply. The food items (wheat, flour, macaroni, beef, pork, fish, herrings, potatoes, sauerkraut, cabbage, sugar, and artificial honey) had allowed the Norwegian government to improve ration scales. Meantime the whole system of transport had been improved by the release not only of liquid and solid fuels but of trucks, trailers, passenger vehicles, automobile parts, tires, motorcycles, bicycles, wagons, carts, highway machinery, railway rolling stock, ships, deck supplies, winches, cranes, and other port and dock equipment. Agriculture also benefited from released supplies and luckily our disposal activities began at the crop-planting season. Pending a systematic plan for the disposal of Wehrmacht-held horses and mules, a temporary arrangement allowed Norwegian farmers to borrow draft animals for spring farm work. As much fodder, oats, rye, barley, and other animal food as possible were released. Essential farm machinery, fencing wire, farm tools, carts, wagons, and other equipment also constituted a welcome assistance to Norwegian farmers who had suffered five years of austerity.

A wide range of raw and semifinished materials were released to Norwegian industries: wolfram, molybdenum, rubber, gypsum, calcium carbide, zinc, graphite, brass scrap, steel, copper wire, paint, glass, charcoal, tinplate, steel wire, copper slag, iron ore, paper, wool yarn, jute bagging, knott (wood blocks for automobile fuel), talcum, and cement. Large quantities of machinery and equipment were also released ranging from stationary engines, transformers, and storage batteries to delicate laboratory equipment. Tractors, farm machinery, winches, cranes, machine tools, metal- and wood-working machines also were passed over to the Norwegians. Nor should one overlook the barracks buildings, warehouses, furniture and office equipment, and the simple household supplies such as brooms, dishes, stoves, refrigerators, and kitchen ware.

Meantime some major installations came under our jurisdiction. The Germans had laid marine cables across the Skagerrak and a legal question arose about whether these should be released to the Norwegian or to the Danish government. An agreement was reached (August 9, 1945) whereunder the cables were divided in ownership on a linear basis by allocating portions to both claimant countries. Meantime we had the problem of disposing of thousands of horses in the Tromsö area and elsewhere,[27] as well as a cargo of industrial materials that arrived in the port of Trondheim (May 23, 1945) from Japan on a German U-boat. Our 19,000,000 bottles of sequestrated alcoholic beverages, as I have already

[27] See below, chapter 20.

explained, were reserved for "operational purposes." All in all it proved to be an exciting and very interesting task.

While we were busy repatriating displaced persons, bringing in supplies, and disposing of enemy property, the Norwegians progressively reassumed responsibility for ordinary routine governmental duties. It had been expected that at least six months would be required to make an orderly transition from the Terboven (German) regime to a full-functioning, restored, royal Norwegian government. Very quickly after his arrival on May 17, in the company of the crown prince,[28] General Thorne realized that so long a period of occupation by his military forces would be quite unnecessary. Some differences between the government in exile and the home-staying politicians did develop, but after hard bargaining they were resolved.[29] Once the crown prince had returned, to the great joy of the Norwegian people, it became clear that the sooner the beloved king could stand again on Norwegian soil the better it would be. But he could not be brought back as the servitor of the Allied Military Command. He must either quite promptly return as king or wait until our occupation work was completed. Since the Norwegians very much wanted the king to come home on June 7,[30] a decision was hurriedly reached to ask SHAEF for a declaration ending the military period in Norway. Our very competent legal officer, Lieutenant Colonel Enrietto, prepared the appropriate documents making it possible for General Thorne to turn over the civil administration to the Norwegian government, and then made a swift trip to Frankfurt to obtain the consent of SHAEF to our drastic change of plans. General Thorne's

[28] The return of Crown Prince Olav was the occasion for a tremendous celebration. I wrote to my wife on that historic May 17, "This morning I stood in a reviewing stand from 9 until 12 while there passed before us thousands upon thousands of deliriously happy Norwegians. For this is their 4th of July, celebrating their independence after 400 years of Danish overlordship. For five years they have not been allowed to celebrate the 17th of May and you can therefore appreciate what an event this was, particularly when it also marked the return of the crown prince. From early morning Karl Johann's *gata* was lined with people although the parade did not begin until nine. First came the 'Home Front' in ski clothes, then the police, fire brigades, nurses, and all paramilitary organizations. Then came all the students in the university and in schools shouting, chanting, 'We are free, we are free.' If I were to live a thousand years, I doubt whether I should ever see such happiness as when the crown prince arrived."

[29] Not without some ill feeling. The Oslo group felt that they had borne the brunt of the German occupation while the government in exile was living comfortably in London; the government in exile had expected to be welcomed back with enthusiasm and gratitude for its faithful service in laying the groundwork for liberation. In the end, by a one-sided compromise, the government in exile had to give up twelve cabinet posts, retaining only three, and the Oslo group named one of their members the prime minister.

[30] There were two very important reasons for the choice of this date. On June 7, 1905, the union with Sweden was dissolved leaving Norway a sovereign state, and on June 7, 1940, King Haakon left Norway on a fishing boat for his five-year exile.

decision proved to be a very wise one. The Norwegian people rejoiced that their king could return so promptly, while the restoration of the legitimate Norwegian government relieved us of a host of responsibilities, making it possible for us to concentrate on the few essential tasks that the Norwegians could not handle.

Never again will I witness such joy or such an outpouring of affection, fidelity, devotion, admiration, and love as I beheld on the morning of June 7, 1945, when the tall and dignified King Haakon VII came ashore at Government House. The thousands of men, women, and children uttered only two words, *Leve Kongen* (long live the king), but the repetition of these two words thousands of times by thousands of voices swelled into a chorus that reverberated from the waterfront to the hills that rise up from the Oslo fjord. It had taken exactly one calendar year from the day the German Atlantic seawall was breached for Allied military victories to make it possible for the indomitable Norwegian sovereign to be returned to his adoring subjects. *Leve Kongen, Leve Kongen*, they repeated over and over and over again, even long after their constitutional monarch had entered the doors of his royal palace. This is where I saw him next when he decorated me with the Haakon VII Cross of Freedom, on October 13, 1945,[31] and handed me a personally signed citation that reads "for outstanding service to Norway during its liberation."

Once the king had returned, the problem of what should be done with the quislings [32] and with Vidkun Quisling himself had to be settled. We helped resolve part of this problem by arranging secretly for a new Norwegian currency. Once the new money had been printed and distributed to the banks, General Thorne's proclamation requiring everyone to convert his old money into the new within a brief, specified time period very neatly dispossessed the quisling profiteers of their wartime profits. Persons who would proffer large amounts of old currency for conversion would actually indict themselves, and practically none of the justificatory

[31] Altogether eighteen officers received the Haakon VII Cross of Freedom of whom only two were civil-affairs officers. The list of officers decorated can be found in *Aftenposten* for October 15, 1945, p. 1. Fifteen received a lower decoration, the Cross of Peace.

[32] Estimates of 47,000 members of Quisling's neo-Fascist party suggest that less than 3 percent of adult Norwegians had been associated in any overt way with Quisling's movement. There is a delightful story of the British dowager who asked King Haakon at a dinner party whether there were any quislings in his country. "Very few," he replied, without any sign of pique or amusement. Demaree Bess put the matter plainly when he wrote, "The Norwegians are acutely conscious of the fact that Vidkun Quisling has made his surname a permanent synonym for treachery in the English language." See "Norway Takes a Holiday," *Saturday Evening Post*, October 6, 1945, p. 90.

documents our legal experts had prepared for such persons were ever used. The profiteers, collaborators, and quislings did not dare to convert their ill-gotten gains into the new currency. Aside from this swift and successful maneuver, we left it to the Norwegians to deal with their disloyal compatriots.

Quisling was charged not merely with treason but with about a dozen other crimes.[33] He had lived like a king when he held power. His house "Gimle," which General Thorne occupied after the liberation, was a veritable palace. In it Quisling had his fabulous art collection, part of which he had bought in Russia just after the Revolution and to which he had added paintings from Norwegian public and private collections. The pictures hung quite naturally in many spacious rooms, without any crowding or museum effect. When one stood in the middle of a room, there were the Van Dycks, Rubenses, Goyas — a whole galaxy of famous creations before you as you gazed at the four walls. Much too busy to attend many sessions of his dramatic trial, I nevertheless did find time to visit the courtroom on a few occasions. Quisling conducted his own defense with disarming, ingenuous forthrightness. I remember particularly the morning when the prosecuting attorney, Annaeus Schjödt, handed Quisling a copy of a letter addressed to Adolf Hitler [34] and asked him whether he had written it. The straw-haired, unflustered, and supremely confident Quisling replied with zestful eagerness. Indeed he had written that letter and, like Peer Gynt, he defended his artless action with unrestrained pride. "History will show me to have been the savior of Norway and the northern countries," said Quisling, in a strong, clear, and confident voice. In the emerging world situation, he argued, there is no longer any place for small, independent countries. For that reason, he said, he had explained to Adolf Hitler that because Norway was a Teutonic nation it must become part of "a great Germanic community" by means of a "voluntary affiliation in a Greater German Reich." Further explaining his letter to Hitler, Quisling said, in his most dulcet tones, that it had been his hope that the integration of Norway into a great Teutonic political community could be accomplished without bloodshed, and it was to this end that he had sought to "paralyze the opposition forces" and had evolved for Hitler an appropriate

[33] E.g. responsibility for the death of more than a hundred Norwegians, stealing public property, purchasing a shipping line with German-supplied money in order to conceal disguised German soldiers at key points on the Oslo fjord and thereby facilitate the German invasion.

[34] The full text of this letter, dated July 10, 1940, has been reproduced in a book of documents that appertain to Quisling's culpability, published under the title *Documenter I Offentlig Straffesak Mot Vidkun Qvisling* (Oslo, 1945), pp. 32–35. A large number of incriminating documents had been found in the archives of Alfred Rosenberg, the Nazi "race philosopher."

plan of action.[35] It was with boastful vanity that Quisling admitted his treasonable acts, while indignantly denying his guilt.[36]

When he was found guilty not only of treason but of a number of other crimes and had been sentenced to death, Quisling asked for a review of his trial record and for a commutation of his sentence. I recall this episode rather vividly because of a strange occurrence. Since I was then about to leave Norway for reassignment in Germany, I had been asked by the crown prince to visit him at his office in the palace. That morning when I went for my car (a wood-burning, old-model Plymouth) I found scrawled on it in chalk these words: "Quisling's dom ar domar's dom, leve Quisling" (Quisling's doom will be his judge's doom, long live Quisling!). I told the crown prince about this and he said it represented the last frenetic efforts of the hard-core quislings. "We know who they are," he said, "and we are not at all worried. But we shall review the trial record with great care to ensure that justice has been done." As far as I could see, the whole tragic event had been handled with impeccable correctness [37] and with great restraint, without any tawdry publicity, or any vindictive rejoicing at the verdict. Quisling's appeal was found to have no merit, and I remember as if it were yesterday the tiny news item that appeared, without headline, in the leading Oslo newspaper; it said very simply and succinctly: "Late last night Vidkun Quisling was taken from his cell, brought to Akershus Fortress, and disposed of."[38] Nothing more was published.

Throughout the whole liberation period the conduct of the Norwegians toward the Germans and toward the quislings showed how successfully they could control their emotions. I remember my first Sunday in Oslo

[35] There is evidence in the Rosenberg documents that Quisling and Rosenberg, with the assistance of the German minister to Norway, may have persuaded Hitler against his better judgment to order the invasion of Norway.

[36] On the first day of his trial, Quisling rose after the reading of the charges and said in a firm voice, "I plead not guilty to all the accusations." The trial was conducted with great dignity in a small courtroom so that only about two hundred tickets were available. It is the argument of Ralph Hewins that Quisling was unfairly judged, that he was a man of exceptional ability and true patriotism, that "Quisling was not really a quisling," and that "his character and career have become completely distorted in history and in the popular imagination at home and abroad." For this eulogy of Quisling and bitter criticism of his judges, see Hewins's *Quisling, Prophet without Honour* (London: W. H. Allen, 1965). I have no way of knowing whether there is any merit in Hewins's argument but his presentation is extremely partial and passionately defensive.

[37] Hewins is of a different opinion. He avers that Quisling had been promised "fair treatment" but was "lured into a trap and seized under false pretenses" and "kept at 700 and 800 calories a day, instead of a proper 3,000" for four months before his trial. *Quisling, Prophet without Honour*, pp. 352, 361. He fails to mention that despite the "liberation" many Norwegians were not yet getting a "proper 3,000" calories.

[38] For Hewins's views about the trial and his account of Quisling's execution by a firing squad at Akershus fortress, see ibid., pp. 366–370, 371–372.

very clearly because on that day the Germans moved out of the city. Long caravans of wagons lumbered through the streets drawn by hundreds of small fawn-colored horses that the Germans had taken from Norwegian farmers. There were no catcalls, only silence as the Norwegians turned their backs and utterly ignored the outgoing Germans who had bullied them for five years. With the same dispassionate calmness, the Norwegians had demonstrated their disciplined character by refusing to sit with Germans on streetcars and by the extraordinary skill with which they built up a resistance movement which the Gestapo could never terrorize. By chance I learned something about the iron discipline that pervaded the *hjemme fronten* by two incidents. One night about a score of British, American, and Norwegian officers were entertained in a large, richly furnished Oslo home. Our Norwegian host explained that although he wanted to show his personal gratitude for what we were doing for Norway he could not because of the rationing rules offer us anything to eat but mutton and cabbage, and in a moving address of welcome he touched us with his apparent patriotism. The next night three of the Americans who had been present were invited to another Norwegian home. When I told our host that we were impressed by yesternight's event he said acidly, "We don't have anything to do with that fellow." I implored him to tell us why since we were very anxious never to associate with anyone whose patriotism might be questioned. After much insistence he told us that during the occupation our eloquent host had come to him in the dead of night to ask advice on whether he should accept an attractive offer the Germans had made for his lovely house. "Did he sell his house to the Germans?" I asked. "Oh no," he replied, "he didn't sell it. But he considered selling it and that's why we don't have anything to do with him." So strict were the rules of the Norwegian resistance!

As we completed the repatriation of P.O.W.'s, displaced persons, and surrendered Germans, as we gradually had less enemy property to allocate, and as our supply operations neared completion, we began to release personnel for reassignment in Germany where experienced civil-affairs officers were urgently needed. In order to do this, we had to dissolve the joint British-American civil-affairs unit, and I had forgotten until I reread the minutes of my brigadier's staff conference that I had been sent to the War Office in London to make these arrangements. As I look back on my five months in Norway I often wonder whether I was too dutiful and preoccupied with my official work. Most of our civil-affairs officers found reasons to travel widely in Norway, indeed one or two of them became rather accomplished tourists.[39] But if many of my associates took their

[39] If my public-utility officer told me that the Norwegian authorities had asked him to check the electric substations in all the Norwegian counties (*fylker*), or if

duties lightly, I must say the Norwegians did not set very exacting examples. They went on a nationwide vacation spree so that the offices with which we dealt were often so thinly populated that sometimes we found ourselves embarrassed by our inability to answer urgent cables.[40] Even if all government offices had been fully staffed, we would have had enough troubles because all Norwegian offices closed by two o'clock in the afternoon.[41] But after their five years of close surveillance by an invading army we could scarcely censure the Norwegians for wanting to enjoy their new-found freedom. My only complaint was that they set a bad example for our personnel when we had so much to do. Even so, we had largely worked ourselves out of a job by the beginning of autumn.

The prospect of an assignment in Germany distressed me since, as I have already explained, we had not been permitted to plan properly for civil-affairs operations there. Yet only one or two officers who had political connections were able to obtain separation at the end of the Norway operation. The rest of us received orders to report to Frankfurt for reassignment. On the eve of my departure, General Thorne pinned the medal of an Honorary Officer of the Most Excellent Order of the British Empire on my uniform; of the three Americans awarded O.B.E.'s, I was the only civil-affairs officer so honored. I prized my citation because it so accurately mirrors the directness and graciousness of the British general whom I so deeply admired. I liked particularly one sentence in the citation General Thorne prepared for the king's signature: "Colonel Johnson is an officer of the highest integrity with a fine brain and a great capacity for work."

But whereas I felt gratified that the Norwegians and the British governments had recognized the work I had performed in planning and implementing Operation Apostle, I was not happy when the military authorities at USFET (United States Forces European Theater) disregarded the strong recommendations of my American commanding officer, Colonel Paul Boyd, that I be awarded the Legion of Merit and gave me instead a Bronze Star, a decoration some of us considered well described as an

my agricultural officer informed me that the minister of agriculture wanted him to make crop inspections, I had to acquiesce even though I may have suspected that the initiative had not really come from the Norwegians.

[40] Demaree Bess wrote a vivid account of this vacation spree. See "Norway Takes a Holiday" in the *Saturday Evening Post*, October 6, 1945, pp. 12–13, 86, 88, 90. Rereading my letters to my wife, I find that by the first of September the Norwegians were "settling down and going to work."

[41] The idea underlying this, to be sure, is very commendable, since by starting work early and holding a luncheon respite to a half hour, all office workers could have eight hours for sleep, eight hours for work, and, in the summer, almost eight hours for daylight recreation.

"officer's good-conduct medal, second class." [42] Although to the ruling brass in Frankfurt operations in Norway may have seemed only marginal, when I reached Germany, and contrasted the way they operated, I could not resist the conclusion that their logic was rather upside down.

[42] My only consolation was the citation which had been prepared by Colonel Boyd: "Lieutenant Colonel Johnson's diplomatic contact and work with the Royal Norwegian Government made possible, to a great extent, the coordination and cooperation between civil affairs officers and officials of that government. His outstanding qualifications as an economist enabled him to render invaluable assistance in the formulation of policies and principles to be used after liberation. His intelligence, aggressiveness and his outstanding professional ability were of invaluable aid to the Royal Norwegian Government and served to reflect credit upon himself and the United States Army."

9

BITTER SOULS
IN A CONQUERED LAND
★★★★★★★★★★★★★★★★★★★★★★★★

BEFORE I was reassigned to Germany in mid-October 1945, I had already made two trips to American headquarters in Frankfurt (USFET). I therefore had some general idea of the physical and psychological environment in which the staggering tasks of occupation would have to be conducted. On the first trip, in early July 1945, Brigadier Hansen and I flew to Frankfurt to consult Air Marshal Arthur W. Tedder, General Eisenhower's deputy, concerning the deactivation of our Civil Affairs Organization in Norway. Quiet, gracious, and decisive, Tedder impressed me as an extraordinarily gifted general officer and our mission was very swiftly and satisfactorily accomplished. What I remember most about that trip, however, was the shocking devastation the war had caused. Bremen, where we stopped briefly, revealed wretched shambles of partly sunken vessels, and crazy, twisted, blackened, rusting frames of burned-out buildings. Hanover, as we flew over at about six hundred feet, seemed to consist mostly of pyramids or ridges of red rubble. I described my impressions of Germany in a letter to J. T. Madden, dean of the New York University School of Commerce:

I have just returned from a trip to Frankfurt. I have flown over about seven or eight hundred miles of Germany. When I tell you that the cities are destroyed, that statement should be construed literally. Hanover from the air was a terrifying sight with almost every visible building open; it resembled a field of huge empty boxes set in great landslides of red rubble, making the area look like eroded wasteland. In Frankfurt I walked for hours through the ruined city. When you were a boy in New England you no doubt had a real heavy snowfall — a three or four foot snowfall, I mean. Do you remember what Worcester looked like a couple of days later? The main streets were probably cleared to the building lines; a few (but very few) side streets

129

were open to the sidewalks where the snow had been piled ten or twelve feet deep. But most of the streets were completely blocked except for meandering paths, perhaps a yard wide, that had been cut through the lesser drifts. This is what a German city looks like now, except that instead of snow, the litter is brick, stone, twisted iron, household effects, plaster, and every conceivable form of wreckage. In this bleak, dismal atmosphere life must go on.

It was when I was in Frankfurt a month later, August 6, 1945, that the news came over the radio that an atomic bomb had been dropped on Hiroshima, and although my associates and I recognized the dreadful military importance of this new form of warfare that had made such wholesale human destruction feasible, I'm afraid none of us could have sensed even a shadow of the vast potential of the atomic bomb for intensifying human fear, dissension, and political confusion. Like other soldiers we mainly hoped the bomb might simply be a means for shortening the war. "If the destruction here is a monument to ordinary bombs," I wrote that evening to my wife, "what incredible destruction will occur from the atomic bomb? Surely this madness has to end. What nation will again dare to wage an offensive war?"

This second trip to Frankfurt brought me into contact with the burgeoning bureaucracy of military government in Germany. The object of my visit was to work out ways and means for facilitating Norwegian exports and imports so that Norway, as a liberated nation, could more quickly achieve that euphoric goal of "viability," a word that became so popular and so fashionable that its plausible sound obscured the imprecision with which it was commonly used. But I soon discovered that our zeal for Norway's prompt economic development was, in Frankfurt, a matter of very marginal importance. I find in the minutes of my brigadier's staff meeting this cynical report: "Lt. Col. Johnson recently attended a conference at Frankfurt on Imports into and Exports from Germany. The import and export procedure is very complicated; it is governed by J.C.S. 1067 which restricts transactions between Germany and other countries. Any requests for exports from Germany must carry proof that they are needed for military purposes."

The myopic view of Frankfurt officialdom made all our planning for prompt resumption of some reciprocal trade with Germany rather pointless. For weeks the Norwegians, at our suggestion, had been busy preparing lists of commodities available for immediate export, including such items as 150,000 barrels of herrings, 2300 tons of salt fish, 3000 tons of dried fish, 2000 tons of klipfish, 25,000 barrels of salted cod roe, 2000 tons of frozen fish fillets, 4000 tons of cod liver oil. Nor was it only food items that I had been authorized to offer to the Frankfurt occupation authorities. The Norwegians were prepared to export 85,000 metric tons of nitrogen, sizable amounts of ferrosilicon, carbide, ferrochrome, chromesilicon, electrolytic nickel, blister copper, pyrites and molybdenum, as well as large quantities of raw minerals such as feldspar, quartz, and talc.[1] Understandably the Norwegians wanted in exchange commodities that would be serviceable for the rehabilitation and reconstruction of their economy. But my efforts were in vain, and when SHAEF was dissolved (on July 14, 1945), the British forces in Norway returned to the jurisdiction of the British chiefs of staff (through Field Marshal Montgomery) and the few remaining American forces in Norway were placed under the commanding general of United States Forces European Theater. When we became part of USFET we could no longer bargain on behalf of the Norwegians, who were now compelled to negotiate for any possible German trade through their Washington embassy.

When I arrived in Frankfurt on reassignment to USFET, on October 20, 1945, I soon discovered that life there took on a grim coloration from the drab rubble, the roofless houses, and the unconcealed bitterness of the German people. In a letter I wrote to my wife, as I sat by the window of my bleak hotel room, I tried to describe the street scene:

Two skinny horses pulling a wagon are passing and at least ten people are sitting on bags and boxes of personal effects. Four of the men wear Wehrmacht uniforms; apparently they are discharged soldiers who are hauling a family's possessions to an undamaged country village. Jeeps and command cars go by, as well as bicycles ridden by Germans. Here comes a German pulling a child's wagon containing a chest and a roll of linoleum (salvaged, no doubt). A German in a Luftwaffe uniform just passed in a decrepit motorcycle heavily loaded with boxes and bags. Here comes another wagon drawn, as usual, by lean horses; and here are two people pulling a child's wagon. An old man has a load of carpets on a pram; he stops and talks with the couple who have the little wagon. Another couple have a ramshackle buggy, loaded with bedding. The next wagon is drawn by horses so thin their ribs can easily be counted; there are eleven women and children riding on this one. I see that the couple with the child's wagon and the old man with the pram are bringing things out from a wrecked house opposite. They shake the plaster off the grimy things they bring out.

No one in Frankfurt exhibited any zest or enthusiasm for his work except a few Americans who, apparently unhappy or dissatisfied with their prewar occupations, hoped to find a new career in military government. In "Supply Control," to which I was quite promptly assigned, the endemic unhappiness was exceptionally intense since, as I have already explained, J.C.S. 1067 had forbidden Supreme Headquarters from making any advance preparation for caring for over three quarters of a million

[1] The Four-Party Supply Committee had authorized me to proffer any of these exportable commodities to the German occupation authorities and had expected me to bring back some corresponding list of possible German exports as payment goods.

displaced persons. The ceaseless task of searching for "excess theater supplies" with which to feed and clothe these hapless people proved extremely difficult and very frustrating. From the field came insistent demands for more food, clothing, fuel, equipment, and medicine. To add to our difficulties an unwelcome stream of semiofficial visitors from the United States would hurry home to inform their congressmen how heartlessly the D.P.'s were treated, and the elected "servants of the people," in most dutiful political patterns, would promptly demand that we make immediate provision of kosher-killed meat for the Jewish D.P.'s and similar adaptations of our dietary care for other minorities. Congressional ignorance of the difficulties we had in providing D.P.'s with *any* food, unfortunately, could not be overcome, despite our repeated efforts to explain the meshes in which we were innocently caught by reason of Washington's fatuous earlier decision.

When I learned that the impending home leave of the head of Supply Control and the temporary absence of his deputy would soon elevate me for a time to that unwanted position, it was agreed that I should make a field survey of our D.P. camps so that I would have some personal understanding of the local care and feeding problems. With winter setting in, the clothing problem had high priority, and I carefully planned a circuit that would allow me to visit Polish, Jewish, Estonian, Hungarian, and mixed D.P. camps, and one that would take me through the French as well as the American zone of occupation. On a bleak, bitter cold November morning I set out, in a command car with flapping curtains, since for so lowly a person as a G-5 lieutenant colonel the USFET command would not allot a sedan. Wherever I went I encountered varieties of discouragement, frustration, bitterness, and apathy. My first stop at Heidelberg confronted me with a quite unexpected complaint. The very morning I arrived, an order had come forbidding the repatriation of any more D.P.'s unless each boxcar, the customary mode of transport, was provided with a cast-iron stove and a supply of coal. The new problem was where to obtain the required stoves, and the length of time that would be involved in their manufacture. This example of ill-coordinated staff work, however humanitarian its purpose, revealed how operations were hampered almost everywhere in Germany. The argument of the Heidelberg officers was that Polish refugees were entirely willing to make their return trip in unheated boxcars, provided enough straw and blankets were made available. But the new order meant that thousands of D.P.'s must now wait an unpredictable length of time while stoves were cast in some undetermined foundry from pig iron that would have to be procured from some already overcommitted source. And while these immobilized D.P.'s waited for stoves to be cast, they would perforce have to be fed, with daily rations which Supply Control by some magic would be expected to find.

In an area we had just taken over from the French, the previous occupation authorities had exacerbated the bitterness of the German civilian population. I was shown storerooms of winter garments, neatly arranged on gas-pipe racks, that had been accumulated by the simple expedient of searching one house after another and taking all clothing considered beyond minimum family needs. Here also I discovered that all CARE packages were being opened and the little boxes of razor blades and cigarettes systematically removed before the packages were released to the supply officers of the D.P. camps. Just what became of the sequestrated razor blades and cigarettes I was not able to find out, but since both items had become forms of currency, great care was taken to keep them out of D.P. hands. As my investigations in the American zone soon revealed, the problem of caring for D.P.'s was not merely one of providing each displaced person with clothing, but also of preventing the distributed clothing from being sold to the millions of ill-clad German civilians. Even the calculation of requirements proved hard to make. The D.P. population was never static; some persons were daily being repatriated while others were moving in from France, Belgium, Luxembourg, Italy, or elsewhere. The clothing came from many sources, in more or less unforeseen or poorly programmed amounts: from American volunteer welfare agencies, military government stocks, United Nations Relief and Rehabilitation Agency (UNRRA) supplies, inter-camp production, levies on German supplies, and current German production. The most irksome problem, to be sure, stemmed from the constant leakages. General Walter Muller of the American 7th Army told me that in one camp every D.P. had received three overcoats but almost all had been bartered "over the wall" before winter set in. This may have been an exaggeration by an exasperated general but the traffic was heavy. With over 400,000 D.P.'s in 164 camps in the American Zone, controls could not easily be enforced.

My visits to scores of D.P. camps filled me with growing apprehension about the capacity of randomly chosen Americans to cope with new and completely unfamiliar overseas problems. The inherent limitations of parochially conditioned Americans, few of whom had ever been exposed to any other culture, were greatly complicated by a sudden decision which had been reached to allow the hastily staffed UNRRA to take over administrative direction of the D.P. camps. I would not have believed any description of the confusion that resulted had I not personally encountered it. A bleak former German army barracks, housing, say, four hundred Polish displaced persons, might have a Frenchman as its senior camp officer, a Norwegian supply officer, and an Italian social director, or any other equally bizarre combination. In some instances I found that the three officials could communicate with one another only with great difficulty, and that the local American military authorities, through whom supplies had to be obtained, were even less capable of understanding the camp officials. Fortunately a number of ex-army officers, British and American, had accepted UNRRA positions; without them the situation would have been almost hopelessly confused. An effort was therefore made to staff all the major D.P. camps with UNRRA-engaged American supply officers. But after I had lectured to about 120 of these recently recruited Americans at Karlsruhe I found myself still deeply disturbed. They were by all odds the most slow-witted, dull, marginal people I had encountered in three years of lecturing to American, British, French, and Norwegian personnel in the European theater of operations.[2] The same pleasantries that brought gales of laughter from British officers or "other ranks," knowing smiles from the French, or guffaws from Norwegians were met with complete silence on the part of the stolid UNRRA group. From this sample I concluded ruefully that UNRRA, last to seek recruits, had been compelled to scrape the very bottom of the manpower barrel.

The influence of ethnic and cultural factors was vividly evident in the D.P. camps. The Polish D.P.'s rather consistently refused to eat in common messes, and silently carried their food in improvised metal containers to dark, dismal rooms where families kept closely secluded. They were suspicious of all the sincere efforts of the social directors to organize community activities. In contrast, an Estonian camp that I visited was organized so effectively and its school functioned with such precision that I was not at all surprised to discover, years later, that a brilliant Harvard A.B. who became a graduate student at the School of Advanced International Studies of the Johns Hopkins University, where he was my advisee, had prepared for college in this very D.P. camp school. Discipline, housekeeping, and daily routine were all exemplary. Jewish D.P. installations had some, but not all, these admirable qualities; an understandable special solicitude for people who had escaped the gas chambers had probably made them somewhat more demanding and less tractable than other displaced persons. Perhaps too this may have been partly because the Jewish camps, like the Hungarian camps, contained relatively more intellectuals and former propertied persons. My Norway associate Lt. Col. Ross Jenney, for example, found a lovely bride in one of the Hungarian camps, a

[2] While in Edinburgh I was asked to lecture to disembarking American officers or enlisted men, at Glasgow, sometimes in groups exceeding a thousand. I lectured several times to the British army study groups at St. Andrews University as well as to British, French, and Norwegian officers in London, and I was invited to give a public lecture at the University of Oslo on August 22, 1945, an event very graciously featured in the Oslo newspaper the next day.

titled lady whose gracious hospitality my wife and I have enjoyed both in Washington, D.C., and in Honolulu, where Dr. Jenney is now on the faculty of the University of Hawaii and of the East-West Center.

I recorded some vivid impressions of the major groups of D.P.'s in a letter to my wife from Stuttgart, dated November 1945:

This morning I visited in and around Ludvigsburg where there is a cluster of D.P. camps with an aggregate population of about 11,000. The UNRRA director for this group of camps, an Australian ex-army officer, had a brisk, bright lady M.D. from New England as his medical officer, and an intelligent ex-social worker from Montana as his welfare officer. Yet there were marked differences between the several camps. In a Polish camp the majority were idle, although it must be said they had been awaiting repatriation. Here, I watched a clothing distribution and was fascinated to see how cautiously the Polish peasants made their choices. This probably was a day they had long anticipated; if they made a mistake now it could probably never be rectified. They would measure a shirt in a dozen ways: holding it over their backs, around their necks, around their wrists. They tried on jacket after jacket, small ones and big ones, until finally they reached a decision. I visited rooms in this camp, specifying what I wanted to see — rooms for men, for women, for families, rooms with small children or growing children. For the most part the Polish D.P.'s seemed morose and enigmatic; except for the old ladies in the kitchen, whom I flattered by tasting their food, no one seemed to show a flicker of interest in my visit. They didn't seem to be annoyed, just indifferent.

In the afternoon I visited a Jewish camp for about 1100 people in Stuttgart. This group was housed in excellent apartment houses requisitioned from the Germans and completely furnished. Radios blared, people were talking and quarreling. There had been an altercation and one chap, about fifty years old, was rather bloody. I saw him later at the infirmary where he was being cleaned and bandaged. He was still mad as an owl. I suspect idleness might have been one cause of trouble in this community since out of 685 males, over the age of fourteen, only 73 were employed. Next I visited a Latvian camp that had just been established in a Stuttgart suburb. The elected leader, a Lettish schoolteacher, had everything under control. The Letts, men, women, and children, were a clean, healthy, fine-looking lot. They had been washed into Germany by the Russian advance and now found themselves stateless. Since they realized they could not go back to Latvia, they set about making their temporary homes as agreeable as possible.

My trip through Baden, Würtemberg, and Bavaria not only gave me an opportunity to appraise the problems involved in feeding and caring for the thousands of D.P.'s but provided me an opportunity to see more of the devastation the war had brought, and to sense more deeply the impact of defeat on the German population. The most cruelly damaged single city I visited was Heilbronn. Using flexible-walled, 4000-pound "blockbuster" bombs, the RAF in eleven minutes (December 7, 1944) completely destroyed the central core of the city and unroofed the buildings in a large perimeter. A lieutenant in charge of an excellent nine-man civil-affairs team told me that of the 9500 houses in Heilbronn over 50 percent were utterly destroyed. Of the remaining houses, more than half had been damaged beyond repair, leaving little more than 20 percent of the houses reparable to shelter survivors. The lieutenant (who turned out to be the son of a colleague of mine when I taught at the University of Oklahoma in the 1920's) took me to the center of this dead city where perhaps as many as 30,000 Germans lay buried under the debris. Not a person was to be seen, not a sound did I hear; and all I could see were the dunes of rubble. The Germans one did meet in such shattered towns were understandably taciturn, bitter, and resentful.[3] So were the members of the pathetic processions of women, old men, and children who went into the countryside to gather fuel or to buy food. Since all good timber-cutting areas near cities were reserved for the American forces or for D.P.'s, German civilians had to range far afield; and whenever I approached a city I would overtake caravans of children's wagons loaded with faggots, pitiful processions of women bending under their burdens and of old people limping along carrying their rucksacks.

Deep winter had already set in, and hence Americans were winterizing their jeeps, accumulating their coal and wood supplies, giving but little thought to the problems of their former enemies. Hotels were being repaired for American occupancy. Even so the Graf Zeppelin Hotel in Stuttgart was unusable below the third floor, and at the Excelsior Hotel in Munich, as at the Carleton in Frankfurt, one filed through debris to the staircases that led to tolerably satisfactory upstairs bedrooms and improvised mess halls. But a number of army recreational centers, such as Garmisch-Partenkirchen, were already glamorous and luxurious. The Berchtesgaden Hof, with its superb setting, was reserved for the fortunate few, indicating that the upper brass and the "chair-borne" would not hesitate to capitalize on privileges that unsung combat soldiers had unwittingly provided.

Armed with at least some firsthand knowledge of the daily vicissitudes of the thousands of displaced persons for whom I would briefly be responsible, I pitched into my work at Frankfurt in our Supply Control offices in the I. G. Farben Building, that extraordinary structure which, by no mystery whatever, had been untouched by British night bombers and American daylight raids. It soon became evident, however, that someone would have to explain more emphatically to our supply authorities in

[3] War, by its very violence, precipitates resentment and counterviolence. I remember the case of five German peasant women who had been convicted of murdering three captured American fliers by stabbing them with pitchforks. I did not witness their hanging but I talked with several emotionally exhausted journalists who did, just an hour or two after the execution (November 10, 1945).

Paris the increasingly urgent need for more supplies for the D.P.'s. I therefore took the shabby night train, which crept along over "slow places" of the trackage and inched its way over improvised Bailey bridges, from Frankfurt to Paris. There I was lucky enough to enlist the cooperation of understanding Americans, and rather happily felt that I had fairly adequately fulfilled my mission. Aside from a brief visit in the late summer, on my way to England, when I had been quite unwillingly grounded by vile flying weather, it had been a year since I had visited Paris, and I found the contrast a heartening one. Rail transport had been fairly well restored and the fuel problem that had been so acute in the winter of 1944–45 no longer existed.[4] All in all, Paris, although still gloomy, had greatly improved. During my visit in Paris I met Lt. William Lovegrove, an old Fort Custer associate and a most conscientious arts and monuments officer, who told me a story that revealed both the naiveté and the innate boorishness of at least one of our general officers. A former Harvard student of mine, Captain J. J. Rorimer (later director of the Metropolitan Museum of New York), and Lieutenant Lovegrove, under the guidance of their superior arts and monuments officer, had arranged an exhibit of hundreds of objets d'art which the Germans had carried away and which had been recovered. These items were being carefully identified so they could be dutifully returned to the museums or to the private collections from which the Germans had taken them. Bursting with justifiable pride, they invited a very senior American general to visit the exhibit. When they were conducting him through the rooms in which the paintings, etchings, drawings, and sculpture were displayed, the general said crustily, "I'm not interested in this stuff. Show me flat silver or something I can use." It took a good deal of tact to explain to the general that arts and monuments officers were not engaged in the sordid business of looting the looters.

Lieutenant Lovegrove, who before the war, as a sculptor, had lived in Paris some fourteen years, was deeply disturbed about the morale of the French people. None of the unity, none of the spiritual awakening, he had expected had emerged. Self-protection and devil take the hindmost seemed to prevail. No meat could be purchased for twenty francs when appropriate ration coupons were presented, but any amount was available for eighty francs and no coupons. Here were reflected some of the psychological consequences of the long, irksome German occupation. Cheating to keep things out of the hands of the Germans had been regarded as patriotic, but

[4] On temporary duty in Paris in February 1945 I saw how the fuel shortage affected the Parisians' daily life. A Free-French friend of London days invited me to his apartment. For their six rooms the only heat the family had was given off by a stove about 20 inches long, 10 inches wide, and 18 inches high. In it they burned twigs they had gathered in the Bois de Boulogne. During the two hours I was with them, only three handfuls of their precious fuel was used.

in the process a set of deceitful habits had developed. The effect manifested itself in a network of black markets, everywhere, for all manner of goods, leading to a grossly unfair system of distribution whereby the rich were well provided for and the poor made miserable. French efforts to punish collaborators had to be abandoned; there were just too many degrees of collaboration to make tolerably satisfactory juridical distinctions. The evil concomitants of the French defeat had released the Gyntian weaknesses of millions.

When I returned to Frankfurt I took over the Supply Control Branch of USFET for some eight or nine days so that the acting head, substituting for the actual head of the branch (who was on home leave), could take a trip. I moved into a handsome office, tried to look wise, all the time trusting that the staff of majors, captains, and lieutenants could give me answers to puzzling questions. Fortunately my rigorous training at Scottish Command stood me in good stead. A good thing about the army is that one must take responsibility, and ordinarily it isn't half as difficult as one may have assumed. Contrasted with our much smaller volume in Norway, supply operations at USFET were wholesale; where we had dealt in thousands of tons, USFET dealt in hundreds of thousands. But all the procedures had been fairly well routinized. The only really sticky problem I had to wrestle with during my short period of responsibility arose from the insistence of certain members of Congress that USFET should supply fresh kosher-killed meat for all Jewish D.P.'s. Since I would not long be in charge I was willing to act as a curmudgeon. Someone had to say "no," because we could at that time neither establish slaughterhouses at each of our food depots nor find enough live animals to slaughter.

When the head of Supply Control returned from his home leave, I had accumulated enough "points" to permit me to return to the "zone of the interior" (the quaint army name for the United States), and I promptly began the processing that would terminate my tour of duty in Germany. When I told the head of Supply Control how eagerly I awaited my return to the States, he replied laconically, "You won't like it," a prophecy that seemed odd when I heard it but one that proved to be all too accurate. The road home took me to Paris again and then to one of the "repple-depples"[5] in the neighborhood of Le Havre. Named for brands of cigarettes, these camps had such names as "Lucky Strike" or "Home Run," the repple-depple marked on my orders. Surly German prisoners of war served as mess-hall waiters and bedroom stewards, sloe-eyed men from whom I could not elicit a single smile, however much I tried, during my

[5] I suspect this familiar army term originally may have meant "replacement depot" although it gradually came to designate a staging center for returning personnel.

138

three-day residence at Home Run. From our staging center high on a bluff we looked down on a wide flatland along the waterfront, where neat piles of brick, salvaged from the bombed-out buildings of Le Havre, now dotted the landscape like wheat shocks do in grain fields. The work of rebuilding would soon begin, and presently this war, like so many other wars fought on French soil, would be forgotten.[6] The blockhouses the Germans built on the bluffs to repel a cross-channel invasion would ultimately be razed, although when I paused briefly at Home Run they stood as grim reminders of the weird kinds of capital formation that war requires.

A rough ocean crossing, through towering winter waves, on a pre-World War I German ship renamed the *George Washington*, brought me to New York three days before Christmas, and I had visions of a prompt reunion with my wife and twelve-year-old son. To my dismay when we docked we were promptly ferried across the Hudson and taken by train to Camp Joyce Kilmer in New Jersey. It took all my forensic skill to persuade the commandant to release me a day later on the understanding that I would dutifully report to Camp Devons in Massachusetts after Christmas for separation from the army. Late on December 23 I traveled by army truck from Camp Kilmer to New Brunswick; I was dazzled by the lights of that city since for more than two years I had lived in a darkened or very ill-lighted world. The Harvard Club in New York, where I had long been a member, found a place for me that night, and the next evening, Christmas Eve, I arrived in Stockbridge, Massachusetts, to be greeted at the station by my wife and son. I could not help thinking of the thousands of soldiers who, over the centuries, had come home from countless wars — and of all those who had never returned.

A week later I was separated from the army by a rather absurd procedure under which each of us wrote our own military record, after having been urged to describe our achievements without any modesty. These truthful or fanciful accounts were then typed and photographed and out we went fully as embarrassed as one is after having written his own *Who's Who* description. Despite these banal aspects of separation, the sense of freedom gratified me and with considerable eagerness I looked forward to seeing my New York University colleagues. A few days later my enthusiasm had waned. Still in uniform I called first on the chairman of the

[6] In *The Silence of Colonel Bramble* (London, 1919), pp. 210–214, André Maurois describes his visit to the battlefield of Crécy. His British companion explained how "the English were drawn up on the hill" facing the visitors, with "their right toward Crécy, their left at Vadicourt," the thirty thousand English who challenged a hundred thousand French. But since no one in the party was quite certain precisely where the historic military action had occurred, Maurois asked a peasant where the battle had been fought. "The battle?" said the old peasant. "What battle?"

economics department in his Madison Square business office. He told me about the troubles he had experienced in keeping a corps of young instructors and the inconvenience that rationing of food and gasoline had caused. He explained how much he had enjoyed playing golf in Arlington, Vermont. He described in elaborate detail his new house with five bathrooms, and his son's wedding, and he spoke in glowing terms of his new daughter-in-law. After his hour-long monologue I excused myself and left. He had not asked one question about my army life, about my activities overseas, or about my future plans except to remark that he was sure I was glad to be back.

When I called at the economics office, one after another of my colleagues came forward to greet me. Almost ritualistically each one said, "I bet you're glad to be back." When I had heard this remark for the third or fourth, or fifth time, I rather mildly replied that I wasn't sure, adding that all I was certain about was that I was older and sadder, although whether I was any wiser, I really didn't know. One colleague thought this remark very humorous and laughed uproariously, a reaction that not only perplexed me but irritated me to such an extent that I told him very earnestly that I very sincerely felt much older, that the evidence of human cruelty I had witnessed had deeply saddened me, and that I had yet to discover what I had really learned. I sensed that no one wanted to talk about the war; to my stay-at-home colleagues it was something best forgotten, finished and over. My trouble was, of course, that I had a prescience that in some changed form the war would go on for a long time. My disenchantment with my university colleagues, however, was not yet complete. When I left the university to enter the army I turned over my most important graduate course to a younger colleague so that he might have the experience of teaching a subject in which he was deeply interested. Even though I was returning in the middle of the academic year, I expected that he would willingly relinquish the course. To my surprise he categorically refused to do so, making it necessary for me, were I to carry a full schedule, to prepare a wholly new course. Still another frustration occurred. I learned that a modest salary increase was about to be made, and when I saw the assistant dean I told him I had heard the good news. "Oh that's not for you," he said emphatically; "this increase is for those of us who kept the shop going while you fellows were out riding the gravy train." After these experiences I began to understand what the colonel who returned from home leave meant when he said, "You won't like it." I therefore decided to ask the chairman of the department to let me teach halftime for the second semester of the academic year 1945–46. It had become rather evident that it might be a bit more difficult to return to my prewar pattern of life than I had expected.

Brooding about this problem, I decided to visit my relatives in Washington, D.C., and in Florida in the free time I had before my part-time teaching duties would begin. En route to Washington my wife and I stopped in Newark, Delaware, to make a surprise visit with an old friend, M. M. Daugherty, who, like myself, had been in the army in the European theater; but when I telephoned his house, I was told that Colonel Daugherty had gone to Seoul, Korea (although actually he had gone to Japan). I knew precious little about Korea although I was not quite as ignorant as the thirty-eight Mount Holyoke College girls who, when asked in an intelligence test "How many legs does a Korean have?" answered either four, six, or eight. But the idea of someone going to Korea intrigued me, and my chance inquiry in Delaware rather conditioned me for a wholly unexpected turn of events in Washington. The people I looked up there included my former Harvard associate Harry Dexter White, who had been one of the chief architects of the Bretton Woods agreements [7] that created, in 1944, the International Monetary Fund and the International Bank for Reconstruction and Development. I knew Harry White very well since not only had we both been instructors in economics at Harvard but as tutors in the division of history, government, and economics we had briefly shared an office in Holyoke House. Unlike my New York University colleagues, Harry plied me with a barrage of questions about my experiences in France, Norway, and Germany. When I said I was planning to resume my academic life Harry said earnestly, "You can't run out on us, Ed; your country needs you now more than ever." Whereupon he picked up the telephone and dialed a number. "General," he said, when he had made telephonic connection, "I've got an old friend with me whom you must see. He's the kind of man we desperately need if we are to fulfill our international responsibilities." The upshot was that I promised Harry White that I would go immediately to General John H. Hilldring's office in the Pentagon. The general was then director of the Civil Affairs Division in the War Department.

Hilldring wasted no time in urging me to accept an overseas assignment. He told me that Harry White's recommendation made it unnecessary for him to review my credentials since he trusted White's judgment com-

[7] Although I do not pretend to understand all the merits or shortcomings of the "White Plan" as compared with the "Keynes Plan," I must, in deference to Harry White's place in history, protest against Robert Triffin's sweeping characterization of the Bretton Woods conference. "On the American side," writes Triffin in *Europe and the Money Muddle* (New Haven, Conn.: Yale University Press, 1957), pp. 108–109, "the whole negotiation was dominated by the powerful personality of Harry White, his immense personal conceit, and his ruthlessness." Admittedly, White was not a modest person, but his impatience with people with slower minds than his, his intellectual enthusiasm, or even his brusqueness, eagerness, and forcefulness could not accurately be described as manifestations of mere "conceit" or "ruthlessness."

141

pletely. When I asked the general where he needed me, I learned to my surprise that it was in Korea. He explained that General Archer Lerch, military governor of Korea, had decided the time had come to civilianize and then gradually Koreanize our governmental organization, and that key personnel were urgently needed, people who had already demonstrated their ability to cope with civil-affairs problems. General Hilldring called in his personnel officer who took me to his office to show me the organization charts and the unfilled slots. Since USAMGIK (United States military government in Korea) was the legitimate successor government to the Japanese, every department of the government temporarily had to be entrusted to an American. For me the suitable vacancy seemed to be that of director of the Department of Agriculture. I agreed to allow my name to be submitted for consideration, reserving my decision until a definite offer was made. But I explained that I would not consider going to Korea unless arrangements could be made for my family to join me, and of this I was assured.

Taking up my teaching duties, I gave but little thought to Korea, although I read a number of books about that country. When no word came from Washington, I assumed that since I had no proper training to qualify me for the agricultural department of the Korean government, the Pentagon's recommendation had probably been disregarded. Then, out of the blue, in May, came a long telegram informing me that I had been appointed the director of the Department of Agriculture in the military government in Korea, CAF-15. I replied promptly by a personal telegram to General Hilldring in which I said, "I am quite willing to go to Korea but what does CAF-15 mean?" So innocent was I then of the mysteries of bureaucracy that I had no idea this was, at the time, a top civil service classification. Reluctantly, the university gave me a year's leave of absence. Little did I realize that it would be not one year but ten years before I would return to academic life, or that government service would take me not only to Korea but to Japan, Greece, and Yugoslavia.

10

POWER WITHOUT GLORY

★★★★★★★★★★★★★★★★★★★★★★★★★★★★

THE urgent need for my services in Korea, which General Hilldring had so emphatically stressed, apparently had not been conveyed to the persons responsible for arranging my travel. For although when I finally reached Korea, I learned that most of the incoming personnel came by air, whether senior officials or Red Cross girls and secretaries, my orders had called for travel by rail to San Francisco and then by ship to Inchon. The two-and-a-half-day train trip was followed by a three-day wait in San Francisco and the "ship" turned out to be a slow-moving tank carrier that plowed along so leisurely that I lost track of time as day followed day on the vast reaches of the Pacific. From letters to my wife I have since discovered that my trip from Stockbridge, Massachusetts, to Seoul, Korea, actually took twenty-eight days, and these four long weeks were only partly useful and certainly not very gratifying. I shared a windowless, chairless, tableless compartment with eleven bunkmates, and hence I had no privacy for study or writing. As far as I could ascertain, the *Marine Devil* was not equipped with a single chair; consequently one had the choice of sitting on one's bunk, on the mess-hall benches during the four hours the mess hall was available as a so-called lounge, or on the steel plates of the decks. I did most of my studying of the dozen or more books on Korea I had brought along in the mess hall, since the decks were usually thronged with people: the ship was carrying over two thousand replacements, officers and men, for the 6th and 7th Infantry divisions, plus about a score of Department of the Army civilians and a few missionaries. The decks were often so covered with sunbathers that, on bright days, the *Marine Devil* from the air must have resembled a floating Brighton or Coney Island.

From three officers returning from home leave who had already served in Korea, from three missionaries impatient to reenter their beloved foster land, and from two Koreans, I learned a great deal about the country where I would soon be living. By lucky foresight I had brought a Korean grammar, and I wasted no time in seeking help from my Korean companions in learning to read and write Korean characters. One of the Koreans had taught Oriental languages at the University of California and I was really very fortunate to have his assistance. "Thank heavens," I wrote to my wife on June 23, "that these missionaries and Koreans were aboard or else there would have been no orientation for officers, enlisted men, or civilians. People are apparently just sent to a theater without any briefing whatever." Of my missionary shipmates, one had lived in Korea twenty-three years, another twenty years. Although I was very grateful to them for the information they supplied about the Koreans and their culture, once I reached Korea I discovered that any working arrangement with the missionaries would be fraught with considerable difficulty.

I arrived in Inchon during the monsoonal rains and found the streets oozing with red-yellow mud. But not even heavy rain could hide the beauty of the countryside that I saw on my ride to Seoul. Rice paddies of all shapes and designs, separated by balks curving with the contours, gleamed with the lustrous color of light green rice. On higher ground barley patches and on house roofs well-trained gourd vines testified to the industry and patience of Asia's diligent small farmers. Women, as erect as the caryatids on the Erechtheum in Athens, carried bundles or jars on their heads, with their babies neatly laced on their backs. The colors of women's clothes in Korea are indescribably beautiful, with carefully considered contrasts between the pastel shades of their long, sweeping, high-waisted skirts and the brighter jackets cut so short they scarcely cover the breasts. My first impressions of Korea have never dimmed; it is a beautiful country inhabited by gentle people, hard to know but so easy to love.

Since I had been appointed director of the Department of Agriculture despite my inadequate training, I had proceeded to read everything I could find about Korean farming. But quite suddenly everything changed. Two days after I reached Seoul, on July 5, a telegram arrived recalling immediately all navy officers on duty with the United States military government in Korea. Since the Korean Department of Commerce had been headed by navy Captain Owen Jones, his impending departure would leave that very important department without a head, and consequently General Archer Lerch, the military governor, promptly switched me from Agriculture, which had a capable acting head, to Commerce. Quite without forewarning I therefore found myself in charge of a government department with more than a thousand employees (United States military, United States civilian, and Korean), an organization responsible for supervising the activities of some two thousand factories and mines, operating the nation's public utilities, formulating policies for domestic and foreign commerce, and coordinating the activities of national and provincial public-works undertakings. Very fortunately Jones had found a superb executive officer in Lt. Col. George D. Burr who guided and counseled me in my difficult first weeks. I had the good fortune also to have a first-class Korean counterpart, Oh Chung Soo, who had been trained at the Massachusetts Institute of Technology. Still another fortuitous coincidence must be noted. James Shoemaker, whom I had known at Harvard, and who, as an army officer, had held key positions under both General Lerch and General Hilldring in Washington, arrived in Korea by air the same day I arrived by sea. His assignment was to head the recently formed National Economic Board whose members, besides the chairman and the executive secretary, were the directors of the departments of Commerce, Agriculture, Finance, and Transportation.[1] I was therefore assured of having at least one very competent economist with whom I could compare views and from whom I could seek advice.

What kind of problems did I encounter in my unexpected new assignment? A letter to my wife dated July 9, 1946, just six days after my arrival in Korea, gives some indication of my daily engagements: "Today I held conferences concerning transferring the street railways of Seoul to the municipality, granting an 8,000,000-won subsidy to a steam-power light plant, and concentrating textile production in six large mills. Tomorrow will bring a set of equally big problems. Fortunately I have some excellent staff officers and a patient deputy who right now is working in his room on a great stack of papers he couldn't handle at the office during the day. He does this every night."[2] Why had all these responsibilities fallen on American shoulders? The answer, of course, was that by reason of the defeat of Japan, the American military government became the legitimate successor government to the Japanese in South Korea.[3] Since

[1] *United States Army Military Government in Korea, Ordinance 90*, dated May 28, 1946.

[2] Before he entered the army Lieutenant Colonel Burr had held important posts in the government of San Francisco. A bronze plaque in the airport building testifies to one of his varied and distinguished municipal governmental activities.

[3] There is nothing that I can say about the division of territorial responsibility between the Americans and the Russians at the 38th parallel. For better or worse this decision had been made at Potsdam long before I arrived in Korea and hence for those of us charged with administrative duties the division of Korea had to be accepted as a given reality. It can be argued, however, as Charles Burton Marshall did in his report to the Foreign Affairs Committee of the 81st Congress, that had this arrangement with the Russians not been made, the Russians could easily have occupied all of Korea since our occupation forces (the 24th Corps) had to travel from Okinawa to the Philippines for refitting before they could embark for Korea.

a decision had been made in Washington that all the Japanese who were in Korea at the time of Japan's surrender should be repatriated with the greatest possible speed, the country was soon stripped clean of all high-grade labor, inasmuch as the Japanese had monopolized almost every executive, managerial, professional, and skilled position and had allowed the Koreans to perform only lowly, unskilled, and routine tasks. With the departure of the Japanese, the administration of government for some 17,000,000 people in South Korea became the responsibility of ill-prepared Americans and untrained and inexperienced Koreans.

Because American policy directives stipulated that all sequestrated former Japanese property should be held in trust for the Korean people, USAMGIK temporarily had to operate the mines, factories, shipyards, power plants, and all other enterprises that had belonged to the Japanese government, to Japanese corporations, or to individual Japanese owners. A large part of these operating responsibilities fell on the provincial governors and their staffs so that the Department of Commerce had more supervisory than operating duties. Many industries, however, had such national importance — coal, textiles, and electric power, for example — that the Department of Commerce had to assume direct operating responsibility. When the United States naval officers were recalled, and after a growing number of army officers became eligible for return to the "zone of the interior," the task of finding plant managers became increasingly difficult. Recruitment of more American civilians therefore became imperative, while progressive Koreanization assumed a corresponding urgency. Although the American occupation forces in Korea were a part of General Douglas MacArthur's command, our appeals to Tokyo for help brought only very meager results. Most unfortunately, in occupied Japan Korea acquired a quasi-Siberian characterization. Officers who were "out of line" or exceptionally marginal were threatened with reassignment to Korea, while oppositely the attraction of good housing, splendid PX facilities, and luxurious clubs in Japan, to say nothing of actual labor scouting, tended to leech away some of the superior personnel from Korea. We had to struggle along with what we had, and hope that civilian recruits could be obtained from Washington. Here, however, we soon discovered we had to compete with Germany, Greece, Austria, and Japan when we asked for experts for coal or tungsten mines, for technicians for textile mills (cotton, wool, silk, hemp), or for electrical and civil engineers, factory managers, accountants, fishery experts, and dozens of other specialists.

Along with our technical problems a host of political and cultural difficulties emerged. I had not been in my new position a week before I was confronted with an embarrassing situation. It came to my attention that the Koreans in charge of the Chosun Coal Distributing Agency, an enterprise under the supervision of a Department of Commerce military-government officer, had spent over 400,000 won on entertainment; and since American (Commerce Department) officials had been present at these festivities, all the costs of food, sake, and Kisang girls had been slyly charged up to the coal company.[4] I'm afraid I did not improve my popularity by forbidding members of my staff to accept invitations to such jolly corporate collations. But it had become quite evident that in the operation of hundreds of mines, factories, and other enterprises through interpreters, vast possibilities for peculation were bound to exist. USAMGIK had engaged its corps of interpreters for the most part through the missionaries, and whereas some of the religious groups, particularly the Seventh-Day Adventists, supplied us with very competent and trustworthy interpreters, many other English-speaking Koreans, though highly recommended by missionaries, turned out to be very skillful wheeler-dealers.

I had a feeling that very few of our American military-government officials could themselves be charged with improprieties, although we did uncover a few cases of flagrant venality and shameful dishonesty. The more typical Gyntian weakness consisted of a rather general willingness to accept gifts that anyone might have known the givers could not personally afford. Unfortunately the early days of the American occupation had not set very high standards for Koreans or for later-arriving Americans to follow. I was never able to discover who made the shameful decision to confiscate the personal property of the repatriated Japanese, but this episode certainly did little to inspire respect for American standards of morality. What happened was this. About three-quarters of a million Japanese had lived in Korea for years. When they had to be swiftly repatriated only a single piece of hand luggage was permitted each train or ship passenger, but firm assurances were given that if all the Japanese families would prepare bundles of their personal property, properly labeled, these chattels would dutifully be shipped to them in Japan. In the city of Seoul warehouses soon bulged with bundles. Time passed, the warehouse space was needed, and then someone made the decision to open the bundles and to sell their contents at nominal prices to American military personnel. The retail store that disposed of these deceitfully obtained family treasures turned out to be under my jurisdiction, but I didn't need to raise any unpleasant issue in order to close it. The sordid truth was that by July 1946 there were no more bundles to open; by then the wholesale looting operation was finished.

When I arrived in Korea, ten and a half months after that country's

[4] At the official rate of exchange this would be $26,666.66; at the more realistic black-market rate about $4000.

(fractional) liberation, quite a number of factories and mines had already been reactivated. But raw-material supplies were woefully insufficient and irregular and uncertain in arriving, partly because of inadequate GARIOA funds (those appropriated by the United States Congress for "Government and Relief in Occupied Areas"), partly because shipping was so notoriously undependable. More plants were being reconditioned, however, as people interested in production gradually superseded those indifferent army officers who had shown no concern whatever about the Korean economy. I recall, as an example, the situation we discovered in Inchon. When American troops were stationed there in the autumn of 1945 some stupid army officer had ordered all the looms, carding machines, and spinning frames of a well-equipped cotton textile mill thrown out-of-doors to rust and deteriorate just so his troops could use the building for a basketball court. In order to have a suitable floor, the open channels that had carried utility wires and pipes were filled in with hundreds of lead ingots, neatly planed level with the floor, ingots taken from a nearby Inchon machine shop. All these rearrangements had been made with utter disregard of the critical importance of both textiles and metal products in the Korean economy. We found, therefore, that the task of rehabilitating industrial facilities consisted partly in repairing damages caused by the war, partly in rectifying those unnecessarily occasioned by our own occupying forces.

Because of the daily pressure of work I found it almost impossible to visit industrial plants to observe at first hand the reactivation of the industrial sector. I did visit a textile plant, a match factory, and a paper mill in the neighborhood of Seoul, and I did fly to Cheju Island to reopen a factory that produced grain alcohol from sweet potatoes. That trip illustrated some of the hazards of life in Korea. When my party arrived at the pasturelike airfield on that island, famed for its matriarchal societal organization,[5] a distressed American provincial governor told us he had tried vainly to intercept our journey because a sudden outbreak of cholera, in the immediate neighborhood of the alcohol factory, had caused over two hundred deaths in the preceding twenty-four hours. Since we had all been inoculated for cholera and a half dozen other infectious diseases, we saw no reason to change our plans and went ahead with our ceremonies without any untoward incidents. Cheju became one of my favorite parts of Korea because of its natural beauty, its wildness, and its superb location in the East China Sea. Kublai Khan had hoped to invade Japan from Cheju and to that end he brought a large number of Mongolian ponies to the island.

[5] The women are the wage earners, diving for sponges, abalone, and seashells out of which buttons are made; while the men care for the children, cook the meals, tend the gardens, and loaf.

148

This venture failed and the ponies, left untended, had to fend for themselves. They reproduced in the mountain fastnesses so that now fierce wild ponies dot the landscape among the pink, white, and red azaleas that make Cheju a blaze of color in the spring.

It must not be assumed that only the Department of Commerce wrestled with problems. Food for the 17,000,000 people, presently to be increased by 3,000,000, had to be assured, a task that the Department of Agriculture and the controller of commodities found baffling and often exasperating. The Department of Finance was confronted with complex problems of taxation, with troubles concerning fiscal monopolies, and with the constant threat of inflation. The Department of Transportation probably had fully as difficult problems: rolling stock, prime movers, manpower, and fuel — all were insufficient. The task of the National Economic Board, and its staff, was to recommend proper policies and programs for all this tangle of occupation problems. One of my letters indicates that we took a rather serious view of the Korean economic situation. "Yesterday," I write to my wife on July 24, 1946,

Jim Shoemaker and I were taken to meet General John Hodge.[6] He must have thought us a brash pair because we told him what we thought without pulling any punches. Korea is being stripped of [American] personnel, week by week, and until qualified replacements come and learn their jobs this assignment is going to be awfully tough. You simply can't imagine what I am called on to decide in a single day. Today I headed off (I hope) a strike on the street railways, approved a loan for 20 million won, discussed coal-production problems with the manager of Korea's largest coal mine, and tried to reach departmental agreement on the price that should be paid for rice in the autumn collection program. Meantime I had another tooth pulled at one o'clock but was back at the office before 1:30. Don't think I am complaining. This is the most worthwhile thing I have done in my life. I only wish I could make more leisurely decisions.

When I think back about the staggering responsibilities that confronted us in occupation tasks, I marvel at the smugness of people like the assistant dean at New York University who had referred to my strenuous Norwegian and German experience as a ride on the "gravy train." It might have been well for such confident pundits to have served a single day in my stead in Korea. In a letter to my son on July 29 I described a typical day:

I got up this morning at 6:30, shaved, took my exercises and my usual cold shower, had breakfast, and by 7:55 was at my office. My deputy, Lieutenant Colonel Burr, had already arrived and he had a number of problems to discuss with me. My Korean counterpart, Mr. Oh, arrived about 8:10. He is a

[6] The commanding general of United States Forces in Korea, whose brilliant leadership of the 24th Corps had led to victory of American forces on Okinawa.

capable man, a graduate of MIT who became the manager of a Corn Products plant in the States and then returned to Korea as the manager of one of their plants here. He, too, had problems to discuss with me. A telephone call from General Lerch's aid informed me the general was coming to see me. He soon arrived to give me some confidential information about a wealthy Korean with whom I had an appointment at 10:00 o'clock. But our discussion went beyond that. The general told me he considered our civilian supply administration much too complex and asked me to prepare a plan for its simplification. When the general left I started to work on papers already accumulating in my "in box." Presently one of my Industry Bureau officers came to ask approval for a manager he had selected for one of our factories that manufactures motors and transformers. While I was talking with him, Colonel Parsons, head of the Communications Department, telephoned to ask how he could get clearance for a ship arriving from Japan that was coming to repair a submarine cable to Cheju Island. My Electrical Section chief wanted to know whether I had read his report on the critical situation in the Seoul street railways. My deputy next told me about the result of our Mining Bureau's analysis of some ferro-tungsten for which our Foreign Trade Bureau was seeking an export market. A telephone call came from Japan informing me that SCAP had agreed to supply Korea with 50,000 tons of coal for July. Aside from a number of other telephone calls, this was about all that happened between 8:00 and 10:00 A.M. when my Korean visitor arrived. He had grandiose plans for opening up direct trade with the United States and proudly showed me the list of manufacturers for whom he allegedly was the exclusive agent. I told him that our import-export regulations would be published soon and turned him over to my deputy so I could attend a meeting of the National Economic Board. When that meeting, devoted entirely to the rice-collection program, was over, I was whisked off to the dentist for a fifteen-minute appointment. Back at the office I signed a large batch of letters prepared by my bureau chiefs. After a hurried luncheon there were more visitors to see. The Korean (deputy) commerce officer from Ch'ungch'ong-namdo (province) told me his situation had become intolerable. Apparently when we, at the national level, had chosen the Federation of Financial Agencies to be the (provincial) distributors of cloth, soap, and shoes, he had "lost face" since he had promised this business to the local "Merchants Association." I consulted the chief of our Bureau of Domestic Commerce who explained why it had seemed best to make firm arrangements with the federation. As the crestfallen Mr. Lee left, the (American) governor of Kyonggi-do arrived. He wanted me to endorse his request to Washington for fifteen more plant managers and also to report some very suspicious activities at MaPo, the port of Seoul on the Han River. Rumor had it that hides were being loaded on Chinese junks despite our prohibitions. We decided to make a quick unannounced visit to MaPo, picking up some policemen en route. We found one junk loading leather and the police arrested the junk's "captain" and ordered guards put on the ship. Since almost every day I heard of someone being arrested, it occurred to me that it might be well to see the jail in which the "captain" would soon be incarcerated. It proved to be an extremely unpleasant place, a long building much like the stables we used to have on American cavalry posts. On either side of a central corridor were the cell blocks, square areas, much like box stalls, about

8 by 8 feet and latticed with four-by-fours. There were no bunks, furniture, washstands, or water faucets in the cells, only a layer of straw on the floor and a clay trough along the wall for carrying off human waste when flushed with water. Each cell contained eight prisoners who, at the sharp command of the warden, sat on their haunches in two well-aligned rows facing the corridor as we reviewed their misery. But our visit had to be a very short one since even an hour away from the office would mean that the pressures would build up all the more.

In contrast to the myopic import-export policy that I had encountered in Germany, I was happy to find that both General Lerch and General Hodge enthusiastically approved the efforts my Bureau of Foreign Trade was making to expand Korea's export-import trade. I held a press conference on July 19, 1946, and outlined our plans. Underlying Foreign Commerce Regulation No. 1, which at our request the Department of Justice would soon promulgate, lay three basic trade policies: to restrict imports to those commodities the Korean economy urgently needed; to permit the export of any or all commodities the Korean economy could spare, and to pay for all imports, not financed by GARIOA funds, or not available from government to government transactions, by exports, thereby ensuring that the future Korean government would not be saddled with foreign debts. Implementation of this policy called for an import-export license system under which approved importers and exporters would be granted import permits authorizing them to bring in commodities that Korea urgently needed or, conversely, export permits for carrying out specific commodities that the Korean economy could spare.[7] No export duties were to restrict such approved exports since the object was to build up maximum possible foreign exchange balances in order to finance needed imports. Because we were under great pressure from both Korean and American businessmen to allow them to sell radios, automobiles, and all manner of consumer goods in Korea, I stated very frankly that I would not allow the importing of unnecessary luxury goods when it was patently clear that essential consumer goods must have priority. Enforcing this program proved extremely difficult, however, since wealthy Koreans, importuning missionaries, and American congressmen (acting on requests from their constituents) all brought pressure for special treatment.

My refusal to bow to these demands did not increase my popularity, and I found that my insistence on the letter of USAMGIK regulations was regarded as something unexpected. "I have acted with more courage than

[7] Section 3 of Foreign Commerce Regulation No. 1 stipulated that "No person, natural or juridical, shall personally or through any agent import or export any goods or commodities into or out of Korea, south of 38 north latitude except pursuant to licenses and terms hereafter provided in accordance with the regulations issued by the Bureau of Foreign Commerce."

any of my four predecessors in this office," I wrote to my wife on August 7, 1946, "but I must say it often takes every ounce of determination that I can summon. There are just too many problems. Everyone wants favoritistic privileges. Factory and mine operators want special arrangements: 'We must have more rice for our twelve hundred workers; we must have higher wages'; these are the daily demands. Then there are the smugglers, shipping out hides or rice and importing such things as wine or watches. Dishonesty isn't a vice in Korea, it's a profession and a fine art." In this unfamiliar cultural milieu we really had an uphill task trying to implement policies which those of us who constituted the National Economic Board considered absolutely essential if the Korean economy was ever to become "viable."

Exactly two months after I took over the Department of Commerce and set it working reasonably well, General Archer Lerch announced that he had appointed me the civil administrator of USAMGIK. The organization chart on page 153 indicates how the office of the civil administrator (OCA) headed the thirteen departments and the nine offices of our government, making the civil administrator the third ranking officer in USAMGIK. As I had been the first civilian to head a department, I now became the first civilian to be chosen civil administrator, an appointment in line with the over-all policy of civilizing and then progressively Koreanizing the government of Korea. Although my swift promotion seemed to indicate confidence in my executive ability,[8] I felt I needed to know much more about the provinces and their problems before I undertook my new duties. It was readily agreed that I should make a week's tour of some of our more distant provincial headquarters. Although I was understandably flattered by my new assignment, it was with genuine regret that I turned over the Department of Commerce to my successor. I had succeeded in building up a very real measure of loyalty in my staff, and more than one officer who could have gone home stayed on because I asked him to do so. Whether I could ever build up such organizational efficiency and engender similar mutual confidence in OCA, I was by no means certain.

My visit to the southwestern provinces abundantly confirmed an impression I had gained several weeks earlier on a short trip to the old walled city of Suwon: that whereas urban Korea was disrupted, unstable, and fumbling, rural Korea reflected a sound albeit a simple culture. I described the countryside in a September 22 letter to my son:

Agriculture is exemplary even though the tools are few. . . . Embankments between rice paddies are planted with lima beans, corn rows shade several

[8] General Lerch said that although I was his first choice for civil administrator, he nevertheless asked his chief of staff and the deputy military governor each to prepare a list of names. I was first choice on both lists.

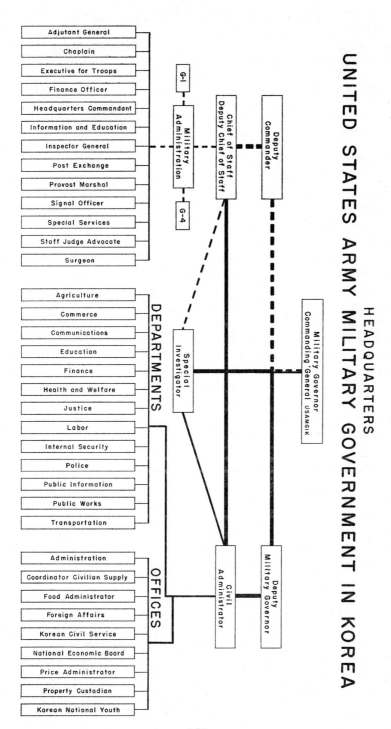

UNITED STATES ARMY MILITARY GOVERNMENT IN KOREA

HEADQUARTERS

Military Governor
Commanding General USAMGIK

Deputy Commander

Chief of Staff
Deputy Chief of Staff

Military Administration

G-1

G-4

Adjutant General
Chaplain
Executive for Troops
Finance Officer
Headquarters Commandant
Information and Education
Inspector General
Post Exchange
Provost Marshal
Signal Officer
Special Services
Staff Judge Advocate
Surgeon

DEPARTMENTS

Special Investigator

Agriculture
Commerce
Communications
Education
Finance
Health and Welfare
Justice
Labor
Internal Security
Police
Public Information
Public Works
Transportation

OFFICES

Civil Administrator

Deputy Military Governor

Administration
Coordinator Civilian Supply
Food Administrator
Foreign Affairs
Korean Civil Service
National Economic Board
Price Administrator
Property Custodian
Korean National Youth

153

rows of lower growing plants. . . . The fields are clean of weeds and most carefully cultivated. The villages . . . are very neat, a street of houses, some with tile roofs, most of them with thatched roofs. Artisans — wheelwrights, mat-makers, carpenters — work in their open, shedlike structures. The streets throng with children, with women carrying their burdens on their heads and their babies on their backs. Stout wagons drawn by huge honey-colored oxen crawl along the roads, whole families of farm folk bend and sway like dancers in a ballet as they weed their rice, while not far away white herons stand fearlessly in the paddies stretching their long, slender necks, watching the faithful workers.

My companions on my trip included the national food administrator, Carroll Hill, his Korean counterpart, Chee Yong Eun, and the head of our Korean Civil Service, Hugh Bledsoe. With two enlisted men and two Korean engineers we set out in a gasoline-propelled railway car. The enjoyment of the trip was somewhat marred by the utter recklessness of our Korean car operators who succeeded in hitting a railway crew's handcar (scattering tools over a wide area), colliding with a flatcar loaded with telephone poles one of which pierced the front window of our car, and hitting a cow that, amazingly enough, wasn't killed even though she slid at least fifty yards on the right-hand rail. Even so we were luckier than another group of military-government travelers had been a fortnight earlier. Their car operator struck a Korean woman who was crossing a high railway trestle bridge. Chee Yong Eun who had been on that trip said very scornfully, "Because someone insisted that we stop to find out what happened to the woman we were delayed twenty-three minutes." Orientals have many, many virtues, but compassion is seldom one of them.

Seven of our ten provincial governors were regular army colonels, professional soldiers who accepted their atypical Korean assignments without complaint but, unfortunately, without enthusiasm or very much imagination. Their greatest fault was their tendency to administer their provinces as if they were separate kingdoms. If they had coal mines in their jurisdictions, they seemed unmindful that it was urgently important for them to obtain the maximum possible output even if only a small portion was needed in their own province. Because all the southwestern provinces produced rice surpluses, the governors protested against our insistence that the rice reserved by producers there ought to approximate the nationally determined daily food ration. We listened carefully to their complaints but we had no choice except to take a very stern attitude toward the governors and toward the Korean officials they supervised as far as rice collection was concerned. After all, we at the national level had to ensure some fair distribution of the nation's food supply, and when we discovered, as we did in Cholla-Namdo, that the richest rice-producing province had collected less than 10 percent of its rice quota we not only removed the Korean counterpart of the provincial governor but threatened the whole cadre of Korean civil servants with punishment unless the rice-collection program was promptly implemented. The trouble stemmed, of course, from the differential between the open-market price of rice (about 8000 won per suk) and the government price (1700 won). But for very good reasons we had to keep the cost of living (which meant the price of rice) low enough so that pressures for higher wages would not build up and further complicate our already serious inflation. About 4,500,000 suk of rice had to be obtained from the growers at 1700 won a suk.

On this trip I had an opportunity to see a number of important provincial cities, Kunsan, Chonju, Kwangju, Sunch-on, Mokpo, Taejon, and Taegu, which not only served as major market centers but constituted fairly important industrial locations. In each province I tried to take a measure of the problems of all our departments: Agriculture, Transportation, Education, Commerce, and Finance in particular, for it would now be my responsibility to harmonize as best I could all the operations of our complex governmental organization. I found that our three provincial governors who were reserve officers approached their tasks in a way that contrasted sharply with the routine performance of the professional soldiers. Colonel Charles Anderson, for example, a Nebraska national guard officer who had been a dentist in civilian life, by honoring his *gunsoos* (county headmen) skillfully persuaded them to fulfill their rice-collection quotas and was busy establishing 4-H clubs in his province, improving schools, and reconditioning factories. Colonel Timothy Murphy, a chemical engineer from New Jersey, was another excellent, energetic provincial governor; while Colonel James Wilson, an advertising executive in civilian life, proved to be a very competent mayor of the city of Seoul, which was a separate province.

If life in Commerce had been strenuous, the tasks in OCA proved to be even more demanding. Messengers brought in a huge volume of requests, reports, recommendations, and other communications from all the government departments and offices. When I discovered a warrant officer in my outer office merely logged in these papers before politely placing them in my in box, I explained to General Lerch that this would never do. We needed a competent administrative officer who could divert, return, or otherwise dispose of at least half of this documentary avalanche. We found such a competent person in a WAC captain, Alba Martinelli, who very skillfully screened out the items that I should not bother with. Even so, the remaining quantity was overwhelming, and since I found myself seeing ten, twenty, thirty or more people every day, I would stagger out each evening with a bulging briefcase of papers to work on at home. Years before he came to Korea General Lerch had written a classic essay on

155

"Completed Staff Work" and he therefore expected that every paper forwarded to him would be ready for his signature, or, if he ought not sign it, the reasons should be so convincingly stated that he needed only to note his concurrence. It was my responsibility to see that the staff work that went to General Lerch was "completed." But the flow of paper was not only upward from the bureaus and departments to the military governor. Another stream came down, through OCA, to the departments: cables from Washington or Tokyo, complaints brought by Koreans to General Hodge or General Lerch, ideas both good and bad about how our operations should be changed, demands from provincial governors or Korean factory managers, and a growing volume of requests from American businessmen, missionaries, and, of course, ambitious Korean politicians.

Who were the people telephoning for appointments with me or waiting so patiently in the anteroom of my spacious office once occupied by a Japanese civil governor? Department heads, or their bureau chiefs, had top priority because my main function was to serve as an intermediary between them and the military governor. But since our government really was a surrogate for the yet unpoliticized Koreans, we perforce had to see all Koreans who thought they had any justification for bringing problems to the attention of the military governor. It would be impossible to describe or categorize my unending succession of Korean visitors. Captain Martinelli diverted as many as she could, but they proved very hard to deflect. Since I had learned to write the Korean alphabet, whenever Koreans were orally introduced to me I would transliterate their names into Korean characters and to their unfailing joy and amusement I would show them my calligraphic efforts.[9] But for the most part I couldn't satisfy their wishes, not those of the principal of a girls' school who wanted a new building, or of an engineer who hoped to harness the tides of the Yellow Sea and thereby solve our electric-power deficit; nor could I accede to the importunities of Koreans employed in our government agencies who coyly suggested that I should remove their corrupt enemies from positions they occupied.

Conferences constantly called me away from my administrative duties. I soon discovered that policy decisions were being made in so many places that coordination became more and more difficult. In name, General Lerch was the military governor of Korea although the commanding general of the United States forces in Korea could, if he wished, override any decisions agreed upon in the military-government organization. What

[9] The learned man has always been held in very high esteem in Korea. General Lerch, who had grown up in a Nebraska village with two Korean schoolmates, very skillfully capitalized on this cultural predilection, always referring to me as "Dr. Johnson" or as "Johnson *paksa*," which is to say "Johnson the scholar."

had actually grown up was a polycentric system in which decisions were made by the commanding general, by members of his headquarters, by a subsidiary (24th Corps) policy section whose function originally had been to deal with the Russians, by General MacArthur's huge Tokyo staff, by certain intelligence agencies, and by the military government. If consultation below the level of the military governor seemed appropriate, any or all of these decision-making agencies would call on me. Meantime, as might be expected, the emerging Korean politicians skillfully played one or more American decision-making agencies against others.

The growing dilemma revealed itself with regard to rice collection. Our job was to feed the Korean people, not merely for the purpose of keeping them healthy but to prevent unrest. But the farmers who raised the rice objected to our collection program because they could sell rice at higher prices in the open market, while wealthy consumers also objected because they wanted more than the daily authorized rice ration (as everyone did) and were prepared to pay the higher open-market prices. But since in September 1946 we had 19,369,000 people to feed,[10] and a rice crop of only so many suk, we could not allow prosperous Koreans to consume more than their share. General Hodge and his military advisers, constantly badgered by Korean critics, felt that we were far too perfectionistic in our rice-collection and -distribution system, and as a result of their objections we reluctantly agreed to engage in some discussions with a group of representative Korean leaders — with the ablest people that could be induced to consult with us.[11] To these earnest and responsible Koreans we explained precisely how the food requirements for all the Korean people had been calculated, how many suk of rice would have to be collected, and how the total national supply would be distributed so that every Korean man, woman, and child would be assured of a daily rice ration of at least one and a half hops for the entire calendar year.

After some preliminary sparring it was apparently agreed that one person would speak for the Koreans, Won See Hoon. He began by thanking us for our solicitude for the Korean people. He said he was convinced that we were not, as was so often said, collecting rice to export, as the Japanese had done. But he went on to explain that for all the unquestioned

[10] For the population figures, 1940–48, see George M. McCune, *Korea Today* (Cambridge, Mass.: Harvard University Press, 1950), p. 327.

[11] Syngman Rhee forbade members of his undercover political organization to take part in these conferences lest he be accused of collaboration with the American military government. All other important political groups except the extreme left agreed to take part, and about a dozen spokesmen for varying shades of political opinion were represented. On the American side General Albert Brown and Arthur Bunce represented the commanding general, and General Archer Lerch, General Gardiner Helmick, and I spoke for the military government.

merits of our plans, for all our fairness and logical correctness, we had failed to understand the wishes of the Korean people. When the rice harvest comes, he said, while his Korean companions nodded approval, the Koreans want to enjoy it; they want to eat not one and a half or two and a half or three and a half hops of rice a day but rather ten hops if they can afford it. And what will they do when the rice is gone? What will happen when by reckless consumption in the autumn there is none left by January or February? The people will suffer, he said, and if worst comes to worst, they will have to eat the tender bark of trees. By the time Won See Hoon's long discourse had been translated for us I was completely convinced of just one thing, namely that we did not understand the workings of the Korean mind.[12] General Brown, who represented the commanding general in these conferences, thought that he did, and proceeded to persuade General Hodge to authorize Koreans to purchase from farmers as much rice as a family head could carry. All our protests were in vain, the unwise concession to the black marketeers was made, and not only were our rice-collection efforts sadly undercut but many millions of GARIOA dollars had to be spent in bringing in food supplies the next spring. Once again a Gyntian weakness had revealed itself: the propensity to avoid problems by compromise!

This experience convinced me that we needed anthropological advice since apparently our concepts of good government did not coincide with Korean ideas. I therefore told General Lerch that we ought to engage the services of a well-trained anthropologist to advise us how we could better articulate military government to Korean needs. General Lerch thought my idea a capital one and asked me to find the right anthropologist whom he could invite to come to Korea to help us. I assigned the job of selecting such a person to Bruce Melvin, a sociologist on the staff of our National Economic Board, and, after consulting scholars in the States, he proposed that we invite Cornelius Osgood of Yale University. Not until the summer of 1947 could Professor Osgood come, however, and when he did, he chose to make his investigations of the Koreans and their culture in a village on the island of Kanghwa that lies in the Yellow Sea just off the northwestern corner of South Korea. Here for two months he gathered data and then without giving us the benefit of his findings he returned to Yale where he wrote a very good book which he called *The Koreans and Their Culture*.[13] But since four years passed before the book was published, we, alas, were none the wiser, and I consider it rather unfair that

[12] In my files I found the penciled note that General Lerch handed me when Won See Hoon finished his explanation. The note said: "The mind of the Korean lacks even the dependability of a ricochet."

[13] Published in New York by Ronald Press in 1951.

Osgood should have berated military-government personnel for their failure to understand the Koreans when we had confessed our inability to do so by inviting him to come to Korea to help us. His exclusive interest in making yet another precise village study leads me to doubt whether anthropologists can be very useful advisers to those unfortunate persons who are saddled with responsibility for devising and implementing governmental policies in unfamiliar milieus. Admittedly Osgood's study was a very thorough one, and his contrasts between American and Russian occupation policies were very thoughtful. My complaint is simply that he missed a golden opportunity to show us how we could have done a better job. Instead he chose, unfortunately, to sit in the seat of the scornful.

So we blundered along. We had power that we really did not know how to use: power over Korean consumption, employment, and the conduct of millions of people, even the power over life or death, a terrible responsibility as I shall explain in a later chapter.[14] Yet our policies could scarcely be consistent when entirely too many people were making policy decisions. Moreover we constantly found ourselves caught between strange and irreconcilable local political pressures. Syngman Rhee, together with his followers, sycophants, and admirers, not only tried to discredit all our efforts in order to advance their chances of seizing power, but actually infiltrated our Korean police organization in shameless ways. Left-leaning Korean leaders, such as the very able Lyuh Woon-heung, considered our policies far too conservative and our programs ineffective.[15] Washington directives instructed us to avoid commitments to either right or left political aspirants, and indicated a strong preference for a center-dominated provisional Korean government to prepare the Korean people for self-government. Beginning in the autumn of 1946 an energetic effort to carry out the Washington policy led to the establishment of a Korean Interim Legislature, the Koreanization of the courts, and presently to the selection of Korean provincial governors and department directors. With the Koreanization of the executive branch I soon found myself very deeply involved.

[14] See chapter 20, "Reflections on a Drop of Dew."
[15] At the conferences we held with Korean leaders Lyuh severely criticized us for our failure to provide satisfactory public transportation, our inability to repair and staff the hospitals, and our apparent unwillingness to assume responsibility for what he considered to be the minimal welfare duties of any modern government.

11

THE DYNAMICS
OF DEMOCRACY
★★★★★★★★★★★★★★★★

As a chapter in the history of American postwar foreign policy the Korean episode must be considered both discrete and important. Our military government in Korea differed from our administration of conquered territories: Germany or Japan. Our purposes in Korea were different. Pending some acceptable evidence of capacity for self-government, the United States decided to establish and operate a government in South Korea that would bridge the gap between Japanese imperialism and Korean independence. Who were the Americans entrusted with this heavy responsibility and how creditably did they acquit themselves? I shall attempt to answer this question by looking at the manpower we had to work with, noting the strange mixture of motives that animated the diverse groups of persons who found themselves struggling with baffling political, economic, cultural, and technical problems. My appraisal has not been sentimentally mellowed by time since it is essentially the same as a military-government typology I outlined quite soon after leaving Korea in the autumn of 1948.[1]

Even though I was trained as a cavalryman, in the days when cavalry meant boots, saddles, surcingles, and horses, and although one necessarily has the deepest loyalty to his original service, I have taken perhaps an even greater pride in my association with the army's units for civil affairs and with military government. We are all of us instinctively creative, and I suspect the keenest satisfaction we derive is from exercising whatever innovative capacity we possess. Despite a few historical precedents,

[1] My analysis of military-government personnel types was first sketched in a paper I read at a meeting of the Military Government Association in New York City on December 9, 1950.

160

military government during and immediately after World War II was something essentially new to the United States army. As a consequence, all of us involved in it had to puzzle out our probable tasks and help design tentative organizations, only to discover that the real jobs were often very different from those we had imagined, or to learn belatedly that the personnel requirements were far different from the ones that had been preplanned. But, for better or for worse, we were the innovators. Collectively, therefore, we are entitled to take whatever credit may be due provided we remember that we must also shoulder most of the responsibility for the mistakes, blunders, and shortcomings of military government as it evolved.

On balance I think we can conclude, without vanity, that there were more hits than misses. We did a fairly good job although sometimes I wonder how we did it. For despite our several specialties, in which we had considerable technical competence, we were really all amateurs in military government. Most of us were reasonably diligent and conscientious; our chief fault was that we were inclined to view new problems not through the window of broad governmental experience but through the peepholes of our much narrower specialties. I say we probably got more hits than misses, and I think this is rather remarkable when one remembers how often we were shooting in all directions! Each man, it seems, had his favorite target, for even presumably homogeneous technical groups had great difficulty in agreeing on their objectives. I have the profoundest admiration for individualism, but there are, I submit, times and places when its free exercise may not be the best recipe for attaining certain objectives.

The most typical shortcoming of military-government officers particularly as I observed them in Korea was an overinfatuation with the importance of their civilian specialties. They seemingly could not appreciate that fertilizer procurement, codification of law, or radio broadcasting was only a small component of an organized government. Consequently, instead of each specialist addressing himself to the all-important task of operating a government which would achieve a tolerable balance and proportion among its many activities, and instead of doing his best to ensure that essential activities were properly coordinated, each set about with missionary zeal to commit the largest possible share of available funds for fertilizer, codification of law, or radio broadcasting. Without guile, these overzealous specialists built up their little empires, choosing subordinates who agreed with their views and measuring the ability of Koreans not in terms of their intelligence, political acceptability, or over-all training as civil servants, but only in terms of their interest in fertilizer, codification of law, or radio broadcasting. The result of this was a continuous internal battle among the specialists, needless albeit bitter; a never-ending attempt to "sell" the military governor on certain far-reaching recommendations; a ceaseless attempt to co-opt men and money so that a particular segment of the economy could be favored; and a tendency to judge the governed people by the way in which they responded to the stimuli of these sectarian proposals.

I think in all fairness, however, I should make it plain that the "honest specialists," however myopic, ought not be confused with the "big idea boys." The "honest specialists" were thoroughly competent in their own fields. They could compute precisely the amount of N or P_2O_5 or K_2O that should be applied to obtain certain crops.[2] They knew how to codify the laws, or how to calculate the listening contours of their broadcasting stations. The "big idea boys" in contrast, by some clairvoyance, without bothering to study the culture of an occupied area, were ready to assert just what the people of that country should do to be miraculously saved from all future sorrows. They should raise peas or hairy vetch, instead of rice; they should mine gold rather than coal; or they should build a chain of tourist hotels. It did not matter, of course, that the proponents of these schemes had never raised a pound of hairy vetch, dug an ounce of gold, or built a tourist cabin. What they really were doing was to invent romantic, easy solutions for the tough daily problems they could not solve.

Fortunately, the "big idea boys" were seldom bitter-enders; they willingly shifted from one dream project to another. In fact their proposals seldom got much beyond the talk-and-imagine stage. In this respect they contrast sharply with the activities of the "get things going" fraternity. Frantically impatient, this type of military-government officer had no concern about whether the economy could afford to get certain types of business going or not. Activity was apparently its own justification. Catch fish whether you can or cannot sell them, lend money to locomotive factories whether anyone knows how to build locomotives or not. Stimulate production was their watchword. And away they went! Before anyone knew what was cooking, they had embarked on fourteen-year programs to raise mulberry trees to feed silkworms to produce silk to sell competitively abroad. Costs and prices did not seem to figure in their calculations. The one thing they did insist on was plenty of GARIOA money for their urgently needed supplies and equipment. Specifications could be rather general as we discovered in Korea, much too late, if I may say so. When war came, and the 8th Army took over the port of Pusan in the summer of 1950, it was imperative that all the warehouses on the piers be completely emptied so that a huge volume of military supplies could be accommodated. That

[2] Dr. Wilhelm Anderson, chairman of our National Economic Board in 1947–48, told me that Japanese agronomical tests had demonstrated that one ton of nitrogen with appropriate amounts of P_2O_5 and K_2O would produce, on irrigated land, ten tons of additional rice.

was when we discovered what the "get things going" enthusiasts had been doing back in '46 and '47. Yes, here were 254 drums of fishnet preservative that the Koreans refused to use; 243,000 fishnet floats that the Koreans said were useless; 542 bales of manila netting and 960 bales of cotton netting that would have been serviceable only if the Koreans had had trawlers, which they did not have. Nor was this all: there were machine parts scaled in inches instead of centimeters, fittings that would not fit, large quantities of expensive but useless good intentions, all so urgently requisitioned only to clutter up the all-too-limited warehouse space. Not all the projects of the "get things going" school were wrong. Probably more were right than wrong, but even when this was the case, there were other mischievous consequences. "Getting things going" usually called for recurring imports of raw materials in sizable amounts: cotton, wool, lumber, sulphide pulp, petroleum products, or coal. Here, quite unintentionally, the "get things going" group committed the United States to very large recurring fiscal undertakings, and misled the people of liberated areas into believing that the United States would continue indefinitely to supply whatever quantities of raw materials the economy might need.

Yet in most ways the "get things going" boys were nearer right than the "do it the American way" brotherhood. They at least were willing to admit that coastal people knew how to catch fish or were willing to let Koreans pull rather than push their saws when they were building a warehouse. The "do it the American way" boys had no patience with this sort of nonsense. They had to have steam shovels and sheep-foot packers to build a half mile of road. They insisted on electric adding machines even though Orientals won every competition between Americans using adding machines and Asians using an old-fashioned abacus. On American standards they designed refugee housing for Koreans that cost ten or twenty times as much as wholly acceptable Korean housing needed to cost, because Korean houses are framed with round poles rather than sawed lumber, have walls made of bamboo and clay rather than matched boards, and use thatch for roof instead of asphalt shingles. But for this group there could be no compromise; the only "good" way was the American way. As a consequence, masses of complicated machinery were brought in that Koreans could not be expected to operate, repair, or maintain. And what a prodigal waste of manpower resulted. Obviously it took a lot of Americans to train people in occupied or liberated areas to work in new and unfamiliar ways, whether it be railroad building, coal mining, or bookkeeping. And the pathetic thing was that the "do it the American way" group never could understand why they had so much trouble getting results. It never seemed to dawn on them that there was more than one way to saw a two-by-four!

The "do it the American way" boys had high enough standards of integrity; they wanted to get a job done swiftly and competently. What they failed to grasp was that appropriate technology is a resultant of a nation's culture, education, population density, and rate of capital formation, not something that can be changed overnight or quickly readjusted. We discovered in Korea that thoroughly good railways could be built entirely with hand labor, and that it was far and away the best plan to let the Koreans do the job in familiar and time-tested ways. The "do it the American way" type of military-government officer, by reason of his cocksure conviction that there was only one way to do things, failed to appreciate the real ability of the people of liberated or occupied areas. Whether French, Belgian, Italian, or Japanese, they were to him odd, stupid, and unteachable. His impulse, therefore, was to let Americans do most of the work which should properly have been assigned to the resident population. In consequence, large numbers of Americans were required, which in turn meant not only a waste of manpower but unnecessary expenditures for their logistic support. But I think the most serious consequence was that fewer members of the indigenous work force were purposefully and constructively employed than would have been possible, leaving a large number to engage in tasks of lesser importance and in black-market operations.

Whether such unsatisfactory consequences of military government might ensue were of little or no interest to another breed of military-government officers whom I can best describe as the "Let 'er roll, we won't be here long" variety. Their casual attitude was, as I see it, blameworthy on two scores. In the first place, they paid little serious attention to the work for which they had been hired and for which they were being paid. In the second place, their indifference to the long-run effects of their actions often had a deteriorating if not a positively damaging effect on the economy which they were partially administering. I regret to say that I found quite a number of this variety wherever I went. They did not worry about whether bank credit was dangerously overextended; they expected to be on their way home long before the inflation they had helped create became rampant. Consequently it was virtually impossible to convince them that it was their duty to turn down loan applications, to be sparing in the use of scarce indigenous commodities, or to adhere strictly to authorized wage rates. If I speak with some feeling about the "Let 'er roll, we won't be here long" fellowship, it is because the Korea Program Division of the Economic Cooperation Administration (which it became my responsibility to direct after I left Korea) inherited the confusion that some military-government officers had so irresponsibly caused. For the "Let 'er roll" boys were by no means as passive as the title I give them would imply. Like the "honest specialists," they were doers. The trouble was that they could not waste time or thought worrying about the long-run consequences of what they were doing. In this regard, they differed markedly from the "Let's not take this seriously" crowd, for whom military government was an enjoyable, interesting sinecure. Pleasantly and agreeably they went through the motions of any task assigned them. But quitting time was a sacred hour which they observed with unfailing exactitude. The very idea of working after hours was foreign to their outlook, and homework was even more unthinkable. Their motto, if they may be said to have had one, would surely have been: "Sufficient unto the day is the evil thereof."

In marked contrast were the "Why not make a career of this" group, who tried to entrench themselves so deeply that no one could ever pry them out. They were diligent in their work in the hope that they would become indispensable. They were even more concerned with establishing their homes in a stay-the-rest-of-our-lives fashion; indeed a comfortable house for their wives and kiddies was their chief ambition. They were the ones, therefore, who brought all their furniture to Korea, Japan, or Germany, who prided themselves on their staff of servants, and who sat up late at night planning how they would modernize their overseas houses and really settle down to the joys of domestic felicity. They were not necessarily "operators" themselves, but they lost no opportunity to court favor with "operators" so that they might get more than their share of furniture, plumbing fixtures, or lumber. That cement was critically scarce in a governed economy was often forgotten by the "Why not make a career out of this" group if they needed some to build a tennis court or a swimming pool. They were true Anglo-Saxons whose chief glory was in their homes.

The home lovers were also great shoppers and collectors, who, in a matter of weeks, became authorities on Meissen, Imari, or Royal Copenhagen porcelain, on Korean chests, or on Persian rugs. But they were not the only emergent "connoisseurs." Subtle and highly critical artistic judgment never was so quickly developed as among military-government personnel. With condescending hauteur, the "connoisseurs" would survey the shelves of the art dealers' shops in their daily after-work perambulations. For the most part these new interests were wholesome and educational. It was only when the temptations became too strong that the accumulators, shoppers, collectors, and connoisseurs were on slippery ground. Then, alas, they began to play too near the edges of the currency-control regulations and not only brought discredit on themselves but set rather bad examples for the occupied population. But like the "Why not make a career of this" group, all the eager collectors were thinking of a home somewhere filled with artistic treasures.

A beautiful art-filled home, however, had no allure for the "Cook's tourist" breed of military-government officer who spent most of his stationary time in planning his next journey. For the most part he was in motion, ever making an inspection, a survey, or a reconnaissance. With his Leica camera to record each interesting sight, he would sally forth by train, sedan, jeep, or airplane. For some strange reason, his duties frequently made it necessary for him to visit distant headquarters. If he was in Norway, something would require a visit to Sweden, Denmark, or France. If he was stationed in Germany, there were urgent reasons why he must go to Brussels or London. Obviously someone had to liaise with other headquarters; obviously someone from Korea had to survey the surplus property in Iwo Jima, Saipan, Manila, or Honolulu. Nor were these insistent travelers attracted only to headquarters cities in neighboring countries. Their interests were geographically microscopic as well as macroscopic. Remote and inaccessible villages had their problems that someone must take care of. By odd coincidence these little places, hidden away in mountain valleys, seemed to possess the more beautiful Buddhist temples, or were otherwise rich in cultural lore. But whatever the pilgrimage, the "Cook's tourist" always had a good reason for going. I had an agricultural officer in Norway whose peregrinations always seemed imperatively necessary. He had traveled throughout the country, investigating the timber the Germans had cut, estimating the fertilizer needed, or looking for fodder for famished cattle. When all plausible excuses had been exhausted, he brought me a letter signed by the minister of agriculture requesting him to make an extensive trip throughout Norway to round up the war dogs that the Germans had unleashed and which were allegedly destroying calves, sheep, and poultry. It was futile to ask "Is this travel necessary," since I knew the parade of arguments he would advance. But when he returned from his two-week journey I had the temerity to say, "Tell me quite honestly, Major, did you find many dogs?" "Colonel," he said, "this time I am going to come clean; I did not see a single dog."

I need scarcely explain how propensity for tourism resembled the activities of the ubiquitous "operators" who were ever with us. They were the boys who had two cars when most of us had none, steaks when the rest of us ate Spam. They could no more be excluded from military government than from any other organization. They represent not incurable selfishness, but merely reprehensible pettiness which led them to seek little, unimportant advantages. They had the tip-off that made it possible for them to be first in line at the PX. They were the "chow hounds" of military government who made life just a little harder for everyone else. They ultimately received their just reward: the disdain and the contempt of everyone who played the game fair.

In this swift parade of military-government types, I have tried to show many of our failings. In doing so I have quite intentionally neglected to mention our virtues. They are many, but it is appropriate, I think, that we should look at ourselves quite objectively to ascertain our major shortcomings. Perhaps our greatest sin was that we, like Peer Gynt, were only little sinners, deserving not some crushing punishment but only the humiliation of being cast into the button-mold of oblivion. What we probably forgot more often than we remembered was that millions of people judged the motives, the character, and the dependability of the United States by each and every one of our daily words and deeds.

Beginning in December of 1946, when members of the Korean Interim Legislative Assembly of ninety members, half elected, half appointed,[3] began their deliberations, a very earnest effort to Koreanize the entire government became our main concern. The courts were presently Koreanized and then, in February of 1947 we rather dramatically reorganized the executive branch. On a chosen day all our military-government officers below the level of the deputy military governor turned over their desks to their understudies and became "advisers" to those Koreans who had been selected to be section heads, bureau chiefs, department directors, or provincial governors. At my suggestion a political liberal, Ahn Chai Hong,[4] was chosen as civil administrator, and by a new ordinance dealing with the reorganization of our government I became the "chief adviser to the government of Korea." The South Korean interim government (SKIG), of which General Lerch had dreamed, at long last had come into being. In our innocence we had rather assumed that the newly installed Korean officials, whom we had selected chicfly because they seemed to possess technical or administrative competence, would avoid political affiliation and concern themselves primarily with public administration. This we soon learned was a vain hope. More and more our interim government came under pressure from ambitious Korean political leaders. Before we knew what had happened we found that arch-conservatives were in control of all important positions in both the Police and the Justice departments; and that Ahn Chai Hong, although formally occupying a position

---

[3] When an effort to let the Koreans elect an Interim Legislature led to a dominance of right-wing candidates, it was decided, with Washington concurrence, that General Hodge should appoint half of the Assembly members, thereby ensuring a broader political representation. The composition of the Assembly has been carefully analyzed by George M. McCune, *Modern Korea* (Cambridge, Mass.: Harvard University Press, 1950), pp. 78–80.

[4] Before the arrival of American troops in September 1945, Lyuh Woon Heung and Ahn Chai Hong had formed the "Preparatory Association for Establishing the Nation," in the hope of bringing important Korean leaders together, whatever their political convictions, in order to preserve order and ultimately to effect a transition of political authority from the Japanese to a Korean republic.

tantamount to prime minister, was not able to obtain cooperation from the rightists in the government and little encouragement from leftists, who had been largely ignored in our selection of Korean understudies.

To many of us in key positions it seemed increasingly necessary to do something decisive to offset the growing influence of the extreme right, something to attract liberal and left-of-center support. We therefore took counsel with Koreans whose judgment we trusted and they agreed with us that it might be a shrewd maneuver to invite the well-recognized left-of-center leader Lyuh Woon Heung to take some important governmental post. At what we thought was a skillfully disguised secret meeting at Ch'angdok palace, we agreed that I should discuss this possibility with Lyuh and, since it did not seem tactful to invite him to come openly to my office in the capitol, we decided that he would be asked to visit me at my house. My wife and my son had arrived in Korea in November 1946, and we had been assigned one of the large brick houses that our American housing authorities had rented from the Presbyterian Missionary Society to whom a whole hilltop compound belonged. As if it were yesterday, I remember how impatiently I waited, with my interpreter, that afternoon of July 19, 1947. I had been told by messenger that Lyuh would come about four o'clock. Four o'clock came, four thirty, and then a furiously driven car swerved into the muddy lane leading up the hill to our house. Mired down, the car could go no further, but a man jumped out and ran stumbling up the hill. Breathlessly he told me that Lyuh had been assassinated less than a half mile from my house. His driver had slowed to round a traffic circle, and at that moment an assassin jumped on the rear bumper and shot Lyuh through the rear window.

The rightist press blamed the murder on the Communists, the leftist press accused the rightists. Lyuh was not the only aspirant politician to meet a violent death. Five months later a rightist Korean leader, Chang Duk Soo, answered a knock on his door late one night and was shot in cold blood by an assassin dressed in a policeman's uniform.[5] It began to dawn on us that Korean politicians, playing for high stakes, might resort to far more desperate measures than we had foreseen, and from the date of Lyuh's murder we found it necessary to take most careful precautions to protect the lives of some of our Korean officials, particularly Ahn Chai Hong, whose courage in continuing to serve as civil administrator I greatly admired. What an unpleasant life he lived. When the time came for him to leave his office each evening his escort had already arrived. Four police waited outside our joint anteroom to escort him to his jeep. Rather jauntily Ahn would set out with one policeman on either side,

[5] Kim Koo, the tough, pock-marked revolutionary who had headed the Korean exiles in China, survived until June 26, 1949, when he too was murdered.

another preceding him, and the fourth following. Three jeeps with motors running stood on the entrance ramp of the capitol, one in which Ahn would ride, one to precede, one to follow, each loaded with armed men.

Because two contentious and fruitless meetings of the Joint U.S.-U.S.S.R. Commission [6] had ended in deadlock,[7] the Korean problem was laid before the General Assembly of the United Nations. In a resolution passed on November 14, 1947, the Assembly declared that "the Korean people themselves should create a provisional government through free and secret election of representatives and that subsequently foreign troops should be withdrawn." [8] Our Korean departments of Information and of Justice proceeded to make all necessary preparations for holding such "free and secret elections" in South Korea, and in January 1948, the United Nations commission appointed to supervise the elections arrived in Seoul. Since the members of that commission were not allowed even to enter the Russian-occupied zone, it became quite clear that South Korea would presently have to be organized as a separate government. By the spring of 1948 all the necessary arrangements for the election of a Korean National Assembly had been made; and on May 10 millions of Korean men and women, 95 percent of the registered voters, went to improvised polls and cast their ballots. Wherever possible the United Nations commission had posted observers, and on the basis of their reports the commission certified that the election had been conducted with reasonable impartiality. The duly elected Korea National Assembly convened on May 31, and after long debate adopted a constitution for the Democratic Republic of Korea on July 12. Eight days later the Assembly elected Syngman Rhee president, and, after the Assembly had rejected his first choice, Rhee proposed that Lee Bum Suk be named prime minister, a nomination that the Assembly confirmed on Aug 3. A Korean government had been established. The next event was mainly ceremonial. On a platform in front of the capitol it was blistering hot that August 15, 1948, when Rhee was inaugurated and the United States military government in Korea formally ended.[9] We had already transferred our files and desks

[6] Created under the terms of the December 27, 1945, Moscow Agreement for the purpose of deciding how a provisional government for the whole of Korea should be formed.

[7] The first meetings of the commission were held between March 20 and May 8, 1946; the second group of meetings took place from May 22 to October 18, 1947.

[8] *Korea, 1945–1948: A Report on Political Developments and Economic Resources, with Selected Documents*, Department of State Publication 3305, Far Eastern Series 28 (Washington, D.C.: Government Printing Office, 1948), p. 122.

[9] General MacArthur who had not once bothered to visit Korea during our difficult military-government years came to share in the publicity. Quite a stir occurred when he discovered that his Bataan cap was missing, and the ceremonies were suspended until the symbolic headgear had been recovered.

to wooden buildings in the capitol compound, but after the ceremony I went upstairs to my former office to gather up a few remaining oddments. In the anteroom I met my secretary, Marie Spradlin, who, with tears running down her cheeks said, "Mrs. Rhee is in there, sitting at your desk." "It isn't my desk any more, my dear," I said. "Yes, I know," she replied, "but it's not Mrs. Rhee's desk either." But in many ways Miss Spradlin had misjudged the situation.

Although we had formalistically turned over the reins of government on the third anniversary of South Korea's liberation from Japanese rule, the actual business of vesting the Koreans with authority and, more particularly, of endowing them with the vast amount of property we had held in trust for the Korean people took about two more months. We had, fortunately, made careful preparations for the transfer of power and property quite some time in advance. I had spent almost six weeks in Washington, April 6 to May 17, 1948, making these arrangements, and I note from a report I prepared on my return to Seoul that I attended seventy-two conferences during my stay in Washington soliciting the views and opinions of eighty-four staff officers in the departments of Army and State. My report lists eleven main tasks with which I was mainly concerned. First in importance was the preparation of a coordinated policy paper to govern the transfer of governmental responsibility from USAMGIK to a new Korean government. But there were many other urgencies: finding an acceptable way for shifting to the Korean government the obligations we had incurred to the Foreign Liquidation Commission, ascertaining what could be done to alleviate the electric-power shortage, working out ways and means for facilitating trade between Korea and Japan, expediting the procurement of necessary supplies so there would be no critical shortage when the Koreans took over, relieving the currency famine without estopping the Koreans from issuing their own new currency soon after the takeover. Other priorities included recruiting a faculty for a Teacher-Training Institute and reaching agreement about how certain specially qualified military-government personnel could be transferred to an aid mission, a problem that involved discussions concerning what agency might appropriately assume operational responsibility for post-transfer Korean aid. It should be recalled that the Economic Cooperation Administration, which ultimately did accept responsibility for the Korean aid program, had not yet begun to function. I flew the Pacific on my way to Washington with Paul G. Hoffman, who had just been appointed the administrator of ECA, but neither he nor I then had any inkling that within six months the Korea program would be a part of ECA and I would be on Hoffman's staff directing its operations in Washington.

On my return to Korea I devoted most of my time to making preparations for an orderly transfer of authority to the government that was being formed after the May 10 elections. Immediately after Rhee's inauguration, when it was agreed that three spokesmen from either side would be appointed to carry on these transfer negotiations, I assumed responsibility for organizing and staffing the United States Negotiating Committee with interpreters, court reporters, secretaries, and legal counsel, and preparing the necessary documentation. Supervising the compilation of an inventory of the property we proposed to alienate proved to be a very complex task, since, as successors to the Japanese, we had come into possession of about a fifth of the paddy land of South Korea; well over a hundred thousand houses; not hundreds but thousands of factories, mines, quarries, and shipyards; the assets of banks, insurance companies, and other financial institutions; and a great many other enterprises. More than that, the American army had brought in 101 locomotives, over 200,000 railway ties, and a large amount of electrical equipment; it had built barracks, warehouses, tank farms, and other facilities, as well as dependent housing for the families of military and civilian personnel. Washington decided that all this property should also be included in our massive inventory volume.

Two issues arose to complicate the negotiations. The first should have caused but little trouble yet for reasons we never could understand it seemed to worry the Koreans greatly. When USAMGIK had control over South Korea it entered into contracts with the Foreign Liquidation Commission for the purchase, on credit, of surplus military supplies from the United States government. In the Philippines and on Pacific islands we bought ships, vehicles, engineering supplies, clothing – a great variety of things at bargain prices ranging from 20 to 30 percent of their cost. As in all other OFLC contracts, there was a provision, in conformity with a proposal of Senator William Fulbright, that repayment need not be in foreign exchange but could be in local currency made available for the maintenance of Americans, students and professors, who came to be known as "Fulbright students" and "Fulbright professors." President Rhee was very reluctant to agree to this extremely generous arrangement although he finally gave his consent.[10]

The other issue proved to be far more troublesome. The new Korean government had made no provision for a Ministry of Supply, and since the United States planned to support the Korean economy with a fairly

[10] Some of the surplus property arrived in deplorable condition so that sometimes several vehicles had to be cannibalized in order to obtain one operable machine. A few instances of this kind gave the impression that the United States was unloading junk on naive buyers.

sizable aid program, our negotiators, General Gardiner Helmick,[11] Dr. Arthur Bunce,[12] and Owen Jones,[13] quite properly took the position that the United States government had to have a responsible Korean official with cabinet rank who could receive and allocate our aid supplies. They went farther than that, insisting that they should be allowed to name the minister of supply to ensure that he would be a man who had the experience and the integrity to receive and distribute aid goods to the value of many millions of dollars. On this issue the negotiations were deadlocked for quite some time but, realizing that the aid his government so desperately needed hung in the balance, Rhee finally agreed to our proposal. General Helmick thereupon asked me whom we should propose as minister of supply and when I suggested Lee Tong Chae he enthusiastically agreed. Lee Tong Chae had been our "controller of commodities," a very competent official who had supervised our difficult and highly controversial rice-collection and -distribution apparatus. When our recommendation had been made abundantly clear, Rhee agreed to create a Ministry of Supply and to name Lee Tong Chae as supply minister. But, as I shall explain in the next chapter, this was by no means the end of that story.

My greatest regret during these closing days of USAMGIK was that the main architect of our Koreanization program did not live to see the end of the vast operation which he had dreamed about, planned, and so conscientiously guided. But our military governor, General Archer Lerch, one of the very ablest of our regular army officers, had died in September 1947 of a heart attack undoubtedly brought on by his unceasing work. His successor, General William Dean, for all his ability, never really took General Lerch's place, since he concerned himself primarily with military problems, leaving all too many of the governmental problems either unsettled or hastily disposed of without regard to the possible effect of quick decisions on the very delicate Korean political situation. On the other hand General Dean probably sensed better than I the growing danger of North Korean infiltration. By early 1948 more than two million migrants had crossed the 38th parallel or otherwise entered South

[11] General Helmick, who had been deputy military governor, was immensely popular with the Koreans because he displayed such unfailing kindness and courtesy. The Koreans nicknamed him "the soft as silk general."

[12] Bunce had headed a State Department advisory group attached to General John R. Hodge's headquarters.

[13] When Jones turned over the Department of Commerce to me in July 1946, he returned to the States, where he was separated from the navy and joined the foreign service. The Department of State then assigned him to Korea where he was temporarily made available to USAMGIK to head the National Economic Board when James Shoemaker left Seoul to assume his duties as a professor at the University of Hawaii.

Korea.[14] Even though most of these "refugees" had come through our elaborate networks of collecting points and reception centers, where they were not merely registered and immunized but carefully interrogated and screened, no doubt many hundreds of well-disciplined agents were able to masquerade as escapees from North Korea.

What can be said of the quality of life that Americans and their dependents enjoyed in Korea? It varied widely, not merely in terms of the motives of the various types of people our large organization included but by reason of chance, circumstance, and events over which we had no control. Our housing for the most part was structurally adequate, consisting of sequestrated Japanese houses, rented missionary property, or newly constructed "dependent housing." The trouble lay in the inability of USAMGIK to ensure heat, light, and water. Heating difficulties stemmed from the poor quality of Korean coal; but this handicap was minor in comparison with the constant inconvenience resulting from lack of water and electricity. The swift increase in the population of Seoul, a 60 percent increase in a three-year period, put such a strain on water facilities that those of us who lived on the top of a hill were lucky if we could accumulate, for all purposes, three or four inches of water a day in our bathtub. Two or three people had to use the same scanty bath water. Our greatest inconvenience, however, resulted from the action of the North Korean authorities who in 1947 intermittently cut off the electricity supply we had been receiving from the North Korean hydro plants [15] and then on May 14, 1948, definitively shut it off. During the winter of 1946–47 my wife, my son, and I used up a whole gross of plumber's candles in our household, and I did my hours of evening homework by the light of a Coleman lantern.

Schools for our children were unsatisfactory despite the efforts of the responsible authorities. Teachers had to be recruited locally for the most part, and when a captain who taught the high school science courses was called away for more urgent military duties the science classes did not meet. Our cultural activities were limited, but people truly interested in the Korean milieu found very interesting and instructive outlets for their curiosity. By modest USAMGIK financial assistance I was able to save the classical Korean orchestra [16] which would otherwise have been disbanded,

[14] As of April 1948 official figures indicated that 2,096,047 Koreans had entered South Korea. Since a sizable number of the inbound migrants did not clear through our entry stations, the arrivals exceeded these official figures. For details, see United States Military Government in Korea, *South Korean Interim Government Activities* (published monthly by the National Economic Board), April 1948, p. 5.

[15] Monthly variations in electricity received from north of 38° during 1947 ranged from a low of 31,000,000 kilowatts to a high of 62,900,000. For the monthly figures, see ibid., p. 116.

[16] The orchestra consisted of lutes, recorders, Chinese violins, and a set of

and I helped organize support for the modern Seoul symphony orchestra by persuading Americans to act as patrons. There were compensations for our domestic frustrations in delightful Korean receptions at Ch'angdok palace, in performances of talented Korean dancers, in the staging of a lovely Korean opera, *Spring Fragrance*, and in dinner parties to which our Korean friends invited us. Yet for all that, life in Korea was not easy; it could scarcely be called a "ride on the gravy train." Fortunately most of our fifteen hundred military-government officials and their wives responded to the challenges that confronted them in most commendable ways. My wife, for example, ran our military-government library, spending long hours at her work so that both Americans and Koreans could have a pleasant, comfortable place to read and relax.

There were, to be sure, irritating events that embittered and rankled us. Despite the stationing of police near our houses, pilferage and burglary could not be prevented. While a policeman stood at the front door of our house, our icebox, in the rear entry, was cleaned out in broad daylight. A new three-speed bicycle that I purchased in Japan for my son lasted just two days before it was stolen, and the electric fans were pilfered from my office. Our most costly loss occurred when accomplished thieves patiently removed the putty from a glass pane of a large living-room window and entered our house, conducting their operations so silently that we heard nothing although we slept directly over the living room and our bedroom door was open. Unhurried, the thieves sat down by our coal fire, sorted out my wife's PX card and driver's license, courteously leaving these essentials but taking a lovely handbag and the money it contained. They took all my son's clothing from a downstairs closet and dozens of tins and packages of food from our kitchen. Most families had similar losses. When I complained about these Korean peccadilloes to my missionary neighbors, somewhat to my surprise I was told that the Koreans were poor and therefore they could scarcely be blamed for stealing. Reluctantly I built a ten-strand barbed-wire fence around our house lot and padlocked our gates.

Our relations with the missionaries can best be described as ambivalent. We depended on them for information, for recommending interpreters, and for advice. But we could not fulfill their ill-concealed hopes that we would design our programs to support their evangelical work. Obviously we could not respond to these oft-repeated suggestions when only about 2 percent of the Koreans could be considered Christians. When information came to us that some of the missionaries were advising their rural parishioners not to deliver rice to our collection points, and when we had

L-shaped marble slabs of varying sizes and thicknesses which when struck with padded hammers produced dulcet tones.

174

indisputable evidence that some missionaries were evading our foreign-exchange regulations, General Lerch decided that we had better have a frank talk with them.[17] We therefore invited all the missionaries to a meeting, and I remember vividly that afternoon when General Lerch and I met with them in Room 207 of the capitol. There sat the Irish fathers who had stayed in Korea during the war, the French and the American Catholics, the Presbyterians, Baptists, Lutherans, and Methodists, the Seventh-Day Adventists, the Anglicans, all in solemn clerical dress except the Salvation Army representatives who wore their uniforms. General Lerch welcomed them, told them that in a sense we were all missionaries. He then introduced me and, after offering some excuse, left. I practically knocked a hundred and twenty-five or more missionaries off their chairs when I began my talk by saying that we were having much more trouble with the missionaries than with the Koreans. The Emersonian approach accomplished its purpose. They listened to me when I explained in no uncertain terms that they must stop advising Koreans not to deliver rice, that we would not hesitate to prosecute missionaries who engaged in black-market operations whether in commodities or in foreign exchange. I certainly did not increase my popularity with the missionaries by my blunt declarations, but from that day on there was a very decided change in the degree of cooperation which we obtained.

In a very thoughtful and penetrating chapter of his excellent book on Korea, Professor Osgood has contrasted the Russian and the American occupation of Korea.[18] He points out that whereas the Russians in their zone were supplied with "a large body of trustworthy agents and interpreters, the United States army landed with practically none."[19] And whereas the Russian occupying authorities largely shared the food and facilities of their Korean associates, the majority of Americans "created a strange and misleading spectacle by their enforced isolation and superior attitudes."[20] I do not propose to quarrel with Professor Osgood's appraisal; it is, I'm afraid, a pretty accurate picture of what happened. And yet for all our shortcomings, our all-too-evident failings, our varied Gyntian weaknesses, we did prevent the Russians from enveloping the whole of Korea. Despite all our blunders, we did keep the South Korean economy operating at a tolerable level. The 17,000,000 people already there in

[17] Not only had all missionary groups been allowed to return to Korea but they had been accorded commissary and PX privileges. In the opinion of quite a few Americans the missionaries abused these privileges by releasing altogether too many commissary and PX supplies to their Korean brethren.

[18] *The Koreans and Their Culture* (New York: Ronald Press, 1951), chapter 16.

[19] Ibid., p. 316.

[20] Ibid., p. 323.

1945 and the 3,000,000 who came into South Korea from Japan and from North Korea in 1945–48 were fed, clothed, and sheltered. Despite the lampoon that described Korea as the land of "the morning calm and the afternoon riot," public order was maintained. Indeed if one wants to look on the bright side, as I did in a rather eulogistic description of our accomplishments in a public address I gave in the summer of 1950,[21] one can make out a case for a fairly creditable performance by our very ill-prepared personnel. Our successes in Korea can be attributed to the degree of cooperation we were able to achieve between the Korean people, the Department of State, USAMGIK, SCAP, the United Nations, and, after 1948, the Economic Cooperation Administration.[22] Despite the allegations of North Korea and of Soviet countries that our program was exploitative and essentially negative, I think the record will show that up to the time of the North Korean invasion (June 25, 1950) steady progress had been made in rehabilitating the South Korean economy.

The record is available for all to read. It tells a dramatic story of progress in the face of great difficulty: in the establishment of representative government; in the production of food, textiles, minerals; in the expansion of exports; in the widening of educational facilities; in the improvement in public health; and in the building up of national solidarity and civic responsibility. I shall never again witness such an outpouring of responsible effort or such dedication of intellectual, physical, and spiritual forces to a collective task as I witnessed in the years that I worked with the Korean people. Admittedly we were inexperienced, Americans and Koreans alike, but how could we have been otherwise? Korea had been a Japanese colony for forty years, administered by the Japanese for their own benefit. The Koreans, however gifted or able, had been given few or no opportunities in government or business. But the Koreans knew their country, their people, their traditions, and we, the inexperienced Americans, learned more from them, I suspect, than they did from us.

We tackled our work together in a sincere effort at mutuality, the task of governing the fifteenth largest nation in the world and the equally complex duty of operating a circumstantially socialized economy since we were obligated to take over all Japanese properties and hold them in trust for the Korean people. Our functions were so many that it would be impossible to prepare a checklist that would summarize all our activities. For obviously no one could describe all the things that a hundred thousand

[21] This address which I gave at Lennox, Massachusetts, on August 20, 1950, and which I entitled "The Dynamics of Democracy," elicited a gracious editorial in the *New York Times* four days later.

[22] The contributions of the Economic Cooperation Administration began with the creation of the Korea Program Division in late November 1949, the activities of which I will describe in my next chapter.

Korean civil servants and three thousand American advisers and assistants accomplished. Yet in our joint activities Koreans and Americans operated across the whole panorama of governmental functions: in agriculture, mining, public health, transportation, education, public works, and law. We laid the foundations of an agricultural program which made it possible for South Korea to feed its rapidly growing population. We repaired the railway system, brought in 101 new locomotives, and allowed Korean firemen, under supervision, to take over the throttles and run the locomotives, a privilege formerly reserved for Japanese engineers. With American help the Koreans rehabilitated power plants, reopened coal and metal mines, and immunized millions of people against cholera, thereby reducing the incidence of that dread disease from 16,000 cases in 1946 to 24 cases in 1947. Meantime cotton mills were reactivated — some 300,000 spindles and 10,000 looms — as were over 1000 machine shops and 86 rubber factories. Foreign trade, which had ended completely in 1945, was gradually revived, particularly with Japan and Hong Kong, thereby building up modest foreign-exchange balances to help finance critically needed imports.

Among our other joint Korean-American operations can be listed the reopening (or establishment) of orphanages,[23] leprosariums, and agricultural colleges, the launching of a program of reforestation, and the continuation of work on 1470 flood-control and irrigation projects begun by the Japanese. All this was done despite persistent, vicious Communist interference that revealed itself in local terrorism, in the dynamiting of bridges, or in attempts to organize nationwide strikes. Yet during these years of military government we patiently tried to find a negotiatory basis for unifying North and South Korea only to be confronted with Russian double-talk, obstructionism, and shameless propagandistic distortion of our sincere purposes. When the Second Joint Commission (May 22–October 18, 1947) like the First (March 20–May 8, 1946) ended in a stalemate, the North Koreans attempted to collapse the South Korean economy by cutting off our (imported) electricity supply. The joint American-Korean efforts to meet this emergency included careful supervision of the few South Korean thermal and hydro plants and the bringing in of a power barge (to Inchon) and a power ship (to Pusan).

Our program for the economic reconstruction of South Korea, suddenly torn out of the prewar economy of Japan, Korea, and Manchuria and further hampered by the division of Korea at the 38th parallel, was in my judgment imaginative, well conceived, and comprehensive; it placed more Korean children in schools than had ever been in classrooms before; it took over all the property in Korea of the Japanese government, the

[23] In this work we received excellent cooperation from missionary organizations.

Japanese army, and Japanese nationals and held it in trust for a properly elected Korean government; and it effected sweeping land reform and saw 700,000 acres of farmland sold on a liberal payment plan to 588,000 tenants. I have said that I have never witnessed such a dedication of people to a task as I did in Korea. At breakfast, luncheon, or dinner the key personnel of USAMGIK talked about Korea; weekdays, Sundays, and holidays we worked. The rehabilitation of South Korea may not have been a challenge to all our American personnel but it surely was to some. One American employee contributed a prize-winning bull so that the Korean herds could be improved. Another brought to Korea, at his own expense, $700 worth of lespediza clover seed to seed down eroding hillsides. These are only a couple of examples of the way in which some Americans reacted to this challenge.

The program of economic development which we could attempt was, to be sure, not as far-reaching as we would have liked. Congressional terms of reference restricted the United States army to short-range assistance to Korea, designed primarily to prevent undernutrition, disease, and unrest, and we were constantly accused of going far beyond these guidelines. Yet it was also the function of USAMGIK to facilitate an orderly transition from a Japanese administration to an independent Korean government. To this end we found it necessary to deviate somewhat from a strict construction of "Government and Relief in Occupied Territories." We realized we had to engage in a great deal of economic rehabilitation if the new Korean government was to be able to provide a tolerably satisfactory administration of its inherited capital plant and its other resources. That our preparatory work had not been in vain was proven by the achievements of the economy during the first year of Korean independence. Coal mining had increased to five times the 1946 output, cotton textile production had tripled, and the index of industrial production, summarizing the output of forty-four commodities, had doubled, 1949 over 1947. More than a hundred irrigation projects were completed, some fifty miles of railway extensions were built into coal-mining areas, and over 546,000,000 seedlings had been planted to reforest the denuded Korean hills; meantime, electric-power generation had reached about 73 percent of the total available before the cutoff of power from North Korea, a remarkable performance considering the technical difficulties. Food production had responded to generous American-financed fertilizer imports, and for the first time since liberation South Korea was not only self-sufficient in food but capable of exporting 100,000 metric tons of rice.

In view of these achievements, I said very frankly in my Lennox, Massachusetts, talk, I had been distressed by the misinformation that had been published about Korea. Duped by their own ignorance, or unwittingly repeating the Communist party-line propaganda, some writers, I said, had contrasted what they called the "dynamism" of the North Koreans with the "apathy" of the South Koreans. But I pointed out that the hasty judgment that the South Koreans would not fight, repeated so carelessly at the outset of the war, was no longer heard once the South Koreans had demonstrated their courage, perseverance, and dependability in the face of terrific attacks. Allegations continued to be made that the North Koreans appeared to have greater fervor to expand their regime than the South Koreans seemed to generate in defending theirs. Why, asked these critics, had not the Americans instilled a comparable crusading zeal in the minds of the South Koreans?

I took pains to answer this naive charge. "The Americans who worked in Korea," I said, "were not there to develop a variety of psychiatric fanaticism. Our purpose was to help the Korean people develop their own form of democracy, not some variant imposed from without. Because we believe in freedom as a way of life, one cannot expect Americans, brought up in this precious tradition, to engage in propagandistic distortions of the truth. They have too much respect for the dignity of the individual to be willing to train human beings to become half-crazed automatons." I argued that there was no need to doubt the devotion of the South Koreans. If they had shown none of the wild, adolescent chauvinism of the North Koreans, this merely demonstrated that they are well-balanced, normal people. "The so-called dynamism of Communist satellites," I said, "was cheap, shoddy merchandise that has been sold to unsuspecting people by the most odious system of mass deception that was ever invented." I asked my listeners to remember that tyranny is always dramatic, must be in fact, in order to persuade people that it is worth keeping. Democracy in contrast is never dramatic; it yields its incremental benefits to all citizens in a quiet, steady stream of social, economic, political, and cultural amelioration. It make no grandiose promises because it does not need to do so. It rests its case on accomplishments, not on glib promises.

The great decisions about Korea were, to be sure, not made by USAMGIK but at Yalta, Potsdam, and Moscow, in flimsy American-Russian "agreements" that were not really agreements at all; other decisions were made in Washington by changing State Department and Pentagon policy-makers; or in New York by the United Nations Security Council and the General Assembly. Those of us saddled with responsibility for implementing such policies ought not be blamed if the American occupation of Korea, as Professor Osgood has said, demonstrated that "a more difficult locale for experimentation could hardly have been selected," particularly when one considers that after two generations of exploitation the country had been "left in dire economic straits which even the Japanese could not resolve." The outcome of being cut in two by mutually suspicious occupying powers was that "the major portion" of Korea depended for guidance on "an occupying force few of whom had any meaningful preparation for the task or any wish to undertake it." Having said all this, with a graciousness that compensates for his less complimentary remarks, Professor Osgood went on to say that "it is a tribute to the American character that some tried so hard to meet the challenge and the responsibility." [24]

Even so, I'm not sure we tried hard enough. We accepted too many compromises that Washington authorities suggested. Too fearful of the Communists, we made concessions to the rightist elements and did little to prevent their infiltration into our Police and Justice departments.[25] To offset Rhee's storm troopers, disguised as voluntary members of a youth movement, we had allowed Lee Bum Suk, under our overt auspices, to form a youth movement of adults that by the end of 1947 may have included almost a half million members. Confused by the complex spectrum of Korean political cliques and parties, we found it difficult to know which factions to favor, which to ignore; and failing to recognize the basic philosophy of an ancient agrarian country, we sought, with far too much energy and impatience, to change and modernize a proud people who loved their traditions.

In 1969 at the East-West Center I was explaining some general principles of spatial reconstruction which form the basis of my most recent book [26] to a very distinguished University of London anthropologist, Raymond Firth. "But that's the trouble with you economists," he said; "you always want to change people. We anthropologists leave them alone and study them." This, to be sure, is a very wholesome and charitable attitude, but I suspect that if old underdeveloped countries are to find a truly meaningful place in a rapidly changing world community, they too must change. To do this they may need guidance, but our experience in Korea indicates that persons who dare to assume the difficult task of

---

[24] Osgood, *The Koreans and Their Culture*, pp. 301, 302.

[25] George M. McCune is very critical of our inability to restrain rightist elements. He points out that USAMGIK "endeavored to institute some reforms in working conditions and to encourage the labor movement to take shape along American lines" at the same time it "was prone to take a conservative or oppressive stand in the increasing labor difficulties generated by the inflation." As a result the "views and tactics of rightist Koreans became increasingly predominant in labor relations" and "the rightist-controlled police and rightist private organizations engaged in open terrorism of striking workers." *Korea Today*, pp. 161, 162.

[26] *The Organization of Space in Developing Countries* (Cambridge, Mass.: Harvard University Press, 1970).

180

charting the paths that may lead to a proper type of modernization need to study very carefully the cultural forces with which they must inescapably deal. Our task in Korea had overtones that many of our American executives could not possibly understand. The trouble was that our responsibility was not merely to serve as an interim government in an ordinary sense. Unwittingly, we had been loaded with the responsibility for liquidating an extensive, deeply entrenched system of Japanese economic imperialism and replacing it with the beginnings of a political, economic, and education system that would reflect the hopes and aspirations of the great majority of the Korean people. All I can say is that we tried.

12

GREAT HOPES
AND DISHEARTENING
FRUSTRATIONS
★★★★★★★★★★★★★★★★★★★★★★★★

WHEN a firm decision had been made by the State Department to request
a congressional appropriation for a Korean aid program, and when agreement had been reached with the Economic Cooperation Administration
that a Korea Program Division could be established under Paul G. Hoffman's direction in that agency, Arthur Bunce and I were summoned to
Washington for consultation in mid-September 1948. In a succession of
morning, afternoon, and evening meetings we explained our views about
the personnel needed for a suitable aid mission, the amount of annual
funds required, and the types of goods and services that would help
facilitate the earliest possible economic independence of the newly created
South Korean state. We met with State Department and Pentagon officials,
with Mr. Hoffman's closest policy advisers, and with his ECA experts on
agriculture, industry, transportation, and electric power. We described
the over-all Korean situation to the ECA advisory board and to the trade-
union representatives detailed to ECA by the American Federation of
Labor and the Congress of Industrial Organizations. To all these groups,
Bunce and I pointed out that if an aid program were to be undertaken
an adequate military perimeter for South Korea would be absolutely
necessary, since unless the United States stood ready to protect its investment, our efforts to create a viable economy in South Korea might tempt
the North Koreans to take aggressive action. A second point we emphasized was that the amount of aid would have to be substantial. Parsi-
monious driblets would not do because, with Korea divided at its 38th
parallel, sizable amounts of capital formation would be required to improve the South Korean economic prospects in agriculture, mining, fishing, and manufacturing.

My mother

My father

When I had curls

Our family and our new house near Orion

My college graduation

My college sweetheart

My pyramid team

Leading the parade

My wife and I in the 1920's

"And gladly teach"

Our eighteenth-century Stockbridge house

Planning the liberation of Norway

General Thorne decorates me with the O.B.E.

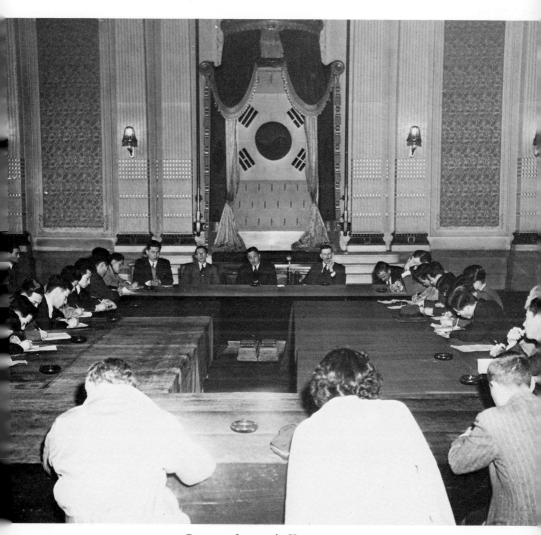

Press conference in Korea

With President Rhee and Ambassador Muccio in 1950

The pool and rose garden of our Belgrade house

A committee meeting in India

Academic marshal at Johns Hopkins (SAIS)

After being kept on tenterhooks for several days, Bunce and I were presently sent for. To his great joy, Bunce had been selected as chief of the ECA mission to Korea, and, to my complete satisfaction, I had been chosen to head the Korea Program Division of ECA in Washington. I knew that both the United States political adviser in Korea, Joseph E. Jacobs, and General John Hodge had warmly recommended me for a Washington assignment, but even so I was somewhat fearful that I might be asked to direct the aid program in Korea. Fortunately General Hodge settled that matter when he told Paul Hoffman that I would be much better assigned in Washington than in Seoul because I was "too hard on the Koreans."[1] Much as I admired the majority of Koreans, my difficult days as civil administrator and my trying experiences as chief adviser to the South Korean interim government had led me to hope for somewhat less hectic duties. Moreover, Bunce had far better qualifications than I for mission chief. First of all he had served six years in Korea (1928–34) as director of rural reconstruction for an international YMCA committee. Trained as an agricultural economist with a B.S. from Saskatchewan University and a Ph.D. from Wisconsin, he could understand the problems of an essentially agricultural country far better than I. His experience as a professor at Iowa State College (1937–43) and with the Federal Reserve Board in Washington (1944–45) further qualified him to undertake the difficult task of supervising a large aid program in Korea.

Our return trip to Korea was long and tiring. From Washington Bunce and I flew to Minneapolis where after a succession of two-hour delays that added up to twenty-six hours we finally took off for Anchorage. Here half the seats were removed from the C-45 to lighten the load before the hop to Shemya began. On that bleak Aleutian island we refueled before beginning the jump to Tokyo where, as usual, we boarded a bucket-seat C-47 for Seoul. Weary but happy we pitched into our next tasks, chief of which was to screen out the very best military-government officers whom we hoped to keep for the emergent ECA mission. We had agreed that we could make do with 150 mission members and, rather arbitrarily, we decided to keep 75 of our true and tested personnel and recruit 75 new people so we could not only have some fresh blood in our organization but hire certain necessary experts that we had heretofore lacked. Screening out 75 future mission members proved to be a difficult task. Some of the people we wanted to keep did not care to stay, whereas others about whom we had doubts used every possible device to ensure their selection.

[1] Very likely only Koreans whose requests I had denied protested to General Hodge. It is readily understandable why, after hearing so many complaints, he felt I was "too hard on the Koreans." I was indeed unbending when unreasonable demands were made.

Although there were a few quite troublesome cases, three of which I shall describe later, we succeeded in choosing nearly 75 outstanding future mission members.

Meantime, in close consultation with John Muccio, the newly appointed United States ambassador to Korea, and with Eric Biddle, an experienced State Department official who was sent to Korea to oversee the transition from a military to a civilian organization, Bunce selected two excellent old "Korea hands" as his deputies. Primary responsibility for program planning and over-all economic policy he entrusted to Wilhelm Anderson, an economist with a Chicago Ph.D. degree who had had long experience in the United States Department of Agriculture, and had succeeded Owen Jones as chairman of our USAMGIK National Economic Board. Fiscal policy and all monetary and financial matters became the responsibility of Allen Loren, who had served with distinction not merely as the United States Treasury representative to USAMGIK but as director of the Department of Finance and, after the creation of the South Korean interim government (SKIG), as adviser to the (Korean) director of the Department of Finance. In addition to these stalwarts, Bunce chose Robert A. Kinney as his special assistant, an excellent choice because of Kinney's exceptional knowledge of Korean economy, as well as his understanding of the Korean culture and language.

With the Korean end of our organizational planning well advanced, my family and I crossed the Pacific by army transport to San Francisco where I left my wife and son to drive across the continent while I hastened to Washington by air to set up the "backstop" for Bunce's mission, supervise the recruitment of the 75 "fresh blood" mission members, develop a defensible aid program, and make plans to justify the program before the appropriate congressional committees.[2]

For my own staff in the ECA Korea Program Division I selected experienced people whose work I had personally observed and in whom I could have complete confidence. For my deputy and senior program officer, I chose Dr. John W. Harriman, my old fellow student at Harvard and my close COSSAC associate in London, who as a colonel had been finance officer of the SHAEF mission to France in 1944.[3] For his assistant, I

[2] Normally four: the Foreign Affairs Committee of the House of Representatives, the Foreign Relations Committee of the Senate, and the House and Senate Appropriation committees. Special circumstances may require appearances before other committees; thus although ordinarily only members of Congress testify before the Rules Committee an exceptional situation made it necessary for me to make a statement to that committee and answer some searching questions.

[3] After his separation from the army Harriman was appointed a dean at Syracuse University. I had to enlist Paul Hoffman's aid to pry him loose from that job, but a direct appeal by Hoffman to the president of Syracuse did the trick. The trouble was that in Washington Harriman demonstrated his exceptional ability so quickly that

selected Fred Bunting, an Oxford fellow student of mine who also had served with COSSAC. My senior procurement officer, Ed Garwood, had been in Greece, where he had been confronted with problems similar to those we would face. As his assistant I was able to get Charley Spreyer split loose from the Pentagon, where he had served as a GARIOA procurement officer for Korea under Colonel Orville Baldwin, who had been our G-4 in Allied Land Forces Norway. My administrative officer, Carl Burness, had served in Tokyo, and since he had been one of the liaison officers between SCAP and USAMGIK, he had a very clear understanding of our Korean administrative problems. From SCAP also I recruited my statistician, Martin Daugherty, who had been a military-government officer in Italy, and who, in Japan, had prepared the data on Korea that appeared in the monthly "Summation" of nonmilitary activities of SCAP. Finally I persuaded Al Fessler, a first-class engineer who had served on the staff of our National Economic Board in Korea, to leave an idyllic life on a Michigan country estate and join my hard-working crew in Washington. This group of men together with Ann Spock, who became our assistant administrative officer, formed a highly competent, intensely loyal, and truly dedicated organization, and I would indeed be remiss if I did not acknowledge my deep gratitude for the wonderful help they gave me.

Since we began our operations in the middle of fiscal year 1948–49 we were allotted some carried-over GARIOA funds and against these appropriations the most urgent procurement could be made: such things as fertilizers, raw materials for textile plants, and a variety of other basic commodities. Our main concern, however, was to build up a wholly new type of program as soon as possible, one that would help animate more of the "going concern" in Korea and, by judicious capital formation, and equally well planned technical assistance, set in motion a cumulatively expanding development of all the basic sectors of the Korean economy. Before we had made much progress in putting this program together, however, we were confronted with a wholly unexpected and most embarrassing situation. Persons we had never heard of in Korea kept coming to see my procurement officers, challenging our right to spend any of the carried-over GARIOA funds. As far as I could determine there were three separate cabals. Yet oddly enough, the spokesman for each group told a story identical to that told by the others, averring that, in requital for funds advanced to Syngman Rhee, his group had been assured that it would be the exclusive purchasing agent for the South Korean government. Since the whole ECA procedure for the European countries had been based on the assumption that duly

I was unable to keep him. He left the Korea Division to become Averell Harriman's assistant in Paris (they are not related) and later filled positions (as White House consultant) in London, Belgrade, and again in Paris.

185

accredited agents of the assisted countries would do the actual purchasing, the alleged agents of the South Korean government hoped to begin very profitable commission operations, first by using the GARIOA funds that were being transferred to ECA and, after that, the congressional appropriations specifically earmarked for Korean aid.

Since we were in no position to ascertain who was, or who was not, a bona fide agent of the Korean government, and since Syngman Rhee professed to have no knowledge whatever of any promises made to any of these groups, we had little choice but to undertake all procurement on behalf of the Korean government; and because neither Mr. Hoffman, Dr. Bunce, nor I was willing to see millions of dollars, urgently needed in Korea, spent on useless and unnecessary commissions,[4] we decided to fight these rapacious opportunists to the last ditch. Our legal counsel therefore prepared an appropriate document under the terms of which the Korean government appointed Paul G. Hoffman as its procurement agent. Fearing that we might not otherwise press for an adequate Korean aid program, Syngman Rhee signed this agreement and we thought our troubles on this score were over, an assumption that unfortunately proved to be quite wrong.

When the carried-over GARIOA funds had been transferred to ECA,[5] we proceeded to use them for the highest priorities to tide over the Korean economy until a more comprehensive aid program had been authorized by Congress. In designing such a separate program we perforce worked in close cooperation with Bunce's mission which supplied the essential data, and with technical experts in various Washington governmental agencies. Our Pentagon advisers strongly urged us to have a Philadelphia consulting firm make a survey of the major nonagricultural sectors of the Korean economy so that the program we submitted to the Congress would have impartial technical justification. As I look back on this episode I must regretfully conclude that we may have wasted a good deal of money on this survey. The handsomely bound report contained very little information we did not already have in our Korean files, and very few novel proposals for the rehabilitation of Korea. From our experience I discovered that consulting firms ordinarily have skeleton staffs, and only after contracts have been signed do they hire engineers or other tech-

[4] At least $146,735,105 had been made available to Korea from GARIOA funds for fiscal year 1949 and approximately half of these moneys were transferred to ECA on January 1, 1949. A 5 percent commission on this fraction of the Korean aid funds, for half of fiscal year 1949, would have amounted to well over three and a half million dollars.

[5] These arrangements were concluded in a letter to Paul Hoffman from General William H. Draper, Jr., acting secretary of the army, dated February 1, 1949. I was flattered to note in this communication that General Draper made special reference to the help I had given in effecting this transfer of responsibility.

nicians to make field surveys. To our surprise we found that the firm we had engaged hired some people whose qualifications we had already reviewed in our recruitment efforts and found inadequate. Worse than that, we discovered that some of the consulting firm's "experts" had had no experience with Oriental technical problems.[6] Consequently for rather routine and even amateurish advice we not only paid the wages of the "experts" but a very high surcharge to the consulting firm. Moreover when the bill was presented to the Korean government, which had in a legal sense contracted for the survey,[7] we discovered that the overseas members of the survey team had been given 25 percent salary increases the day they departed from the United States. When I advised the Korean ambassador not to pay this factitious salary bonus, I quite unwittingly precipitated a fierce storm of protest. It turned out that all the consulting firms that sold their expertise to government agencies were thus padding their overseas salary costs, and by challenging this procedure I came under attack for upsetting an accepted principle of operation in the huge system of consulting contracts. Little by little I was discovering tactics with which I had no experience, business ethics that seemed both strange and unsavory. I had a feeling that Peer Gynt might have understood Washington much better than I. Leaving Harriman in charge of the Korea Division I posted back to Seoul.

The object of my trip back to Korea, March 11–28, 1949, was not only to obtain essential data for our program but to visit the more important electric-generating plants and mining centers, for which sizable amounts of money would be requested, so that I would have a firsthand appreciation of the technical problems. An excellent electrical engineer, Carl Giroux, a man of proven technical competence, accompanied me. Bunce's mission had made faultless plans for our travel to South Korea's largest thermal power plant at Yongwol, to the Sangdong tungsten mine, and to the Samchok coal and steel complex. Benefiting from Giroux's remarkable capacity for finding critical elements in the fragile South Korean power system, I came to realize how extremely important the fullest possible utilization of the Yongwol thermal plant would be for the Korean economy.[8]

[6] I flew out to Korea with the group hired by the consulting firm. Among them were two "experts" whose task was to make recommendations for enlarging the domestic production of salt for the Korean fishing industries. As we reached the southern coast of Korea I pointed to the network of salterns and said to the salt experts, "There are your laboratories." To my utter amazement I learned that neither one had ever seen a saltern before.

[7] It being understood that ECA would provide the Korean government with the necessary funds.

[8] A number of difficult technical problems had to be solved. The coal that came to the plant by an aerial cableway over two mountain ranges not only was inadequate

A rather strange turn of events occurred while we were at Yongwol. Our party had traveled, from a railhead, to Yongwol in two jeeps in which, next day, we planned to cross over a mountain range to the Sangdong tungsten mine and processing plant. That night just when I was about to retire, the *goonsoo* (county chief) came to see me. Ho told me that we would have to fly American flags on our jeeps when we crossed the mountains. "But we have no flags," I said, and explained that I could see no reason why we needed flags. He left very unhappy and soon returned with the military commander of the Yongwol area who insisted that we must have American flags on our jeeps. "But we have no flags," I protested. "Then your servants must make them," the commander replied. So all night long the servants worked, ruling stripes on linen, drawing ninety-six stars, and then coloring the two flags with red and blue ink. When we started the next morning the work had been so recently finished that wet red ink smeared one of the white stripes on my flag. Off we started with our flags flying and just when we reached a point where the road begins to creep up the mountain on frightening cornices four jeeploads of soldiers were waiting to escort us over the mountains. If this seemed strange, I found it even more unexpected to see four more jeeploads of soldiers waiting for us on the other side of the mountain to relieve our Yongwol guards and to escort us to Sangdong.

Our investment plans called for new, larger, more efficient jaw crushers and ball mills at the tungsten processing plant so that Korea could greatly increase its production of this valuable metal, which would supply a much-needed export item. Hence we gathered all relevant data not merely to document our request for funds but to supply Allis-Chalmers with figures to enable that firm to estimate the cost of the requisite new machinery. At Sangdong our military escort had been replaced by four jeeploads of police and under their protection, from whom we had no idea, we went on to Samchok. Here we verified the need for new equipment for both the coal mines and the steel plant; next day, still under escort, we set out for the airfield at Kangnung where we were to board a DC-3 for our flight to Seoul. As we approached the airfield we drove between a mile-long line of police spaced at ten-yard intervals, each man facing outward. Not till we reached Kimpo airfield near Seoul did we discover what had inspired this unprecedented solicitude for my welfare. Mrs. Horace Underwood, the wife of a second-generation missionary, had

in amount but had a high ash content and a very low percentage of fixed carbon. More and better coal could be brought in if a railway were built to Yongwol and if the poor coal could be beneficiated by the use of a device which screened out noncombustible elements at the pitheads. These items had to be included in our capital-investment program.

been murdered, presumably by a Communist assassin, and the Korean police chief, an old friend, Chang Taik Sang, had apparently feared that any or all Americans might be in danger particularly those of us who were traveling in "Communist-infested" areas, as certain interior regions were rather infelicitously called.

On my return to Washington my staff redoubled their efforts to prepare a sound, defensible aid program. Hearings on H.R. 5330 [9] began on June 8 and ended on June 23, 1949. I testified on all the nine days that the Foreign Affairs Committee devoted to this bill. Aside from an introductory statement by James E. Webb, undersecretary of state, a capsule summary of our program by Paul G. Hoffman, and a brief explanation of the achievements of USAMGIK by General Gardiner Helmick, the burden of explaining how the aid program would help ensure the viability of South Korea, and thereby serve American interests in the Far East, fell largely on my shoulders. Mr. Webb called our program of economic assistance for Korea one of "the most important which the Department of State is supporting at this session of Congress," [10] while Mr. Hoffman emphatically pointed out that the program we were submitting was a recovery not a relief program.[11] He argued that whereas a continuation of a relief program would "result in progressive pauperization of the people of South Korea," the combined commodity-import and investment program that we were submitting could make a vigorous independent state out of a former Japanese colony.[12] About $110,000,000 would be requested for fertilizer, raw materials, petroleum, and other commodities to assure full utilization of the Korean "going concern," and about $32,000,000 for capital investment to improve, expand, and modernize mines, factories, fisheries, and electrical generating plants; the latter was roughly 20 percent of the requested funds, a fraction which Mr. Hoffman called "the key 20 percent." [13] But for all his persuasiveness there were misgivings expressed by several members of the committee [14] that he could not allay. How could Korea be protected against Communist expansion, Dr. Walter Judd asked, when China was being engulfed? [15] He

---

[9] *Hearings before the Committee on Foreign Affairs, House of Representatives, Eighty-First Congress, First Session, on H.R. 5330: A Bill to Promote World Peace and the General Welfare, National Interest, and Foreign Policy of the United States by Providing Aid to the Republic of Korea* (Washington, D.C.: Government Printing Office, 1949). The printed transcript of the *Hearings* ran to 207 pages.

[10] Ibid., p. 3.

[11] Ibid., p. 9.

[12] Ibid., p. 11.

[13] Ibid., p. 15.

[14] See the statements of Mike Mansfield, Walter Judd, John Lodge, and Abraham Ribicoff in ibid., pp. 23–33.

[15] Ibid., p. 28. With parallel frankness Mr. Ribicoff said he thought "the time

warned us that we would "have to bring up a lot of good answers" before the Congress could justify an expenditure of $150,000,000 for a "fragmentary approach" to Northeast Asia. After Dr. Judd's announced intention to relate our Korean aid program to the China controversy, which had long embittered the defenders and the critics of General George C. Marshall, I began to realize, on the first day of the hearings, that we might have real trouble, however sound our program might be technically.

The second day confirmed my fears. I had asked General Helmick to summarize the achievements of USAMGIK and to explain, on the basis of his experience as deputy military governor, why the kind of a reconstruction program we had designed was necessary in the military interest of the United States.[16] Since General Helmick had no prepared statement, the committee peppered him with questions: about who had decided that the Russians should be given control over North Korea, who had authorized MacArthur's General Order No. 1 which set the 38th parallel as the boundary between the Russian and the American occupation zones, and did he not think the Russians would be tempted to invade South Korea if the economy were improved by American aid. When the general agreed with the premise of one of his questioners (Congressman Donald Jackson) that a cold war existed, and admitted "that our front extends from the Bering Straits to Indonesia," he was brusquely told that the committee was being asked to make a decision on the equivalent of a "company front" without "any adequate knowledge of what our side proposes to do in case the enemy does certain things."[17] Then Dr. Judd, an old-China-hand congressman, made a sharp criticism of General Hodge's decision to appoint half the members of the Korean Interim Legislature after a trial election had returned only extreme conservatives. Using an editorial "we," Dr. Judd satirically described what had been done in these blistering words: "We decided what is democratic after they had decided democratically what they wanted. We did not like their choice so we changed it so it would fit our idea of what we thought they ought to want."[18] General Helmick could have pointed out, had he not been so unfailingly courteous, that we had plenty of reasons for believing that the

has come to formulate an American policy for the entire Far East," not merely for Korea. Ibid., p. 33.

[16] "Very early in our occupation," said General Helmick, "we realized that giving bare relief — just keeping [South] Korea on its feet — would not get us anywhere. This would have to be continued indefinitely unless we built them up so they could take care of themselves." Ibid., p. 37.

[17] Ibid., p. 51. "We are being asked to do, as a country," said Congressman Jackson, "what the youngest second lieutenant in the military service would be court-martialed for doing, that is to embark upon a program which is based on no reconnaissance and no overall policy."

[18] Ibid., p. 57.

election of members of the Interim Assembly had not been quite as "democratic" as Congressman Judd implied.[19] But Judd's question alerted me to the probability that we might well be criticized for assuming control over procurement operations rather than entrusting these to Rhee's putative agents. Unfortunately my fears proved to have been well founded.

I had contributed points of information and detail during the testimony of Messrs. Webb, Hoffman, and Helmick, but my substantive explanation and defense of our proposed $150,000,000 Korean aid program began on June 14, 1949. Armed with large, vivid, colored charts, maps, and other visual aids, I made, I believe, a very convincing presentation. After my long experience as a college teacher, and my opportunities to brief British, Americans, and Norwegians in London, Edinburgh, Oslo, and Frankfurt, I had few worries about addressing the Foreign Affairs Committee of the 81st Congress. For me it was like a graduate seminar, and my listeners proved attentive, alert, extremely curious, and uniformly courteous and gracious. I explained what the program included and how the commodity and investment content had been determined with the help and the approval of the Koreans. I described the expected effects the projected aid inputs would have on the Korean economy, on production, exports, and external accounts. I attempted to visualize the growth-generating capacity that could result, and how our reconstruction program would facilitate the ultimate termination of our economic responsibility in Korea. "This is not . . . something cooked up in a perfectionist sense. It is a program related to the immediate specific needs of South Korea." [20] I pointed out that our program had been scrutinized by thirty top officials of the Korean government and reviewed again and again by the ECA mission to Korea, and that relevant parts had been vetted by the Food and Agriculture, Transportation, and Industry branches of ECA Washington, by the economic staff of the State Department, by the Bureau of Mines, by the Army Corps of Engineers, by technical laboratories, and by machinery manufacturers. Then I went through the whole program, item by item, showing not only why the proposed commodity imports, the increments of investment, and the several types of technical assistance were necessary, but

[19] I would be most unfair to Dr. Judd if I did not mention that he stated that USAMGIK had done "an extraordinary job under most difficult circumstances. . . . There is no country I visited in Europe or Asia where I felt the situation was in saner hands than in Korea from the American standpoint — Hodge at the top and you [General Helmick] and your associates in the economic field and Joe Jacobs on the political side, and I want to compliment you for the remarkable progress you have made toward sound development of democratic trends." Ibid., p. 59.

[20] My verbatim description of the program together with reproductions of the explanatory charts is available in ibid., pp. 22, 49, 61–107, 123, 142, 145–153, 165, 173, 175, 185.

how the outlay on aid could be expected to fructify in greater production from Korean resources.

My picture of the Korean economy and the manifold ways in which our carefully planned program could improve it seemed to satisfy the members of the committee who had before appeared so critical. The senior member, Congressman Charles Eaton, rather extravagantly commented on my testimony by saying that "in 25 years [in Congress] I have never heard a more sound statement of a proposition than you have made today, and I am wondering how in heaven's name they ever got a man of your ability into public service." [21]

But although the committee willingly recognized that our program had been carefully planned, skillfully related to Korean needs, and examined technically by the best experts we could find, the fear that our efforts to make South Korea viable would precipitate aggressive action from North Korea, Russia, or mainland China persisted. To obtain more information about this troublous political-military aspect of the Korean situation, the committee asked the undersecretary of state, James E. Webb, to meet with them again and also took testimony from Walton Butterworth, assistant secretary of state for Far Eastern Affairs, and from George F. Kennan, the former director of the Policy Planning Staff of the Department of State. Two army officers also appeared at the committee's request, as did one air force officer and a rear admiral.[22] Finally, upon his return from abroad, the secretary of state, Dean Acheson, at the insistence of the committee, met with them on June 23, 1949. What disturbed the committee proved to be the very thing Bunce and I had brought up the preceding September. Congresswoman Helen Gahagan Douglas put the issue succinctly: "The question troubling the Committee is whether or not United States troops should withdraw from Korea [on] July 1 [1949]. Is it sound to withdraw United States troops . . . leaving only technical forces to train the Korean army?" [23] The Department of the Army answer to this query was given by General Bolte who said, "We feel that they should come out now." [24] Mr. Kennan agreed, pointing out that were the

[21] Ibid., p. 93. A night's sleep had not diminished Congressman Eaton's enthusiasm. Next day before I began further explanation of our program he said, "I want to say for myself personally, and I am confident that this will express the view of our whole committee, that we have never heard a finer or more sound and sane presentation of a great issue before this committee than Mr. Johnson gave us yesterday. I am profoundly thankful that the Economic Cooperation Administration has been able to obtain the services of so able and accomplished a leader." Ibid., p. 94.

[22] Major General Charles L. Bolte, Brigadier General T. S. Timberman, Brigadier General P. M. Hamilton, and Rear Admiral E. T. Wooldridge.

[23] *Hearings on H.R. 5330*, p. 120.

[24] Ibid. A view supported by the air force and the navy in later testimony. See ibid., pp. 159–189.

United States to reject the United Nations' recommendation that American troops be withdrawn, the Russians could say, "We obeyed this demand and the Americans did not. We do not maintain troops [in Korea] without permission and the Americans do." [25] It became crystal clear that the decision to withdraw American tactical units had definitely been made, and, despite repeated expressions of their misgivings, the members of the committee received no assurances from Secretary Acheson that any effort would be made to protect either past or future investments in Korea by military means. "We cannot possibly guarantee the southern Koreans their independence by American military power," said Mr. Acheson.[26] "We cannot tell you that [South] Korea is going to stand up under all pressure. . . . but there is a good fighting chance that the Koreans can take care of themselves." Yet for all the Olympian confidence with which he expressed this view, many members of the committee remained very much dissatisfied. Dr. Judd had already announced his agnosticism: "It is hard for me to support a program half fish and half fowl," he said. "We continue to give economic aid without doing the military things necessary to protect it." [27]

I had not expected to be caught in crossfire between the China lobby, the Department of State, the Pentagon, and members of Congress who were deeply worried about the possibility that South Korea would ultimately be engulfed by Communist forces. With amazement I listened to angry accusations against the Department of State by members of the committee and, with equal astonishment, observed the cold, condescending hauteur of the secretary of state and some of his senior staff toward the more aggressive members of the committee. We had been so much concerned with our immediate Korean problems that we had, I fear, given far too little thought to the question of how our program fitted into the whole Asian policy of the United States or indeed into our country's global foreign policy. What seemed to confuse and irritate the Foreign Affairs Committee most was the inability or the unwillingness of the army, air force, and navy spokesmen for the Joint Chiefs of Staff to explain why it seemed so imperative to withdraw American tactical troops as soon as possible.[28] Their endorsement of our economic development program

---

[25] Ibid., p. 127. [26] Ibid., p. 191.

[27] Ibid., p. 162. At another time (ibid., p. 186) he expressed his misgivings even more pessimistically, "I believe sincerely that the Korea economic program, accompanied by military withdrawal . . . does not have more than a 25% chance of success and therefore I question whether we are justified in approving this."

[28] The precipitate action of the Joint Chiefs in withdrawing the American tactical forces from Korea is evident from two documents. In the hearings on H.R. 5330 on June 21, 1949, the three representatives of the Joint Chiefs spoke rather vaguely about when the troops would be withdrawn. Yet it now seems quite clear that when they were testifying a decision to withdraw the troops had already been made and

had a rather hollow sound; the army, air force, and navy were "bugging out," leaving the rest of us unprotected.

Despite the sharp differences of views, the Foreign Affairs Committee went ahead and prepared a Korean aid bill, in which our recommendation for an appropriation of $150,000,000 was accepted, and formal approval of the bill by the committee was voted on June 28, 1949.[29] That same day Mr. Webb, Mr. Hoffman, and I appeared before the Senate Foreign Relations Committee to give testimony concerning S. 2319, the parallel Senate version of H.R. 5330. In contrast to the charged atmosphere of the House committee, the relaxed attitude of the Senate committee was a welcome relief. After Mr. Webb's short introductory statement, the chairman, Senator Tom Connally, said that the committee had most urgent business before it and could hear no more testimony. The "urgent business," he explained, was to approve the appointment of Perle Mesta as minister to Luxembourg. Mr. Hoffman said he would not take a minute of the committee's time but he begged the chairman to "let Dr. Johnson have just ten minutes" to explain the charts that my statistician had so neatly arranged on easels. I must have been in exceptionally good form that morning because one hour and forty-five minutes later my listeners were still pelting me with questions. Perle Mesta had seemingly been forgotten, and when we finally adjourned I had been asked to come back again on July 7.

Senator Connally began the second session on Korean aid by asking if there were questions, and when Senator Alexander Wiley raised a point that I had discussed in detail on June 28, Senator Arthur Vandenberg interposed to ask, "Senator Wiley, did I understand you to say you did not hear Dr. Johnson's presentation [on June 28]?" When Senator Wiley replied, "I do not recall," Senator Vandenberg answered, "If you do not recall it, you did not hear it, because it was the best presentation that has been made, in my opinion, in specific justification of a proposal that I have heard, and I was greatly pleased with it."[30] A week later the committee

most of the troops had probably already left Korea since John Muccio, the United States ambassador to Korea, informed the United Nations commission (on July 8) "that the withdrawal of the U.S. Military forces in Korea was completed on June 29, 1949." See *U.N. Document A/936. Add 1 Volume II Annexes*, p. 36. The only troops remaining in Korea after June 30, 1949, were 50 air force personnel to operate Kimpo airport until civilians could take over these duties, and 500 officers and men of a Military Advisory Group under the command of Brigadier General W. L. Roberts.

[29] *Aid to Korea: Report of the Committee of Foreign Affairs on H.R. 5330* (Washington, D.C.: Government Printing Office, 1949), p. 3.

[30] *Testimony before the United States Senate Committee on Foreign Affairs, July 7, 1949* (Washington, D.C.: Government Printing Office, 1949), p. 80. Senator Connally had been equally gracious on June 28. "I want to congratulate you on your marvelous grasp and understanding of the [Korean] situation." Ibid., June 28, p. 65.

questioned Major General W. E. Todd and Brigadier General Timberman, and that same day, July 12, voted to recommend favorable action by the Senate on the $150,000,000 Korean aid bill. But just when we felt happy about a successful defense of our program before the gracious and courtly senators, new storm clouds had already appeared and presently we found ourselves in deepening trouble.

The Foreign Affairs Committee had complained about our bringing the Korea aid program to their attention so late in the legislative year. I could not very well explain that the Korea Program Division had been ready to defend its program two months earlier but had been repeatedly told by Tyler Wood, who was in charge of congressional presentation for ECA, that our little Asian operation could not be scheduled until the "main show," the European Recovery Program, had been steered through the congressional mazes.[31] Quite unfairly I had to take most of the blame for asking the Foreign Affairs Committee to reach an instant decision since the carried-over GARIOA funds would finance our operations only until July 1, 1949. The exemplary cooperation of the Foreign Affairs Committee is attested by their prompt preparation of a bill, on June 28, only five days after they heard Dean Acheson as its last protagonist. But although both the House and Senate committees had marked up their bills by July 12, it seemed impossible to persuade the leadership to bring the House bill to a floor vote. Mr. Hoffman talked with Sam Rayburn, the speaker of the House; he and I together saw John McCormack, the majority leader; and Mr. Hoffman received promises from Joe Martin, the minority leader. Meantime our GARIOA funds had been exhausted, and in this emergency Public Law 154 was passed on June 30, 1949, which provided us with enough funds to continue the Korean program for one month on the 1949 (GARIOA) level; on August 1 Public Law 196 extended this level of aid for another fifteen days. With these appropriations, totaling $17,500,000, we had to make do — not for six weeks but for over three months, since not until October 10 was another authorization made, one which netted us another $12,500,000.[32] A fortnight later another $30,000,000 was appropriated under Public Law 430 for use for the period October 15, 1949, to February 15, 1950. What had occurred, therefore, was that for seven and a half months of fiscal year 1950, we had received $60,000,000 instead of the $93,700,000 we had requested.[33]

[31] I often thought that Wood's appointment as ECA mission chief in Korea after the Korean war savored of retributive justice. He then learned what I had been up against much earlier.

[32] Public Law 349 made $30,000,000 available for the period July 1 to October 15, against which the funds appropriated under P.L. 154 and P.L. 196 were charged.

[33] For further information on this succession of stopgap Korean aid appropriations, see *Economic Assistance to Certain Areas in the Far East: Report of the*

But the 27½ percent shortfall was not our main handicap. What we received came in driblets [34] so that we could not program the long-range investment items on which we had laid such stress and on which the growth and development of the Korean economy so very much depended.

After all these frustrating delays, which profoundly disturbed the Korean government, H.R. 5330 finally was brought to a vote on January 19, 1950. An amendment reduced the authorization from $150,000,000 to $60,000,000, and since we had received $60,000,000 the effect would have been to decrease the total aid for fiscal year 1950 to $120,000,000, a reduction of 20 percent. With the bill so amended the voting began. I sat in the distinguished visitors' gallery with my friend Dr. John Chang, the Korean ambassador. I saw Joe Martin in earnest conversation with each member of his party as they proceeded down the well of the House to vote and assumed he was carrying out the promises he had made. Presently the voting had been completed and the result was announced. The bill had failed of passage by one vote! I shall never forget Dr. Chang's unconcealed distress. He could not believe what he heard, "How could it have happened?" he asked again and again. Several days later I would be able to tell him.

It had of course been expected that the opponents of any or all foreign aid, Representative Otto Passman and his group, would vote against Korean aid. Equally predictable was the attitude of those members of Congress who accused the Department of State of neglectful action in China.[35] But the tactless criticism of the "China Lobby" by one member of the Foreign Affairs Committee, in the caucus held to determine Republican party policy, broke up an anticipated agreement, and left Republican members of the House free to vote as they chose. Finally, an altogether extraneous event occurred. Bitterly resentful of ECA's refusal to let Rhee's alleged "purchasing agents" engage in procurement activities with ECA funds, one of the cabals circulated a letter to all members of the House urging them to vote against the Korean aid bill because the funds would not be made available to the Korean government to spend. It is my firm

Committee on Foreign Affairs on S. 2319 (Washington, D.C.: Government Printing Office, February 1950), p. 13.

[34] The very thing Bunce and I had warned against. See above, p. 182. What actually happened was that we received "$17,500,000 for 6 weeks; then nothing for 6 weeks; then $12,500,000 for 6 weeks; then nothing for 10 weeks; then $30,000,000 for the 10 fallow weeks and for the next 9 weeks." *Report on S. 2319*, p. 13.

[35] Secretary Acheson apparently thought these two groups were responsible for the defeat of the Korea aid bill. "We neglected our usual precautions," he writes, "and were caught off guard by a combination of China-bloc Republicans and economy-minded southern Democrats and defeated on a snap vote." *Present at the Creation: My Years in the State Department* (New York: Norton, 1969), p. 358. This explanation, I fear, is much too simple.

conviction that this shameful lobbying operation turned just enough votes to ensure the defeat of the program in which we had invested so much time, thought, work, and worry.

It took only a day for responsible members of Congress to realize what an incredibly stupid blunder had occurred. Most unfortunately, Secretary Acheson, in a public declaration at the National Press Club on January 12, 1950, had already implied that Korea was not within the American defense perimeter.[36] By defeating the aid bill the House of Representatives had gone even farther, denying ECA any funds to be spent on behalf of Korea. These two developments when taken in conjunction with the withdrawal of American troops could very easily be construed to mean that the United States had virtually written off South Korea politically, militarily, and economically. Lest this conjuncture of events encourage North Korean aggression, leaders of both parties in Congress, with exceptional promptitude, prepared a new aid bill which would be acceptable to enough congressional dissenters to ensure its swift enactment. To enlist the support of the China bloc, a new version of S. 2319 (the original Senate bill for providing aid to Korea) was renamed "An Act to provide economic assistance to certain areas of the Far East."[37] By the addition of a section providing for economic assistance to "non-communist areas of China," it was believed enough votes could be attracted to ensure passage. In the surprisingly short period of ten days the bill had been recast,[38] further testimony from Secretary Acheson was heard, and on February 9, just twenty days after the defeat of the Korean aid bill, the House voted an authorization of $60,000,000 for Korean aid to cover the remaining four and two-thirds months of fiscal year 1950.[39]

In the autumn of 1949 when we were being harried by our troubles with Congress, I received so many reports about political discord in Korea that

[36] See George M. McCune, *Korea Today* (Cambridge, Mass.: Harvard University Press, 1950), p. 255. For Acheson's explanation of why he took the position, see his *Present at the Creation*, pp. 355–358. For a fuller discussion of this unfortunate remark see below, pp. 212–213.

[37] For its provisions and its justification see *Report on S. 2319*.

[38] To placate members of Congress who feared that Rhee's government might fall and be succeeded by a coalition government, the bill provided that "the Administrator shall immediately terminate aid . . . in the event of the formation in the Republic of Korea of a coalition government which includes one or more members of the Communist Party or of the party now in control of the government of North Korea." Ibid., p. 1.

[39] The reduction in Korean aid from the $150,000,000 that both the House and Senate committees had approved originally to a total of $120,000,000 was justified by none-too-skillful casuistry. The reduction, said the committee report on the (revised) S. 2319, "is not because the $150,000,000 was not needed at the time it was requested" but because "at this late date . . . the spending of $90,000,000 over a 4- to 5-month period . . . would result in gorging the Korean economy with materials and supplies in excess of its assimilative capacity." Ibid., p. 17.

I decided to visit our mission to ascertain how the aid operations were proceeding, with the uncertain and unpredictable driblets of aid we were receiving. When I arrived at Kimpo airport, on November 24, 1949, the governmental delegation that greeted me included a new minister of supply, and when I had an opportunity to ask Dr. Anderson, the deputy chief of our aid mission, what had become of Lee Tong Chae, he told me that for some months Lee had been languishing in a Korean prison and that I must see Syngman Rhee about this unfortunate affair. Very promptly I had the embassy ask for an appointment, and next day, armed with all the information I could gather, Everett Drumwright, the deputy chief of our diplomatic mission, and I called on President Rhee. With a show of deep gratitude, Rhee told me what a true friend of Korea I was and that the Korean people would never forget my solicitude for their welfare. It was an opening I very much needed.

"Mr. President," I said, "I deeply appreciate your gracious remarks because I have a favor to ask of you."

"Anything you ask, my dear Dr. Johnson," said Rhee, "I will grant."

"Mr. President," I said, "I'm so glad to hear you say that because it is most important that you grant me this favor. You see there is something quite cruel that I have unintentionally done and you must help me to correct it."

"Anything you ask," said Rhee, "I will grant."

"Mr. President," I said, "I want you to release Lee Tong Chae from prison because I am responsible for his being there."

My statement took President Rhee completely by surprise and he replied: "What nonsense are you talking? How could you be responsible for his imprisonment?"

"Mr. President," I said, "I am not talking nonsense. You will recall we insisted there be a minister of supply in your government. If we had not done so, there would not have been a minister of supply. And if I had not suggested to General Helmick that Lee Tong Chae be named minister of supply, you, Mr. President, would not have appointed him. If Lee Tong Chae had not become minister of supply, he could not have misappropriated the public funds for which act he is now in prison. No, Mr. President, my logic is impeccable. I am responsible for his imprisonment and I want you to release him."

For quite some time Rhee said nothing. Then finally he spoke. "I said I would grant any favor you asked. I will release Lee Tong Chae."

Rhee was as good as his word. I could scarcely wait to hear Lee Tong Chae's story. This is what he said:

"*Paksa,* I know that you suggested that I be minister of supply. But how could I know what I would be expected to do. Two days after my appointment President Rhee sent for me.

" 'Lee Tong Chae,' the president said, 'you have four million won in the Office of the Controller of Commodities.'

" 'No, Mr. President,' I replied. 'I have almost eight million won.'

" 'Oh, that's even better,' said the president. 'This is what I want you to do with this money' and he proceeded to list the amounts I should give to this person, or to that organization.

" 'But Mr. President,' I said, 'I can't do what you ask. Those are public funds.'

" 'I am president,' Mr. Rhee said sternly, 'and you will do as I say.'

" 'Very well,' I answered, 'but you must give me instructions in writing so I will have some proof that I have been authorized to distribute these moneys.'

" 'Of course you may have it in writing,' said the president and he wrote out on a sheet of paper the way I should distribute the funds. I asked that he sign this instruction and took my leave.

"A day or two after I had distributed the funds as ordered, the prime minister, Lee Bum Suk, learned about it and very swiftly charges were brought against me. I was arraigned, tried, and found guilty of the misuse of public funds. I threw myself on the mercy of the court asking that I be permitted to see the president. My request was granted. The president received me coldly.

" 'Mr. President,' I said, 'I am being prosecuted for carrying out your wishes.'

" 'What nonsense are you talking?' asked the president. 'Did I tell you to misappropriate public funds?'

" 'You not only told me to distribute these funds as I did, but you gave me this written instruction.'

" 'Let me see that forgery,' said President Rhee, and when I handed him the piece of paper he tore it into small pieces. Then I went to prison, *Paksa*, and there I stayed until you obtained my release."

This was the story Lee Tong Chae told me. Both he and Syngman Rhee are now dead, and no one will ever know whether Lee Tong Chae told me the truth. Before another year had passed, however, I had other encounters with Syngman Rhee that led me to believe that he was quite capable of unblushing duplicity.

At a second meeting with President Rhee, during which neither he nor I mentioned Lee Tong Chae, he explained once again to me the two projects he wanted ECA to finance. The first was a set of sewage filtration beds for converting the night soil of the city of Seoul into granular fertilizer. He was convinced that such a plant would provide all the fertilizer that South Korea would need, and he pooh-poohed my objections that according to his experts and our experts no less than 110,000 metric tons of contained nitrogen would be needed plus 313,000 metric tons of super-phosphates; and that the right solution would be to build modern fertilizer plants that could produce at least those quantities. But such projects would call for a very marked increase in South Korea's electric-power output. Rhee kept insisting that all that was needed would be a sewage-disposal plant for the city of Seoul.

His second project had an equally romantic quality except that it also had, known or unknown to him, a very sinister aspect with which I was very familiar. Rhee's argument that the Yellow Sea teemed with fish had merit, but his proposal that ECA purchase a gigantic floating fish factory, together with a covey of trawlers to gather the fish for the floating cannery, had already been considered and rejected. It seemed most unlikely that the Koreans, without any experience in deep-sea fishing, could operate the *Northern Explorer* which Rhee wanted us to purchase. Built by the Maritime Commission during World War II to increase food production, the hugh floating cannery had turned out to be a white elephant which none of the American west-coast fishing companies could operate at a profit. We knew that one of Rhee's "purchasing agents" had persuaded him that this unmarketable giant was precisely what Korea needed, and we had a fairly good idea of what the purchasing agent's commission would be. So regretfully I had to tell the president that we had consulted fish and wildlife experts who had recommended that we purchase one trawler and ascertain from experience with that single vessel whether the Koreans could make a beginning in deep-sea fishing.

Fortunately the ministers of the Korean government and their bureau chiefs had more realistic program proposals. They wanted to complete the scores of irrigation and reclamation projects the Japanese had begun. They realized that if South Korea was to balance her external accounts she would, once again, have to export not merely silk, marine products, tungsten and other metals and minerals, but rice; and that to increase rice production very large inputs of fertilizer would be needed. They appreciated also that Korea needed a wide range of raw materials and large quantities of repair, replacement, and maintenance equipment for the industrial plant South Korea had inherited from the Japanese. Above all, they recognized that technical assistance would be imperative in order to obtain full use of the "going concern."

When I returned to Washington I addressed myself personally to this latter problem. After calculating what it would cost to train technicians by bringing them to the United States or to Hawaii, I concluded we could get far more mileage out of our aid money if we set up an American-staffed

Technical Training Institute in Korea. I asked the president of the Illinois Institute of Technology, Henry Heald,[40] to recruit a faculty for such an institute, which he did with his customary good judgment and dependability. Meantime we had arranged for a cadre of machine-tool operators to be trained in Minneapolis.[41] During the spring of 1950 we sorted out our priorities, making do with our $120,000,000, and every night when I left my office I reminded myself that I had been responsible for spending more than a third of a million dollars of other people's money.

When President Heald had completed recruiting the faculty for our Korean Technical Training Institute he needed someone to serve as a coordinator. Very reluctantly one of his close associates at the Illinois Institute of Technology agreed to undertake this task after I had urged him to do so. We arranged to have the group assemble in Minneapolis, and here, on June 20, President Heald and I briefed them before they enplaned, two days later, for Anchorage, Shemya, Tokyo, and Seoul. They arrived at Kimpo airport on Saturday, June 24. The very next morning enemy forces invaded South Korea on a broad front, and on Tuesday, June 27, after two days in Korea, the members of the faculty of our intended Technical Training Institute were evacuated to Japan by air, all but one, who had died of a heart attack brought on by the excitement of that hectic experience. I have never been able to forget that he probably would not have gone to Korea had I not helped persuade him.

[40] Who later (1952) became chancellor of New York University and (in 1956) head of the Ford Foundation.

[41] For some details about the proposed institute and about the training of Korean technicians at Dunwoody Industrial Institute in Minneapolis, see the *Minneapolis Tribune*, June 20, 1950.

13

TERRIBLE CONSEQUENCES
OF RECKLESS RISKS

★★★★★★★★★★★★★★★★★★★★★★★★★★★★★★

WHEN the Korean aid bill failed to pass for lack of two more affirmative votes, I realized for the first time how a small, well-organized lobby can influence public policy. Those of us in ECA who had been subject to their flattery, cajolery, and threats knew very well the motives of Syngman Rhee's "purchasing agents" and sycophants. We stood our ground in face of all their efforts to misrepresent to President Rhee, to the Korean people, and to the American public what we were earnestly trying to do. We had not dreamed, however, that they would attempt to engineer the defeat of the aid bill. But they did; and there is no doubt in my mind that the rejection of the Korean aid bill helped embolden the North Koreans. Hence each and every one who contributed to the defeat of that bill, wittingly or unwittingly, must bear some responsibility for a terribly cruel war, one that resulted in the death of 400,000 Koreans and the maiming or pauperization of at least five million more; the sacrifice of the lives of 33,629 American soldiers and the wounding of another 103,284; and the destruction of millions of dollars' worth of property much of which had been contributed by American taxpayers.

The invasion caught us unprepared. We had been lulled into a sense of false security by the crafty tactics of the enemy. For whereas in 1949 there had been an alarming number of border incursions as well as persistent guerrilla activity on Cheju Island [1] and in the mountains of Kangwon-do, the four months preceding the June 25 invasion were so

[1] I explained to the Senate Appropriations Committee, on June 13, 1950, how these guerrilla forces were surrounded and destroyed. *Foreign Aid Appropriations for 1951, Hearings before the Committee on Appropriations, United States Senate, 81st Congress, Second Session* (Washington, D.C.: Government Printing Office, 1950), pp. 317–318.

singularly calm that in retrospect it seems odd that this period of quiet did not raise suspicions that a major offensive might be in preparation. But the copies of the cables from the Military Assistance Group that we saw in Washington were very reassuring, and on the basis of these reports, to my later embarrassment, I put words of confidence in the mouth of the deputy administrator of ECA that neither he nor I could retract, and, most unfortunately, we were not even permitted to explain why we had taken so complacent an attitude. That unhappy episode, exacerbated by Soviet distortions, I shall presently explain.

After returning to Washington on June 23, 1950, from Minneapolis, I looked forward to a restful weekend. It proved quite otherwise. Late Saturday night, June 24, the telephone rang. The message, urgent and brief, was only this: "South Korea has been invaded. Please come at once to the State Department." [2] But although I was at the department that fateful night, I had nothing to do with the historic decision to lay the invasion problem before the United Nations.[3] I had plenty of other things to worry about, however, and although I did not return to my house until four o'clock in the morning, by eight o'clock that Sunday forenoon all my Korea Division staff had arrived for consultation. We had enough information to realize that the enemy actions could not possibly be construed as a series of minor forays: a front extended across the entire Korean peninsula; and the depth of penetration clearly showed that sizable forces with large reserves were being used. Understandably our immediate concern centered on the safety of the members of our mission in Korea and their dependents, and we set about doing what little we could at our end to facilitate their evacuation to Japan.

Fortunately by the late afternoon, after we had been in touch with Tokyo, we were able to get through to Bunce by telephone and to learn that plans were already well advanced for the embarkation, at Inchon, of the women and children on a Norwegian fertilizer ship, and that aircraft from Japan would begin an airlift of all the men. By these arrangements over a thousand Americans departed from Korea for Japan on June 26 and 27. Of our ECA personnel, their dependents, and our consultants, all but three were evacuated. One member of our ECA mission lay

[2] By Korean time the invasion began on Sunday morning, June 25, but because of the time difference we learned about the invasion on Saturday, June 24 (Washington time).

[3] Dean Rusk, assistant secretary of state for the Far East, telephoned Secretary of State Acheson at his farm, who in turn called President Truman in Independence, Missouri. Acheson and Truman decided to lay the issue before the U.N. Security Council and a call went to Trygve Lie, the secretary-general of the United Nations. For details of how the president reached "the toughest decision" he had to make, see Harry S. Truman, *Memoirs*, vol. II: *Years of Trial and Hope* (New York: Doubleday, 1956), chapter 2.

dying in the Seventh-Day Adventist Hospital, another could not be found;[4] the third was the newly arrived faculty member of our projected Technical Training Institute who died of a heart attack. A situation of this kind tests emotional stability, but even so we were somewhat surprised to learn that two quite senior members of our mission were so disturbed that they had to be evacuated with the women and children.

Having burned all their classified papers, the members of our mission in Korea hurriedly left their posts in Seoul and elsewhere.[5] Meantime we were extremely busy in Washington drastically revising our policies to meet the critical emergency. After what the *Baltimore Sun* called a "top level conference of Marshall-plan officials,"[6] I issued a press release on June 26, 1950, explaining the emergency action we were taking. Our "immediate action program" involved (1) diverting all vessels carrying ECA-procured commodities that were nearing Korea into ports where they would not fall into enemy hands;[7] (2) rearranging shipping schedules so that all available vessels could be used to rush military supplies to the beleaguered peninsula; (3) ensuring that deferrable nonmilitary supplies, such as fertilizer, would be directed to non-Korean ports in order to keep Korean dock workers free for unloading guns, ammunition, and other military supplies; (4) switching procurement to militarily essential commodities, such as petroleum, engineer supplies, and foodstuffs, and giving these items priority over peacetime supplies; (5) coordinating our activities with those of the United States army forces in Japan, and emphasizing procurement activities in Japan in order to hasten deliveries to Korea. I arranged for Charley Spreyer to fly at once to Japan to coordinate our ECA program with the efforts at military support of Korea that SCAP had been instructed to provide. Meantime in Washington urgent conferences on the Korean situation were called, not merely by ECA and the Department of State, but by the Maritime Administration, the National Federa-

[4] Much later we learned that he was taken by North Koreans on what came to be known as the "death march," when United States army prisoners, missionaries, nuns, journalists, and diplomats were force-marched through North Korea in the bitter winter of 1950–51. Like several other of my friends, he did not survive this terrible experience. A vivid account of this shameful episode was written by Philip Deane in *I Was a Captive in Korea* (New York: Norton, 1953).

[5] Quite a number of our engineers and technicians were not in Seoul but at outlying power plants, mines, or factories. One of our engineers was very seriously injured after he had succeeded in removing certain critical parts, thereby putting a power plant out of commission before it fell into North Korean hands.

[6] "Emergency Basis Set for E.C.A. Program," *Baltimore Sun*, Tuesday, June 27.

[7] The hijacking of an American ship, carrying a cargo of ECA-financed salt (en route from Pusan to Kunsan) and its diversion to a North Korea port, on September 21, 1949, had alerted us to the possibility that such predatory action might now be attempted on a larger scale. About fifteen United States merchant ships were believed to be nearing the port of Pusan when the invasion occurred.

tion of American Shipping, the Department of Agriculture, and the main suppliers of petroleum products to the Far East.[8]

Just before the invasion we had been engaged in justifying our proposed Korean aid program for fiscal year 1951 (July 1, 1950, to June 30, 1951). This time our request (for $100,000,000) constituted part of an over-all ECA program, and consequently we did not have to defend a program for Korea separately as we had to do the year before. The invasion, however, soon intruded all manner of new difficulties, since, in quite an unforeseen way, our program became part of a military assistance operation. Both programming and procurement would now have to be discussed with Pentagon officials, who, very likely, would want to revise quite markedly the order of priorities. Fortunately most of my staff had served in the army or in the navy and therefore had the requisite experience to work effectively with our Pentagon planning partners in reaching acceptable agreement.

Meantime William C. Foster, the deputy administrator of ECA, and I were being severely criticized for testimony we had given before the Senate Appropriations Committee on June 13, 1950. I had prepared for Mr. Foster an assessment of the over-all Korean situation based on my intimate knowledge of the economic situation, on the information we received concerning the improved political situation, and on the cables describing the military situation. As an opening statement Mr. Foster therefore said:

I am happy to tell the Appropriations Committee that in my judgment the trend of events in South Korea is more favorable than it has been at any time since the liberation of that country in 1945. The reasons for optimism are military, political and economic. It is my considered opinion that in the face of great difficulty the Government of the Republic of Korea is now steadily gaining strength in each of these three sectors:

1. A rigorous training program has built up a well-disciplined army of 100,000 soldiers; one that is prepared to meet any challenge by North Korean forces; and one that has cleaned out the guerrilla bands in South Korea in one area after another.

2. The political sector is equally reassuring. On May 30 a national election was conducted in a peaceful and orderly fashion. . . .

3. In the economic section very definite signs of improvement are evident. The danger of inflation . . . has been met honestly and courageously. New taxes were voted by the outgoing legislature, tighter controls over bank credit have been enforced. . . . Black market rates for dollars have fallen from 4000 won in January, 1950 to 2000 won in June, 1950. . . . the index of industrial production . . . now stands at more than 175 percent of the monthly average for 1948.[9]

[8] See "E.C.A. Halts New Authorizations for South Korea," *New York Journal of Commerce*, June 27, 1950.

[9] *Hearings before the Committee on Appropriations*, pp. 305–306.

To the extent that appropriation committees are ever satisfied with the testimony of witnesses, this very honest statement seemed to be accepted in good faith, and although I was sharply questioned about border raids and marauding attacks that had been made by guerrilla bands, there seemed to be far more interest in exports, in a proposed fertilizer plant, and in the development of coal mines than in military issues. The topic on which Dr. Wilhelm Anderson [10] and I were most severely questioned centered around the likelihood that most industries in Korea were already nationalized or would be. Patiently we explained, as clearly as we could, that USAMGIK had indeed nationalized all Japanese properties because our State Department directives stipulated that all such properties and assets should "inure to the benefit of the Korean people." We pointed out that we had alienated sequestrated Japanese paddy land since it seemed appropriate that these lands be sold in small parcels to tenant farmers; by that means, the payments would "inure to the benefit of the Korean people." To have undertaken the sale of mines, factories, banks, shipyards, or other "lumpy" parcels of property would have involved us in unintended favoritism, and we therefore had left the disposition of all nonagricultural property to the Korean government.

Almost immediately after the invasion, when it seemed as if the South Koreans would be utterly routed by the tank-led aggressors, the Appropriations Committee released our testimony, and Mr. Foster's statement about the "well-disciplined army of 100,000 soldiers . . . prepared to meet any challenge by North Korean forces" quickly made big headlines in the newspapers.[11] Then Senator Harry Byrd called on the White House to explain why the ECA intelligence given the senators had been so faulty, the implication being that Mr. Foster and I either had distorted the facts to mislead the committee or had shown ourselves incapable of making a correct appraisal of the Korean situation. Gleefully one of Washington's leading columnists described our predicament under the stinging caption "A Prophet Stubs His Toe," an article that nettled Mr. Foster more than any other news item, as well it might when one considers that there were very few more sure-footed men in the government service. Since I had brought this misfortune on him, I tried to take the blame, but Mr. Foster told me to forget about it and just charge it up to "occupational hazards."

The trouble was that we weren't allowed to forget it. Senator Byrd

[10] He had come to Washington to provide us with the latest data for the Appropriations Committee hearings.

[11] "Events Show E.C.A. Wrong about Korea," *Washington Post*, July 6, 1950; "Over-optimistic E.C.A. Blushes at Playback of Its Report on Korea," *Washington Daily News*, July 5, 1950; "Senate Was Told Korea Was Ready: E.C.A. Deputy Said 12 Days before Invasion That South Korea Could Meet Any Challenge," *New York Times*, July 5, 1950.

asked the White House to explain why such an erroneous estimate of the situation had been made, and Mr. Foster and I were summoned to the White House to discuss the issue with an ad hoc committee selected to make some suitable answer to Senator Byrd. I therefore carefully assembled, in proper chronological order, all the cables, so that we would be prepared to explain why we had taken the position we did. But when Mr. Foster suggested at the meeting that our dossier of cables should be shown to Senator Byrd, a State Department representative sharply interposed to say that no classified cable whatever would be shown to the senator. And despite our vigorous objections, that was where the matter ended. "Show the senator one cable," said the State Department spokesman, "and he will want to see all our cables. The Senate is not in charge of foreign affairs; the president is. You may not show any of your cables, or any of our cables, to members of Congress or paraphrase their contents." Mr. Foster and I left the meeting not only unhappy but rather angry, knowing that we would have to keep on taking the blame. "Who was that fellow from the department?" Mr. Foster asked me. When I told him the name of the dogmatic official, Mr. Foster said, "He's the most obnoxious person I've met in all my governmental experience."

For me this unpleasant episode was soon followed by another spate of trouble. Something happened that might have been considered ludicrous had it not been fraught with so many international implications. On July 4, 1950, Andrei A. Gromyko, deputy foreign minister of the U.S.S.R., issued a statement in which he asserted that the "so-called" North Korean invasion was nothing of the sort; it was, instead, a defensive operation against "a provocative attack" by South Korean troops on "border areas of the Korean People's Democratic Republic," which North Korean forces had repelled.[12] Gromyko then proceeded to argue that the "attack" on North Korea had been planned long in advance, and I was dumbfounded to learn that I had been a party to this conspiracy. I read with amazement that I had assured "the Commission of Appropriations of the United States House of Representatives" that "100,000 soldiers and officers of the South Korean Army, fitted with American equipment and trained by the American military mission, had finished their preparations and could start war at any moment."[13] Mr. Gromyko explained that my assurance to the members of Congress clearly was a part of a Korean-American conspiracy since "only a week before the provocative [South Korean] attack on the border districts of the Korean People's Republic," Syngman Rhee had said, "in the so-called National Assembly," with John Foster

[12] An English translation of Gromyko's statement was printed, from a Reuters dispatch, in the *New York Times*, July 5, 1950.
[13] Ibid.

Dulles listening attentively, "We shall reach victory in a hot war." Gromyko went on to say that such statements would not have been made unless the South Koreans had been assured of American support; and "It is known that only a few days before the events in Korea the War Minister of the U.S.A. [Louis] Johnson, the Chief of Staff of the Armed Forces of the U.S.A., General [Omar] Bradley, and the adviser of the State Department [John Foster] Dulles arrived in Japan and held there a special conference with General MacArthur, and that Dulles after that visited South Korea and journeyed to the border areas on the thirty-eighth Parallel." Gromyko said that when Dulles spoke to the South Korean legislature, on June 19, 1950, he assured them "that the United States was ready to give all necessary moral and material help to South Korea which is fighting against communism." These facts, said Gromyko, "are sufficiently eloquent by themselves and do not require comment."

As far as I am concerned they do indeed "require comment." My testimony before House Appropriations subcommittees can be found in a public document [14] that anyone who wishes can read. I quote the main questions addressed to me that appertained to the military situation in Korea and the answers I gave.

Mr. Gary. What is the United States foreign policy in the Far East, and how are we implementing this policy through the Korean aid program?

Dr. Johnson. The American foreign policy as far as Korea is concerned — I am not prepared to speak on the American foreign policy in the Far East — is to assist economically the Korean people so that the Korean republic can survive as an independent nation. To that end, the policy of the State Department is to implement the resolutions of the United States General Assembly, that is, the resolutions of November 14, 1947, which were, first of all, that the security forces of South Korea should be trained. To that end, we have a military advisory group of 500 officers and men, and they have trained a Korean army of 100,000 soldiers. . . .

Mr. Gary. Is eventual unification of Korea an objective of that policy?

Dr. Johnson. It is. But that can only be achieved when some global solution to the Russian question is found. I do not believe there is any local solution. . . .

Mr. Gary. Therefore you say we have no plans at the present time for obtaining unification locally?

Dr. Johnson. No, sir. And we have discouraged the Koreans from efforts to unify North and South Korea by military action.[15]

The only other discussion I had on military subjects with the House Appropriations Committee occurred on May 11, 1950. The questions addressed to me and my answers were these:

[14] *Hearings before Subcommittees of the Committee on Appropriations, House of Representatives, Eighty-First Congress, Second Session* (Washington, D.C.: Government Printing Office, 1950), pp. 707–763.

[15] Ibid., p. 727.

Mr. Wigglesworth. Am I correct that there are no American troops in Korea?

Dr. Johnson. There are no American troops in Korea now. There is, instead, the Korean Military Advisory Group composed of 500 officers and men. Korea has a trained army of 100,000 Koreans, one which our advisers state is a well-trained and pretty well seasoned army. It was seasoned first by the operation against the Communists on the island of Cheju. The Communist concentration was in the center of the island, and from that center they would make marauding raids on all of the coastal villages. It was necessary, then, for the Korean army to start from this perimeter and press in and overcome the Communists. . . . It took a good deal of courage and tactical experience to tighten that perimeter. . . . This portion of South Korea . . . (pointing to map)

Mr. Wigglesworth. That is the northwest portion?

Dr. Johnson. The northwest portion of South Korea was most unfortunately arranged as far as military occupancy is concerned because there was no land access. The thirty-eighth parallel went here (pointing to map) . . . and during the period of military government in order to service our American troops on the Onjin Peninsula General Hodge had an arrangement whereby American convoys could get through the Russian territory in order to supply our forces. But after the creation of the Korean Republic, such arrangements were not possible, because North Korea . . . took a very hostile attitude toward the government of the Republic of Korea, and very soon thereafter pressure from the north began to develop.

The Onjin Peninsula is therefore the second place where the Korean Army was battle-tested. Their troops had to be moved in by boat, and this was fought out last summer. So the Korean Army has had battle experience here and here (indicating). They have deployed their forces now partially along the frontier and partially throughout South Korea for suppressing guerrilla activity. . . .

Mr. Taber. Are they fairly well equipped?

Dr. Johnson. They are well equipped but not quite adequately equipped. We left equipment for 65,000 men, and they have 100,000 men. Our equipment in the American Army is, of course, pretty abundant, so that each man would have two weapons. If one [Korean] man has a carbine now, he won't have a pistol.

The amount of equipment left was to cover 65,000 and the Koreans felt . . . that they should have a somewhat larger army than that. . . .

The rest of the work of the Korean Army has been to eliminate the guerrilla elements in South Korea, and that work has gone forward very effectively. We have a dispatch which indicates the number of active guerrillas in South Korea has been reduced in the last six months from around 3,200 to approximately 350. Of course, the northern Koreans send in a small group every so often.

Mr. Taber. The policy at the moment seems to be that we would let the Koreans themselves meet any Communist drive rather than for us to become involved in it; is that it?

Dr. Johnson. That is correct. And what would occur if there was a strongly supported operation by the Russians, I am not advised.[16]

[16] Ibid., pp. 739–741.

Our American embassies, confronted with newspaper comments and queries about Gromyko's allegations, were understandably concerned about what I might have said. In reply to their reports and inquiries the State Department cabled a verbatim account of my testimony, the text being that which I have given above. But the Russians persisted in their distortions. I listened with consternation to the radio broadcast of Jacob Malik's repetition of Gromyko's fatuous charges, at the August 14 meeting of the Security Council of the United Nations. Again it was stated that 100,000 Korean soldiers "equipped with American equipment and trained by the American military mission *had completed their preparations* and were prepared to begin the war at any moment." [17] Mr. Malik then added the commander of the Military Advisory Group, General Roberts, to Gromyko's list of American warmongers (John Foster Dulles, E. A. J. Johnson, General Omar Bradley, and Louis Johnson) and quoted General Roberts as saying that in the Korean soldiers "the American taxpayer has an army which is an excellent watchdog protecting the [American] capital investments in that country . . . a force which represents a maximum of results with a minimum of input." Mr. Malik further alleged that American officers were assigned to every Korean division and "were with them at the front on the thirty-eighth parallel." All this goes to prove, said the U.S.S.R. representative to the United Nations, that "American monopolists want to transform [Korea] into their colony"; that the Korean army was established and trained "to protect American capital investments in Korea," and this army (as I had presumably told members of Congress) "was, at the beginning of June, in full battle readiness to carry out the provocative incursion into Northern Korea" that started the war. These attacks on the Korean People's Democratic Republic, said Mr. Malik, were "unleashed by the Syngman Rhee clique on instructions and with the connivance of official persons in the United States of America."

How different the reality! At four o'clock on Sunday morning, June 25, 1950, the North Korean "People's Army" began an artillery and mortar barrage which preceded a rapid advance across the 38th parallel by seven infantry divisions, an armored brigade equipped by 150 Russian T-34 tanks, plus other smaller units deployed on a 150-mile front stretching across the Korean peninsula from the Sea of Japan to the Yellow Sea. Altogether the invading forces numbered about 90,000 men,[18] probably

[17] The verbatim text of Mr. Malik's speech was printed in the *New York Times*, August 12, 1950 (italics supplied).

[18] For more details, see David Rees, *Korea the Limited War* (London: Macmillan, 1964), pp. 3–20; and for the tactical history of the war, see Matthew B. Ridgway, *The Korean War* (New York: Doubleday, 1967).

The most detailed analysis of the military aspects of the Korean war will be twice the strength of the opposing forces, consisting of elements of four divisions none of which had armor since American tacticians had confidently asserted that tanks could not be effectively used in a country as mountainous as Korea. Very swiftly the invading forces pressed their advantage, advancing by four main routes, but with the greatest fire power and armor concentrated on the historic invasion route that the Mongols and Manchus had used. On Sunday afternoon, while members of our mission were frantically destroying their classified documents, North Korean aircraft attacked railway stations, airfields, and petroleum storage tanks in the Seoul area.

Meantime deceitful radio broadcasts from the North Korean capital kept telling listeners that the South Koreans had invaded North Korea, while actually the aggressors were surging southward. Seoul fell on June 28, and units of the Republic of Korea's army, fleeing from the tanks and aircraft of the North Koreans, crossed the Han River without attempting to establish a defense line there. Their 37-mm. anti-tank guns had proved "hardly better than pistols against the T-34s," and their few bazookas could destroy a tank only "if fired close up and at a vulnerable spot." [19] While the South Korean government started to move to Taegu, leaderless soldiers and panic-stricken refugees by the thousands hurried southward. In an ill-advised attempt to prevent the North Korean tanks from crossing the Han River, the sole highway bridge was dynamited while loaded with fleeing people, before thousands of South Korean soldiers, with their vehicles and heavy weapons, had crossed to the southern bank of the river.

All this wretched news, which we received in Washington with growing dismay, was only the prelude to further disasters. With the South Korean forces confused, scattered, and disorganized, a decision to send in American ground forces from Japan brought General William Dean back to Korea in command of elements of the 24th Division. But hastily flown-in troops, lacking high-powered bazookas and heavy equipment, could not stem the North Korean advance as it had been hoped they could until sea-borne units arrived to organize a defense north of Taejon. To make things worse, my old friend General Dean was captured,[20] and the retreat continued until finally enough troops, weapons, and armor had arrived

found in Roy E. Appleman, *South to the Naktong, North to the Yalu (June–November 1950): U.S. Army in the Korean War* (Washington, D.C.: Washington Office of the Chief of Military History, Government Printing Office, 1960).

[19] Robert Leckie, *The Korean War* (London: Barrie and Rockliff, 1962), p. 44.

[20] For an account of his experiences after his capture, see *General Dean's Story* (New York: Viking Press, 1954). The general told me that our former USAMGIK associate Ahn Chai Hong was brought to his cell in Seoul by the North Koreans and asked to certify that the American captive was indeed General Dean. I can well imagine Ahn's intense embarrassment.

to allow the American and South Korean forces to establish a defensive line on the Naktong River, thus saving a beachhead, roughly seventy miles long and sixty miles wide, an area provided with three good ports (Pusan, Masan, and Pohang), precious territory that became both a military mobilization area and the seat of a beleaguered government until enough troops and material could be concentrated there to permit the reconquest of South Korea. It was to this shrunken, crowded, salvaged corner of Korea that I returned in September 1950.

Why had the newly established South Korean Republic, which we in ECA were expected to make "viable," been left so defenseless? I have already explained the unsatisfactory answers the spokesmen for the Joint Chiefs of Staff gave to the Foreign Affairs Committee during our hearings on the Korean aid bill in June of 1949. Despite those evasive replies, it is now evident that a firm military decision to withdraw all American tactical troops from Korea had been reached more than six months before Secretary of State Dean Acheson made his very unambiguous statement to the National Press Club on January 12, 1950, startling his listeners by saying that the American defense line in the Far East "runs along the Aleutians to Japan and then goes to the Ryukyus [and] . . . from the Ryukyus to the Philippine Islands."[21] Very clearly Korea lay outside that perimeter, but Mr. Acheson was making no new policy when he spoke to the Press Club; he merely confirmed that the Joint Chiefs of Staff had been insisting, at least since May 1947, that all American troops be withdrawn from South Korea.[22] This decision, which proved to have been so patently unwise, apparently had been taken on the basis of the unanimous recommendation of our Far Eastern military policy-makers. Only when the remnants of the South Korean army and their inadequate American reinforcements were cooped up in the Naktong perimeter did the reckless risks which the hasty withdrawal of American forces had precipitated become painfully evident. The fact that the military policy-makers agreed, for reasons they considered compelling, that the troops should be with-

[21] The full quotation is given in Acheson, *Present at the Creation: My Years in the State Department* (New York: Norton, 1969), p. 357.

[22] For details of the recommendations of Robert Patterson, secretary of war, (May 1947), of General Albert Wedemeyer (September 1947), of the Joint Chiefs of Staff (Eisenhower, Nimitz, and Spaatz) soon thereafter, and of General MacArthur (February 1949), see Rees, *Korea the Limited War*, pp. 13–15. Secretary Acheson was entirely explicit as far as Korea was concerned. After having traced the "defensive perimeter," he said, "So far as the military security of other areas in the Pacific is concerned, it must be clear that no person can guarantee these areas against military attack. . . . Should such an attack occur . . . the initial reliance must be on the people attacked to resist it and then upon the commitments of the entire civilized world under the Charter of the United Nations." *Present at the Creation*, p. 357.

drawn does not absolve them or Secretary Acheson of blame. Learning that American troops had been withdrawn, that the secretary of state had said publicly that Korea was not in the American "defensive perimeter," and that the Congress had defeated an initial Korean aid bill, the North Koreans and their Russian mentors might very well have concluded that no American resistance to their southward movement need be feared. Mr. Acheson has argued that it is "specious" to suggest that his Press Club speech "gave the green light" to the North Koreans. Admittedly, he says, Korea was excluded from the American "defensive perimeter," but so were Australia and New Zealand.[23] But the comparison of these two unthreatened countries with South Korea is really not very convincing. There had been a long series of incursions at the 38th parallel, but none whatever on the beaches of Australia or New Zealand.

Four days after the invasion the decisions of the Security Council of the United Nations had converted the war into a U.N. effort to repel the North Korean invaders. To add to our problems in the Korea Division of ECA we now had to coordinate our procurement and logistic activities not only with the Department of State and the Pentagon but, to some extent, with the United Nations. Much of the latter activity turned out to be a sheer waste of time. The appeal of the secretary-general to the member nations for contribution of supplies to aid homeless and destitute Koreans at first brought rather pathetic results, and we found ourselves required to acknowledge, in formal diplomatic style, such things as a dozen white shirts, or five kilograms of antiseptic gauze. With our small staff we needed to concentrate on larger and more pressing problems, such as finding the shipping space for urgently needed bulk supplies.

The precipitate evacuation of our mission had created additional vexing difficulties. Since our personnel in Korea had to be moved out promptly before the North Koreans captured Seoul, they were flown to various Japanese airports. The task of locating and reassembling the mission proved time-consuming since no rallying place had apparently been selected. Husbands were hunting for wives and children, wives for husbands. Moreover long before the invasion we had heard mutterings of discontent with the mission leadership, and the confusion resulting from the separation of mission members from their families brought all manner of intensified and bitter complaints. Although Arthur Bunce possessed very great analytical ability and an excellent understanding of the Korean people, he had had no executive experience, and consequently, largely from a failure to delegate tasks, he tried to do far too much himself. Several months before the invasion our senior ECA officials had considered

[23] *Present at the Creation*, p. 358.

transferring him to a less demanding post, and when, after the invasion of South Korea, time passed and the Japan-based mission remained dispersed and ineffective, a decision was reached to find a more experienced executive with Far Eastern experience as mission chief. Until such a person could be found, Mr. Hoffman begged me to go to Tokyo to reassemble the mission, rekindle morale, and get our people ready to return to Korea when military progress would make that possible. Bunce had meantime been reassigned as mission chief to Thailand and had already taken up his new duties there when I arrived in Tokyo on September 16, 1950. I found that 27 members of our ECA mission were in Pusan, 49 in Tokyo, and 6 on Cheju Island. Of the rest quite a number had resigned and gone home, while some were still scattered around various places in Japan. An unenviable task faced me. First of all I had to placate my dear friend Wilhelm Anderson, whose appointment as mission chief I had recommended to no avail, and who now felt that no one in Washington had any confidence in him. What I set about to do I explained in a letter to my wife.

I didn't sleep well Monday night [September 18] for two reasons. It seemed hopeless to offset Anderson's unhappiness — that was one reason. The other reason was that although I went to bed early, by 12:45 for me it was morning as a result of retarding my watch as I traveled West. So I had about six wakeful hours to puzzle things out. What I did on Tuesday morning was to call all the mission together and talked to them for almost two hours, honestly, frankly, and very modestly. I praised Anderson, complimented the staff, explained the new policy, and asked each and every one to contribute their ideas on our mutually difficult tasks. It was a very personal, indeed almost sentimental talk. But it had an unmistakable effect. I think I have already succeeded in reanimating the mission members here in Tokyo and to my amazement I even swept Anderson along in the general current. Today [September 20] I had a meeting with the ten key people and it was enthusiastic in every way. . . . If I can do in Pusan what I did in Tokyo I will have the hardest job licked. I expect to go to Pusan on Friday [September 22]. . . . On the army side I saw General Eberle yesterday. . . . Everything went very well. The general is an old friend of mine and he was most gracious and completely understanding.

When I arrived in Tokyo in mid-September the fortunes of war had already begun to turn in our favor. The brilliantly executed amphibious assault on Inchon, September 15, 1950, and the recapture of Kimpo airfield, on September 17, made possible the liberation of Seoul, on September 28, exactly three months after its capture by the North Koreans.[24]

[24] But at very heavy cost: "Few people," wrote a British correspondent, R. W. Thompson, in the *Daily Telegraph*, "have suffered so terrible a liberation," because the immense American firepower "brought down a deluge of destruction." I saw the shambles this battle had made of parts of the city when I reached Seoul six days after its liberation.

The Inchon landings came at the very time when the North Korea forces were making furious efforts to breach the Naktong perimeter. Intensified American air attacks, the severing of major enemy supply routes after the Inchon landings, and the skill with which General Walton Walker employed his combined American, Korean, and United Nations forces began to tell. Cracks in the enemy lines soon became wide passages through which the liberating forces moved swiftly. I witnessed this breakthrough from the air when Everett Drumwright and I flew all along the collapsing Naktong perimeter in an observation plane piloted by Jack Seifert, Ambassador Muccio's navy air attaché. Far above the battle lines the spotter planes were directing artillery fire, while on the ground the smoke of burning napalm, of exploding shells, and of rifle fire revealed the areas of concentrated activity. At my request we flew far beyond the enemy lines to see whether the power plant at Yongwol had survived the war. It was intact. More than any other single installation, Yongwol would be needed in our planned rehabilitation effort.

Before I left for Pusan I had set the Tokyo part of our mission at work on a comprehensive rehabilitation plan. For me the situation seemed to be, in many ways, Norway all over again, except that whereas in Norway (except for a relatively small but extremely difficult operation in winter-scorched territory) very little damage had been done to cities, factories, power plants, or railways, in Korea we faced a very large area that had been summer-scorched so cruelly that with winter coming the relief and rehabilitation operations would have to be both very large and very swift. Food, housing, and medical care became the short-range top priorities. The food problem would have been fairly manageable had not shipping been such a bottleneck. Even so, we had rice ready for distribution in Seoul (actually across the river at Yongdongpo) by October 7, just nine days after the capture of the city. Housing would be a much more difficult problem and I suggested that our engineers estimate the amount of pine poles (for studdings and rafters),[25] of sawed lumber for doors, and of bamboo (for wall lattices) which, together with a kit containing the minimum tools, could be combined into a package some Koreans could use to build their own houses, with local stone for foundations, clay for walls, and thatch for roofs.

Just before I left for Pusan, on September 22, an old friend, Kim Woo Pyung, who had served very effectively on our USAMGIK National Economic Board, came to see me, as a special emissary from President Rhee in Pusan. He explained with some embarrassment that Rhee had commis-

[25] I had hoped that United Nations countries such as Canada might contribute whole shiploads of eight-foot poles with about five-inch tips, while Asian countries might be asked to supply bamboo.

sioned him to ask me to release half of our ECA funds (about $45,000,000) because Rhee had the means to bring in relief supplies much faster than we could do. I told Mr. Kim that his proposal was quite unrealistic. How could the Koreans, I asked, find the shipping even if they were able to obtain the supplies? How could they unload ships (if they could charter any) when the military forces had control of all harbors and docks? Behind Rhee's request I promptly detected the scheming of his "purchasing agents," trying once again to get their greedy hands on ECA funds. "Tell your president," I said to Mr. Kim, "that the answer is no." Two days later, in Pusan, Ambassador Muccio and I called on the president. "Oh, Dr. Johnson," said Rhee as soon as he saw me, "the first thing I want to do is to apologize for the very foolish and unreasonable request that Kim Woo Pyung made. You are so right. We have no experience in procurement, no ships, nor any unloading facilities. So I hope you will forget about this unfortunate request because we are so profoundly grateful for the wonderful work you are doing to help Korea."

For all this dissembling Rhee made still another attempt to loosen up some American funds for his "purchasing agents." When I arrived in Seoul, on October 4, I met my old friend General Crawford Sams who had charge of all the military medical assistance the army was providing for the wounded, sick, and orphaned Koreans. "What sort of a deal did you make with Syngman Rhee?" he asked me. "Suppose you tell me, General, what Rhee has told you." "Rhee asked me," said General Sams, "to turn over to him half the funds allotted for health and welfare because he has the means for bringing in supplies much quicker than I can. And to show why I should do this, he told me that 'Dr. Johnson has just agreed to turn over half of his ECA funds to me.' But I knew damn well," General Sams continued, "that you had done nothing of the sort."

On my return to Tokyo from Pusan we worked at fever heat getting ready for our return to Korea. I had arranged that the Pusan element, which Allen Loren had organized into a very effective team, would precede us as an advance party, and we would come direct to Seoul as soon as circumstances there would permit and whenever we could get transport.[26] But as the time of our departure for the war-torn capital approached, the Gyntian weaknesses of some of our mission members revealed themselves. No fewer than four out of the ten key men of the ECA mission in Tokyo refused to go into a recent combat area. All of them, to be sure, had quite willingly stayed on in Japan for three months, doing

[26] Because in daylight hours all the Japanese airfields were being used by American bombers and fighters, my flight to Pusan took off at 02:30 hours. At Tachikawa airfield, while we waited for a plane to fly us to Seoul, military planes with rockets and napalm bombs were taking off two abreast in a steady procession.

very little until I arrived to initiate some urgent planning. Now a retired navy captain, a wartime lieutenant colonel, a highly recommended program officer, and our senior legal officer all showed their inherent moral infirmities. One had slyly gotten himself reassigned to Washington; two simply refused to go back to Korea and insisted on their right to resign; while our legal officer, like a truant schoolboy, came bashfully with a piece of paper signed by a surgeon in the 49th General Hospital saying that he needed an operation for a hernia. I telephoned the surgeon and asked how long my brave lawyer had needed the operation. "Oh, about ten years would be my guess" was his answer. When I suggested to our legal officer that he go at once to the 49th General Hospital he protested vigorously that he couldn't possibly trust an army doctor to perform so delicate an operation; he would have to have it done in the States. To be sure, when I discovered their failings I didn't want any of these chronic cowards to accompany me to Seoul, but I made it abundantly clear that if they had not intended to go back to Korea they should have resigned in early July as many others did.

I arranged for some members of our mission to remain in Tokyo to coordinate our procurement activities with the army, and then split the rest into three echelons, the first of which would accompany Anderson and myself to Seoul and would include those experts who needed to make the soonest possible reconnaissance. When we arrived at Kimpo airport, with its twisted hangar skeletons, I was reminded of the Bremen airport where Brigadier Hansen and I had landed five years earlier; while Seoul, 65 percent destroyed, recalled the wrecked German cities. The railway yards were a wasteland of crater holes; the capitol, blackened by fire, stood gaunt and desolate; our embassy, the Banto Hotel, had had one corner blown away, and in Anderson's windowless office the calendar had not been changed since June 25. A press photographer accompanied me wherever I went since *Life* magazine had planned to prepare a feature article on the return of ECA to Korea, a plan that was abandoned when new disasters occurred after the entry of the Chinese Communists into the war. But I have all these photographic records of the wanton destruction that Seoul had suffered.

Because we hoped to launch a swift rehabilitation program, it was imperative that Anderson, Loren, and I survey the more important industrial installations in the Seoul-Yongdongpo-Inchon area. We hurried out to the municipal power plant to see whether it had been damaged. Fortunately it was intact, but when we visited the plant, which stands on a bluff overlooking the Han, we were faced with the gruesome sight of bloated bodies floating down the river. At Inchon we discovered that the textile plant we had reactivated (after its conversion into a basketball court by some stupid army officer in 1945) had been stripped of its looms and that the Inchon machine shops had been systematically looted. Fortunately the 1st Marine Division scaled the seawalls of Inchon before much of the loot had been moved north. Machine tools — lathes, planers, boring machines — stood coated with cosmoline and well camouflaged on flatcars ready to move north, while machines not yet loaded, but ripped from their foundations, were carefully covered with layers of sandbags lest they be damaged by American bombers.[27] Clearly, a tremendous amount of rehabilitation would be involved, and we tried to estimate as best we could what could be salvaged.

If one lives in a place even for only a couple years an inevitable attachment develops. It was with sadness that I saw what had happened to the capitol compound where I had worked, and which, aside from the capitol itself, contained a lovely Oriental palace, now badly damaged. Fortunately the nearby large house where I had lived in the summer of 1946 had escaped injury, and both the diplomatic and the ECA missions promptly moved into this lovely residence so recently evacuated by high-ranking North Koreans. Here we found a curious manifestation of a North Korean administrative decision. When our advance party arrived they found in one of the large rooms a veritable pyramid of ladies' shoes, obviously assembled from all the vacated American houses. Neatly tied together in pairs were scores of white, black, gold, blue, red, and green ladies' shoes. Whereas it was entirely clear that the machine tools from Inchon were going to be transported to North Korea for installation in factories there, no one seemed to be able to divine what the North Koreans planned to do with their carefully assembled cache of ladies' shoes. My own lovely Japanese house — one I acquired after all the plaster ceilings in our missionary house fell — had been taken over by squatters, and Bunce's house, which stood nearby, had very recently been converted into a children's hospital where rows of pitifully injured children lay in their misery.

After having made a courtesy call on President Rhee, now comfortably reinstalled in his palatial residence, I left the ECA mission in the capable hands of Anderson and Loren and hurried back to Tokyo to speed up, if possible, the shipment of urgently needed relief supplies. We had under procurement about $500,000 worth of lumber from Japan, $2,000,000 worth of rice from various countries plus about $1,300,000 worth of barley; and we had spent $172,000 for textiles, $468,000 for antitoxins, and $420,000 for ration biscuits fortified with minerals and

---

[27] Although relatively little machinery had been moved out of South Korea before the Inchon landings stopped these looting operations, large stocks of raw rubber, iron, chemicals, salt, and cement had been taken from warehouses, and our tank farms had been emptied of their petroleum products.

vitamins. We had also engaged tents for refugees, and some 350,000 paper bags so that rice rations could be easily distributed. Yet these items would only constitute a small beginning. With virtually all railway bridges bombed, most locomotives destroyed or inoperative, and hundreds of railway cars burned, the entire railway system would have to be reconstructed and re-equipped. Meantime trucks would be urgently needed as well as petroleum products, repair parts, and tires.[28] Raw materials for the surviving factories, machine parts, and skillful technicians to supervise the restoration of plants would be equally essential. The magnitude of the rehabilitation task clearly required the services of a first-class experienced executive, someone with Far Eastern experience. After I returned to Washington we were able to find just such a person in Clarence E. Meyer, a retired vice-president of the Standard Vacuum Oil Company, who had served his company in the Far East from 1913 until the time when he was imprisoned by the Japanese during World War II.

Meantime with reckless disregard for the repeated warnings that the Chinese Communists would not stand idly by if the United Nations forces pressed on to the Yalu River, the war went from momentary victory to a disastrous retreat. Our mission had hardly settled down to their manifold duties and our new chief of mission had just arrived when the reinforced enemy split through the middle of North Korea and routed the United Nations forces. Seoul fell for a second time on January 4, 1951; General Walker died in a road accident, and it was left to General Matthew B. Ridgway to form a new defense line across the peninsula roughly fifty miles south of Seoul.

Although when I left Tokyo on October 15 things looked fairly hopeful, I had not been back in Washington long before news came that the Chinese had entered the war. The whole attitude toward our ECA operation now had to be reassessed; indeed ever since September, when Secretary of State Acheson had proposed that the United Nations undertake responsibility for post-hostilities Korea, sentiment for a curtailment of ECA's commitment had been growing. We nevertheless went ahead and persuaded "Chief" Meyer to hurry out to Korea, but his opportunity to direct rehabilitation activities melted away when Seoul fell again to the enemy, and when the best that General Ridgway could do, in his really heroic stand, was to establish a defense line running from Pyongtaek to Samchok. As a result, our mission found itself back in Pusan, with elements in Taegu and Tokyo. Until the war could be brought to some conclusion, until a tolerable degree of security could be ensured, very little

---

[28] I visited the burned-out ruins of the excellent tire-molding factory we had financed and which had just gone into operation when the invasion occurred.

foreign assistance beyond the provision of relief supplies would be feasible. Since the arrival of British, Australian, Turkish, Canadian, New Zealand, Indian, South African, French, Greek, Dutch, Thai, Philippine, Belgian, and Swedish forces had made military activities multilateral, it seemed logical that relief and rehabilitation should likewise become more of a United Nations responsibility. In ECA we made no attempt to influence this decision; we stood ready to continue our work if that was wanted, or to turn over the task to the United Nations should the General Assembly so desire. Steadily sentiment in the United Nations moved in the latter direction, and on December 1, 1950, the United Nations Korean Reconstruction Agency (UNKRA) was authorized.[29] In order to effect a smooth transition I sent my program officer, Dr. Fred Bunting, to Lake Success to advise and assist the United Nations personnel who would take over our duties, and I arranged for senior U.N. officials to consult with Mr. Hoffman, Mr. Foster, and the members of my Korea Program Division in Washington.

While this work was going forward, I found it both necessary and appropriate, because of the nationwide interest in Korea, to accept a large number of speaking engagements. Among the groups I addressed were bankers in Seattle, the United Nations Association of Maryland in Baltimore, the annual meeting of the American Automobile Association in New York, and the national convention of the Military Government Association, also in New York. I pointed out in these talks to thousands of deeply interested people that the reconstruction of war-ravaged Korea offered a "tremendous challenge to the resourcefulness, the ingenuity, the perseverance and the moral fiber of the free nations of the world."[30] I tried to show the magnitude of the task by describing what had happened to the serene, beautiful "Land of the Morning Calm."

The destruction of homes, bridges, factories, power-stations, railway marshaling yards, port installations, urban buildings, farmsteads, livestock, tools, equipment, and warehouses has been terrific. Fully two-thirds of the textile plants and their machinery have been utterly destroyed. Three hundred and fourteen thousand homes have been turned into rust-colored ashes. Three million farm animals have been killed, almost two-thirds of the all-too-few

[29] Since so much of the relief expenditures came out of United States military budgets, and later out of a resuscitated American aid program (ICA), UNKRA administered only some $148,000,000 of aid funds from the time of its creation in 1950 to its dissolution in 1958. But whereas United Nations bilateral aid had been insignificant before the end of 1950, during the next few years it totaled $474,000,000 worth of supplies that were contributed by more than thirty U.N. member countries. For more details, see Chae Kyung Oh, *Handbook of Korea*, Office of Public Information, Republic of Korea (New York: Pageant Press, 1958), pp. 383–384.

[30] "Planning the Peace in Korea," address given before the United Nations Association of Maryland, November 27, 1950 (mimeographed), p. 5.

animals that the hard-working Korean farmers had owned. Factories that once produced such necessary commodities as shoes, cotton cloth, and silk yarn have been gutted by fire, charred by high explosives and reduced to tangled shambles of twisted steel. Some of this awesome destruction was caused by U.N. artillery, rockets, and napalm; some by enemy mortars, mines, and artillery; and some, quite needlessly, by the malicious arson of the retreating enemy. With exemplary realism the Koreans recognize that the destruction attributable to the U.N. "police action" was necessary and inevitable. Even so, great areas of the land lies waste, and Korea, all too poorly equipped with houses, schools, and factories before the invasion, is now infinitely poorer.[31]

I tried in these talks to mobilize public opinion in support of an energetic United Nations relief and reconstruction effort. "There is no disagreement," I said, "about whether the relief, rehabilitation, and reconstruction of Korea should be a U.N. responsibility." But I would have been less than honest if I had not pointed out that "there is considerable difference of opinion as to how comprehensive this program should be, and whether this responsibility should go beyond the provision of relief and the repair of devastated areas." [32] My contention was that United Nations military action would not suffice if in driving out an invader a nation were to be left prostrate. Unless collective action was taken to repair and reconstruct an economy from the ravages of war, threatened free countries could scarcely be expected to look forward to "liberation."

In these talks I satirized the allegations of Gromyko and Malik that the basic objectives of American military policy in Korea were to protect American investments there. Yes, I said, we are indeed protecting our investments in Korea, but what Gromyko and Malik completely failed to understand is that we Americans "do not make all our 'investments' with the idea of obtaining private gain." [33] However much the U.S.S.R. propaganda machine may "vociferate about our imperialistic intentions," the truth is, I said, that Americans had "only nickel and dime private investments in Korea." When I spoke about "protecting our investments" I was not talking about the few oil tanks and bulk stations of American oil companies, the minuscule investments of a few private firms, or the property of the missionary foundations. I was referring rather to "the billions of dollars we have invested since 1945 to make Korea a free and independent nation," investments we made "in exactly the same spirit in which we invest in schools, hospitals, and other worthy causes." And whereas

[31] Ibid., p. 6. For a gracious newspaper report about this talk, see "Korea Called a Laboratory," *Baltimore Sun*, November 28, 1950.

[32] "Planning the Peace in Korea," pp. 9–10.

[33] "Protecting Our Investment in Korea," address given before the American Automobile Association, New York, October 24, 1950 (mimeographed), p. 1.

we have long thought it "good business" to have educated citizens and a society free from pain and disease,[34] I argued that

> We have reached a position of responsibility in the family of nations . . . where concern must . . . transcend our national boundaries. We have come to realize that it is both inhumane and politically dangerous not to concern ourselves with the health and vigor of other nations in the world community. We need, therefore, make no apology for the "investments" we make in the stability and productive strength of other nations. This policy is at once wise and decent . . . an extension of the kind of community investments we have been making at home since the beginning of our history. . . . We may not be very clever at explaining ourselves to other nations (and for this reason we are very often misunderstood) but we do have, nevertheless, a rather peculiar national characteristic: we have an intense desire to let other people experience some of the privileges we have been permitted to experience.[35]

I went on to say that if we really wanted to "exploit" Korea we certainly had a golden opportunity when, by right of conquest, we "came into temporary occupancy of South Korea . . . a nation of 20,000,000 people who had been exploited for forty years." But the idea of utilizing the Korean people for our own ends "never occurred to any American."

> The question never was what can we get out of Korea but rather how can we help these people to get going so they can become a free, independent and self-dependent nation.
> And so we began making our investment in Korea. We invested our money in fertilizer, in raw materials, in machinery. We loaned Korea ships and floating electric plants. We supplied locomotives, rails, and railway ties. We hired engineers and technicians, agricultural experts and economists. We brought Korean doctors, foresters, and scientists to the United States for further training. We had spent over $500,000,000 on this comprehensive program . . . either under the army or under ECA when the shameful, criminal invasion occurred.[36]

But whereas during the military-government period this "investment in international peace" had been unilaterally an American expenditure, after the United Nations resolution on June 28, 1950, urging member states to "furnish such assistance to the Republic of Korea as may be necessary to repel the armed attack and to restore international peace and security in that area," an "investment" was made by almost a score of nations that dispatched military forces, and by twoscore that contributed civilian supplies. In one of my talks I pointed out how new circumstances in Korea had alerted large numbers of people to novel ideas and concepts. "It took the Second World War to make people generally aware of the

[34] Ibid., p. 2.
[35] Ibid., p. 3.
[36] Ibid., p. 4.

need for some adequate international agency if the world community was to be saved from another barbarous recourse to war." [37]

It was Korea that supplied the particular circumstance that transformed a "visionary, remote, and impersonal" idea into a program of action and thereby gave "a personal meaning to the urgent need for genuine international cooperation." The collective action program led not merely to a unified military command or to integrated logistic arrangements for supporting the troops provided by United Nations members; it produced supply arrangements for bringing in food, medical supplies, and all manner of relief supplies; it involved contributions of services of machines, particularly civilian aircraft, and of men and women. "In the work of caring for refugees, for the homeless, the civilian wounded, and orphans, U.N. personnel were called forward, temporarily integrated with the military doctors and nurses, and then, as the battle lines moved, given full responsibility for these tasks. Wherever we look, therefore, we find that Korea has been the great laboratory for working out the techniques of international collective action." [38]

I tried to convince my listeners that the experience that had been provided circumstantially by the war should be seized upon to unite those nations in the world community that recognized the leverage that is latent in collective action. In Korea, I said, "The U.N. can demonstrate to all nations how a planned, cooperative approach can be made to post-hostilities difficulties. It can demonstrate to threatened nations that if they resist aggressors they will not be left alone to struggle with a war-harvest of human and material wreckage. It can give an assurance that there is an international responsibility that nations can fall back upon and on which they may rely." [39]

Oddly enough it seemed easier to persuade the public of the propriety of United Nations action than to persuade the Department of State and the Pentagon to transfer responsibility for the relief and rehabilitation of Korea to U.N. agencies. Ever since the December 1, 1950, resolution, wherein the United Nations General Assembly declared its intention to assume responsibility for Korean relief and reconstruction in the post-hostilities period, we had tried our best to liquidate the Korea Program Division of ECA. We had not anticipated that disagreements between the departments of State and Defense, the United Nations, and CINCFE (the Far East Command) would take so much time to resolve. We could do nothing to settle some of these difficulties, the wrangle, for example,

[37] "Planning the Peace in Korea," p. 3.
[38] Ibid., p. 5.
[39] Ibid., p. 10.

between John Hickerson's staff and Dean Rusk's staff [40] over the extent to which the United States should receive credit for its relief expenditures in Korea against the 65 percent it had pledged of the $250,000,000 United Nations program. Within the United Nations, politics, jealousy, and indecision delayed the appointment of an agent-general; while meantime CINCFE and the 8th Army made it plain they had no enthusiasm for replacing ECA with UNKRA.

The army reluctantly agreed that UNKRA could be allowed to come to Korea as a segment of the United Nations command, but it would have no operational duties until peace and security had been restored in Korea, or in some designated part thereof. On the assumption that this had at last resolved the difficulties, we asked permission from the Bureau of the Budget to transfer enough money to the Department of the Army to ensure an adequate pipeline of relief supplies, pending preparation of legislation permitting us to transfer all our funds to that department. But the State Department now very emphatically took the position that all funds appropriated for civil assistance in Korea must be given to UNKRA, and that UNKRA in turn would decide what funds it cared to pass on to the Department of the Army. To this proposal Army tartly replied that it could not be beholden to an international agency for funds needed to prosecute a war, and laid before the Bureau of the Budget a request for $205,000,000 for civilian relief in Korea during the fiscal year 1952. Suddenly, without even consulting ECA, the Department of State capitulated, accepted the Army thesis, and we were put into the embarrassing position of being asked to appear before the Bureau of the Budget to defend a budget we had not screened or even seen.

I have given the details of this episode to explain how difficult it can be to conduct affairs in the welter of overlapping bureaucracies. It took over five months to close out the Korea Program Division, something that might have been done in two weeks if there had been a reasonable degree of agreement between State, Defense, CINCFE, and the United Nations. In the end, however, we terminated our procurement contracts, disposed of our funds, our pipeline supplies, and our Tokyo inventories, set up proper accounting procedures for the administration of counterpart funds, and, finally, disestablished our mission and my own staff. Those of my able associates who wished to remain in government service were eagerly sought by other divisions of ECA and reassigned. For myself I agreed I would go to Greece as economic adviser to the ECA mission chief after I had taken part in a special summer school program on Korea at the University of California at Berkeley. Closing the Korea Division

[40] Hickerson was assistant secretary of state for international organization affairs, Rusk assistant secretary for Far Eastern affairs.

called for an acknowledgment of my indebtedness to my loyal associates and I therefore wrote:

> You have helped me so immeasurably that I cannot hope to express adequately my deep gratitude and my profound respect. You may, however, have the satisfaction of knowing that you have been engaged in a task that is eminently worthwhile. It is a matter of some importance whether twenty million Koreans remain independent and democratic. Ours has been a heavy responsibility, but the richness of life depends on our response to challenging tasks.
>
> To some people Korea may be unreal and far away; to us it is familiar, near, and most vividly real. That is why you and I can appreciate so clearly the cruelty, the wastefulness, and the terrible wrongness of this war. Everything we were trying to build, war is destroying; everything we tried to make better, war has made worse; all the hope we had sought to engender, war is obliterating. From our experience we see the wasteful, disorganizing, destroying impact of war, and hence we can so keenly appreciate the constructive benevolence of peace.

In early June of 1950, my wife and I picked up our son at Valley Forge Military Academy and started on our drive to the West Coast. The best five years of my life had been given to Korea with a full knowledge that I would probably receive little praise for anything useful I may have done but very likely plenty of criticism for my mistakes. Yet these five years of very hard work, of intense emotional experience, had seemed so eminently worthwhile that I found it hard to understand why we had had such trouble in recruiting the talented people we so desperately needed. I remember how shocked members of my own guild of economic historians were when, at the September 1949 meeting of the Economic History Association, I pleaded with them to leave their peaceful academic quads and help us in manning the frontiers. I reminded them that on the tombstone of one of the greatest French economic historians of my generation there is only his name, the date of his death, and four words, "Killed by the Germans," for Marc Bloch had given up the cloistered university for the battlefields of the Maquis. My 1949 remarks were met with stony silence, and I was not flattered a year later when dozens of people told me how vividly they remembered not only the clairvoyance with which I foresaw the Korean war but the ringing challenge I had so courageously declared. I was not flattered because I could not forget that not one person had offered to help me find the economists we needed so badly and not one person had complimented me in 1949.

14

A MISFIT
AMONG LOTUS-EATERS
★★★★★★★★★★★★★★★★★★★★★★★★★

IN ALL my thirty years of college teaching I have never made more elaborate and thorough preparation than I did for the "Korean Program" that Professor Hiram Bingham arranged for the summer session of 1951 at the University of California in Berkeley. The program included three undergraduate courses: on Korean history, art, and economics respectively; three parallel graduate seminars; a weekly discussion session for all registrants; and a series of public lectures. Dr. George Paik, president of Chosen Christian College, had charge of the history courses, Professor Kyoicki Arimitsu of Kyoto University dealt with art, and I was responsible for economic problems and policies. Graduate students from about a dozen universities participated in the program, together with a number of junior specialists on Korea from the Department of State and the Library of Congress. Evelyn McCune, whose *Arts in Korea* is such a model of scholarship, was one of the authorities on Korean culture who enriched our Thursday evening sessions. For my students I prepared a forty-five-page syllabus for my twenty-four lectures, and I brought with me more than four hundred slides to illustrate major aspects of Korean economic life, as well as all the charts and other visual aids I had used in justifying the ECA request for congressional appropriations for Korean aid.[1]

I lectured four times a week, dealing with major aspects of the Korean economy;[2] and at each of the fifth sessions, I showed from fifty to seventy-

[1] I gave all these charts, displays, books, and documents to the University of California library, a rich collection that I hope graduate students can use.

[2] The land, the people, and spatial aspects of the economy; the country's capacity to feed her people and, beyond that, to develop agricultural exports; Korea's manufacturing potential for domestic consumption and for export; the mineral resources that Korea could exploit; the infrastructure needed for an efficient economy; the

five slides, carefully chosen to illustrate the topics I had been discussing during each week. Most of my undergraduates (approximately fifty) were of Oriental extraction, while all but one of my graduate students were Occidentals. Altogether it proved to be an exciting interlude even though we were all painfully aware of the tragic impact the war was producing. I spoke with some feeling about this in my public lecture, pointing out that whereas in the military sphere South Korea's right to be an independent nation was being defended skillfully and effectively, in the economic sphere the United Nations had not shown a corresponding willingness to deal adequately with urgent relief and reconstruction tasks. During an entire calendar year following the invasion, less than $100,000,000 had been made available for civil assistance by the combined contributions of the United States Department of the Army, ECA, and the United Nations, a total sum representing not 1 percent of the gross national product of the so-called free nations, not ½ of 1 percent, but actually only about 1/50 of 1 percent. Nor was there much prospect of improvement, since the U.N.-approved program could only be recommended to member states; even if every Allied nation provided its adequate share, this would involve less than 1/17 of 1 percent of the gross national product of the Allied nations. I therefore concluded my public lecture by asserting that if the United Nations were really trying to defend the fabric of freedom in Korea, it was high time that they "prove emphatically to people who dare to declare themselves on the side of freedom that they will not be repaid in misery and poverty for their courage, loyalty, and heroism. This . . . is the challenge that faces us . . . in Korea; and I very much fear that unless we meet this challenge forthrightly, we shall have missed one of those rare moments in human history when a real opportunity has been offered us to demonstrate, not only the fundamental humanitarianism but the basic decency and true liberalism of practical democracy." [3]

Immediately after the completion of my work in the Korean Summer Program I left Berkeley for my new assignment in Greece. A delay en route for needed repairs to a Pan American airplane gave me a day to visit one of the islands of the Azores (Santa Maria), while a stop for some consultations with our MSA [4] mission to Portugal allowed me to see something of Lisbon, that charming and extremely interesting city. I arrived in Greece during

fiscal requirements for economic progress; and ways or means for achieving a satisfactory balance of payments. An outline of these topics was detailed in my "Economic Problems of Korea" (mimeographed; Berkeley, 1951), copies of which are available in the University of California (Berkeley) library.

[3] "The Reconstruction of Korea, a Test of Democratic Decency," a lecture given at the University of California, June 22, 1951.

[4] All the former ECA missions had been renamed Mutual Security Administration (MSA) missions.

the hottest part of the year and physical discomfort may have contributed to my prompt dissatisfaction with our MSA mission and with the Greek officials with whom mission members dealt. I had been forewarned that our mission was overstaffed,[5] and I had been asked to take a hard look at the whole operation, but even so I had not expected to encounter such an atmosphere of relaxed complacency. After the dreadful urgency of our tasks in Korea, I found the leisurely pattern of life in Greece not only frustrating but rather irritating.

Although all our mission offices presumably opened at 8:00 A.M., most people drifted in to suit their convenience; moreover many would just check in and then leave to visit the PX or to have coffee on the roof. Secretaries would disappear, leaving their offices unattended. The daily staff meeting of the mission chief scheduled for 9 A.M. actually began whenever a suitable group had convened. The usual procedure was for the public-affairs officer to open the meeting with a recapitulation of the main news items and the editorials in some half dozen Athenian newspapers. This ritual finished, the activities of the several divisions of the mission were reported seriatim, all in all a routine, time-consuming daily formality. Since four days were "short," ending at 2 P.M., with closing time even earlier on Saturday,[6] the mission personnel could spend their afternoons on the beach, at their villas in Glyfada, Philathea, or Kiphisia, or sailing on the blue waters of the Aegean. Except for a few serious and really dedicated "honest specialists," work and worry did not seem to bother the majority of the two hundred and fifty members of the MSA mission. Our mission chief, Roger Lapham, entranced everyone who knew him with his courtesy, his charming amiability, and his innate kindness. But as a successful politician (he had been mayor of San Francisco) he benevolently assumed that all his staff members knew their jobs and that they therefore required no supervision. As a consequence, there seemed to be no over-all plan, no mission goals or targets; instead each division was virtually free to do as it pleased. This lack of coordination had almost made a "Rabelaisian monastery" out of the mission, whose motto could well have been *faire ce que veux*.

I sensed this fragmentation when I began talking with people in the several divisions. I found, for example, that although divisions such as Program, Agriculture, Trade, Finance, and Transportation all had "econo-

---

[5] A senior MSA official, who had himself served in Greece, put it this way: "It's as if when you're building a house the excavators would stay on after their work was done, setting an example for the masons, carpenters, plumbers, electricians, and painters who would do likewise. Because Greece is so pleasant a place to live in, everyone tries to stay on whether needed or not."

[6] Monday and Friday were "long" days when office hours were 8–2 and, after a siesta break, 4–6. On Tuesday, Wednesday, and Thursday, office hours were 8–2, while on Saturday, our shortest day, office hours were 8–1.

mists" on their staffs, as did the adviser to the Bank of Greece, the economists had not once met together to discuss over-all policies, and my suggestion that we inaugurate regular meetings came as a most revolutionary proposal which met strong objection from the mission chief's deputy and from members of the Finance Division. Nor was it welcomed by strong-willed individualists in several divisions who wanted to be entirely free to design their own programs and specify their particular budgetary needs. One of the ablest of this type, Walter Packard, certainly was a true friend of Greece, a man so highly respected by the Greek government that a statue was erected to honor him several years before his death; but his single-minded ambition to make Greece self-sufficient in rice production led to strange economic contradictions that I will presently describe.

During my first week in Athens I lived in a small room on the fifth floor of the King George Hotel. Fortunately I had a balcony facing Constitution Square, and, as I said in a letter to my wife, I could "look down on literally thousands of people, sitting at little tables drinking their resin-flavored wine or their anis-flavored liqueur, all, no doubt talking politics, under a big white moon that hangs in the sky bathing the Parthenon in a misty light." But much of the pleasure I might have derived from this romantic view was dissipated by the insufferable heat. It reminded me of one summer in Norman, Oklahoma, when the heat was exceptionally offensive; "Athens," I wrote before the first week was half spent, "is Norman all over again which, as you recall, meant three baths a day." Rather reluctantly I therefore moved to a mission hotel in Kiphisia, twelve miles from Athens, a pleasant place, some sixteen hundred feet higher than Athens, a cluster of villas and hotels in a community near Mount Penteli that had been a summer resort at least since Roman days. Here I met quite a number of the seven hundred American families in Greece, most of whom really seemed to be enjoying their newfound comforts, particularly their large villas cared for by three or four maids and yardmen. I rather dreaded the prospect of establishing such a ménage, and I wrote to my wife, "I have a feeling that the Americans in Kiphisia are party-mad, and I am not at all anxious to get involved in a competition to show who can give the most elaborate party. I want to do a creditable, honest job in Greece, and yet learn all I can about the classical world."

I had been advised against trying to find a house in Kiphisia in August because wealthy Athenians always bid up rentals during summer months. It took me only a few days to discover that wealthy Greeks used all manner of tactics to capitalize on any money-making or money-saving opportunities. I learned, for example, that the long line of elegant automobiles neatly parked each morning by the Grand Bretagne Hotel were not really for hire even though each sported a "Taxi" sign. Instead the wealthy owners of these vehicles were merely complying with a favoritistic legal provision which allowed them to license their Cadillacs or Mercedeses as public vehicles at less than a tenth of what the fees otherwise would be, provided their cars were "for hire" two hours a day. The chauffeurs, of course, were nowhere to be found. This same type of venality was brought more sharply to my attention in another context before I had been in Greece ten days. I learned that a retired American general in charge of the port of Piraeus had become so embittered that he would soon leave. I went to see him to find out what lay behind his disenchantment. He told me that he was unwilling to take the blame for excessive unloading costs which he estimated might exceed a hundred thousand dollars a year.

"Instead of bringing our colliers up to the wharfs and unloading coal directly into the bunkers with the ships' winches, we have to anchor out in the harbor and lighter the coal to the bunkers."

"Why don't you moor at the bunkers?" I asked, innocently.

"Because," he replied tartly, "of that big floating dry dock that's anchored right in the channel."

"Why don't you move the dry dock?" I asked.

"Because six hundred men who work on that dry dock go over that catwalk," to which he pointed, "and buy resina wine in that little *taverna* you can see over there."

"But this is ridiculous," I protested. "Here you are in charge of the port of Piraeus and you let the owner of a little wine shop impose huge, unnecessary costs on American taxpayers. Why do you do it?"

"You'll learn something about Greece after you've been here awhile," he answered. "I do it because that damned wine shop belongs to the prime minister. But I'm getting the hell out of here. I'm not going to be responsible for this mess."

Seventeen days after I arrived in Greece, Paul Porter, who headed the Paris office of MSA, telephoned to Roger Lapham asking that I be released for thirty days to go to Belgrade, Yugoslavia, on an urgent assignment. He argued that since I had not been long in Greece, I surely could be spared for such a short period. Although both Lapham and John K. Peurifoy, our ambassador, were reluctant to release me, they consented, but with a firm promise on Paul Porter's part that the temporary duty in Belgrade would not exceed thirty days. So instead of going to Epirus, as I had planned to do on August 28, 1951, to get a firsthand view of the problems of Greek peasants on the Albanian frontier, I flew to Belgrade, never suspecting that my "thirty days" would, after a brief return to Athens, grow into a three-and-a-half-year sojourn in Yugoslavia.

In order to explain why I had been asked to go at once to Belgrade I must very briefly review the circumstances that led to the 1950 American food program for Yugoslavia and the joint British-American-French decision to underwrite Yugoslavia's balance-of-payments deficit for 1951–52. After the Tito-led Partisan faction came to power in 1945,[7] its leaders made arrangements with their Eastern wartime allies whereunder major shares of Yugoslavia's exports would be sent to East Germany, Poland, Czechoslovakia, and the U.S.S.R. in order to build up credits with which to finance the importation of capital equipment needed for an elaborate investment program designed to industrialize and modernize the Yugoslav economy. By 1948, exports to a value probably exceeding $400,000,000 had been sent eastward; but before any machinery and industrial equipment had been received irreconcilable political differences developed which led to the expulsion of Yugoslavia from the Cominform and the termination of all trade relations between Yugoslavia and the Soviet bloc countries. Rather sheepishly the Yugoslavs now had to turn to Western nations for help. But here they found themselves at a very great disadvantage because, in 1945–46, they had rather arrogantly nationalized all the property of Western nations without compensation. To the Yugoslav requests for investment credits with which to purchase machinery and equipment for scores of industrial projects, on which huge local outlays (e.g., for foundations, buildings, access roads, power lines) had already been made, the consistent reply was that there could be no consideration whatever given to these proposals until the Yugoslavs had made restitution for all sequestrated property. The roughest sort of estimates indicated that these claims might exceed $155,000,000. When I arrived in Belgrade I discovered that my tidy little thirty-day task was to work out, in consort with the British, the French, and the Yugoslavs, some arrangement for funding these (nationalization) debts. "When Yugoslavia occupies at this very moment such a critically important place in the European defense puzzle," I wrote to my wife on September 4, 1951, "it is nothing short of fantastic that in thirty days I am expected not only to make proposals for debt adjustments with Britain, France, Belgium, Switzerland, Holland, Germany, the United States, and eight other countries, but concurrently to serve as 'principal economist' and make recommendations for the judicious spending of over $50,000,000 of American aid."

This bizarre situation, which would have been ludicrous had the East European outlook not been so ominous, had been precipitated by a serious drought that had brought about a very sharp reduction of the Yugoslavian

[7] As early as 1942 with the formation of AVNOJ (Anti-Fascist Council for the National Liberation of Yugoslavia), plans were developed to convert the Partisan military organization into a political movement. Regional branches of AVNOJ were formed, making possible a wide enough representation by 1945 so that a government could be organized. For a brief account of this chapter of Yugoslav history, see Basil Davidson, *Partisan Picture* (Bedford: Bedford Books, 1946), pp. 318–331.

wheat and barley crop in the summer of 1950.[8] The upshot had been an American ad hoc decision to provide food relief on a generous scale in order to allow Yugoslavia to survive as an independent nation without knuckling under to Cominform threats. The object, in short, was to enable Yugoslavia to remain outside of the Russian orbit. A seasoned Red Cross veteran, Richard Allen, was put in charge of the food program and given, as I recall, five assistants to supervise the food distribution in as many hastily defined districts. Meantime rather prompt agreement had been reached at a London conference, in June 1951, between British, American, and French diplomats that it would be to their mutual interest to "keep Tito afloat" by underwriting the Yugoslav balance-of-payments deficit for one calendar year.[9] A very capable American economist, Emile Despres, had been sent to Belgrade to advise Richard Allen and the ambassador, George Allen, on these complicated problems, but since he had to return to his teaching duties at Williams College in early September, I was whisked up from Greece to take his place temporarily while a permanent replacement was recruited.

Looking back on this weird conjuncture I am still appalled at the naiveté that lay behind the Washington attitude toward Yugoslavia. Whereas in Greece an overgrown MSA staff, far in excess of any actual need, was almost without exception underemployed, in Yugoslavia a retired Red Cross official, a professor borrowed for three months, a diligent Mount Holyoke graduate posted as an economics officer in the embassy, a former Red Cross official who served as program officer and controller, and two very bright but quite inexperienced young "end-use" auditors[10] represented the total personnel Washington thought necessary to deal with one of the most critical situations that had faced our policy-makers since 1945. This handful of Americans, particularly Richard Allen and I, working in concert with our British and French associates, Sir Francis Mudie and Alphonse Sicard, were expected to find some fairly prompt solution for the "nationalization" debts of the Yugoslavs, and also for another cluster of debts that were further complicating the relations of Yugoslavia with the West. Cut off abruptly from trade relations with the Cominform countries in 1948, Yugoslavia had rather hastily entered into bilateral agreements with a number of West European countries. Under these arrangements Yugoslav

---

[8] An observant agricultural attaché, John J. Haggerty, had accurately forecast this crop reduction in the spring of 1950.

[9] Provided it did not exceed $120,000,000. The fiscal responsibilities of the underwriting governments were to be shared: 65 percent by the United States, 23 percent by the United Kingdom, and 12 percent by France.

[10] Their function was to visit factories or other enterprises and verify that American aid goods were being purposefully used and properly recorded on receipts required by the mission controller.

exports were to pay for imports, but since any day-by-day equilibrium could obviously not be maintained, the agreements provided for "swings" whereby one or the other of the trading partners could receive temporary credit pending a capacity to make full payments (for imports) by requiting exports. What had happened, however, was that the Yugoslavs had regularly fallen behind in their export commitments and had therefore become indebted to each of their trading partners for the full amount of the "swings," and, in many cases, for more than the agreed-upon swing credits. Some solutions therefore had to be found for these "swing" debts as well as the "nationalization" debts.

Fortunately our British and French associates proved to be extremely competent men. Sir Francis, who had been governor of Sind, brooked no nonsense, and although he was too harsh with the Yugoslavs to suit Richard Allen, he helped set a tone to our conversations with the Yugoslavs which daily put them on their mettle. Sicard had had experience in international business, and took a very practical attitude toward the debt problem.[11] We met every forenoon with the Yugoslavs who, with exemplary forthrightness, supplied us with whatever data we required. Then each afternoon, jointly or individually, we would work out possible settlement plans, country by country. We had, of course, no authority to settle anything; all we could do was to reach agreement among ourselves and with the Yugoslavs concerning desirable types of settlement which the Yugoslavs could proffer to their trading partners through diplomatic channels. We had, however, hoped to go further than this; what we really wanted to do was to put together an integrated settlement that could be strongly supported through diplomatic channels by the British, French, and United States governments. But for fear of offending bitter critics of the Tito government, our State Department, to our embarrassment, categorically refused to lend the support we requested, thereby undercutting the promised British and French diplomatic assistance and leaving it to the Yugoslavs to negotiate as best they could, a process that took not a matter of months but the better part of two years.

Although we worked diligently, we had only been able to rough out first approximations of possible settlement proposals for the nationalization debts when the time came for me to return to Greece. We had, however, been rather more successful in finding solutions for the swing debts.[12]

[11] It should be recalled that Yugoslavia had been a critical part of the *cordon sanitaire* and consequently the French government had made large grants to Yugoslavia and had encouraged private French investments. Altogether the French had invested the equivalent of about $400,000,000 in Yugoslavia in the interwar period, and they hoped for some reimbursement.

[12] In some cases the swing debts were funded, in other instances the swings were enlarged to absorb deficits not covered by previous agreements.

During that busy month I had come to have a profound respect for the Yugoslav leaders we dealt with. Because it is always easy to color past impressions by the views of the present, I have carefully reread all the letters I wrote to my wife from Belgrade in August and September 1951. The following excerpts indicate that my very favorable impressions of the Yugoslavs were formed during this initial month of daily association:

There is pride, energy, and real purpose in Yugoslavia, and everyone comments on the complete honesty and trustworthiness of the Yugoslav people. The men I meet with are really brilliant. . . . One has a feeling that this is indeed a key spot and that, of course, is why the operation is tripartite. . . . I suspect the Yugoslav situation (political and economic) is just about the most important development in Europe. It calls for the greatest diplomatic tact. Tito has broken with the Russians and the task is to get this remarkable country solidly lined up with the Western nations. . . . The Yugoslavs hope to achieve something better than [Russian] communism and something more liberal than capitalism. . . . I tell you in all frankness that the situation looks infinitely more hopeful than that in Greece. This country not only has resources but people who have energy, imagination, and a real sense of progress. . . . I am still greatly impressed with the Yugoslav officials. They are so young, bright, and serious. You can analyze an economic problem with them as you would in a graduate seminar. They are still Communists, but they have enough objectivity to see that they made a lot of mistakes in 1946 and 1947 by slavishly following Russian patterns. What they are earnestly trying to do now is to find some workable compromise between central planning and private enterprise. I am not certain how stable such a compromise can be, but it is patently clear that the 10,000,000 Yugoslav peasants are staunch individualists who will have to be given a much larger measure of market freedom. . . . I am going to miss these bright, clever, witty, forthright Yugoslavs when I get back to Athens. What I saw of Greek ministers and bureaucrats certainly did not please me. They are maneuverers and "operators"; they have few long-range plans; they don't think through their problems. . . . I have a very certain feeling that this is a far sounder place to invest foreign-aid money than any other I have seen. What I can't understand is why about 250 people have been assigned to the mission in Greece whereas here there isn't even a handful. . . . There is one basic difference between the Yugoslavs and the Russians. The Yugoslavs have a sense of humor not merely at the dinner table (where the Russians, as you remember from our experiences in Korea, can be pleasant) but at the conference table (where the Russians are frozen-faced). One can twit the Yugoslavs about their new-style Marxism and they enjoy the pleasantry immensely.

As the foregoing excerpts from the letters I wrote during my thirty days in Yugoslavia so clearly indicate, I became somewhat apprehensive about my return to Greece. But since I had succeeded in persuading my very capable friend John W. Harriman, who had been my deputy when I directed the Korea Program Division of ECA, to resign his position as deputy chief of the MSA mission to the United Kingdom and come to Yugoslavia as "principal economist," I had a feeling that I was leaving Yugoslavia in very good hands. I therefore took the fabled Orient Express to Venice, where I saw for the first time the exquisite architecture of that dreamlike city, and then went on to Naples where I met my wife when she arrived on the S.S. *Constitution*. After two days in Rome, we flew to Athens and took up our residence in Kiphisia in a small villa temporarily vacated by an American family on home leave. But my thirty days in Yugoslavia, unfortunately, made the whole Greek picture seem even more blemished. The planlessness of the whole aid operation, the absence of targets and goals, and the pedestrian level of discussions by contrast were not only disheartening but downright chafing. I began to ask more and more embarrassing questions as I came to appreciate the unsatisfactory way in which resources, both pecuniary and human, were being utilized. I soon sensed that I was not alone in my misgivings but that they were shared by embassy officers including Harry Turkel, the economic counselor, Charles Yost, the deputy chief of the mission, and John Peurifoy, our ambassador to Greece. I found another skeptic in the very able Treasury representative, Gesualdo Costanza.

One of the most glaring examples of many foolish concessions that had been made to the sly Greek politicians in the early days of American intervention was an arrangement whereby the American government purchased gold sovereigns for dollars and sold them to the Greeks for drachmas. Before I went to Athens I had been warned again and again by State Department experts on Greece that the stability of the whole Greek economy depended on this right of convertibility, and that this system must under no circumstances be tampered with. I could see no justification for this doctrinaire view. That suspension of this arrangement would lead to a capital flight seemed very improbable since unwittingly we were already engaged in subsidizing Greek capital exports. It was not only wealthy Greeks who bought sovereigns, which they deposited in Swiss banks or hoarded as a hedge against inflation, but workmen, maids, and merchants as well. Hence instead of stimulating domestic investment, which is always a critical factor in development, our sale of sovereigns was facilitating a systematic and continuous efflux of Greek savings. Turkel, Costanza, and I soon found ourselves agreed on two points: the silly sale of gold sovereigns should be ended, and the currency should be revalorized to make imports more expensive and exports cheaper.

Walter Packard had the right idea when he argued, as he did so passionately on every possible occasion, that Greece could, by proper land reclamation, become much more self-sufficient in food production. But although I found myself in complete agreement with Packard's objectives, I took sharp issue with him about the methods he was using to attain his entirely laudable ends. On his part he was so certain that he could convert me to his point of view that he organized a trip to his reclamation projects so that a number of us could see how his work was conducted. We went by train to Thessaly and Thrace, stopping at points where he had scheduled his demonstrations. As a hard-boiled economist I was appalled at what I saw. In a country cursed with endemic underemployment, Packard was using the most modern capital-intensive methods of operation in a region where poor tobacco farmers were normally employed on their hard-scrabble patches of ground for less than ninety days a year. Instead of using this redundant labor[13] and providing underemployed farmers with supplemental incomes, Packard had ordered huge, heavy-duty Caterpillar bulldozers that could uproot seventy-five-foot trees in three minutes, and the largest Caterpillar crawler tractors and scrapers for building earthworks and leveling the future paddy fields. The trees removed in the reclamation operation were heaped into huge brush piles by machines and burned, thereby depriving poor farmers not only of fuel but, once again, of needed employment. In this man of most excellent intentions I detected a dogmatic combination of the "honest specialist" and the "do it the American way" overseas American. He told me he had ordered the very latest-type combines for harvesting the rice. "But," I said "in these small paddies, surely the rice could be cut with sickles." "Oh no," he replied, "in California we use combines in much smaller paddies."

A day later when Packard, with equal pride, had shown us a reclaimed valley that had been a torrent in the rainy season and a buffalo-wallow wasteland the rest of the year, I suggested we go up to a *taverna* that we could see on a hillside and talk with the tobacco farmers. "That's a good idea," said Packard, "I've never done that." I had been told that if Americans wandered into a wineshop it would not be long before some local customer would open a conversation. When such an overture had been made by a self-appointed spokesman, I told our interpreter to ask the countrymen what they thought of the improvements that were being made. The answer rather surprised Packard.

"We think it most unfortunate," said the Greek farmer, "that you Americans are wasting so much money."

"But we're not wasting money," I answered; "we're making rice paddies for you so that you will have an opportunity to raise more food and make more money."

[13] It has taken a surprisingly long time for the designers of development programs to recognize the simple fact that underdeveloped countries are long on labor and short on capital. A recent report by Edwin M. Martin, chairman of the Development Assistance Committee of the Organization for Economic Cooperation and Development, which advocates labor-intensive industrial projects, is heralded as news. See "O.E.C.D. Aide Urges High Use of Labor in Poor Lands," *New York Times*, February 20, 1970.

"We're poor tobacco farmers," said the spokesman. "We can't take care of the rice paddies you're building. We can't buy the seed or the fertilizer, or maintain the levies and water channels. In two or three years this valley will just be a buffalo wallow again."

Here then was an idea that had real merit but one which had not been properly related to the cultural situation, and this failing of the "do it the American way" officials can be documented by dozens of examples. In many ways, a worse fault stemmed not from any shortcomings of the MSA mission but from the policies of Congress and the Washington executive departments. Before World War II, tobacco farmers in Turkey, Greece,[14] Bulgaria, and Yugoslavia found good markets for "Oriental leaf" (Turkish) tobacco in Germany, France, Britain, Holland, Belgium, and Italy. The war, and particularly the occupation of Germany, had turned most of these tobacco markets over to American tobacco companies, and they, in turn, wasted no time in obtaining strong support from congressmen not only from Virginia, the Carolinas, and Kentucky, but from tobacco-growing states in New England. When a score of congressmen visited Greece, I brought up this issue, only to be informed that the tobacco question was not anything for us to be concerned about. As Joe Martin of Massachusetts put it, the issue was "closed." Ever critical of how foreign-aid money was spent, these members of Congress must have understood that if the United States destroyed the market for Greek, Turkish, or Yugoslav exports, compensatory dollar grants would be necessary if "viability" was ever to be attained. But, as I discovered, the tobacco issue was not to be debated.

Some of the things the Agricultural Division of our mission had promoted I warmly approved. In the rich lands of the Peloponnesus efforts had been made to persuade farmers to produce tomatoes (rather than "Oriental leaf" tobacco) by building small canning plants. One other excellent innovation was the "mechanical cultivation service" whereby every two or three years heavy tractor-drawn plows could turn up the humus that the Greek farmers could not possibly reach with their light steel or wooden plows. Little had been done, however, to improve the marketing of farm and orchard produce. On a trip to Epirus I made an experiment to get some rough measure of the adverseness of the terms of trade between Athens and rural areas. Before I left Athens I spent the equivalent of one dollar for oranges and the retailer gave me exactly eight oranges. When I spent an identical sum of money in Arta, the town in the very center of the orange-growing region, I received seventy-five oranges. As far as I

---

[14] Tobacco exports provided 45 percent of prewar Greek export earnings but in 1951 Germany, which in 1938 imported 20,000 tons, took only 2000 tons. See L. S. Stavrianos, *Greece: American Dilemma and Opportunity* (Chicago: Henry Regnery, 1952), p. 213.

could discover nothing was being done to correct this situation, which not only was inequitable but was holding down the buying power of the rural population and thereby arresting growth.

Since the United States was providing Greece with about $250,000,000 a year in grant aid, I thought it wholly appropriate that I investigate the uses the Greek government and Greek businessmen were making of their foreign-exchange earnings. What puzzled me was that the mission had not insisted on more rigorous controls. I found, for example, that approval had been granted for the purchase of a string of racehorses from Egypt, and that generous foreign-exchange allocations were regularly being made for the importing of private passenger automobiles and a wide range of luxury goods. Meantime on a long list of quite necessary goods high import duties were levied, and the proceeds of some of these customs duties had been legislatively earmarked for special beneficiaries. Thus hack drivers, whose employment steadily fell off as automobiles replaced horse-drawn carriages, received part of the revenues derived from sugar duties, while aged priests were the recipients of other "third-party" taxes. Strong representation should have been made to the Greek government that unless they put their house in better order they could not expect American aid to continue on the lavish scale that had been permitted by a listless and uncritical mission.

The United States aid program was less than four years old; it seemed almost unbelievable that an operation could have become so confused and the policy patterns so misshapen in such a short period of time. Apparently all manner of experiments had been made by "honest specialists" and other varieties of overseas entrepreneurs. On a trip to Joannina, the capital of Epirus, for example, I passed through a large village with perhaps two hundred houses that had been built, in Levittown style, in 1948 or 1949. Not 5 percent of the houses were occupied because there simply was no employment available for prospective tenants. What mastermind had located the houses in this ill-chosen place, and thereby wasted large amounts of American money, I never could discover. Yet on the same trip I visited the future location of a small run-of-river hydroelectric plant for whose construction a French company had been engaged. No work had begun on the project, but a large compound of houses for workers was being built, houses which within a year or two would quite likely stand vacant. All this ill-planned housing had been or was being built in a country desperately short of housing in permanent employment centers. Yet the over-all plan to electrify Greece certainly was praiseworthy and, for the most part, had very good technical direction. My friend Walker Cisler, now president of Detroit Edison, who helped me in Norway and in Korea and whose advice I later sought in Yugoslavia, had personally scrutinized the electrification plan, insisting on a proper balance between hydro and thermal plants and urging that thermal plants be built near the abundant beds of lignite. Unfortunately not all technical programs had the benefit of such wise and experienced advisers.[15]

The American mission to Greece, to be sure, had had no experience to build on, since it was the first of our aid missions, antedating the Marshall Plan organizations by almost two years. Each mission chief in Greece seems to have experimented with a wide range of policies. In the process people came and went, as one venture after another was tried. Moreover each division became semiautonomous, and within each branch of the divisions an extraordinary freedom of action developed. Lapham had four regional officers whose task presumably was to keep him informed about areal problems and to coordinate activities in northern, northeastern, and northwestern Greece and in the Dodecanese Islands. But the job of the island representative seemed to be chiefly one of entertaining the "Cook's tourist" mission members when they came, as they did in a steady stream, to the island of Rhodes. If there had been a few "tourists" on United States payrolls in Norway and Korea, in Greece there were dozens who had found a paradise for their peregrinations. "Have you not been to Crete?" I was asked again and again. Actually the only Greek island I visited was Rhodes where my wife and I went for Christmas[16] just before we left Greece.

My departure from Greece came much sooner than I had expected. About a month after his arrival in Belgrade, on October 1, 1951, my successor, John W. Harriman, learned that for compelling personal reasons, he could not remain in Yugoslavia. As a consequence, strong pressure was brought to persuade me to accept the position of deputy chief of the emergent Belgrade mission. Because I wanted my wife to see what life in Yugoslavia would be like, we flew to Belgrade for Thanksgiving. The strong representations that Richard Allen and I had made in September had resulted in agreement by Washington and the Yugoslavs to enlarge the planned MSA mission by adding industry, technical training, agricultural, and trade and finance officers. For the industry position I had warmly recommended Robert Hochstetler, who had served on the ECA mission to

[15] Two American highway construction advisers were asked to leave Greece, a dozen Greek contractors were investigated, and the Greek government was asked to rebate to MSA over $100,000 when irregularities were discovered in a single road project. See Stavrianos, *Greece*, p. 215.

[16] At my personal expense. When the director of the Greek Airlines learned that we planned to go to Rhodes, he sent open round-trip tickets by messenger. Since I was then recommending a sharp reduction in United States aid to Greece, I certainly could not afford to be beholden to any Greek official. I therefore ascertained the regular fare, drew a check for that amount, and had the messenger delivering it obtain a receipt.

Korea and who had willingly gone back to that war-wracked country in September 1950. When we reached Belgrade for our two-day visit I learned to my satisfaction that he had agreed to come to Yugoslavia.

Although Belgrade is cloudy and gloomy in late November, my wife seemed quite willing to live there, and I agreed to report for duty in Belgrade on January 1, 1952, on one condition, namely that the Yugoslav government would have a house available for us when we arrived. I made this stipulation because during my thirty-day temporary duty I had become aware of the unsatisfactory way in which our few people were housed. Since the Yugoslavs had expressed a keen desire to have me come back to their country, I thought I had a good bargaining position. It turned out that I really did, but, as I shall explain in my next chapter, things turned out very differently from what I had expected. Meantime, as we flew back to Greece, I suddenly realized that I had just another month in which to complete a lot of work in Greece that I had projected. Above all I felt duty bound to put together the basic elements of an economic plan before I left Athens.

That plan which I developed in close collaboration with Harry Turkel and Al Costanza was on the whole essentially orthodox. It contemplated five interlinked basic policies looking forward respectively to an increase in domestic productivity for the purpose of reducing imports and increasing exports; stabilization of prices, wages, and business expectations so that living standards would be protected, hoarding would become unprofitable, and private investment would be stimulated; holding the Greek governmental deficit to manageable proportions, so that more counterpart funds could be devoted to reconstruction projects;[17] comprehensive currency and foreign exchange reforms designed to increase exports, terminate the sale of gold sovereigns, and give the Greek people a currency in which they could have confidence; and appropriate fiscal policies which would make it possible for the Greek economy to support the required military forces with the least possible amount of foreign aid. I prepared a number of charts to indicate how satisfactorily or how unsatisfactorily these five goals of policy were being realized, and in relation to these trends I tried to make some tenable projections. Once I had completed my analysis, I realized that the over-all situation actually showed considerably more promise than I had initially assumed. But I became certain that progress

[17] Because the Greek aid mission began its operations during a virtual civil war, a sizable amount of counterpart funds (the drachma equivalent of the value of United States aid imports) had regularly been allocated to reduce the budgetary deficit of the Greek government. Consequently in order to free more drachmas for rehabilitation projects, the governmental deficits would have to be systematically reduced. In 1949 almost 75 percent of counterpart funds were used to cover budgetary deficits, leaving only a fourth for investment purposes.

could be accelerated only if certain rather drastic policy decisions were reached promptly.[18]

My import chart showed that the trend line of current-needs imports had passed a 1948–49 peak and was bending downward;[19] and my projections were based on the assumption that as more reconstruction projects (such as those undertaken by Walter Packard) were completed, imports could further decrease. My export chart did not show corresponding progress, since by clinging to an overvalued drachma, the Greeks had priced themselves out of many markets. My projections were therefore based on the assumption that the Greek government could be persuaded to devalue. My balance-of-payments chart revealed one promising trend: an upturn in in-payments from invisibles (tourism, freight earnings, immigrant remittances) and my projections were based on the assumption that more Greek shipowners could be persuaded to repatriate shipping registered in Panama, Honduras, Liberia, and elsewhere, thereby further increasing invisible credits. My fiscal and budgetary charts showed rather contradictory trends, for whereas improved tax collections had narrowed the gap between total expenditures and total revenues, new pressures, resulting from inflation, were perpetuating budget deficits. Subsidies, pensions, and a wide range of new expenditures for civil purposes had been steadily increasing, and the resulting budgetary deficits seriously interfered with the investments that should have been made with counterpart funds to increase productivity. Unless more drachmas could be allocated to rehabilitation and reconstruction projects, many of these worthy ventures, already begun, would have to be suspended.[20]

The inferences were to me quite clear. Devaluation of the drachma, abandonment of the sale of gold sovereigns, and a much more rigorous control over government deficits had become policy desiderata. Systemati-

[18] Although I took the initiative in drawing up an over-all mission plan, I obtained data and a great deal of assistance from all the divisions of the MSA mission, from the embassy staff, from the Treasury representative, from the Bank of Greece, and from the Greek government. But the charts and projections were my own work. I showed my charts and explained them to a group of visiting journalists at Charlie Yost's residence after which I turned them over to the Finance Division for criticism. About a week later a delegation of congressmen arrived, and unknown to me a briefing was scheduled. An urgent message came summoning me to the conference room. There sat two members of the mission with my charts ready to explain them had not Charlie Yost's sharp eyes recognized that they were my charts which he thought I should myself explain. It was not I who was embarrassed.

[19] Mainly because of the greater domestic production of food and fibers, and a greater economy in consumption.

[20] I ascertained that 504 projects had been launched, of which 177 had been finished, while the other 327 projects were in varying degrees of completeness. The drachmas needed to finance all these projects were, for lack of over-all planning, far in excess of any reasonable expected counterpart-funds accumulation.

cally Turkel, Costanza, and I laid these issues before the mission chief and obtained his consent for Turkel to fly to Washington to persuade the State Department and MSA to take steps to implement our drastic proposals. The key to the whole program, however, would be some adequate compulsion that could be used to make the Greek government and Greek businessmen take over more responsibility for the economic health of their country. As it was, the government could run deficits, year after year, on the safe assumption that the (drachma) proceeds from the sale of United States aid imports would cover shortfalls in revenue. Meantime the businessmen, instead of investing in productive apparatus and machinery, were hedging against further inflation by accumulating inventories, by sending their sovereigns to Swiss banks, or by building luxury apartments for wealthy tenants.[21]

The only effective solution for this defensive and negative attitude on the part of both government and business would have to be a very sharp reduction in United States aid. This would compel the government to take steps to close the budgetary gap, and it would, when legalized capital exports were no longer facilitated, induce businessmen to begin investing in productive operations. The whole package of policies that Turkel, Costanza, and I proposed therefore included devaluation, fiscal reform, ending the sale of sovereigns, a drastic reduction in foreign aid, and, associated with that, a reduction of the mission to about a fourth of its 1951 size. Actual implementation of this program took place after I had left Greece, but I had the satisfaction of knowing that I had played a part in introducing some dynamic elements into the Greek economy. For as soon as the Greek businessmen saw that their arbitragist activities would no longer be abetted or condoned, they began to invest in domestic enterprises, and a moribund economy began to grow.

The rain came down in torrents the morning of January 1, 1952, when my wife and I entrained for Belgrade. For us Greece had been a joy and a disappointment. A joy because of the beauty of Grecian sunrises, when indescribable surges of salmon, purple, blood-red, and gold sweep over

---

[21] Before I was urged to return to Yugoslavia, I assumed I would remain in Greece for some time and therefore began a search for suitable living quarters. My wife learned about a small penthouse in Athens and we tried to rent this. I say "tried" because the terms kept changing. My rental allowance of $3300 would not cover the $4800 which was the least the owner would take. When we decided to splurge and take it at that price, we were informed that two years' rental in advance would be required. When we reluctantly agreed to this after being assured we could sublet if we left Greece, we were then informed that the two years' rental in advance would have to be paid in gold and deposited in a Cairo bank. At this point we terminated our discussions and continued to live in one room in the Pentelic Hotel in Kiphisia, which we considered a very fortunate turn of events when we learned our stay in Greece would be so short.

the multicolored mountains; because of the never-ending charm of the Parthenon crowning the Acropolis rising in the center of Athens; because of the gray softness of the olive groves; and because of the "staggering impressiveness" of the Lion Gate to the citadel of Mycenae, in comparison with which the pyramids "are but a boring exercise in solid geometry."[22] All these precious memories we cherish. Yet Greece for us had none of the sweetness we had known in Korea, nor did the Greek people have the warmth we found among the blunt and forthright Yugoslavs. We had, alas, met all too few of the rural people, and it is always hazardous to form opinions of a nation from the sophisticated culture pattern of city-dwelling patricians. But for all its rusticity, we found in Belgrade a measure of understanding that had so strangely eluded us in the cradle of democracy.

[22] Osbert Lancaster, *Classical Landscape with Figures* (Boston: Houghton Mifflin, 1949), p. 116.

15

HELPING TO
"KEEP TITO AFLOAT"
★★★★★★★★★★★★★★★★★★★★★★★

THE Hochstetlers met us at the grim Belgrade railway station and took us to the drab Hotel Majestic. The promised house had not yet materialized, so for the next five months a bedroom and a sitting room that looked out on a dreary street would be our home. I had lived at the Majestic during my "thirty days," and hence I already knew what had once happened at the Café Zagreb across the street. There, at that very sidewalk café we could look at from our window, Gavrilo Princip and his companions had made their plans, meeting again and again with other co-conspirators. Then one night they took a "sugar box" of bombs, pistols, and prussic acid down the hill to the small terminal of a meter-gauge railway, and here they boarded a little train that wound through the Serbian hills into Bosnia and on to Sarajevo. There, as everyone knows, Princip shot the Austrian archduke, Franz Ferdinand, on St. Vitus's Day, June 28, 1914, the anniversary of the fateful battle of Kosovo, that terrible day in 1389 when the defeat of the Serbian army by the Turks ushered in five hundred years of thralldom. Little did Princip realize what a holocaust he would ignite, and the tablet in Sarajevo that commemorates his deed mentions him only as the "initiator of liberty" for the Bosnians and Herzegovinians. Whenever we walked by the Café Zagreb, or even when we heard, night after night, "Over the Waves" played by the little orchestra, we wondered whether other conspirators were making plans there.

The plans my Yugoslav associates evolved were of a very different character: plans to enlarge and modernize the small, outmoded steel plants at Zenica and Jessenica; to utilize the vast beds of lignite at Kolubara and in Kosovo; to lace the country with electric-power lines; to build modern plants for manufacturing a wide range of nonferrous products; to open up new deposits of copper, chrome, lead, zinc, and antimony; to begin the production of generators, turbines, Pelton wheels, switchgear and machine tools; to establish factories that could build farm machinery, tractors, pumps, and all manner of implements; to develop industries capable of making ceramic products ranging from table china to insulators and modern plumbing fixtures. The dreamers in the government offices lacked none of the idealism of their predecessors who had planned the liberation of Serbia from the Turks or of Bosnia from Austria. Their objectives, however, were far more exact and proximate. They had fought the Germans successfully, waged a desperate national revolution, and dared to defy the Russians so that they could realize their own vision of a more productive, more equitable, better society for all the Yugoslav people.

All these plans they explained to us in detail, emphasizing the capacity of the new installations to improve the standard of living of the Yugoslav people, to generate exports, and to replace imports by domestic production. The break with the Cominform had compelled the planners to scale down the investment program originally projected, reducing it to the most essential projects,[1] but, even with this contraction, 105 installations remained in the "key investment program." Since the Yugoslavs realized that the likelihood of any direct United States governmental assistance for financing this elaborate industrial scheme was very small, they sought from us grant aid to cover a sizable share of current imports so that they, in turn, could devote some of their own export proceeds to the purchase of industrial machinery and equipment. Indirectly, then, the United States was making it possible for the Yugoslavs to engage in more capital formation than would otherwise have been possible and pious official governmental pronouncements explaining that we were in no way subsidizing socialized enterprise were actually the kind of half truths that government spokesmen so often employ. It might have been better if we had not resorted to such subterfuges since had we made some direct investments on a joint-venture basis there might have been distinct political and economic advantages.

In early 1952, the Yugoslav planners had an ill-founded impression that the International Bank for Reconstruction and Development (the IBRD is popularly called the "World Bank") would finance their entire investment program. When the World Bank, instead of making an allocation of $140,000,000, which the Yugoslavs had confidently expected, offered only a first *tranche* of $28,000,000, the Yugoslavs realized they would have

---

[1] There was, however, some enlargement of the program. The Yugoslavs decided to build plants (Rade Končar in Zagreb and Litostroi in Ljubljana) for the domestic manufacture of heavy electrical equipment so that they would not again become dependent on external sources for critically important machinery. This decision, however, increased the time span that would elapse before many electricity-generating plants could go "on stream."

to earmark even more of their export earnings for machinery imports, and they pointed out that they could only do so if we increased our aid to cover a larger fraction of current imports. Meantime they hoped to borrow investment funds from West European enterprises and governments. The trouble lay in the unwillingness of machinery manufacturers in Belgium, Switzerland, Britain, Germany, France, and Austria to provide any long-term credits.[2] The World Bank negotiators had taken an unexpectedly "hard" attitude, explaining that until the Yugoslav government had established "creditworthiness" it would have to pay cash for most of the machinery and equipment needed to complete the "key investment" projects. In this emergency, the Yugoslavs began increasing their estimates of needed tripartite grant aid.

Certain differences of opinion arose about what constituted essential imports. Northern Yugoslavia possesses some of the finest agricultural land in Europe; indeed as one travels through Voivodina, north and east of Belgrade, the wide stretches of black earth resemble the rich lands of Iowa or the Ukraine. It was our contention that grain yields could be greatly increased by planting hybrid corn, by the adoption of soil-building crop rotations, and by encouraging better farm practices. But the Yugoslavs, who had hastily collectivized most of the land in this region, were misled by the specious teachings of Trofim Lysenko, and rejected the plant-breeding techniques that had doubled acre yields of corn in the American Middle West and very greatly increased yields in the nearby Italian province of Venezia Giulia. Moreover even though the collective and cooperative farms had fallen far short of their promised output goals, the Yugoslavs, in 1951, nevertheless launched a strong drive to collectivize more land in order to demonstrate to their Russian critics that they were not tainted with bourgeois revisionism but had remained true Communists despite the 1948 break. We had no interest whatever in these doctrinal disputes; what concerned us was that a country capable of producing enough bread grains would, by importing food, be wasting precious foreign exchange much better used for industrial raw materials and capital equipment. But the Yugoslavs insisted they had to have enough bread grains "to control the market" so that peasant farmers who had not joined cooperatives would be prevented from selling their marketable surpluses at high prices in the black market and thus making a profit.

Since neither the French nor the British would be called on to provide grain, this issue had to be resolved by agreement between the Yugoslavs

---

[2] Most of the equipment credits the Yugoslavs received did not exceed one year; as a consequence, repayment of these credits plus the servicing of other debts required the equivalent or about $54,000,000 in 1952, which represented about a third of all Yugoslav export proceeds.

and the Americans. We scrutinized the proposed volume of grain imports with the greatest care for two reasons. Not only did we think it unfortunate that the Yugoslavs should waste foreign exchange on low-priority imports,[3] but we were unwilling to let our aid be used to coerce certain groups who were dissatisfied with the policies of the Yugoslav government. Our agricultural attaché, Sherwood Berg, albeit ever courteous, could hold his ground against the best Yugoslav experts because of his sure knowledge of agricultural economics.[4] He and I reviewed the food requirements and, in relation to expected harvests, estimated what the very maximum imports ought to be. A really ironical situation had developed: the agricultural output of the West European nations (OEEC figures) had risen to about 18 percent over prewar levels and was continuing to rise, whereas in Yugoslavia, despite her rich alluvial lands, the output had fallen 9 percent below prewar tonnage and promised to fall further as inefficiency spread in the socialized sector and as a systematic and willful reduction in farm output occurred in the private sector. When, after our careful analysis and hard bargaining, we had convinced the Yugoslavs, who had asked for 800,000 tons of wheat, that we could under no circumstances recommend any imports in excess of 300,000 tons, it was maddening to have an emissary come from Washington to tell us that the prospect of American wheat surpluses had necessitated a revision of policy and we would be expected to convince the Yugoslavs that they must accept at least a million tons.[5] Because we could not inspire much confidence if our policies had so little consistency, we asked that a tripartite (United States, French, and British) meeting be held in Washington so that all requirements for fiscal year 1953 could be programmed in a more certain and less capricious way.

Aside from our differing views concerning the volume of grain imports, we had little trouble in agreeing with the Yugoslavs about other items in the (1952) aid program. Raw materials of various kinds were needed[6] as were liquid fuels, certain agricultural supplies, chemicals, and a long list of other items designed to improve the operation of the "going concern." The British, among other things, programmed improved breeding stock for pig farmers, while the French, mindful of pressures at home, insisted on the inclusion of a variety of consumer goods. Although the United Nations

[3] From their political point of view they, of course, regarded food imports as a high priority. When I said at one of our meetings, "You don't really want to control the market, you want to control the peasants," the Yugoslav with whom we were discussing the food requirements said, "It's the same thing."

[4] He is now dean of the Institute of Agriculture at the University of Minnesota.

[5] Under pressure from Washington a new mission chief gradually allowed food imports to increase, so that within two years they reached 1,300,000 tons.

[6] Thus although Yugoslavia has abundant limestone, her cement mills cannot operate without imported gypsum; similarly a new plastics factory required certain critical imports.

247

financed quite a sizable technical assistance program, we nevertheless reserved some American funds to bring hybrid seed experts and other technical specialists to Yugoslavia, and, oppositely, to facilitate the travel of Yugoslav technicians who wished to acquaint themselves with production methods in American factories and mines. In great detail the Yugoslav commodity and industry experts explained their export plans, the foreign exchange they hoped to earn, and the uses they proposed to make of their export proceeds. Although we did not always see eye to eye with the Yugoslavs, we were very much impressed with the systematic way in which they approached their many difficult and complex problems.

Actually they had attempted to do far too much by means of centralized administration. In modeling their 1946–51 policies on Soviet precedents, they had created a grotesquely overcentralized system whereunder all planning and virtually all basic implementation decisions were made in Belgrade.[7] Under a Federal Five-Year Plan, with which parallel republic plans were presumably coordinated, decisions were made about what should be produced, and how much of the national income should be consumed, saved, and invested. Output quotas were assigned not only to republics or districts, but to particular factories or specific farm areas; and all conditions of work, credit, costs, prices, and distribution were factored out by the planners.[8] This whole system, which, unfortunately, led to the coexistence of shortages and gluts and to a "staggering increase in officials and paper work,"[9] was soon to be discarded, giving those of us who were in Yugoslavia at that time an opportunity to observe the transition from a Soviet-type centralized economy to one progressively entrusted to market forces.

In these first few months in Yugoslavia I observed an essential difference between centrally planned and volitional economies, a difference that might make it possible for the more authoritarian countries to quicken their rate of growth. In a basically volitional economy, the first (and largest) allocation of national income is for consumption, because the recipients of

[7] The actual enforcement of policies was entrusted to people's committees of which there was a pyramidal structure beginning with the local *savet* (committee) in the *opština* (village or group of hamlets) and laddering up through committees in the *srez* (district), the *okrug* (circuit), the *oblast* (region), and the republic. Since the committees in this hierarchy were all too large to perform the requisite executive functions, implementation of policy fell largely into the hands of full-time chairmen, secretaries, inspectors, and other officials. It was this new elite who exercised power, often with favoritism, sometimes with ruthless discrimination. For further details, see my *Organization of Space in Developing Countries* (Cambridge, Mass.: Harvard University Press, 1970), p. 282.

[8] Ibid. For a clear, nontechnical account of this highly bureaucratic period in Yugoslav history, see Phyllis Auty, *Yugoslavia* (New York: Walker, 1965), chapters 4 and 5.

[9] Auty, *Yugoslavia*, p. 135.

personal incomes consider this most important. If this share happens to be 70 percent, and if 10 percent is needed for military purposes and another 10 percent for nonmilitary governmental expenditures, then only 10 percent would be left for investment. An authoritarian state can operate in reverse fashion. It can arbitrarily allocate, say, 25 percent for investment, and if military costs are 10 percent and government 15 percent (because relatively more functions are performed by such a government) then only 50 percent would remain for consumption. As contrasted with a volitional society, where investment is the residual, in this context consumption is what is left after the other claims have been met. I tried to quantify this phenomenon in Yugoslavia, and my 1952 results indicated that only about 47 percent of Yugoslav national income was then available for consumption. As the economy became a little more efficient and as controls were somewhat relaxed, I saw the fraction available for consumption slowly rise. But the change proved to be small, and my 1954 figures showed only about 53 percent of national income was used for consumption. Although a country engaged in forced draft investment may appear to be poor and unprogressive, actually, by its extensive capital formation, it may be building up important productive forces. Yet this sort of regimentation may not be all clear gain. Persisting restrictions on consumption may weaken the incentives to produce, as the falling output of agriculture in Yugoslavia testified.

While we were discussing a wide range of problems with the Yugoslavs, week after week passed and no progress in locating a house for me seemed to be made. As a consequence, both Richard Allen and I became a little nettled. After all, a definite promise had been made, and we received only evasive answers to our repeated inquiries. One morning Allen said he would engage in no further discussions until the matter was settled. "But we are doing everything we can," said Stanislas Kopčok, the Foreign Office official with whom we ordinarily dealt. "Let's just forget about the whole matter," I suggested. "I have talked with our ambassador, and he tells me that two prefabricated houses have been purchased in Austria. These prefabs will be erected on our embassy residence grounds, and I am to have one of them. So let it be put into the record," I said, pointing to the secretary who was recording our conversation, "that a promise was made by the Yugoslav government, that this promise has not been kept, and for that reason I have had to resort to other means to find a place to live in Yugoslavia."

The effect was electric. "Oh, please, Dr. Johnson," said Mr. Kopčok, "don't be so hasty. We will find a house for you." "But I'm not being hasty at all," I replied. "I have been more than patient and nothing has happened." True to his word Richard Allen refused to discuss any other matter, and we left the Foreign Office and walked back to the embassy. I had scarcely reached my office when the phone rang. It was Mr. Kopčok. "I want you to do me a favor," he said; "please make no decision about your house until tomorrow morning. Please do me this favor." I saw no reason why I shouldn't accede to this request and therefore agreed to wait another day. Early next morning Mr. Kopčok called. "Please come to my office," he said. When I arrived he told me that he had been up until four o'clock in the morning trying to prove that when a Yugoslav makes a promise he intends to keep it.

Vladimir Velebit, one of Tito's closest associates during the war, had been appointed Yugoslav ambassador to the United Kingdom. His house had just been vacated and Kopčok had insisted that it had to be assigned to me. But the bargaining had been very difficult. "Six generals claimed priority," said Kopčok, "and, worse than that, Peter Stambolić, prime minister of Serbia, said he had to have Velebit's house. But I have convinced the allocation board," he said, "that you must have this house, and for that reason I want you and Madame Johnson to go this morning and look at the house. You won't like it because it's in such wretched condition; but we will repair everything and furnish the house completely. I just want you to say you'll take it and let me have your affirmative answer before eleven o'clock. I've already telephoned Madame Johnson and she will be ready to go. A car is waiting for you downstairs." And so we went to Andre Nicolića 5. The sight both rejoiced and frightened us. One approached the house through a great, handsomely wrought iron gate. A wide walkway, flanked by huge boxwood plants, led to a sunken rose garden bounded by great pergolas covered with climbing roses. I learned later that 165 fruit trees grew in the hectare of grounds. Back of the large stone house we found a swimming pool surrounded by a crescent of blue spruces and nearby a separate building for servants' quarters. The estate certainly had unusual possibilities but only after all manner of problems had been solved. Copper gutters now hung rakishly from the eaves, the lovely stone-balustered porch had apparently been struck by a truck and needed expert repairing. The parquet floors in the salon and in the huge dining room were black with grime. The grounds had evidently been used as neighborhood garden plots, so that what had once been greensward had the ragged appearance of neglected cauliflower patches. The trees had not been pruned for years, and their unkempt appearance added an element of wild sadness to the whole outlook.

We nevertheless agreed to take the house and within two days I had engaged, on the recommendation of the Canadian ambassador, a strong retired railway worker to prune the trees and the roses, level the garden plots so that new lawns could be planted, rake, clean, burn, and tidy up every part of the lawns, fences, and orchard. Meantime the parquet floors were sanded, the gutters repaired or replaced, the stone steps and balusters remortared. We were invited to visit warehouses where quantities of furniture, apparently sequestrated from the houses of expropriated patricians, had been assembled. The rooms of our house were so large — our dining room measured 18 by 32 feet — and the ceilings so high that choosing suitable furniture turned out to be a difficult problem. But, little by little, the bleak house became an elegant home. My yardman asked for eighty floribundas to fill in gaps in the rose gardens and seven thousand annual plants for borders along the entrance drive. Friends who went to Trieste purchased items we could not get in Belgrade, and, fortunately, I had arranged to have electrical appliances sent out from the States. By June 8 everything had progressed so well that our first cocktail party, for about 175 guests, was an affair long remembered. Dressed in neat black clothes, my yardman opened the car doors as our guests arrived. Ushers conducted our visitors through the rose garden and into the lovely salon where my wife and I received them. They passed through the baronial refectory to the rear gardens where five butlers and three maids served drinks and canapés. We, of course, established no new precedents; we merely followed the entertainment patterns of the *corps diplomatique*, dutifully repaying our long overdue social debts in the approved manner.

Our house had a fabulous history. The central portion, a sturdy stone cube, had been built by Milan Marković-Cossa, who at one time had been Serbian minister of finance. He rented the house, one year, to Amed Zog, the king of Albania, who lived in the villa with his sisters and a small harem. After Zog left, Marković-Cossa sold the house to a gentleman who later emigrated to America, and he, in turn, sold it to a successful Jewish businessman. With excellent taste the new owner laid out the rose gardens, added a large wing to the house, built the swimming pool, and planted the orchard.[10] This talented man, named Lovric, owned one of the largest lumber companies in Yugoslavia. He lived in the house until the eve of World War II when he sold it to a *folksdeutscher*[11] who had been born in one of the Baltic states. Two differing accounts of what happened next were related to me. According to one story, the *folksdeutscher* married a Belgrade prostitute who came to live in "our" house. The other story alleged that very high-ranking German officers lived with the *folksdeutscher* and that much of the military planning for the conquest and military control of Yugoslavia took place at Andre Nicolića 5.

When the Germans occupied Belgrade, Lovric, the Jewish business-

[10] There were many varieties of apples, pears, plums, peaches, apricots, and cherries as well as mulberries, grapevines, and walnuts.

[11] An ethnic German, not necessarily born in Germany.

man, hurriedly left Belgrade even though he had been converted to the Catholic faith when he served in the Austrian army during World War I. He assumed another name, and lived in a West Serbian village until the liberation. When the Gestapo had learned he was a Jew and begun searching for him, his wife, who had not renounced her Jewish faith and who had remained in Belgrade, fearing she would soon be taken to the gas chambers the Germans had erected just across the Sava River, had taken poison and died. The Lovrics had two sons. The eldest joined the Partisans and became an artillery officer and a prominent Communist, while the younger son went into hiding with his father. After the liberation, Lovric and his two sons returned to Belgrade. For a time he served in one of the governmental ministries; then he married a Jewish woman, and the two of them emigrated to Israel.

If Lovric had shown foresight in selling his handsome estate before the Germans seized it, the *folksdeutscher* was equally prospicient. Just before the Russians and the Partisans joined forces and came thundering into Belgrade, he sold the villa to a Mrs. Čavić from Zagreb, and left Yugoslavia under the protection of retreating German troops. The rest of the story Mrs. Čavić related to me. She told me how happy she was to have been able to buy an elegant estate in such a splendid part of Belgrade.[12] Her happiness did not last long. Three days after she moved into her house, a convoy of trucks loaded with about forty Partisan soldiers and their boxes lumbered into the driveway. Mrs. Čavić was whisked up to an attic servant's room while the soldiers took over the rest of the house. In desperation Mrs. Čavić, who belonged to one of the "first families" of Zagreb, appealed to General Velebit, who belonged to one of Belgrade's "first families." She offered him the use of her house in exchange for his small apartment provided he could assure her that the soldiers would be moved out and that she would not be evicted from the apartment.[13] General Velebit and his family occupied the house for two years. But the Velebits made no effort to improve or repair the house. The ruts made by army trucks in the rose garden were still there when we

[12] In this section of the city, Topčiderski Brdo, other fine houses were soon occupied by such senior Communist leaders as Moša Pijade, Edvard Kardelj, Marshal Tito, and Svetozar Vukmanović. Milovan Djilas, later to gain fame for his criticism of the new Yugloslav ruling class (for which he was imprisoned), lived about a block distant and his peacocks often flew from his grounds to ours, roosting in a high linden tree where sometimes for days they eluded all the efforts of Djilas's servants to capture them.

[13] A rather complicated legal issue had apparently arisen, the question being whether the *folksdeutscher* (who left with the Germans and whose property could therefore be considered enemy property) could give title to the property. This must have been resolved in Mrs. Čavić's favor because during my last three months I paid rent not to the Yugoslav government but to Mrs. Čavić. But I know she has not yet obtained occupancy.

took occupancy. Moreover Velebit, who during these two years served as ambassador to Italy, had allowed his poorer neighbors to dig up the lawns and plant their little gardens. It was left to us to rescue this lovely house from accelerating deterioration.

Envious people thought us fortunate to have so imposing and pretentious an establishment, and I would be untruthful if I did not say that we enjoyed it in more ways than one. We could entertain graciously, and in my tenure as deputy director of our MSA mission not a week passed without guests. But the place was just too large; and since only two bedrooms could be closed off, the heating costs were distressingly high. Moreover my wife had many unhappy moments not only because the maids disagreed ideologically and were therefore often at loggerheads with each other but because something always needed repair; and since so many Yugoslav resources were mortgaged for new factories, new housing, and other new construction, it became next to impossible to get a waterpipe, a window, or a door lock replaced because there was no pipe, no solder, no glass, no hardware. Meantime my yardman could obtain no spray for the fruit trees, could not get the cesspools cleaned, could not purchase waterhoses and other items because they simply were not available. The servants wanted housing, CARE packages, and all manner of things they thought we could supply. We realized that they all spied on us, as they were required to do, and we assumed that they reported to the secret police about each other. Therefore although our house proved to be a joy, at the same time it became an irksome responsibility. To say the least, its administration was an unforgettable experience.

We gave up the house in the autumn of 1954 so that we would not have to spend $800 for another winter heating bill; and it was almost ironical that we chose to move into one of the prefabs that had been erected in 1952 on the grounds of our ambassador's residence. Despite efforts of many foreign diplomats to lease "our house," it was assigned, in 1954, to Vladimir Popović, who had been Yugoslav ambassador to the United States. When he went to Peking as ambassador, the Chinese ambassador occupied the house. After his return, Popović again lived there, but now Aleksandar Ranković, once the heir apparent to Marshal Tito but summarily replaced as vice-president in 1966, occupies in political retirement the house I did so much to restore, furnish, and improve.

Because I had never had an opportunity to study a Slavic language I resolved to learn to speak and read Serbo-Croatian, and very soon after my return to Belgrade from Greece I asked our embassy whether instruction in Serbo-Croatian might be given. The answer from a crusty assistant administrative officer, to whom I was referred, was a caustic, categorical no. Since this attitude seemed very shortsighted, after getting Richard

Allen's approval, I decided to use some of our MSA counterpart funds to cover the costs of a competent teacher. It did seem odd to me, however, that neither our embassy nor the United States Information Service took the initiative; and I found it very interesting that once I got the project started personnel from both the embassy and USIS availed themselves of the opportunity to learn Serbo-Croatian. I am grateful, however, that USIS did find our teacher, a talented, diligent, and most beautiful lady who made the study of a very difficult language a real pleasure. My study of Serbo-Croatian made it possible for me not only to talk with peasants in the field, with factory workers, drivers, and our servants, but even to give the impression during official conferences that I could understand the remarks of my opposite numbers before an official translation was made. Best of all my study of their language enriched my appreciation of the history of the south Slavs, led me into a survey of monastic and church architecture, and introduced me to the wonderful ballads which give perhaps the best reflection of the culture of the Balkans.[14]

My years in Yugoslavia gave me a better opportunity to observe the activities of American embassy personnel than I had had in either Korea or Greece. During the time I was in Korea the military completely overshadowed the few State Department representatives, while in Greece the MSA mission, by virtue of its size, dominated Anglo-Grecian relations. In Yugoslavia, although we were a separate aid mission, a close integration of our work with that of the embassy was attempted. Thus the chief of our mission served concurrently as economic counselor of embassy, while the agricultural attaché and the embassy economic officers were essentially part of our organization. This attempt at forming a "country team"[15] under the direction of the ambassador led to real advantages but at the same time there were shortcomings. Presumably there would be two advantages: duplicating functions could be eliminated, and by working as a team it was hoped that all Americans would be aware of the governing objectives of our diplomatic, economic, and military activities. But although a few senior people did see the total picture, I discovered, to my surprise, that no attempt was made to explain to incoming junior personnel why we were in Yugoslavia and what our basic aims were. Admittedly some classified information could not be divulged, but it did seem rather bizarre that newly arrived young people had to organize their own orientation groups and invite people like myself to explain to them what we were trying to do. It seemed to me that formal briefings should have

[14] Many of these ballads have been described and partially translated by Dragutin Subotić in his *Yugoslav Popular Ballads: Their Origin and Development* (Cambridge: Cambridge University Press, 1932).

[15] The country team also included the Military Advisory Group (MAG).

been arranged for every arriving American, whether secretary, clerk, or attaché.

One other shortcoming of the close embassy-mission relation should be mentioned. Before World War II, diplomatic missions had been small; the presumption was that the members of the foreign service represented a well-chosen elite so that an ambassador could ordinarily assume that the personnel assigned to his mission had the requisite training and experience to fulfill their respective assignments. With the burgeoning of State Department personnel in the post-World War II period, and with the rapid increase and growing complexity of overseas duties, these presumptions were no longer valid. The State Department might assign persons to an embassy who were not qualified to fill the exacting requirements of a particular situation. We ran into this difficulty on several occasions because of the effort to combine embassy and MSA functions wherever possible. I recall that Richard Allen and I protested that one of the embassy double-duty officials simply couldn't fill the MSA slot to which he had been assigned. But our ambassador was unwilling to let us recruit a better qualified person. He told us very frankly that he had been brought up in a tradition whereunder a chief of mission accepted the persons assigned to him without complaint. Very obviously, such a quietistic attitude would leave no blemish on an ambassador's personnel record, but to me the important thing was to ensure that our essential tasks would be competently performed. Fortunately a special task force had to be rather quickly organized to itemize and appraise the value of particular parcels of the property that the Yugoslavs had nationalized (and for which they had made a lump-sum settlement) so that the United States Treasury could compensate the former owners. To this organization we were able to transfer several persons who lacked the training and experience for the positions to which they had been initially assigned.

The close affiliation of our aid mission with the embassy led to another situation that caused irritation among career foreign-service officers and at the same time embarrassment to some of us who were carried on the diplomatic roster. My own case can be used as an illustration. As deputy director of our MSA (later FOA)[16] mission I had been appointed a foreign reserve officer, Class I. This was eminently fair since I had entered government service at the top administrative level (CAF-15) and when "super-grades" were authorized, in 1950, as director of the Korea Division of MSA, I had been promoted to a super-grade (GS-17).

[16] Once again the name of the agency was changed when Harold Stassen became the administrator in 1952. The new name, Foreign Operations Administration, proved not only inelegant but confusing, since the abbreviation FOA was often mistaken for FAO, the Food and Agriculture Organization of the United Nations.

But seasoned, very capable foreign-service officers had a much slower advancement, so that both Jacob Beam and Woodruff Wallner served as counselors of embassy in Belgrade as Class II officers. Both these excellent career officers accepted this bureaucratic aberration with becoming courtesy and understanding. Others in the embassy, unfortunately, did not, and members of my staff were often treated as second-class citizens in their applications to the embassy for housing, transportation, and other facilities. They found it hard to understand why they should be penalized because Washington recruitment procedures just happened to have given them higher salaries in relation to seniority than their embassy associates received. Surely this was not their fault.

Meantime a number of Washington agencies had grown into formidable bureaucracies by the 1950's, each with expanding overseas units. Organizations such as FOA had to some extent become part of a patronage system as business groups, farm organizations, and trade unions laid claim to some of the top positions. Thus when Richard Allen signified his desire to resign, we learned to our surprise that the mission director's job had been given to a trade-union official who had no special knowledge of socialist economies, no linguistic preparation, and no formal education beyond high school. Fortunately James S. Killen had sharp eyes and a capacity to learn, but because he was ruthlessly ambitious, he attempted to build up a record of personal achievements. Every telegram or dispatch had to be recast in some way to show evidence of his handiwork, and his revisions often did violence not only to English grammar but to the argument of the drafters of a message. I found it quite annoying to discover that my literary style, which distinguished scholars such as Samuel Eliot Morison, Frank W. Taussig, and J. M. Keynes had complimented, always needed revision. I thought it odd that a British general trained at Eton and Sandhurst had found my writing accurate, vivid, and forceful enough to require no recasting. Even more distressing was Killen's unwillingness to give any credit to members of his staff in dispatches to Washington. Here is just one illustration.

After a tripartite Washington conference held in the spring of 1952, while Richard Allen was still our mission director, at which it was decided to continue tripartite aid for another year, we instituted a thoroughgoing study of the Yugoslav development program so that we could wisely utilize the $100,000,000 in grant aid that had been agreed upon for the coming year. Since Richard Allen made me responsible for the American participation in the tripartite study panels, I enlisted the help of everyone in our FOA mission as well as all appropriate embassy officers. One study group — all were tripartite — dealt with aid requirements, another with exports and imports, while a third tackled the very complex investment problem. With excellent cooperation from Yugoslav experts, and from our British and French associates, we developed a large mass of data all of which was rigorously sieved and analyzed before our conclusions were incorporated into carefully reviewed studies. These analyses were just being completed when Killen became mission director. For each study I had written a preface, noting the specific contribution which each of our people, whether in the FOA mission or in the embassy, had made to the joint effort. Killen removed these acknowledgments, substituting letters of transmittal which he signed personally. His argument, that any accreditation of authorship was inappropriate in a government dispatch, strangely enough had not deterred other mission chiefs from carefully noting, for the Washington record, the faithful work of their staff officers.

Yet for all these Gyntian vanities Killen proved resourceful, energetic, perceptive, reflective, and very diligent. But, like Bunce in Korea, he found it very difficult to delegate responsibility, and, as a result, more and more negotiations became personal rather than group activities. Shrewd and ambitious Yugoslavs, particularly Svetozar Vukmanović, minister-president of the Council for Industry and Construction, encouraged this sort of in camera discussion and we often discovered, when we saw copies of outgoing cables, that decisions had been summarily reached on issues which merited very careful consideration by our staff. I recall one particularly exasperating experience. The Yugoslavs had alleged that with their depleted industrial inventories it was impossible to ensure any satisfactory, sustained employment of their manufacturing facilities. They therefore asked for a supplemental United States grant to be wholly earmarked for the purchase of essential inventories. I put Robert Hochstetler on this job because he had been trained as an industrial engineer at MIT, and because he had had long experience with such firms as Monsanto Chemical and Lukens Steel. Day after day he carried on his consultations, getting estimates of the period for which normal inventories ought to be provided in all the major industries. It took time to assemble such data and meantime Vukmanović kept pressing Killen for a decision; he in turn asked me to turn the heat on Hochstetler. When at long last the data were consolidated, the best engineering estimates indicated that about $9,500,000 would cover the really essential inventories. I prepared a suitable cable, informing Washington that a dispatch was being mailed containing detailed justification for the requested additional aid allocation. I felt very proud that so careful an appraisal had been made. But not for long. Killen sent for me and angrily told me he had waited patiently for Hochstetler's figures and since nothing seemed to happen, after a conversation with Vukmanović he had sent a cable asking for $20,000,000, and since the dispatch had to document his cable he would give me just two hours to revise

HE COULD RESIGN ON THE SPOT

Hochstetler's figures to show that the need was not $9,500,000 but $20,000,000. I had no choice but to accede to this imperious instruction, but I made it very plain that I would never doctor any more figures for him. In this instance I merely lengthened the time period for which inventories were to be provided, but what shocked me was the impulsive, cavalier way in which a decision had been made about other people's money. Yet I fear that such carelessness in making large decisions has become quite typical in our bureaucratic society and particularly in our new imperialistic ventures.

By 1952 the talented and perceptive Yugoslav leaders realized that centralized administration based on Soviet models had failed to animate the Yugoslav economy. Actually the poor performance in manufacturing, mining, and distribution did not present the most serious immediate difficulty. Peasant farmers bitterly resented the inequity of the Soviet-type "scissors" policy whereunder the selling prices of farm produce were artificially depressed while the prices farmers had to pay for industrial products were kept at levels that farm families considered extortionate. Nor was this their only grievance. In order to buy any consumer goods or farm supplies a farmer needed both money and "bons" (coupons doled out in proportion to agricultural deliveries made at controlled prices).[17] Against these discriminations, Yugoslav farmers took typical peasant countermeasures. Without any outward evidence of collusion, they gradually reduced the amount of land under cultivation, and with studied carelessness disregarded the traditional standards for the care of fields and animals. Farm output, already seriously reduced by severe droughts, decreased further, despite the fulminations of the government press. Meantime those farmers who had joined one or another of the several varieties of farm collectives were disenchanted when the predicted paradise failed to materialize and when an authoritarian regime emerged characterized by venom and conflict more than by happiness and harmony. I was appalled at the number of inoperative tractors I saw when I visited the collectives, the rapid deterioration in farm tools from lack of care, and the crass indifference toward maintenance so out of character for traditionally frugal peasants. On both private farms and collectives the necessary incentives for conservative, bourgeois-minded, land-loving peasants were not being provided. The effort to force peasants to join collectives had bogged down, while within the collective

[17] "The currency in this strange country," I wrote in a letter to my wife when I first came to Yugoslavia, in 1951, "is the damnedest thing you ever dreamt of. Prices in dinars are astronomically high. But there are at least three kinds of discount currency. Thus a worker who fulfills a production quota gets a set of 'bons' which give him a discount; a farmer who delivers his assigned amount of produce gets another kind of discount money, while foreigners receive 'putnik' certificates which authorize a 70 percent discount."

258

and cooperative farms a tolerable level of efficiency could no longer be maintained. Peasants wanted the right to plant the crops they thought best, freedom to sell their produce or their livestock at prices they considered satisfactory. It had become quite clear that if agricultural output were to increase, farmers would have to be allowed to function once again in a market-directed economy in ways largely of their own choosing.

After five years of unsuccessful experimentation with collectivized agriculture, and after five years of centralized administration of factories, mines, and distribution, the Yugoslav leaders conceded that very different principles of organization were needed if farmers were to have incentives to farm better, raise more crops, and deliver larger surpluses to markets, and if factory workers and miners were to increase their productivity. After searching inquiry and long doctrinal disputes, there emerged in 1952 the idea of decentralization based on a spatial approach to economic and political development. It took fully another two years before the whole new system had been publicized, introduced, tested, and generally accepted. In agriculture, however, changes were immediate, decisive, and dramatic. Farmers who had joined collectives or cooperatives were authorized to withdraw, if they chose to do so, and the great majority did. Our agricultural attaché, Sherwood Berg, and I made a long trip through Voivodina, Slavonia, and other important farming regions just after the new policies had been promulgated. We talked with scores of farmers who planned to withdraw from collective or cooperative farms. Uniformly bitter about their experiences, they could hardly wait for the day when they could revert to traditional farming.[18]

Decentralization called for both political and economic change and we watched the transition to an emergent new order with great interest. The 1946 constitution was superseded by "a New Fundamental Law" designed to set in motion the "withering away of the states." Under the new scheme, planning became the responsibility of republics, of districts, and particularly of "communes," the new spatial entities conceived not merely as units of local government but as the means for building a wholly new societal structure. The idea of the commune had been developed by a number of Yugoslav theoreticians, particularly Edvard Kardelj[19] who defined

[18] "All I want to do is to get out so I can farm as one ought to farm" was a typical reply to our queries about whether an interviewed farmer planned to leave the *zadruga* he had once so hopefully joined. "I contributed four horses, a plow, a harrow, and a wagon," said one hard-bitten farmer. "They can keep it, what's left of it; all I want is my freedom."

[19] Kardelj had been advocating decentralization since 1950. His ideas were crystallized in a speech at Kragujevac in the summer of 1953 when he laid down the principle that the federal government and the republics should draw off as little of the profits of enterprises as possible and leave the basic control of investment and social-security expenditures to the lowest levels of government.

it as "a politico, sociological, economic fusion of all the inhabitants of a given area into one organic whole." Elsewhere I have described in some detail just how Yugoslavia was transformed into a spatial system of 581 communes integrated into a unified national market by a hierarchy of cities of graduated size.[20] Here I can give only a very brief general description of the new organizational scheme, and say just a few words about the effects it had on incentives, output, and economic efficiency.

The basic idea underlying the spatial restructuring of the Yugoslav landscape was to disperse industry so that almost all communes[21] would comprise an industrial-commercial urban core surrounded by an agricultural hinterland. Some small cities or large towns already fulfilled this condition, but more frequently a number of villages (opštine) had to be combined to form a new agro-urban community. Moreover, new investments would usually need to be made in order to provide the appropriate processing facilities or the suitable types of local manufacturing. During a transitional period, while the nation's leaders were engaged in "building socialism" (and showing its advantages) the new economic system contemplated the coexistence of socialized industries (in the urban cores of communes) and private agriculture (except for the few surviving cooperatives and the greatly favored state farms). But in both the public and the private sectors a market-oriented system of production would come into being.[22] Farmers would be allowed to raise the crops that promised to be most profitable, while the workers' councils, which were entrusted with responsibility for enterprises in the public sector, were expected to make net profits over and above all their costs by effectively attuning their production to market demand.

During the years I served in Yugoslavia there was as yet little evidence of the really great stimulating effect that decentralization, within a few years, would have on the Yugoslav economy. All we could do, therefore, was to hope that the sluggish rate of growth, which had averaged about 1.9 percent from 1948 to 1952, would quicken.[23] Although we approved of the abandonment of dirigisme and applauded the progressive reliance on

[20] *The Organization of Space in Developing Countries*, pp. 286–288, 294–296.

[21] Some communes would be spatial fractions of cities which would not have discrete agrarian hinterlands. Thus if a large city consisted of six communes, they would, in some variable way, share the city's total agricultural hinterland.

[22] The extent to which this new scheme of things has actually been realized and the stimulating effect it has had upon growth and development has been well described by Svetozar Pejovich, in *The Market-Planned Economy of Yugoslavia* (Minneapolis: University of Minnesota Press, 1966).

[23] Which indeed it did, averaging 8.4 percent per annum for the 1953–56 period and reaching an average of 13 percent in the 1957–60 period. For an account of this extraordinary performance, see Janez Stanovnik, "Planning through the Market – the Yugoslav Experience," *Foreign Affairs*, vol. XL (January 1962), pp. 252–263.

market forces, the seemingly endless succession of changes introduced, we felt, needless instability, and made it extremely difficult for us to attune our aid program to precise and explicit objectives. The whole process, admittedly, had to be empirical, but we often felt that before the probable effects of one policy could be determined it had already been replaced by yet another. But our American views of the situation did not mesh with other interpretations. I detected at least five different attitudes toward Yugoslav development policies, and harmonizing these disparate views proved difficult.

The Yugoslav leaders, ever concerned with creating a new variety of socialist society, insisted on more and more investment, whether in state farms, in infrastructure, in large heavy industries, or in the lighter types of manufacture suitable for most emergent communes. They made every possible effort to borrow funds abroad and kept us constantly worrying about how they would be able to service their rising external debt. They pressed us to increase aid so that they would need to devote less of their exports to finance current imports. Our British associates looked with some disfavor at the Yugoslav effort at industrialization on such a broad front. Still influenced by nineteenth-century imperialist concepts, they urged selective investment in export industries, such as metals, nonmetallic minerals, foodstuffs, meat, or timber products. With these ends in view, they earmarked some of their aid for better breeding stock, such as Hampshire hogs, and asked permission for British timber experts to make a survey of export potentials for semiprocessed hard and soft timber products. The French shared this British preference for increased primary exports, not so much because they objected to Yugoslavia's ultimate industrialization as because they hoped that a quick expansion of exports might allow the French to recover at least something on the large investments that the French government and French businessmen had made in Yugoslavia during the interwar period. Meantime the World Bank took a rather different view, emphasizing investment in infrastructure as a precondition for a slow, cautious program of industrialization, one which would require external borrowing and would therefore depend basically on the "creditworthiness" of the Yugoslav government.

The American attitude differed from all four of the foregoing development purposes. Our overriding objective, far more military and political than economic, was to "keep Tito afloat" and to prevent, if we could, a return of Yugoslavia into the Soviet orbit. Our Military Advisory Group hoped to find an ally who could, in an emergency, defend the pass in the Dinaric Alps known as the "Ljubljana gap"; and with this and other military objectives in mind, they supplied the Yugoslav army and air force with military hardware. They favored any or all industrialization that would

261

increase the capacity of Yugoslavia to equip its military forces. As part of a "country team" we perforce recognized the great importance of direct military assistance and of indirect "defense support." But our FOA objectives went beyond these ally-attracting purposes. As we saw the over-all situation, Yugoslavia could remain "unaligned" only if genuine economic vigor could be imparted to the whole economy; if enough reciprocally beneficial trade between Yugoslavia and non-Warsaw Pact countries could be developed; and if the growth of creditworthiness would allow Yugoslavia to borrow enough funds for her essential capital projects at reasonable rates on long enough terms so that projects could be self-amortizing. We therefore agreed with the Yugoslav planners' ultimate investment plans, but we urged a tailoring of projects to the availability of investment resources.[24] Like the World Bank, we emphasized the critical importance of creditworthiness, but we favored far more immediate industrialization than the Bank did.

There is a Balkan epigram that in many ways reflected our predicament: "It's wonderful to be a Serb but difficult." For although it was ever exciting to appraise the Yugoslav situation and relate our aid activities to some tolerably satisfactory objectives, problems constantly crowded in, and to reconcile our differences with the British, the French, the Bank, and the Yugoslavs was not easy. We worked hard at our tasks, and because we all were busy good morale existed. Since travel involved poor roads, very simple hotel accommodations, and plain food (and since journeys to Italy or Austria involved three-hundred-mile trips just to reach the Yugoslav frontier), we had few "Cook's tourists." Yet we were constantly called upon to entertain a stream of "official" visitors from the Paris headquarters of FOA. For some quaint reason not one but four, five, or six officers had to survey our agricultural problems, and almost always wives found it necessary to accompany their husbands. Nothing ever seemed to result from these high-priority visits; and when we needed a replacement for our agricultural officer when he resigned, Paris had great difficulty in finding someone who was willing to serve in so benighted a land. Admittedly we had few attractions to offer, no golf courses, limited and none-too-satisfactory housing, a makeshift small commissary for which each family con-

[24] In the enthusiasm which characterized the Yugoslavs' initial planning of their investment program, three large nonferrous metal-processing plants were begun. In an attempt to complete these projects (which ultimately was done) funds were doled out to all three ventures and hence all stood inert and unproductive, whereas if one after the other had been completed there would have been a much quicker usufruct. For an analysis of this propensity of developing countries to overestimate see my "Problems of 'Forced Draft' Industrialization: Some Observations Based on the Yugoslav Experience," in *Contributions and Communications, First International Conference of Economic History* (Paris and The Hague: Mouton, 1960), pp. 479–488.

tributed $250. We did have a primitive embassy club, and, for the most part, we all tried to make the best of things. We had to be content with the very little music Belgrade afforded, but we did have splendid ballet performances and excellent but infrequent operas. Fortunately everyone in our FOA mission played chess, and this gave us an intramural sport. James Killen was a superb player whose excellence provided a challenge to us all. We organized a chess tournament, and one night the Uruguayan minister played against all fourteen members of our chess group. As I recall Killen and our air attaché both won their games while I was more than pleased to settle for a draw.

The remarkable thing about Yugoslavia was precisely what I had noticed when I first came there in 1951: the energy, the devotion, and the idealism of the Yugoslavs. Perhaps I can point this up by contrasting my circumstances with that of my Yugoslav opposite number. I lived in an elegant, well-furnished house staffed by four servants, whereas he lived in a two-room apartment, and his wife shared a kitchen with another family. I received a salary of a thousand dollars a month while he had to be content with about seventy dollars. I had a car, a radio, a refrigerator, an electric stove, and other appliances; he had none of these conveniences. I worked about eight hours a day at the office and two hours each night at my Serbian; I would guess he worked fifteen or sixteen hours each day. This type of dedication could not be ignored; no one scoffed at the Yugoslavs or as much as suggested that they were a group of opportunists who were feathering their own nests. Oddly enough my admiration for the Yugoslavs got me into trouble as I shall recount in my next chapter.

16

THE PERILS OF PATRIOTISM

★★★★★★★★★★★★★★★★★★★★★★★★★★★★★★★★

AFTER two extremely busy years in Greece and Yugoslavia I looked forward, as my wife did, to our home leave in the summer of 1953. But if we thought it would be a vacation, we soon learned differently. We had run into extremely bad luck with our Stockbridge, Massachusetts, house, a charming structure built in the eighteenth century that I had restored with museumlike accuracy. A good, dependable tenant had been transferred to another location and our local real-estate agent had obtained a successor she thought would be ideal. On the assumption that the rental would be paid, as it always had been, into our account at the Housatonic Bank, we gave the matter no thought until, about a month before my home leave, when I sent the bank book to Stockbridge so we would know the current balance. Only then did we discover that our new tenant, who had occupied our house for eight months, had paid no rent whatever. Deeply concerned with the Yugoslavs' affairs I had foolishly neglected my own. Now I had to engage a lawyer in order to have our faithless tenant evicted and in addition to the loss of rent I had to pay the lawyer for his services. Then came almost a month's hard work putting everything in order. My son and I painted the house, resanded the floors, pruned the trees, repaired the roof of the guest house, and worked long hours on the grounds. For what end? So the place could be rented to some tenant we hoped would be more worthy. Our other house, in Washington, D.C., did not require such a thoroughgoing refurbishing, although here a good deal of neglect, by a fairly satisfactory tenant, had left all too many tasks for us.

One need only return on home leave to realize how overseas residence interferes with many routine needs and responsibilities. Initial appointments must be made with one's dentist and usually these lead to a series of subsequent visits that conflict with other plans. Fortunately we had been able to obtain emergency dental care in Yugoslavia, but anything beyond that had to be postponed. Appointments with an ophthalmologist were equally important since the uneven quality of documents in most overseas governmental work and unsatisfactory lighting had put heavy strains on my eyes. In addition to medical and dental matters, a large number of other neglected tasks confronted us on our all-too-short home leave. Investments and insurance had to be tidied up, our wills needed to be revised. Time had to be found to search for those unusual purchases that we required for our Yugoslav house, and for parts for our automobile that we had been unable to find in Trieste or even in Paris. Only when all these commitments had been finished could we find a little time to visit friends and colleagues or discuss our son's progress at Johns Hopkins with his professors, most of whom, fortunately, were old friends. Even so we had worried about him, as all overseas parents do about the problems children must resolve without any parental assistance.

Separation from son and friends was but one of the serious disadvantages of overseas governmental service. My academic career had been interrupted; indeed because of my long absence from my university post I had been required to resign my professorship. Yet — although I had not sought any of my governmental assignments — I accepted these "costs" willingly in order to perform services presumably in the public interest; it helped to know that General Lerch and General Helmick in Korea, Paul Hoffman and Bill Foster in ECA, Roger Lapham and Charles Yost in Greece, and Richard Allen and Ambassador George V. Allen in Yugoslavia all seemed pleased with the work that I did and the fidelity with which I acquitted myself. Before we went on home leave I had agreed to return to Yugoslavia for another two-year assignment even though this would put me even farther behind professionally inasmuch as once again there would be no time for research and writing outside of my official duties.[1] I recalled wistfully that four years earlier I had forsworn a golden academic opportunity when, at Paul Hoffman's strong urging, I reluctantly turned down an invitation that had been extended to me to spend a year with the Institute of Advanced Studies at Princeton, an appointment which is a professor's most cherished ambition.

We returned to Europe on the *Andrea Doria*, an ill-fated ship that later collided with the S.S. *Stockholm* and sank in the waters of the continental shelf. Among our fellow passengers we would remember a plump, energetic clergyman for two reasons: because he took a dozen or more turns

---

[1] Some of my very best economic analysis is buried in government files, classified and unavailable. I have tried to have some of these, now quite innocuous, papers declassified but to no avail.

around the deck before breakfast, as my wife and I did; and because, just before we landed at Naples, he very insistently engaged us in conversation. He wanted to know where we were going. When we said Yugoslavia, he told us that he had been born in that country, near Osijek, and for that reason he was intensely interested in the changes that were taking place there. He wanted to know why American aid was being given to the "Communists" and I explained as accurately as I could that our object was to keep Yugoslavia independent of the Cominform. When he asked my opinion of the Yugoslav leaders I said with some enthusiasm that they were very talented and dedicated officials. He wanted to know whether we liked living in Belgrade, how we were housed, questions to which I gave forthright answers. Then he asked why the Yugoslav leaders were "persecuting" Cardinal Stepinac. Had I been an experienced career foreign-service officer I would no doubt have known how to evade answering this question, but rather innocently I said that the Yugoslav leaders alleged that Cardinal Stepinac had aided and abetted the Ustaše, the violent Croatian Fascist organization that had ruthlessly fought the Partisans, murdered thousands of Serbs,[2] and set up a German puppet state in Croatia. "Well, you must know," my ecclesiastical conversationalist said, with what I erroneously took to be the cynicism of a Slavonian, "the Croats are all politicians." Little did I dream that this brief conversation would lead to such untoward consequences. I had no idea that the cherubic clergyman was a bishop of the Uniates[3] who would soon denounce me in a letter addressed to the president of the United States.

As I look back on this episode I am appalled at my naiveté. As guileless and artless as an unbaptized Parsifal, I had allowed myself to be interviewed by a person who did not welcome any words of praise about "the other side." All of which illustrates the hazard of entrusting para-diplomatic tasks to amateurs. After what I had seen and heard in Washington, I should have been on my guard, since during my home leave the ideological hysteria that Senator Joe McCarthy worked so hard to stimulate had reached frightening dimensions. I recall a visit I made to the State Depart-

[2] For an unpleasant account of Ustaše cruelty, see David Tornquist, *Look East, Look West: The Socialist Adventure in Yugoslavia* (New York: Macmillan, 1966), p. 274. For specific references to Ustaše depredations and atrocities, see Vladimir Dedijer, *With Tito through the War: Partisan Diary 1941–1944* (London: Alexander Hamilton, 1951), pp. 62, 86, 96, 200, 202, 208, 257, and particularly 163–165, 229, 233.

[3] The Eastern Christians, usually called Uniates, accept the authority of the pope at Rome and agree with the Roman Catholic Church on matters of faith. They differ on points of discipline such as the procedure during the Communion service, the marriage of priests, and the choice of liturgical language. For the most part the Yugoslav Uniates are descendants of Orthodox Serbs who emigrated to Voivodina, Slavonia, and Croatia in the eighteenth century.

ment where I found the foyer thronged with photographers eagerly awaiting someone's arrival. "What foreign dignitary is coming?" I asked in astonishment. "No head of state would call for all this preparation," answered the hard-bitten photographer to whom I had addressed my question; "we're waiting for Joe McCarthy who has notified the secretary of state that he's coming to see him." With whomever I talked the story I received reflected the same pessimistic conclusion: no one dared challenge the Wisconsin senator since by doing so the critic might raise a suspicion that he had Communist leanings. I had been warned, for example, that it would be "unwise" for me to introduce the talented Yugoslav ambassador to the United Nations, Leo Mates, to a Washington audience; but I did so without suspecting that even this act of courtesy would be misconstrued.

A couple of months after our return to Yugoslavia our mission chief informed me that an investigation of my loyalty to the United States had been ordered. Although I was entirely confident that no evidence of subversive activity could possibly be found, the prospect of having security officers interrogating friends and neighbors both in Washington and in Belgrade was disturbing and humiliating. Nevertheless I took the unhappy consequences of my fifteen-minute conversation with a suspicious Uniate bishop rather philosophically chiefly because I recognized that security investigations are, after all, necessary devices for screening out undesirable persons from government or for clearing the blameless. I recalled three very interesting cases we had encountered when we were staffing the Korea ECA mission which demonstrated the usefulness of careful security investigation. All three cases revealed that rather important facts may sometimes be concealed behind wholly satisfactory efficiency reports.

I have already mentioned that when we began selecting personnel for our Korea ECA mission we decided to keep seventy-five old Korea hands and recruit an equal number of people who had not served in Korea under USAMGIK in order to infuse fresh blood into our mission and obtain certain needed experts. Out of fifteen hundred veterans we therefore chose one in twenty, and until we received some unexpected security reports we felt confident we had chosen all really outstanding people. To our amazement this is what we discovered. One very competent woman, who had prepared excellent graphic displays and engaged in dependable data processing, alleged in her Form 57[4] that she had an A.B. from Radcliffe and an M.A. from Stanford. But neither Radcliffe nor Stanford had any record that she had ever been a student there. Security did find, however, that she had been a corset salesperson in a Chicago department store and that she had disappeared from her Chicago address to avoid the garnisheeing of her

---

[4] All applicants for government employment fill out this form showing their education, professional experience, and other qualifications for particular positions.

salary to cover unpaid debts. A second case, although it had a sinister side, reflected rather favorably on the investigated person. His wife had been found guilty of embezzlement and sentenced to imprisonment in Ohio Penitentiary. When she entered prison her husband divorced her, but when she was paroled two years later and came out friendless and despondent, compassionately her former husband remarried her, sought employment abroad, and brought her with him to Korea. I knew them both, and I saw no reason why her transgression, for which she had been punished, should in any way disqualify her able husband from employment. We therefore hired him and his work was exemplary as was his wife's conduct.

The third case involved me more directly since I was accused by a United States senator of denying employment to a young man whom he described as "a fine, loyal and completely dependable . . . veteran who is one of my constituents." The object of the senator's solicitude had considerable experience in textile manufacturing and had supervised some of our Korean textile plants, demonstrating entirely satisfactory technical competence. He was eager to stay on in Korea, and, since we needed such a person, we intended to hire him provided there were no security objections. But there were. Two years of his employment record were unaccounted for, although he alleged he had been self-employed during this interval. The senator's office kept calling me at the Korea Program Division of ECA and when all I could do was to report that we were still awaiting security clearance the senator himself called and informed me in no uncertain terms that he would brook no further delay. Fortunately the next day the security report came, explaining quite fully the gap in the Form 57 employment record. The senator's "fine," "dependable" constituent had spent those two years in Atlanta Penitentiary, having been found guilty of operating a confidence racket. I put in a personal call to the senator to explain the matter, but before I could even say a word he wanted to know when his young constituent would be appointed. "I can do so immediately," I said, "but I'm afraid I shall have to inform the press that I have done so at your insistence." When I explained what the security investigation had revealed and that the veteran's preference, which the young man had told the senator he had, did not exist inasmuch as he had received a dishonorable discharge from the army, the senator very quickly changed his tune, begging me to forget the whole affair.

These cases, in one way or another, involved misdemeanors or crimes. My sins presumably represented some degree of political turpitude such as aiding or giving comfort to an external enemy. Yet it was difficult for me to understand how we could "keep Tito afloat" if we did not help his government, and I could feel no sense of guilt whatever for saying that the Yugoslavs, not I, alleged that Cardinal Stepinac had had some association with the Croatian Fascist leaders. Presently a very decent security officer arrived in Belgrade to make the local part of the investigation and I felt sorry that Woodie Wallner, our capable counselor of embassy, had to waste so much of his time on this rather silly affair. Thanks to my father's example, I had joined no organizations, other than professional associations, and hence not one of the scores of suspected organizations on the attorney general's list could show any record of my membership. I had associated with no Yugoslavs other than those I met officially. Nothing I had written had a leftist flavor, and most of my public addresses dealing with Korea had been sharply critical of the North Koreans and their agents who had infiltrated South Korea. After the wastage of quite a lot of public money, I learned, about a year after my alleged offense, that I had been cleared and for this I was probably indebted, if that is the proper verb, to James Killen and Woodie Wallner for their intercessions. The long delay in notifying me had apparently been caused by a Washington decision to allow the Paris regional inspector to "close" the case. After months of waiting this was comforting news but I thought it odd that Washington, which had initiated the investigation, had not had the courtesy to inform me that the case had been closed. I had reason to believe that politics interested Washington more than justice.

When my secretary informed me that a bumbling administrative officer, who had been imposed on us when the Oslo aid mission was closed out, had been searching my files at night, and when I sensed that our mission chief would not be displeased if I were to resign, I became increasingly disenchanted with government as an employer. Evidently the whole Washington intellectual climate had changed after 1952, and many of us began to look back on Truman's administration as a golden age.[5] The Berlin Blockade and the invasion of Korea had, to be sure, shattered the hopes of postwar cooperation with the Soviets. But the gnawing fear that was to in-

[5] Like so many other Americans, I had grave misgivings about Roosevelt's wisdom in choosing Truman for his running mate, and I regretfully recall what I said in Edinburgh on April 13, 1945, the morning after President Roosevelt's death. A British air vice-marshal, who lived at the Roxburghe Hotel, as I did, pointed to the headline on my *Scotsman*, "Roosevelt Dead, Truman President," and said, "Sir, what does this mean?" "Sir," I answered, "it's a national disgrace and an international tragedy." I was completely wrong on both scores. Truman's enlightened domestic and foreign policies have given him a claim for inclusion in the short list of America's great presidents, and I gladly acknowledge the mistake I made in foolishly prejudging him. But in my misgivings about Truman's qualifications I suspect I reflected rather typical skepticism. In a letter I wrote to my wife on April 13, 1945, I said, "Why is it, in our governmental system, we can never elect a vice-president who is worthy of becoming president? It's all well and good to advance from county judge to vice-president in ten years (with the help of the Boss Pendergast machine), but it's foolhardy to turn over the chief office of the foremost nation of the world to a Missouri machine politician. Yet that is precisely what has happened."

fest American society in the McCarthy era came only when suspicion became endemic, when everyone sensed he was being watched but did not know why. Quite suddenly only two colors seemed to remain: white and red, and since communism was evil by definition, every loyal American would be expected to "fight communism." Our capable ambassador to Korea, John Muccio, fell from grace because he failed to obey this new commandment. He allegedly told a member of Congress who visited Korea that we weren't fighting communism; we were repelling an invasion. For that correct and honest answer he incurred the displeasure of John Foster Dulles and was rusticated in Iceland.

My only meeting with Dulles occurred before he became secretary of state. As an adviser to the State Department he planned a trip to Korea in the spring of 1950 and I was asked to answer any questions he might raise. Among other things he wanted to know how many Christians there were in Korea. I said that I understood that only about 2 percent of the Koreans could be counted as Christians. He asked about Buddhism and Shintoism, and after I had said something about the persistence of Buddhist thought I volunteered my opinion that the Japanese had made a very serious mistake when they built a Shinto temple on Nam San (South Mountain), a revered eminence within the walls of ancient Seoul, and the proof of Korean resentment was the promptitude with which the Shinto symbols had been destroyed after liberation. Yet less than three days after my talk with Dulles, we received news from Seoul that the very first thing Dulles did was to conduct a Christian prayer meeting on Nam San, to the great embarrassment of our embassy.

The Dulles era was characterized by both dogmatic certitude and strange contradictions. Because neutrality or nonalignment was regarded as "immoral" conduct, nations presumably sovereign and independent were expected to join a crusade against communism. Even the nonbelligerent, gradualist socialism of Scandinavia was obliquely disparaged when the president in one of his most simplistic and artless moments attributed the high rate of suicide in Sweden to the corrosion of socialism.[6] Yet by odd coincidence, the Eisenhower years witnessed a steady expansion of the public sector of the American economy. Never before in times of peace had such a large share of capital formation been undertaken in the public sector. Moreover the boundaries between the private and the public sector became increasingly blurred as old and new (presumably private) enterprises obtained investment funds from the government and sold increasing fractions of their output to the selfsame government. While professing patriots railed against socialists such as Nehru, in whose country less than

[6] Unmindful of the very low rate of suicide in Norway, a country fully as "socialistic" as Sweden.

5 percent of national income came from the socialized sector of the economy, the American dependence upon government rose to perhaps five times that fraction. Semantics and reality conveniently parted company, making it possible for American defenders of the folklore of private enterprise to castigate socialists while advocating a steady increase in the share of American property socialized by direct or indirect government investment, an expansion of social services provided by the state, and by these means and others the co-opting of more and more of national income by the state. Very good reasons prompted our lawmakers to embark on these quasi-socialist ventures. The absurd paradox was that at the very moment when the economic functions of American government were expanding as never before, our secretary of state and our president tried to persuade people in other countries that we were implacable enemies of socialism. Victims of myths, our leaders lacked the wit and the shrewdness to explain to the unaligned nations that an American brand of socialism was achieving welfare goals much more quickly than the archaic variety of nineteenth-century Marxism. Actually our lawmakers allowed the owners of enterprises to wrestle with all the difficult management problems and to suffer the losses if their ventures failed. But if enterprises succeeded, made money and developed, the government socialized 52 percent of all corporate profits.[7]

These strong trends toward widening the scope of government in the American economy were occurring at the very time when the Yugoslavs found it expedient to abandon their agricultural collectivization program, at the moment when they sharply curbed the authority and duties of central planners and, by swift decentralization, reduced the number of federal employees from the 1948 level of 43,000 to fewer than 8000 by 1955, a manpower shrinkage in the central public sector of 80 percent. In the new scheme of things a search was being made for incentives that would induce workers on farms and factories to produce more, improve the quality of goods and services, and increase per-man productivity. Yet these conservative tendencies received no praise from Washington, where demagogues by threats and distortions had frightened most politicians so badly that they ran like the fabled Gadarene swine. The situation reminded me of the story of the politician who looked out of the window and saw a mob bent on some mischief surging down the street. "There go the people," he said; "I must follow them for I am their leader."

We faithfully reported the redirection of Yugoslav economic policy to-

[7] I explained the pragmatic mixture of private and socialized elements in our economy to an Indian audience in 1964. This lecture has been published under the title "Capitalism and Communism: Problems of Coexistence" in *Conspectus* (New Delhi, India International Centre), First Quarter, 1965, pp. 28–46.

ward a market-directed economy, but I can recall no effects that our dispatches seemed to have on Harold Stassen's foreign-aid headquarters. Rather than applause for the Yugoslav policy changes and articulation of an appropriate American response, a succession of short-range improvisations continued, making it all but impossible to fathom what over-all objectives we should strive to achieve. The simplest way to have tested the sincerity of the announced Yugoslav preference for a market-oriented economy would have been to reduce sharply the unrequited grain exports from the United States, thereby compelling the Yugoslavs to abandon their efforts to "control the grain market" and forcing them to find in the open market a proper relation between agricultural prices and farm costs. Nothing of the sort happened. The Yugoslav requests for more wheat imports coincided with willing Washington concessions to the farm bloc. Meantime the American tobacco lobby, by its control over German markets, effectively negated the hope of the Yugoslavs to increase (Oriental leaf) tobacco exports from their excellent production, grading, and processing facilities in Macedonia. Similarly the Yugoslavs found it impossible to sell their lead, zinc, and other metals in the United States because of our high tariffs. Yet whereas mission recommendations for well-considered projects, such as enlarging Yugoslav copper mining, were rejected or ignored, we were expected to urge the Yugoslavs to purchase old steam locomotives that the Pennsylvania Railroad had replaced with diesel engines; to act, in short, as junk dealers for American railroads. The mutually reciprocal international principles that Hoffman, Harriman, and Foster had worked so hard to incorporate into our initial Marshall Plan aid program had virtually disappeared, and the negativism of the Stassen administration was paralleled by its intense fear of criticism, particularly from self-appointed enemies of "communism," a term never defined and consistently misinterpreted. Consequently when, on the basis of a fifteen-minute conversation, a complaint was lodged against me, cowardly little men in Washington acted precisely the way Peer Gynt did when the ship on which he had embarked began to sink. Ruthlessly he pushed the cook into the water to save himself:

> THE COOK Spare me, please!
> Think of my children, what they'll lose!
> PEER GYNT I'm more in need of life than you.[8]

My growing discontent, although exacerbated by the readiness of Washington to believe any charges however fatuous, really stemmed from a growing realization that Washington officialdom seemingly no longer had

[8] Henrik Ibsen, *Peer Gynt: A Dramatic Poem*, a new translation with a foreword by Rolf Fjelde (New York: Signet Classics, New American Library, 1964), p. 193.

any cognitive theory of international relations within which the Yugoslav situation could be meaningfully subsumed. Aside from an earnest, and successful, joint effort to resolve the Italian-Yugoslav boundary dispute in the Trieste area, admirably handled by our very competent embassy officers, American-Yugoslav relations represented for the most part planless improvisation. When the tripartite aid arrangement ended, as it did because the proposed British and French inputs had become too negligible to justify three-way discussions on program problems, our FOA mission became mostly a post office that transmitted Yugoslav requests for aid to Washington. But day-by-day decisions cannot be made wisely unless some general policy exists, and, beyond that, unless fairly specific goals and targets are envisaged.

Instead of any realistic analysis of what our American-Yugoslav economic relations should be to subserve worthwhile objectives for both parties, Washington supplied little beyond imprecise rhetoric. Yet surely in this situation someone should have puzzled out what decisions a superpower such as the United States ought to reach in relation to a very strategically located middle power. Hasty conferences on ephemeral problems could supply no tolerably appropriate answers to such overriding issues. The essential content of any intelligent imperialism must be a well-reasoned concern with relatively long-range purposes. Moreover the goals of an imperial nation, if they are to be attainable, must be articulated to the direction of policy changes that occur in each country that fits into the imperialist matrix. Once well-considered decisions have been reached, there must be a consistent effort to implement them, a condition that cannot be realized if the policy-makers are so fearful of currents of public opinion that they pander to every vocal minority out of fear of political recrimination. Stassen's attempt to curry favor with the advocates of governmental economy humorously illustrates the ironical consequences that can result. In a brave show of rhetoric he announced that the number of persons with salaries over $12,000 in his organization would be reduced by one third. Very dutifully the Personnel Division reduced my salary from $12,000 to $11,995 and stripped me of my classification as foreign reserve officer, Class I. But since I no longer had FRO rank, I now became automatically entitled to hardship post allowances so that my actual salary increased to $14,400.

The shortcomings of Stassen's administration of our aid program might not have been so manifest to newcomers. But to those of us who had worked under Hoffman and Foster, and who had watched the skill with which planning and operations were coordinated in Paris by Averell Harriman, the contrast was discouragingly evident. I therefore decided to return to the academic world although I refused to be hurried by the

273

pressures for my resignation I knew were being put on James Killen. Having volunteered for two world wars I had a "veteran's preference" which could not be disregarded, and having been cleared in writing by security officers I could not be removed for cause. When I was good and ready I helped Killen out of his predicament by resigning, recalling that he had once told me: "I've got to make a go of this job; I can't afford to return to my trade union at $125 a week." The moral of this story should be crystal clear. No one ought to accept government employment unless he has an outside income, for only then can he be protected against the capricious power of timid bureaucrats. In my case I had double protection: I had had the wisdom and good fortune to achieve financial independence before I reached my fortieth birthday, and I had the professional training which would allow me, if I wanted more income, to find an academic position to my liking.

I had no difficulty whatever. In order to catch up at least partially on the books and articles I had not had time even to look at during twelve years of military and government service, I wanted only part-time academic duties for an initial year. Moreover since my son would be beginning his graduate work at the Johns Hopkins School of Advanced International Studies, my wife and I wanted to live in our Washington house so that our little family of three could once again be reunited after four years' separation. I therefore agreed to give graduate seminars on economic development, as a visiting professor, at both the University of Maryland and the University of Pennsylvania. The next year, after having received another tempting offer, which regretfully I declined to accept, I joined the Johns Hopkins University, first as professor of international economics at its Bologna Center and then, after three fruitful years in Italy, as professor of economic history at the School of Advanced International Studies in Washington. Of these happy years I will have something to say in my next two chapters. For the moment I must point out a few more things about our relations with the Yugoslav leaders who have made the recent history of their country a success story of economic development.

They were by no means of one mind. The sharpest disagreement centered around the question whether they should look east or west.[9] Despite the Stalinist efforts to brand them as bourgeois revisionists there can be no doubt of the devotion of all the Yugoslav leaders to socialist ideals. We sensed, however, that considerable difference of opinion existed about the strategy to be employed, the institutions needed to realize socialist goals, and the priorities in the elaborate investment program. Although the de-

[9] Quite appropriately David Tornquist has called his very interesting account of the Yugoslav economy *Look East, Look West: The Socialist Adventure in Yugoslavia* (New York: Macmillan, 1966).

termination to remain independent of the Soviet bloc was, I believe, shared by all the leaders, whether a defiant or a conciliatory attitude toward the Warsaw Pact countries should be followed became a critical issue. The Washington guidelines, as far as we had any, might be subsumed in the trite epigram that "the enemies of our enemies are our friends." Washington therefore approved the designation of one of our industry officers to serve as a defense-support counselor to our Military Advisory Group and, through them, to the appropriate Yugoslav military and civilian officials. But since our FOA mission believed that the main purposes of our aid ought to be to ensure the macro-economic health of Yugoslavia, we repeatedly expressed our misgivings about the diversion of what appeared to us to be an excessive amount of resources to military and para-military consumption[10] or investment.

When I had decided to leave Yugoslavia I turned my attention away from the short-range daily problems and concerned myself as much as I could with an effort to envisage how Yugoslavia would, over the longer run, fit into our international commitments. In doing so, however, I did not disregard the dominant immediate issues.[11] I accompanied our end-use auditors, visiting soap factories, aluminum-processing plants, glass factories, and textile mills to see how our aid supplies were utilized. I made a long tour with our industry officer, visiting a new rayon plant, several metal-fabricating plants, and an automobile assembling plant where, under arrangements with Italy's FIAT works, a gradual process of domestic manufacture of components had begun. The more I saw of the far-flung industrial ventures, the more I became convinced that Washington's short-range interrelation with Yugoslavia failed to sense the ultimate importance of a liaison with this dynamic economic and political development; something more effective and substantial was being created in Yugoslavia than the narrow vision of Stassen and Dulles could appreciate. For here was being forged an imaginative new mix of the public and the private, one which rejected both the rigidity of central planning and the wasteful and purposeless drift of uncoordinated private enterprise. Admittedly the entrusting of the destinies of seventeen million people to the presumed wisdom of relatively few planners involved not only statistical but ideological risk, although, fortunately, decentralization progressively diluted the power

---

[10] Yugoslav security regulations prevented us from exercising our "end-use audit" privileges in military installations and hence we could not ascertain whether aid goods were used as we had "justified" them.

[11] When overseas production of ball ammunition and artillery shells became an insistent Pentagon injunction, I did everything I could to expedite the program. Not only was I present one cold November morning when the first 104-mm. howitzer shell produced in Yugoslavia was fired but I have the shell case.

of the doctrinaire, and gradually related policies, purposes, and programs much nearer to the needs of local communities.

My last five or six months in Yugoslavia gave me an opportunity to appreciate even better the enchantment of the Balkan region. In my trips to factories or mines I planned side excursions to the exquisite churches and monasteries that had been the glory of the Nemanja dynasty:[12] Dečani, "the most beautiful [monastery] in all Serbia,"[13] Sopočani with its remarkable frescos whose lustrous colors even shameless exposure to the elements for hundreds of years could not destroy, and Gračanica, the perfectly balanced Byzantine church with its five cupolas and three tall apses, built in 1321 on what became the battlefield of Kosovo. One weekend my wife and I drove to Studenica, perhaps the greatest of the surviving Nemanja monasteries, with its three churches, in one of which the great Dušan was entombed. It was late at night when we turned off the main highway up a narrow rocky road, and here by chance we overtook Father Simeon, the abbot, who was returning to Studenica after having given work assignments to his monks on an outlying farm. Because the great oak doors of the compound were locked, it took some time before a sleepy monk let us enter. Our arrival wakened the peacocks who screamed their raucous sounds, unseemly for creatures so beautiful. Once we were seated on the balcony cloister, an unkempt but most gracious dean gave us each a spoonful of (Studenica) honey, the symbol of hospitality as venerable as it was delicious. In a dreamlike medieval atmosphere we slept, and next morning, after a simple monkish breakfast, we visited not only the churches but the vegetable gardens, the weaving room, and the apiary of beautiful, peaceful Studenica.

I'm afraid that on one of my last trips through Yugoslavia I almost became a "Cook's tourist." There were parts of Serbia, Bosnia, Herzegovina, Montenegro, and Metohija to which my official trips had not taken me. I planned, therefore, to accompany our industry officer on a rather long trip that would take me through these neglected areas and I arranged for my wife to accompany us. I gave as the main reason for my trip the "urgent" need for someone to inspect the 53,000,000 Yugoslav plum trees, to see whether they were in full blossom and therefore promised a good crop of plums (*šlive*) on which the nation's supply of plum brandy (*šlivovica*) so

---

[12] The founder of the Nemanja line of kings, Župan Stefan, was born in Ribnica (now Titograd) in 1164. He organized a dukedom that grew into a kingdom. Under Dušan, who died in 1355, it became an empire that awakened an artistic renaissance which really flowered in the gorgeous frescos still to be seen in the monasteries and museums of Yugoslavia.

[13] Lovett F. Edwards, *Introducing Yugoslavia* (London: Methuen, 1954), p. 124; by all means the best book that deals with the topography, history, art, and culture of Yugoslavia.

obviously depended. We wound through the Serbian hills to Sarajevo by way of Tito-užice, where the Partisans consolidated their forces before their assault on Belgrade. Sarajevo we had visited twice before, but the frowning, walled town of Travnik and the little water mills at Jajce let us taste the simple charm of the Bosnian highlands. Although the calendar said April, snow still lay in the forests and only when we reached the Adriatic at Zadar could one believe that spring had come. This lovely medieval city had been badly damaged by Allied bombing, but, fortunately, the establishment where the most luscious of all liqueurs (Maraschino Maraska) is made had not suffered. We saw how the grapes are fermented, with their leaves and stems, in underground vats, how the basic emulsion is distilled and stored for aging before the secret condiments are added. We had already purchased two cases to bring home with us but the genial director of Maraska told us to cancel that purchase because he could arrange for us to have fifteen-year-old liqueur, which we very gladly purchased. This sort of courtesy, hospitality, and bonhomie we encountered everywhere in Yugoslavia whether from Communist party members, déclassé patricians, orthodox priests, peasants, or factory workmen.

We left Belgrade in May 1955, drove the two hundred fifty miles to Zagreb, then over the new road to Rijecka that our counterpart funds had financed, across the Istrian peninsula to Trieste, over the great stone escarpment behind the city, down into the Po Valley, and on to Turin by way of Vicenza, Verona, Brescia, and the other elegant north Italian cities. At Turin I lectured at the Institut Universitaire after which we laddered down the *lancets* of Savoy to Nice. We had booked passage from Gibraltar, and a delightful first visit to Spain lay before us. En route we stopped at the same hotel in Saint-Raphaël where we stayed twenty-five years before, when we made our first automobile journey on the Continent. We entered Spain at Figueras, not without some worriment since two years earlier one of our mission members had been denied entry because his car, like ours, bore Yugoslav license plates. But nothing adverse happened, and we threaded our way through the Catalan pastures, studded with cork trees, on our way to Barcelona. Our only trouble occurred two days later, when, crossing the bleak country toward Saragossa, I stopped at a pump dispensing what I thought was gasoline but which turned out to be diesel oil. In a blue cloud of exhaust fumes I popped along several miles to a village where a quick-witted mechanic sized up our problem, took the carburetor apart and cleaned it, unbolted the gasoline tank and its fuel line, cleansed everything, and smilingly sent us on our way.

Spain is a visitor's joy. The Prado Museum in Madrid, which we had long wanted to see, met all our expectations despite its old-fashioned display methods. Toledo thrilled us not merely because of the El Grecos and the fascinating architecture but because one could have luncheon in a garden of rose trees and enjoy the refreshing sangría. A former associate of mine in Korea, who then served as the agricultural officer of the FOA mission to Spain, had arranged for us to stay at one of the *paradores*, castles converted into luxury hotels by the Spanish government. Ours stood on a hill, overlooking thousands of acres of bull pastures near the Portuguese border. We shall never forget Oropesa with its courtyard bull ring, its great hall through which we passed to our room, the beautiful wrought-iron balustrade that framed our bedroom windows, the excellent meals, the delicious wines, and the unbelievably low prices. The only trouble is that there are so few *paradores* and normally they must be booked months in advance. In vain we tried to engage rooms at the *paradores* in Mérida and in Granada, but we at least did have the memory of Oropesa, and of Seville, Córdoba, Granada, and Málaga — all beautiful, exciting, and each so exquisitely different architecturally and culturally even though they symbolize a unity amid differences. Gibraltar, more British than Britain, proved an excellent point of departure. From the Rock Hotel we looked out to the harbor where the S.S. *Constitution* would arrive next morning to take me back not merely to the states but to a profession I had left twelve years before to embark on my strange military and governmental career. It had been incomparably challenging, exciting, and instructive. I most surely would not have wanted to miss this unpredictable bundle of experiences. Yet for all that, I now felt a sense of release, of freedom, of independence that buoyed my spirits.

17

LO STUDIO
E BOLOGNA LA GRASSA
★★★★★★★★★★★★★★★★★★★★★★★★

WHEN I was nine or ten years old my mother let me have the prize coupons we received when we made purchases at Wayne's store in our native village. Finally I had enough for a framed picture I wanted badly, a reproduction of a painting which carried as its printed title "Israel Putnam Leaving the Plow at the Call to Arms in 1775." Across a partly plowed field an eager young woman, whom I took to be Mrs. Putnam, is running toward a plowman, carrying his flintlock, three-cornered hat, and blue uniform, while Israel hurriedly unhitches his spirited horses from the plow. With what boyhood admiration I gazed hundreds of times on this picture, symbolizing, as it did, the patriotism first-generation Americans so instinctively reflect. Many years later, my fun-loving wife used to remind me that like Israel Putnam, I ought to be memorialized because the stone wall I had begun at Stockbridge, Massachusetts, in 1943 stood half built when I "went to war." But I also left unfinished a manuscript I had worked on for more than three years; and it is an interesting, if trifling, indication of the sheer nuisance of wars that although almost three decades have passed not a stone has been added to the Stockbridge wall nor a sentence to the manuscript, two projects to which so many hours of fatiguing work had been devoted. All I have thus far salvaged from the manuscript can be found in the presidential address I delivered to the Economic History Association in 1962.[1] Thomas Wolfe's contention that "you can't go home again" isn't wholly true, but when, after long absence, one does return to a place, an institution, or a profession, the adjustment can be difficult because the returnee is not really the same person who left years before. The

---

[1] "Federalism, Pluralism and Public Policy," *Journal of Economic History*, vol. XXII (December 1962), pp. 427–444.

manuscript I was working on in 1943 is unfinished because other types of inquiry and more timely and immediately relevant research still seem to merit priority.

Although I had long been concerned with analyzing economic development as a historical phenomenon, my years in Korea, Greece, and Yugoslavia revealed facets of growth, development, and transformation that I had really not noticed or appreciated in my studies of seventeenth-century colonial history, seventeenth- and eighteenth-century Britain, or nineteenth-century America. Moreover the swift postwar liberation and decolonialization of vast areas of Asia and Africa gave an urgency to policies and programs which did not exist when development could be surveyed leisurely as chapters of history. When I began to prepare an initial bibliography for my seminars on economic development I became aware of the small fraction of the huge new literature I had read, thereby sensing how ill prepared I actually was to return to the groves of academe. Professor Arthur H. Cole of Harvard, my close friend and ever-helpful critic, characterized my 1955 limitations rather succinctly when he said that in my writing I was "at least two books behind" my stay-at-home academic contemporaries, indicating that catching up might prove to be quite a task. He was absolutely right. Aside from a collaborative book that Herman Krooss and I had published in 1953,[2] in which my contribution consisted almost entirely of essays I had originally written seventeen years before,[3] and aside from a few book reviews, the period from 1943 to 1960 is almost a bibliographic blank. I could not immediately begin writing in 1955 since a great deal of careful research would have to come first. Contrary to a view entertained by people who have never been subjected to a professor's exacting training, and who erroneously assume that any superannuated foreign-service officer or retired army colonel is qualified to teach, the academic discipline is extremely rigorous, indeed actually severe in the standards expected from its members. Whereas it rewards exactitude and intellectual precision, it scornfully repudiates hasty, unproven assertions and flimsy generalizations. These canons of proper academic conduct derive from the learning, the intellectual dedication, and the essential humility of medieval scholars whose concern with epistemology laid the basis for the erudition, the curiosity, and the zest for learning that became the great intellectual contribution of an age otherwise blemished by war, caste, and arrogance.

I soon discovered that a large portion of the spate of books and articles devoted to economic development that had poured from the presses after

[2] *The Origins and Development of the American Economy* (New York: Prentice-Hall, 1953).

[3] *Some Origins of the Modern Economic World* (New York: Macmillan, 1936).

1945 deviated widely from these traditional scholarly standards. Many items were little better than tracts, whether they favored private enterprise or an enlargement of the public sector. A distressingly large proportion of the books and articles either betrayed an abysmal ignorance of economic history, particularly of the agrarian sector, or, worse yet, engaged in naive distortions of historical factors. All too many writers proffered simplistic solutions for endemic and deep-seated poverty, attributing wonderful, almost magical, transforming power to such imprecise strategies as balanced growth, broad-front industrialization, land reform, community development, or the provision of "infrastructure," a word borrowed from military lingo that captivated a generation of political and economic analysts — and which, admittedly, I have sometimes found useful. To weed out the dross and find the truly scholarly items in this burgeoning literature proved a wearisome task, and I owe a real debt to my graduate students at both Maryland and Pennsylvania for their help. Among their other tasks I asked each student to prepare critical reviews of a dozen monographs, after we had devoted enough attention to methodology to provide them with the essential tools. In view of the ill-assorted and poorly prepared undergraduate population at Maryland, I was rather pleasantly surprised by the quality of some of the graduate students. Largely owing to the presence of a cadre of stimulating professors, such as Dudley Dillard, Daniel Hamburg, and Alan Gruchy, in the economics department, a number of really good graduate students had been attracted. My Pennsylvania seminar, however, had more uniform excellence, and at least three of the fourteen students in that group had exceptionally acute minds. I found them truly challenging, and, despite the rather fatiguing weekly four-hour round trip to Philadelphia, on deteriorating railway cars, I profited intellectually from this partial and unhurried return to academe.

By happy coincidence I was offered a professorship of international economics at the Bologna Center of the School of Advanced International Studies (SAIS) of the Johns Hopkins University beginning in the autumn of 1956, the same academic year when my son (B.A., Johns Hopkins, 1955) would go to the Bologna Center for his second year of graduate work. Consequently our whole family — the three of us plus Song, our Siamese cat — could travel to Italy together. I arranged to have a new European car, a Sunbeam Rapier, delivered to us at Genoa, and from that interesting, but tourist-neglected city, we drove to Bologna, charmed by the churches and *palazzi* of North Italian Romanesque cities such as Piacenza, Parma, and Modena, or smaller towns like Fidenza. In architecture and in all the fine arts, Italy is simply inexhaustible. The opportunity to live a number of years in Bologna, located so strategically that scores of fascinating cities and towns are contained in a circle whose radius is less than seventy-five miles, filled us with gratitude to Dean Philip Thayer of SAIS and to C. Grove Haines, director of the Bologna Center, for inviting me to join the Hopkins overseas venture, and deepened my indebtedness to my long-time friend William C. Johnstone, who first proposed my name for the Bologna position.

The prospect of living in Italy constituted only one of the attractions of Bologna. A light teaching schedule would give me time for research and writing, an opportunity that I seized with my customary zest and energy. During the three stimulating years I spent in the city of the studious and the well-fed, I gave each year two seminars on European economic history, and I planned, staffed, and supervised an annual sequence of thirty-two lectures on European integration, a topic of burning interest during that period (1956–59). This very interesting task brought me into contact with scholars, technical experts, high-level bureaucrats, and statesmen from virtually all West European countries. From Britain, for example, I invited Sir Eric Roll, an old friend whose excellent *History of Economic Thought* was published in my Prentice-Hall Economics Series; Lionel Robbins, now Lord Robbins of Claremarket; Alexander Cairncross from Glasgow; and Max Beloff from Oxford. From France, among others, came Raymond Aron of the Sorbonne; Paul Chamley from Strasbourg; Claude Fohlen from Besançon; Jean Majorelle, president of the Comité Professionel du Petrole who was also a professor; and Paul Delouvrier, who then served as director of finance in the European Coal and Steel Community. Since during the three years ninety-six lecturers participated in the "integration" course, I will not attempt to list them all. But as other examples I can mention Ingvar Svennilson from Sweden; J. W. A. Huibregtse and H. J. Witteveen from the Netherlands; A. J. Vlerik from Belgium; Heinz L. Krekeler and Fritz Hellwig from Germany; Giovanni Malagodi, Aldo Garosci, Pietro Quaroni, and Paolo Baffi from Italy; Michael Heilperin and Jacques Freymont from Switzerland; S. L. Mansholt, Richard Mayne, and Pierre Matijsen from the European communities; Patrick Gordon Walker and Frank Figures from Britain; and Frederick Vogt from Norway. Entertaining such distinguished visitors was not only pleasurable but intellectually rewarding.

The student body of the Hopkins Center in Bologna in my day consisted of from forty-five to fifty students, of whom about half were Americans, the other half West European. Every seminar therefore represented a cultural mixture from which all profited. But cross-cultural contacts were not confined to the classrooms. In an apartment house that served as a dormitory, a very worthwhile experiment with international living took place. Thus if four young men shared an apartment, one might be an Italian, another a Belgian, a third a German, and the fourth an American. Although the lingua franca of the center was English, a professor could, with the approval of his students, give his course in Italian, as Mario Toscano did, or in French, as Alfred Grosser and Claude Fohlen usually did. Meantime in the domitory apartments, agreements could be reached concerning the language to be used, often alternating to distribute the learning benefits. Since students had taken their first degrees in German, French, Austrian, Belgian, Dutch, Spanish, British, or American universities, very interesting contrasts in academic emphasis revealed themselves; but I saw little or no evidence of intellectual snobbishness or academic chauvinism. Very deep attachments grew up, obliterating boundaries of culture or language, and a number of happy international marriages occurred.

The students spent only one year at the center. The European students, like the Americans, were carefully chosen and personally interviewed before acceptance. If they wished to become candidates for the Hopkins M.A., for which the minimum residence is two years, they had to arrange to go to SAIS in Washington for their second year of graduate study. The majority of Italian and Austrian students were preparing for foreign-service examinations and a surprising number of successful candidates proved to be alumni of the Hopkins Center. After their year at the center most of the Germans continued their graduate work for their doctorates at German universities, although some, like the Belgians and the Dutch students, hoped to use the center as a steppingstone to positions in international organizations. The American students fell into three main categories. One group consisted of second-year SAIS students who had chosen Europe as their area of concentration; a second group reversed the procedure, spending the first year for the M.A. in Bologna, the second in Washington; while a small third group comprised students who did not plan to become candidates for a Hopkins M.A. but who wanted a year's study in Europe.

The program attempted to open up as many important vistas of international relations as possible and therefore included seminars on international law and organization, international economics, comparative government, diplomatic history and practice, plus a rather flexible variety of special courses on labor problems, political parties, and political theory, some of which dealt with particular European countries. The faculty, as international as the student body, consisted of American, French, German, and Italian professors, but unfortunately too many of the Europeans were peripatetics who came once a week from Rome, Florence, Milan, and Trieste, or once a fortnight from Paris, Besançon, or Freiburg. Only the Americans and those Italian professors connected with the University of Bologna were therefore regularly available to advise and assist the students. This situation produced little complaint from the European students, accustomed as they were to professors who confined their contact with their students to the lecture halls. But the aloofness and particularly the inaccessibility of many of our professors distressed American students who had been nurtured in a less formal academic environment. The adaptation of European students to American teaching methods was exemplary, except for their repeated protests against written examinations, which they feared almost as much as the Americans dreaded the final oral examination for the Hopkins M.A. degree. All in all, however, the Bologna Center has proven to be a unique institution that has enriched the education of all its participants and concurrently done much to deepen and strengthen international understanding among the future leaders of the North Atlantic Community countries.

Indeed this larger horizon of the center has been and still is its real raison d'être. Like many other ventures of this kind, the center has been subsidized, although by no means as generously as Europeans have assumed. Indeed, from my experience with the "integration" course I concluded that almost every European politician, bureaucrat, or professor had the idea that all the costs of the center were covered by generous American governmental grants. Perhaps we contributed to this assumption by our generosity. We gave each visiting lecturer an honorarium, paid the cost of travel, and reimbursed all incidental expenses by an ample per diem allowance. During the three years, I invited about eighty visiting lecturers to Bologna (some of the lectures were given by our Bologna Center faculty) and entertained each one in my home at my personal expense; yet only three in any way reciprocated my courtesies, in Paris, Milan, and London respectively. Seemingly convinced that the whole Bologna operation represented some variety of political blandishment, none of our lecturers had any compunctions about presenting their expense accounts and pocketing their honoraria.

Although during the first years, when the center was small, a government grant did cover most costs, gradually, as more American and European students applied, the director and founder of the center, C. Grove Haines, who had been professor of diplomatic history at SAIS, discovered that academic administration entails the unpleasant task of raising money. For a time this largely consisted of persuading one agency of our government to take over some of the fiscal responsibilities relinquished by another agency. But when he had to seek outside sources of money, Haines, who had hoped to convince European governments and business enterprises to underwrite portions of the center's budget, discovered that European politicians feared criticism if they were even to suggest the use of Italian, French, or German tax revenues to support an American institution; while European business enterprises seemingly had not yet reached a state of civic responsibility that yielded more than token contributions. In this emergency grants from the Ford Foundation saved the useful institution. But the growing fiscal difficulties were compounded, rather than resolved, by the center's application for a block of money with which to construct its own handsome building. These funds originated in the lira counterpart derived from the sale, by the Italian government, of American grain made available under U.S. Public Law 480, passed by the 83rd Congress. To qualify for funds under that legislation, Haines had to create a European Center of American Studies wherein courses on American government, history, economics, and sociology would be made available to European students. The addition of this program to the original instruction in international studies doubled the size of the student body and the faculty, and more than doubled the budget, in a decade when relatively fewer governmental subventions were made available for the social sciences. Indefatigably the director has searched for funds, obtaining some from foundations, from government agencies, from Italian and German industrialists, a little from local benefactors and from European organizations, only to be faced each year with larger deficits which the parent university has been compelled to shoulder.[4]

The issue is much larger than the mere question of whether an American university should have a graduate school outpost in Europe. By some means or another a nation that acquires, by choice or accident, heavy international responsibilities must, if it is to acquit itself creditably, prepare personnel for a variety of difficult, varied, and changing overseas duties. The British civil service, by one means or another, trained a cadre of officials versatile enough to serve in a variety of administrative positions. Indeed, even before the British government formally accepted responsibility for the imperial governance of India, the East India Company had trained key personnel for administrative tasks tantamount to governmental functions. For that purpose the company established the famous Haileybury College which had as one of its professors Thomas Robert Malthus, perhaps the most brilliant economist and sociologist of a remarkable generation of seminal social scientists. Little of this systematic approach to the training of American personnel for our new imperial tasks has occurred; instead there have been a series of improvised arrangements, usually abandoned or changed before their usefulness could possibly be measured. The Bologna Center, so rich in possibility, has been the victim of such checkered and unpredictable vacillation.

The early attempts to conceal or deny the rather evident fact that the

[4] A deficit of $10,000 in 1967 rose to $40,000 in 1968 and ballooned to an estimated deficit of $125,000 for 1970. See "International Center in Bologna Threatened by Fund Crisis," *Johns Hopkins Journal*, vol. IV, no. 4 (March 1970), p. 4. Increased contributions from several donors and a grant from the Italian Ministry of Education reduced this deficit to manageable proportions. Yet since no real solution to the fiscal problem has been found, the center lives precariously from year to year.

center was being subsidized by the American government seemed to me to be rather foolish. Most Europeans just took it for granted, and the cover story that a benevolent American foundation was financing this venture in international education, although it did have verisimilitude, was politely but skeptically accepted. I suspect our inexperience accounts for the Gyntian roundabout way in which all manner of American activities were camouflaged during the first postwar decade. The silly thing was that we thought it necessary to be so apologetic about doing something useful and perhaps really necessary. I never could understand why we should be covert, devious, or ashamed about training Americans abroad to qualify them for overseas assignments, or for discovering capable foreign students and exposing them, by means of an American-directed educational discipline, to the decent and scholarly side of our culture, thereby increasing the understanding and friendly reaction of talented young foreigners who very likely would occupy important governmental posts in coming years. Little by little the masks had to be discarded as direct appeals to foundations and to more governmental agencies became necessary, and as some para-governmental activities, such as maintaining an American reading room, made our dependence on government aid more explicit. Meantime excellent arrangements with international organizations, such as NATO and GATT (General Agreement on Tariffs and Trade), and with European communities — Council of Europe, Coal and Steel Community, European Economic Community — not only opened the way for the Bologna Center students to visit these organizations and see them function, but made possible field investigation and research with the aid, sponsorship, and assistance of these organizations. By these means the Bologna Center students came into direct contact with the architects of a changing Europe, indeed of a changing world community.

To be sure the rhetoric extolling the educational virtues of the center did not necessarily coincide with the actual motives of the students. In the early days of the Bologna branch we had perhaps more than our share of professional fellowship seekers, young Europeans aged twenty-seven, twenty-eight, twenty-nine, or even thirty-one, who, beyond their baccalaureate, probably had already studied at Bruges, Nancy, Dijon, and Stockholm, often repeating the same courses; but fortunately these opportunists gradually disappeared as bureaucratic opportunities for well-prepared applicants (and some of these people were indeed well prepared) steadily increased. For the Italians, and to a lesser extent for the Austrians, the center, however, became something of a cram school where they could repeat, review, and organize the subjects on which they would be questioned in their foreign-service examinations. The Germans, recognizing the academic limitations in their traditional universities, seized the opportunity to broaden rather than deepen their studies, and our problem with them always centered around their insistence on registering for six, seven, or eight courses rather than the customary four. The few French students that came to the center seldom represented the best of their college generation because the rigid French educational system looked with frowning disfavor on any student who dared to deviate from its inflexible curriculum. Hence a year at the Bologna Center would really put the very best French scholars a year behind their fellows.

European students accustomed to a large measure of collegiate freedom fitted readily into the undisciplined procedures of the center's European professors and only a few were nettled by the far more precise demands of their American teachers. But some of the American students, accustomed to rather rigid week-by-week requirements, fell into bad academic habits under European teachers. Thus first-year American students who registered in courses taught by European professors often neglected their studies and traveled too much, even though short-range travel was not only condoned by the director but encouraged. The American second-year students, faced with an oral examination for their degree, could not afford to be equally cavalier, although their relative lack of application is attested by the comparatively higher number of failures on the oral examinations in Bologna than at SAIS in Washington. Yet the extracurricular activities ought not be underestimated. The real shortcoming of Americans in their overseas work has stemmed largely from their intellectual parochialism. Bologna provided splendid opportunities for talented American students to overcome their socio-cultural limitations.

As I look back on my three years in Bologna I wonder whether I could have found a better place to repatriate myself in academe. At the center the challenge of bright, well-trained students with varied university preparation constantly put me on my mettle, making it necessary for me to keep abreast of the currents of changing European political and economic realities; and since new problems called for improved methodological tools, these too had to be found or forged. Every honest graduate-school teacher will admit that he probably learns as much from his students as he imparts to them, particularly if a proper seminar method is employed. But to be effective graduate classes must be small; a "seminar" with fifty or a hundred students is a semantic contradiction and an educational perversion. At Bologna we seldom had more than ten students in our seminars, and consequently the research plans of each participant could be rigorously criticized *ab initio* and progress reports could be frequent, thereby providing opportunity for continued evaluation. Ever since the founding of the Johns

Hopkins University the small seminar method of guided research has been a cherished tradition, one that the first president of Hopkins, Daniel Coit Gilman, borrowed from the German universities, where, alas, it has now virtually disappeared as all too many students have thronged into all too few universities because German university numbers and faculties have by no means increased in proportion to the growth of the student population. I shall never forget the praise lavished on our Bologna seminars by German septuagenarians who visited them. "Oh, this is what a seminar used to be in Germany," one old scholar said. "Here your students can really learn."

Yet there is no magic in the institution itself. It takes time, effort, perseverance, and imagination to conduct a fruitful seminar. For if students engaged in research are to reinforce each other intellectually, there must be general agreement about a seminar theme. Once a tentative consensus has been reached, the seminar leader will be well advised to suggest a whole spectrum of possible topics, far in excess of the number of participants, so that the full range of the seminar theme may be revealed. From such a checklist, a set of derived topics, manageable in scope and interlinked in some meaningful way, can then emerge, allowing a dispersion of talent and yet a focusing of all students on central issues. Quite a number of the papers prepared for my Bologna seminars were publishable, and the hope of such an outcome proved to be an extramural incentive for careful research, as well as for precise and yet felicitous writing.

Because I devoted myself quite conscientiously to my seminars, assuming full responsibility while my students spied out their research terrain, and because the "integration" course took a sizable share of time, my own research proceeded somewhat more slowly than I had anticipated. Moreover I decided that before I began anything essentially derivative from my Korean, Greek, and Yugoslav experiences, I would give top priority to a rather drastic rewriting of the book that Herman Krooss[5] and I had published in 1953. Whereas in the first edition of this historical evaluation of the American economy we had laid the emphasis on "growth" and "development," the new version added to these essential concepts the idea of "transformation," a type of change that had been explored, described, and evaluated with great insight and methodological precision by Ingvar Svennilson in his brilliant and revealing study of Western Europe in the inter-

[5] Herman Krooss, who had been my student and my assistant, succeeded me as professor of economic history at New York University. While he and I were preparing our revision of *The Origins and Development of the American Economy*, a Serbo-Croatian translation (*Podrijetlo i Rasvoj Američke Ekonomije*) was published (Zagreb, 1958). Since our revision very greatly improved the argument, the organization, the analysis, and the historical documentation, we were sorry the Yugoslavs could not have waited and translated our new version.

war period.[6] I therefore pointed out in a chapter devoted to "Introductory Explanations and Concepts" that

It is not enough that an economy should merely grow and develop if it hopes to be genuinely progressive. For even if output were to increase, through time, not only as a total, but as a per capita quantity, this would merely mean the production of more wheat, candles, cotton or other traditional consumer goods; and more wagons, grindstones, hand looms or other time-sanctioned capital goods. It would not supply a community with such things as automobiles, electric power, vacuum cleaners, machine tools, television or frozen vegetables. Real progress therefore implies something more than growth; it involves a much more far-reaching concept of change, yet one in which growth is nevertheless a basic characteristic.

What, then, is involved in the idea of transformation? It comprehends first of all an improvement in production methods, normally in the direction of using relatively more capital and relatively less labor. At the same time, it brings about changes in input-output relations, so that larger amounts of better quality end products will result from the incorporated raw materials. Thus the same amount of iron will have greater strength in the form of steel than in the form of wrought iron, or the same amount of timber when converted into plywood will cover a larger area of wall or ceiling. Meanwhile the development of new end products may drastically change patterns of consumption and production. The availability of electrical appliances, for example, can largely obviate the need for domestic servants and thereby release a portion of a community's labor supply for other productive purposes.

The use of hitherto unused natural resources such as petroleum (originally for lighting purposes) may obviate the import of certain non-indigenous resources (whale oil), although it is possible that new end use products (automobiles) may, conversely, necessitate the import of other non-indigenous products (crude rubber for tires). Far-reaching changes are set in motion by the transforming process, not least of which is a re-distribution of manpower among various sectors of an economy. As agriculture, for example, is progressively mechanized, fewer and fewer people will be needed to produce food and fibers, and hence relatively more manpower can be devoted to other occupations, such as manufacturing and the service industries.

. . . It is evident, then, that a really dynamic economy must be based on some combination of growth, development and transformation. But whereas growth and development can result simply from increases in manpower and capital, transformation must come essentially from exogenous sources: from experimentation, scientific advances, research and business innovations.[7]

Reconstructing the economic history of the American economy with the aid of newer, sharper, and better analytical tools gave me a splendid opportunity to evaluate the developmental problems of less-developed countries, and allowed me to relate many of my observations in Korea,

[6] Ingvar Svennilson, *Growth and Stagnation in the European Economy* (Geneva: United Nations, 1954).

[7] E. A. J. Johnson and Herman E. Krooss, *The American Economy: Its Origins, Development and Transformation* (New York: Prentice-Hall, 1960), pp. 16–17.

Greece, and Yugoslavia to a more comprehensive framework. The decision to rework the American book before I turned my attention to less-developed countries proved eminently sound. My experiences had persuaded me that much of the macro-economic emphasis in the burgeoning literature of development, although theoretically valid, had little relevance to low-income countries cursed with spatial isolation of most producers, a condition which not only had stultifying effects on the capacity to save and invest but resulted in economies so fragmented that producers had wholly inadequate incentives to change their low-productivity practices. Aside from two articles on Europe and the United States, occasioned by lectures I was asked to give in Rome and in Padua,[8] I devoted my time to analyzing critically some of the development practices I had observed in less-developed countries. I started with Yugoslavia because the strategy there had been so drastically revised in 1952–53 when it had become clear that plans and policies borrowed from the U.S.S.R. were ill suited to the Yugoslav situation.

A rather fortuitous circumstance set me to work on the Yugoslav appraisal. A proposal had been made for the knitting together of British, American, Italian, French, German, Russian, and other economic history associations into some kind of an international organization. At an initial meeting in Paris, where I represented the (North American) Economic History Association,[9] we agreed to hold a first International Congress at Stockholm in the late summer of 1960. I was asked to contribute a paper for that meeting, and this circumstance led to the preparation of the first of quite a number of studies exploring contemporary development policies and practices. Since the "commune," which would become the quintessential element in the Yugoslav program, had not yet really crystallized, I decided to appraise merely one part of the Yugoslav program, the efforts at swift industrialization on a broad front. I therefore called my paper "Problems of 'Forced Draft' Industrialization: Some Observations Based on the Yugoslav Experience."[10]

The assumptions that lay behind industrialization policies, so enthusiastically adopted by most less-developed countries, had seldom been rigorously analyzed, and, as a consequence, a great deal of rather impulsive capital formation had been hastily undertaken. Too frequently it was as-

[8] "Riflessioni Sull'Esperienza Americana in Materia di Monopoli," *Rivista Della Società*, vol. II (July–August 1957), pp. 878–895; "Cambiamenti Nell'Orientamento E Nella Composizione Del Commercio Estero Dal 1918 in Poi," in *Lezioni Sul Commercio Estero* (Padua: Cedam, 1958), pp. 205–219.

[9] I was one of the founders of this flourishing organization and the first editor of the *Journal of Economic History*. See above, chapter 6.

[10] It was published in *Contributions and Communications, First International Conference of Economic History* (Paris and The Hague: Mouton, 1960), pp. 479–488.

sumed that any country could emulate the U.S.S.R., and the Yugoslav experience stemmed essentially from this hopeful belief. But the rather obvious assumptions — that the minimally necessary capital installations can be wisely planned, that equipment components that must be imported can be financed, and that a sizable portion of the required installations can be built with local funds and local labor — are by no means all there is to the problem. The newly built factories, mines, mills, cokeries, shops, furnaces, laboratories, and other varieties of specialized industrial equipment will depend for their functioning upon a number of complementary institutions, agencies, and instrumentalities. An adequate infrastructure to provide power, transport, water, and other utilities must be concurrently provided; and, for all the sacrifice involved in its creation, industrial capital will yield no social benefits unless an appropriate supply apparatus for raw material, and a marketing and distribution network for the end product, can be developed before the capital installations have been completed. Yet such an intricately interlocked mechanism cannot function unless competent managers, technicians, administrators, foremen, skilled workers, and ordinary laborers can be recruited, trained, apportioned, and seasoned in their varied tasks. The achievement of these essentially technical ends rests, however, upon certain cultural, political, ideological, and psychological assumptions, far less precise in character and always subject to unforeseen variations. These factors are critical, since unless incentives exist there will be little motivation for savers to invest in new enterprises, for entrepreneurs to move out of safe and customary activities into new and untried ventures, or for workers to acquire, by arduous application, the skills requisite for a new order. Progress will require a great many people to reorder their activities. Consequently the planners must address themselves to much more than the simple construction and financial problems; they must tackle the far more complex problems involved in achieving administrative and price harmony.[11]

My observations in Yugoslavia had convinced me that production is really the simplest activity of an industrialized economy. Marketing and

[11] "Slaughter houses must have hogs and steers not only of the right age and weight, but at a regular, dependable daily rate; copper wire drawing mills must have a steady input of electrolytic copper, rosin, plastics and fibers; cement plants must have fuel, limestone and gypsum; paper mills a stream of pulp-wood and chemicals. Can all these raw materials, and many others, be augmented in adequate volume at prices low enough to make the infant industries reasonably competitive with manufacturing operations in nearby countries? Can one deprive farmers of some of their essential production goods (by devoting an inordinate share of lumber, cement, or hardware to the new industries) and yet expect them to stand ready and willing to deliver corn to starch factories, animals for slaughter houses, or sugar beets to refineries in adequate quantities once the industrial plants are finished"? "Problems of 'Forced Draft' Industrialization," ibid., p. 484.

distribution systems are far more complex, much more difficult to develop because they "must be patiently and skilfully attuned to national habits and customs"[12] on the one hand, to highly competitive, quality-conscious, and delicate export markets on the other. Although there is little doubt that industrialization can be hastened by forced-draft measures, new patterns of economic activity will call for different skills and mental attitudes, a peculiar type of discipline, and, above all, a continued search for productive efficiency. The nub of the problem, as I pointed out, is not so much a question of inadequate intelligence (intelligence is often very high among the leaders of underdeveloped countries) as it is the want of a particular type of institutional wisdom which an antecedent agrarian-commercial culture had not generated. The insights into the development problem which my Yugoslav experience had provided presently led me to a number of explorations. In a series of lectures at the University of Madrid (May 1961), I analyzed the factors that influenced the economy of scale. Three years later I began my investigation of spatial factors in development in a book on India,[13] a subject I explored further in my essay on "The Integration of Industrial and Agrarian Development in Regional Planning."[14] Meantime in a lecture at the Second International Conference on the Development of Science and Technology and Their Impact on Society (Herceg-Novi, Yugoslavia, July 1, 1966), I had analyzed the process whereby latent creativity can be released.[15] Gradually these several topics began to knit themselves together, leading me to attempt a rather comprehensive synthesis in my *Organization of Space in Developing Countries.*[16] The Bologna years were extremely important, not so much for what I actually wrote or published, but because I had time for reflection and for a preliminary visualization of the detailed research and writing that would occupy my attention for the next decade.

Busy though I kept myself, life in Bologna was not all work. Within a hundred miles of that charming city, which in Dante's day boasted scores of baronial towers a few of which still stand, one can reach fifty and more mellow, beautiful cities, each crowded with artistic treasures and possessing structures of amazing architectural elegance. Singling out one city after another, my wife and I planned our weekend journeys, carefully preparing

[12] Ibid. p. 485.

[13] *Market Towns and Spatial Development in India* (New Delhi: National Council of Applied Economic Research, 1965).

[14] In *Regional Perspective of Industrial and Urban Growth: The Case of Kanpur,* ed. P. B. Desai, I. M. Grossack, and K. N. Sharma (Bombay: Macmillan, 1969), pp. 171–190.

[15] This paper was published in one of the journals of the Polish Academy of Science. See *Zagadnienia Naukoznawstwa,* vol. IV, no. 8 (1966), pp. 164–173.

[16] Cambridge, Mass.: Harvard University Press, 1970.

ourselves in advance so that we would not waste a precious minute. Serious tourism is hard work. I remember our first trip to Florence which we took when we were living in Yugoslavia. On the assumption that we would probably not again visit that fabulous city, which fortunately proved to be wrong, we allotted a full fortnight to Florence. What a regimen we followed. By seven in the morning one of us was already reading aloud, the other taking notes in order to plan our morning expedition. Then after breakfast more reading and planning before we set out for a 9:30 to 11:30 visit to some chosen church or museum where we knew what we wanted to see. The noon hour was given over to planning the afternoon trip, and the entire evening to the next day's exploration. Yet even with this rigorous and disciplined procedure, we could only make a beginning in our fourteen days.

With Bologna as a semipermanent base our cultural sorties could be smaller in scope and far less exhausting. In spare moments over the span of one, two, or three weeks we could plan each journey, whether to Parma, Modena, Cremona, or Piacenza; to Lucca, Siena, or Verona. We seldom visited more than a single city on each trip, and customarily we would stay overnight so we might have two days for a leisurely visit. For some of these cities volumes in the Medieval Town Series[17] could be purchased, thereby providing us with solid historical background material, as contrasted with the flimsy content of most compact guidebooks. These rich and rewarding visits to Ferrara, Perugia, Arezzo, Pisa, Urbino, Mantua, Forli, and other North Italian cities, and our repeated trips to Ravenna, Verona, Padua, Venice, and Florence provided never-ending surprises. Feudalism in Italy had laid such an emphasis on uniqueness that no two cities are alike in architecture, style of painting, or even in food. Bologna, for example, is a blood-red city in color, Florence is pale yellow; the churches in Verona bear little resemblance to those of Siena. I think the greatest joy came from discovering the atypical artistic creations; the unbelievable colored terra-cotta frieze on the Ospedale del Ceppo in Pistoia that Giovanni della Robbia fashioned between 1514 and 1525 to portray the Seven Works of Mercy;[18] or Piero della Francesca's "Resurrection," which one must seek out in the town hall of San Sepolcro, a painting so startlingly real that my friend Lionel Robbins, who told me where to find it, has called it the "greatest single piece of Christian art."

Yet for all these exciting peregrinations, Bologna itself was not to be despised. In what other city were the most impressive sarcophagi carved

---

[17] Published by J. M. Dent and Sons, in London. Unfortunately some of these excellent volumes are no longer in print.

[18] Clothing the naked, receiving strangers, nursing the sick, visiting prisoners, burying the dead, feeding the hungry, and comforting the sorrowing.

for great scholars rather than military leaders? Where else have practically all the streets been arcaded so that scholars can go, as they have for nine hundred years, to Lo Studio, the oldest university in Europe, without fear of rain or sun? It takes quite some time to learn enough about the lofty towers, the ancient churches, the great palaces of the bankers or notaries, and the museums to appreciate the artistic richness of this wonderfully homogeneous medieval city. Fortunately Alethea Wiels's splendid book in the Medieval Town Series[19] provides every serious student of Bologna's history with an enchanting introduction, for she has done what the librarian of the Biblioteca Communale told her she must try to do: "Make the stones of Bologna speak to you." Yet one need not listen only to the message that the stones of this "dark, turreted city" offer, for Bologna has for centuries been one of Italy's great musical centers. The walls of Sala Bassi are covered with pictures of artists who have performed in that venerable hall, from Mozart to Segovia. The glorious chamber music we heard there, and the equally thrilling music in the Sala Mozart, made our life in Bologna not only pleasant but thrilling. Although the Bolognese symphonic music could not compare with the quartets and trios, the operatic offerings were nothing short of lavish. At the acoustically ideal *teatro communale* we heard a succession of operatic spectacles: *Otello*, *A Masked Ball*, *Aïda*, *Prince Igor*, *Nabucco*, *Il Trovatore*, and a dozen others; while at a smaller opera house we listened to glorious readings of small-cast operas, *La Bohème*, *Madama Butterfly*, *Tosca*, *Lucia di Lammermoor*, *La Traviata*, and *Rigoletto*. What a contrast with Greece, where we heard only one amateurish rendition of *The Bartered Bride*, or even with Yugoslavia where ballet was superb but, aside from a glorious *Boris Godunov*, opera too seldom was heard. Because of the variety, the richness, and the innate artistry of its music, for us Bologna will be forever blessed. And in the same way that Lo Studio, the university, honored the scholars, the city has remembered its musicians. Each day as I walked to the Hopkins Bologna Center, I would pass the Largo Respighi and the Piazza Rossini.

[19] *The Story of Bologna* (London: Dent, 1913).

18

A HALCYON
ACADEMIC AUTUMN
★★★★★★★★★★★★★★★★★★★★★

WHILE World War II still raged in its unpremeditated fury, destroying millions of people and hundreds of cities, confusing customary ways of life, uprooting time-honored institutions, and weakening faith in man's capacity to order rational political and diplomatic conduct, a group of thoughtful American governmental and business leaders, apprehensive about our ability to cope with emergent international responsibilities, began to formulate plans for a new type of educational institution that might better prepare talented young men and women for governmental, diplomatic, and international business careers. Although many other people contributed ideas, as well as funds, the most active member of this group of innovators was Christian Herter. Born in Paris of American parents, Herter prepared for Harvard at the Ecole Alsatienne in Paris and the Browning School in New York. After several years with the Department of State, he turned his talents to governmental problems in Massachusetts, serving in the state legislature until he was elected to the United States Congress. More than anyone else he was responsible for the creation of the Foreign Service Educational Foundation which financed the School of Advanced International Studies. Later when he was elected governor of Massachusetts, appointed undersecretary of state, and then became secretary of state, he still found time to devote to SAIS.

Although twenty-eight persons are listed as "founders," Herter's chief associates in this educational venture included Paul Nitze, Joseph Grew, Edward Burling, Frances Bolton, and William Burden. After his graduation from Harvard, Nitze became an investment banker. The war brought him to Washington where he served in the Board of Economic Warfare, the Foreign Economic Administration, and the War Department. The Vice-chairmanship of the United States Strategic Bombing Survey and the directorship of the Policy Planning Staff of the Department of State were only two of his other important assignments. During the Kennedy and Johnson administrations he became secretary of the navy and then deputy secretary of defense. Like Herter and Nitze, Joseph Grew also graduated from Harvard. Entering the foreign service he served in Cairo, Mexico City, St. Petersburg, Berlin, Vienna, Paris, Copenhagen, Bern, and Tokyo where he distinguished himself for exceptionally good judgment in a most difficult diplomatic situation. Edward Burling, after taking a first degree at Grinnell College, went to Harvard for another B.A. degree, then received an A.M. and an LL.B. Chief counsel for the United States Shipping Board during World War I, Burling remained in Washington as a member of a prominent law firm. Mrs. Frances Bolton, a member of Congress from Ohio, had maintained a long and deep interest in a wide range of educational institutions, professional and academic. William A. M. Burden, like Nitze, graduated from Harvard and made his mark as an investment banker. From this activity he branched into mining, civil aviation, and a host of civic activities, not least of which was his association with the Foreign Service Educational Foundation which financed the School of Advanced International Studies.

This group of gifted and earnest government and business leaders envisaged a rather unorthodox type of graduate school that would concentrate on basic international problems of business and government, and they foresaw, quite wisely, that an adequate training for our rapidly increasing "imperialism," to use Carl Becker's word, would call for greater college concentration on law, diplomatic history, and international economics. By reason of the availability of many competent people in the government departments and agencies who were capable of serving as lecturers, because they combined academic qualifications and practical experience, the founders were of the opinion that Washington, D.C., would be the proper site for the new graduate school. In this expectation they were indeed richly rewarded since a succession of brilliant governmental analysts, beginning with scholars such as Herbert Feis and John Dickey, have given SAIS students the benefit of their experience as experts in economics, law, diplomacy, and political science, supplying the school with a galaxy of distinguished, albeit part-time, teachers.

Central to the thinking of the founders was the idea that the school's main function should be to train young Americans for active careers in international affairs and international business; indeed the initial assumption was that the two groups should be approximately equal in numbers. Instruction in international business proved, however, quite difficult to arrange, and progressively the emphasis shifted toward diplomacy, international politics, and area studies. Meantime a conviction that linguistic proficiency would be indispensable for anyone who was to represent the United States properly and effectively in the international sphere underlay a recommendation for emphasis on oral language training; and a belief that fluency could only be assured if all language instruction were to be provided by native teachers added another reason why the new school should be located in Washington where the embassies could provide the school with native teachers.

Out of these deliberations the School of Advanced International Studies was born, modeled in some ways on the Fletcher School of Law and Diplomacy[1] yet different enough to give it a number of unique characteristics. From the Fletcher School came not only the first dean, Halford L. Hoskins, but two other persons whose contribution to the school became extremely important. Philip Thayer, Harvard A.B. and LL.B., who had been engaged in business in the Far East for a decade, and who had taught in the Harvard Law School and the Harvard Graduate School of Business Administration as well as the Fletcher School, became the second dean of the school. He brought with him as his administrative assistant a talented graduate of Smith College and of the Fletcher School; and it was Priscilla Mason who assumed responsibility for the hundreds of day-to-day decisions leaving Dean Thayer free to deal with policy issues. One will seldom find examples of such dedicated service as SAIS received from both these capable executives. Miss Mason was not above typing professors' letters or manuscripts, addressing envelopes for corporate conferences, or running the telephone exchange if necessary. Yet with her extraordinary versatility, she could prepare scholarly reports, help the controller with the budget, or see to it that a student could find proper medical assistance. Moreover, Miss Mason's work was almost entirely voluntary and unrequited since she and her mother have been among the most generous benefactors of the school.

Fearful that hackneyed, conventional, and traditional educational principles and practices would assert themselves if the school were to be established as a part of an existing university, the founders originally opted for a completely independent institution, small enough so that close contact between student and teacher would be assured, adequately distinctive and creditable so that very capable students could be attracted, and staffed with a faculty so few in numbers and so catholic in scholarly interests that

[1] Founded in 1933 as a joint educational venture of Tufts College and Harvard University, the Fletcher School has been more traditional in organization and in course offerings than SAIS. All instruction falls within four "divisions" dealing respectively with international law and organization, diplomacy, international economics and relations, and international politics. There are, however, two area professors.

they would not isolate themselves in fissiparous departments. The "area" organization of course and seminar offerings, which ultimately led to the appointment of professors of Soviet, Latin-American, Asian, Middle Eastern, African, European, and Canadian studies, does not seem to have been part of the founders' initial plans. It just happened that the first dean[2] had the Middle East as his primary interest, and after one "area" had been blocked out for didactic and heuristic purposes, the organization of courses for other areas seemed equally appropriate. Meantime appointments were made in a few basic disciplines apposite for training young men and women in international relations: diplomacy, economic history, foreign policy, international economics, international politics, international law, and political science. The outcome therefore proved to be a discipline-cum-area approach, one that has served the school's students extremely well.

The founders' dream of a completely autonomous institution proved increasingly difficult to sustain. Bright, talented, and exceptionally promising students had reservations about working for a degree unfamiliar in the educational world; while the mature scholars that SAIS really needed understandably compared the advantages of a new, untested school with the academic security of Ivy League or other outstanding graduate schools. When financial stringency made it necessary for the school to seek aid from foundations, it discovered that the foundations preferred to allocate their funds to prestigious academic institutions. It became apparent that a merger of SAIS with some well-established university might be eminently desirable, and through the intervention of John Gardner of the Carnegie Foundation an agreement was reached with President Detlev Bronk of Johns Hopkins University for the incorporation of SAIS as a separate graduate school. The reciprocal advantages of a merger of SAIS with Johns Hopkins were readily apparent; SAIS needed a university connection, while Hopkins, by absorbing SAIS, could have a specialized graduate school of international relations already organized and functioning in precisely the right place. In September 1950, after six years of autocephalous existence, SAIS became an integral part of the Johns Hopkins University.

Although I had taught at the school's Bologna Center for three years, because of the center's semiautonomous status my formal connection with the Johns Hopkins School of Advanced International Studies began only in 1959, just fifteen years after the school's establishment. At SAIS I found colleagues who were scholars of distinction but who had also, at one time

[2] Halford L. Hoskins, Ph.D., Pennsylvania, taught at Trinity College (now Duke University) and then at Tufts College where he helped organize the Fletcher School of Law and Diplomacy and became its first dean. He served as dean of the School of Advanced International Studies from 1944 until 1949. Thayer served as dean for the next eleven years.

or another, been engaged in some kind of governmental activity. Let me cite merely five examples of the kind of tasks my associates had performed: William Johnstone, professor of Asian studies, was once chief public-affairs officer in India; Vernon McKay, professor of African studies, had served as the deputy director of the Office of Dependent Areas Affairs in the State Department; Philip Thayer, dean of the school, had held a foreign-service appointment in Chile and spent ten years in Singapore; William Phillips, professor of international economics, had been deputy coordinator of foreign-aid programs in the Department of State; while Paul Linebarger, professor of Asiatic politics, had participated in the formation of the Office of War Information as a Far Eastern expert and served as a liaison officer in the China-Burma-India theater of military operations. This combination of scholastic achievement and active service in government was later typified by Francis Wilcox, who succeeded Philip Thayer as dean. He had occupied a succession of governmental posts, culminating in his appointment as assistant secretary of state for international organization affairs. Meantime the part-time faculty, almost to a man, consisted of scholarly experts occupying important positions in the federal government. With my academic, military, and governmental background, I fitted into this fellowship readily. In a very real sense we were comparable to the fellows in an English college, each one presumably competent by training and experience, each first among equals since no academic hierarchy existed; it was altogether a very happy situation.

When I joined the SAIS faculty, in 1959, the student body numbered fewer than two hundred because only about seventy-five first-year graduate students were admitted. The admissions committee could choose the candidates they considered most promising from among the well over five hundred applicants who sought admission, and as a result our students proved to be not only exceptionally bright and well prepared but by reason of the competition properly motivated. For the most part they came from relatively small arts colleges, although each year we had a cadre of students from Yale, Brown, Harvard, Princeton, and Stanford. Many of our very best students came from schools such as Hamilton, Occidental, Oberlin, Smith, St. Olaf, Beloit, Carleton, Amherst, Wellesley, Dartmouth, and Pomona, although students of exceptional ability would sometimes bob up from rather less distinguished schools, and the admissions committee found some real nuggets in rather unlikely places. By 1960 the school had become a truly national institution, and the resulting cross-fertilization of students from many parts of the country had a wonderfully stimulating effect in our small classes. I offered two seminars: one on the West European economy, the other on the American economy. Virtually parallel in the time span treated (from 1914 to the present) they gave me an opportunity to direct my students' attention to the economics of war on both sides of the Atlantic, the distressing and costly consequences of interwar stagnation, the dislocations in trade caused by World War II, and the attempted remedial measures for the resulting economic malaise, particularly those that involved international cooperation. Many splendid seminar research papers emerged, some of which were abbreviated and published in the *SAIS Review*.

Meantime for some seven years, I conducted a rather comprehensive educational experiment. My colleague Bill Phillips, who, alas, died all too young, had agreed to supervise at SAIS a training program for foreign-aid officials at mid-career in age and experience. He soon discovered that all too many of these overseas bureaucrats lacked a knowledge of the holistic interconnection of economics, sociology, political science, diplomacy, technology, and foreign policy. He therefore found it necessary to bring in experts from a half dozen or more disciplines, and since these visiting lecturers were received with obvious enthusiasm he argued that something similar should be attempted for all our first-year students. Because I had organized the European "integration" course at Bologna, my colleagues thought I ought to be given an opportunity to see whether some useful academic *omnium gatherum* might be incorporated into the SAIS curriculum.

I'm afraid that my course, which appeared in the catalogue as "The United States in a Changing World Environment" but which the students promptly nicknamed "The Wide, Wide World," attempted at first to do far too much. Meeting twice a week throughout the year, it required fifty-six lecturers, and to obtain that many speakers of reasonably uniform excellence proved difficult. Moreover, even though I prepared a syllabus which, by the use of suggested subheads, defined each topic, and related each lecture to the analyses that preceded and followed, not all my lecturers made a conscientious effort to knit their discourse into a planned progression. During the first and second year the course was given, I made another mistake by including "big names" and high government officials. Rather painfully I observed the feigned interest of threescore and ten thoroughly bored students when a career diplomat or a senior governmental official artlessly and superficially talked about a subject without any attempt at thematic development. One by one I dropped the speakers who had no platform expertise, concentrating on lecturers who had the capacity to intrigue and entertain as well as to instruct. For I was not alone in recognizing that college professors, despite all the jocular lampooning to which they are proverbially subjected, do possess extraordinary expository skills. In a survey I made at the end of the second year of the "Wide, Wide, World" there was a consensus among my students that it would be best to

300

drop the ambassadors, the senior government officials, and the politicians, and select scholars who knew how to organize a lecture, how to draw out the major themes, and how to build them into a developing didactic sequence.

Each year I revised, restyled, and restaffed the "Wide, Wide World," concentrating on the quintessential aspects of international relations. Whereas during the first years I attempted to deal with geographic, anthropological, religious, and areal aspects of the world community, progressively I reduced the emphasis to four major sectors, dealing respectively with power, ideology, diplomacy, and values. Only those lecturers who had proven their ability to galvanize student interest were asked to participate, and after three years the course had been very greatly sharpened. Next I reduced the lectures to twenty-eight, one each week, and introduced a seminar critique of each lecture by dividing the class into syndicates of about ten students. Under the guidance of group leaders, these syndicates would make preparations covering the topics to be dealt with by a visiting lecturer. The syndicates met during the two hours that followed each lecture, thus making it possible for the lecturer to visit briefly with each of the groups. The group leaders and I did everything we could to encourage the students to criticize our visiting lecturers, whom I had, of course, forewarned that their conclusions might be aggressively challenged. The system worked well, and elicited lavish praise from my carefully screened lecturers.

As more of our students laid plans to go beyond the M.A. to the Ph.D. degree, it appeared unwise to mortgage a full fourth of their first year for this useful, yet diffuse, approach to international relations. In 1967–68 I therefore reduced the formal instruction to one semester, with, of course, a further contraction of the topics to be covered, and attempted still another innovation. Continuation beyond the (required) semester in the "Wide, Wide World" now became voluntary, and those students who elected to stay were allowed to form "workshops" in which topics of their own choosing would be explored. These workshops were entrusted to senior Ph.D. candidates who were themselves deeply interested in the chosen workshop themes. As students became more concerned with immediate and current problems, the workshops allowed them to explore very timely topics in a systematic way. One workshop on the "Morphology of Revolution" proved extremely intriguing and resulted in some very good papers. But less dramatic topics were equally well explored, such as "The Impact of Domestic Policies on the Pattern of Foreign Policy." I made it a point to visit all the workshops so that I could appraise the consequences of this effort at "induced" rather than "guided" instruction.

During my halcyon years at SAIS I devoted some of my time to further-

301

ing the progress of economic history as a discipline both nationally and internationally. I have already mentioned that I played a small part in forming the International Economic History Association and that I contributed a paper to the 1960 Stockholm meeting. Two years later I attended the Aix-en-Provence Congress, and in 1965 the Munich Congress. Meantime, in 1960, I was elected president of the (North American) Economic History Association for a two-year period, and, following that, chosen head of the Council on Research in Economic History, an organization that eight of us had formed in 1940 to administer research funds provided by the Rockefeller Foundation. Because I thought it organizationally inefficient to have two organizations supervising activities that one could perform, I persuaded the members of the council to turn over their remaining funds, and assign any incoming revenues from royalties on books published under council auspices to the association, thus making what had been a separate agency a committee of the Economic History Association.

Between 1959, when I returned to Washington from Bologna, and 1969, when I retired from full-time teaching, I made several trips to Europe. In Spain I delivered a series of lectures on "The Importance of the Economies of Scale in Development" at the College of Industrial Engineering of the University of Madrid; while, as I have already mentioned, at the Second International Conference on the Development of Science and Technology and Their Impact on Society, organized by the Yugoslav government and held, in 1966, at Herceg-Novi on the beautiful Gulf of Kotor, I read a paper on "The Nature and Significance of Creativity."[3] Because I began this lecture by speaking in Serbo-Croatian and, more likely, because my analysis made a strong appeal to my audience of two hundred "hard" scientists from a dozen or more countries, no fewer than fourteen speakers who followed me on the conference program made reference to my paper. Even more gratifying was the decision of the organizers of the Third International Conference to build their entire program around the concept of creativity. Accordingly, I was invited to give the opening lecture at Herceg-Novi on June 29, 1969. I wrote the lecture and obtained my airplane tickets, planning to leave Washington for Dubrovnik on June 26, 1969. But, alas, on June 25, I suffered a serious accident that put me in the hospital for weeks where I lay with all my ribs fractured, two vertebrae impacted, and one lung punctured. Yet even in the intensive-care ward of

[3] Until recently the text of this essay was only available in Polish (*Zagadnienia Naukoznawstwa*, vol. IV, no. 8, 1966, pp. 164–173) but at the request of a group of Indian scholars, I agreed to include it in a *Festschrift* for Professor B. Kuppuswamy of the University of Mysore. See *Contributions to Psychology* (New Delhi: Institute for Social and Psychological Research, 1968). Because of its relevance I have also incorporated this essay as an integral part of chapter 11 of my *Organization of Space in Developing Countries* (Cambridge, Mass.: Harvard University Press, 1970).

Sibley Hospital I insisted on verifying the language of my lecture, which was read for me at Herceg-Novi by Dr. W. W. Grigorieff of Oak Ridge Laboratory.

Since my duties at SAIS, my learned society commitments, and my overseas lecturing took a great deal of time and effort, not until 1965 did I complete any sizable piece of research.[4] I did, however, write the first chapter for a big UNESCO volume on the economics of education[5] an essay that I entitled "The Place of Learning, Science, Vocational Training and 'Art' in Pre-Smithian Economic Thought."[6] To inaugurate SAIS's new building at 1740 Massachusetts Avenue, I arranged a series of lectures on diplomacy which were given during the academic year 1963–64 by McGeorge Bundy, Henry A. Kissinger, W. W. Rostow, James R. Killian, Jr., Adolf A. Berle, and Livingston Merchant. I edited these essays and they were published in 1964.[7] Meantime I wrote a number of book reviews, a type of scholarly writing frequently underestimated but nevertheless extremely important since a constructively critical review involves not only a very careful reading of the book being appraised but often the collating of disparate material from other sources. Some of my very best scholarship has been incorporated in reviews, and I have made both friends and enemies by the candor with which I have evaluated the marshaling of facts, the methodology employed, and, above all, the actual objectivity of authors.[8] My essay on "The Nature and the Price of Economic Progress," which appeared in the 1962 summer number of the *SAIS Review*, although actually not a review, nevertheless used the same techniques. It focused attention on the shoddy methodology and the factual superficiality of W. W. Rostow's *Stages of Economic Growth*, a book that in my judgment has utterly oversimplified the process of economic development and misled the leaders of scores of underdeveloped countries into believing that there are simple, easy, and universally applicable recipes for economic progress. Aside from such disagreements about the facts of economic history and the inferences we can draw from them, my ten-year academic autumn at SAIS was for the most part tranquil although intellectually exciting. Only two untoward events marred this decade of happy academic life, an exist-

---

[4] *Market Towns and Spatial Development in India* (New Delhi: National Council of Applied Economic Research, 1965). The two trips I made to India, in 1964–65 and in 1966–67, will be described in chapter 19.

[5] *Readings in the Economics of Education* (Paris: UNESCO, 1968).

[6] Although specifically written for the UNESCO book at the request of the editors, in order to make it comparable to all other sections of the book, which had already been published in learned society journals, my chapter was prepublished in the *Journal of Economic History*, vol. XXIV (June 1964), pp. 129–144.

[7] *The Dimensions of Diplomacy*, edited by E. A. J. Johnson (Baltimore: The Johns Hopkins University Press, 1964).

[8] For a list of my book reviews, see pp. 333–335.

ence in which I had respected and admired colleagues, students eager and challenging. The first of these unpleasant events revealed again the dirty McCarthy-fostered pollution in our government, the second an endemic Gyntian weakness of our domestic culture. Both episodes were saddening, both disgraceful.

Owen Jones, from whom I took over the Korea Department of Commerce in 1946, and who soon thereafter, as a foreign-service officer, was assigned to Korea where for a time he was loaned to USAMGIK to head our National Economic Board, was asked in early 1961 whether he would accept the position as director of the United States aid mission to Yugoslavia. He sought my advice, and I strongly urged him to accept the assignment. Once he arrived in Belgrade it occurred to him that it might be very helpful if I were to come to Yugoslavia for several weeks to survey the entire economic situation, assess the contributions that United States aid had made over a decade, and indicate what could now most fruitfully be emphasized. Jones felt that since I had been in Yugoslavia from 1951 to 1955, I would have a far better perspective than any consultant unfamiliar with the ten-year history could possibly have. The idea appealed to me and, at Jones's suggestion, I discussed the proposed assignment with the appropriate people in the International Cooperation Administration (as the aid organization was then called) and in the Department of State. Contracts were proffered me and I prepared to go to Belgrade in late August. The day before I was to leave I had a telephone call from the State Department. With a convenient excuse that the sharp criticism of the United States by Marshal Tito at the summit conference of uncommitted nations then meeting in Belgrade had strained diplomatic relations between the countries, I was informed that my visit to Yugoslavia had been canceled. Completely bewildered by the turnabout, Jones could obtain no explanation whatever for the department's decision. I knew at once what the trouble was: the dead hand of the Uniate bishop had risen out of my files, proving once again that the closing of a security investigation means little or nothing to politically fearful, pettyfogging, pusillanimous bureaucrats. Oddly enough I had experienced no difficulty in getting security clearance for three other far more sensitive missions, but apparently for Yugoslavia the risks would be too great. It made little difference to me whether I did or did not go to Yugoslavia, but I was very nettled to discover that I was still carried on a list of persons whose loyalty could be conveniently suspected whenever it suited some timid, fawning maker of little decisions.[9]

[9] That government files contain adverse comments on many people revealed itself when my son, in applying for a Library of Congress position, gave the name of one of my most dependable and patriotic colleagues as a character reference. Like many

The other unpleasant episode centered around a civil-rights controversy in which I became involved, a series of events that revealed how widespread and virulent Gyntian weaknesses are, even in the scientific and scholarly realm. It had to do with the refusal of the Admissions Committee of the Cosmos Club to admit Carl T. Rowan to membership in that prestigious organization of eminent people who, in the language of the club's bylaws, "have done meritorious original work in science, literature, or the arts; or, though not professionally occupied in science, literature, or the arts, are well-known to be cultivated in some field thereof; or, are recognized as distinguished in a learned profession or in public service."[10] No one may apply for membership; the procedure is for two members to sponsor a nominee, demonstrating by a recapitulation of his achievements and by the submission of his books, articles, or works of art why the nominee is "eligible" for membership in this well-known meritocracy. Carl Rowan, who then held the position of deputy assistant secretary of state for public affairs, was formally nominated in the spring of 1961 by two members well acquainted with his qualifications, and his posted nomination elicited dozens of supporting letters from club members who were journalists, editors, lawyers, scientists, engineers, anthropologists, foreign-service officers, sociologists, political scientists, psychologists, and historians. But at the same time that all these distinguished members wrote letters in support of Carl Rowan's nomination, several dozen other members wrote letters opposing his election. The explanation was simple: Carl Rowan had a first-class mind but a black skin!

It normally takes about eight or nine months from the time a nominee's name is posted[11] until a case comes before the Admissions Committee, and normally only a few members bother to notice the posted names. But all through the summer, the autumn, and the winter of 1961 the nomination of a Negro became a topic of animated conversation. There could be

other scholars this man of unimpeachable integrity, for very legitimate reasons in the interwar period, had been quite properly associated with the Institute of Pacific Relations. Yet this was enough to brand him as dangerous, and my son received a letter requiring him to explain "in writing" how he had been associated with his referee and the extent to which the referee had "influenced" my son's political opinions. Once entries are made in personnel files, scarlet letters can seemingly never be erased. As Philip M. Stern has pointed out in *The Oppenheimer Case* (New York: Harper and Row, 1969), the Atomic Energy Commission board that investigated this security episode concluded that "in a very real sense this case puts the security system of the United States on trial."

[10] Cosmos Club, *Articles of Incorporation and Bylaws* (Washington, D.C., 1969), p. 3.

[11] Which occurs when a sponsor and a co-sponsor have filed a nomination form, written a statement attesting the nominee's eligibility, and submitted letters recommending his election, and when at least four supporting letters from other members of the club have been received by the secretary of the Admissions Committee.

little doubt that Rowan was "eligible" under any strict construction of the club bylaws because his achievements were truly outstanding. Only fifteen years after he graduated from Oberlin, where he majored in mathematics and was elected to Phi Beta Kappa in his junior year, Rowan had been designated "one of the nation's most honored journalists."[12] The only newspaperman to win three successive annual medallions from Sigma Delta Chi, the leading organization of professional journalists, he was cited for his outstanding contributions. Indeed from the time he began reporting for the *Minneapolis Tribune*, he received awards every year.[13] Meantime he had been sent by the State Department to lecture in India and Pakistan (1954–55), he covered the Bandung Conference (1955), and he surveyed the African countries south of the Sahara (1956). By 1961 he had written five books dealing primarily with race relations, all of which had been praised by reviewers. Despite these qualifications, when his name came before the Admissions Committee, of which I was then a member, he was denied admission. Behind this disgraceful action lies a shameful story.

About a fortnight before Rowan's name was scheduled to appear on the Admissions Committee agenda the Cosmos Club's Board of Management invited the members of the Admissions Committee to a dinner. When the comestibles had been finished, the president of the club explained the purpose of this wholly unprecedented meeting, which he said, was to reassure the members of the Admissions Committee that it was "an autonomous body, uninfluenced by any other committee or group except the Club membership itself."[14] Yet a parade of speakers from the Board of Management proceeded to point out the serious harm that would be done to the club if the "particular objects and business of this association" were to be compromised, reminding us that among these "objects and business" was not only "the advancement of its members in science, literature and art" but "their mutual improvement by social intercourse."[15] Two past presidents of the club detailed the divisive effects that the election of a Negro would have on the morale of the club, while the treasurer reminded us that the club had recently borrowed $400,000 to enlarge dining facilities and mentioned

[12] When he was awarded an honorary doctor of letters degree by Simpson College.

[13] Among them the Sidney Hillman award for the best newspaper reporting in 1951. The same year he was named Minneapolis's "outstanding young man," and two years later he was selected as one of America's ten outstanding young men by the Junior Chamber of Commerce. In a letter to me, dated February 23, 1962, Ernest K. Lindley, one of Washington's eminent journalists, wrote that, "with the possible exceptions of Walter Lippmann and Joseph Alsop, I can think of no journalist who achieved high distinction as quickly as Carl Rowan did . . . Mr. Rowan rose not through the Negro press, but through wide-open competition in the regular 'white press.' "

[14] *Cosmos Club Bulletin*, vol. XV, no. 3 (March 1962), p. 2.

[15] Cosmos Club, *Articles of Incorporation and Bylaws*, p. 1.

that the likelihood of resignations of disaffected members could have serious financial consequences. An eminent historian pleaded with us to maintain the "traditions" of the club, and a professor of medicine prophesied that unless a firm stand were taken against desegregation, future American generations would have a uniform chocolate coloration. Despite all this passionate preachment, the unctuous president again reassured us that we were entirely free to reach our own decision.

Drew Pearson forecast the outcome of that most unpleasant meeting of the Admissions Committee on January 8, 1962. Since by the rules of the club I am not permitted to describe what occurred, I can only say that within eight hours after the committee adjourned newspapers, radios, and wire services broadcast what had happened: a fellowship of scholars had excluded a distinguished journalist from their club, and, despite any proffered excuse, the great majority of people believed this action had been taken because Carl Rowan was a black man. My colleague in Bologna C. Grove Haines wrote me that "*Time* magazine spread the shocking news of the Rowan case all over the Continent." Letters of protest poured in from hundreds of members. More than that, some very eminent members of the club resigned: Bruce Catton, Harlan Cleveland, Raymond Swing, Lyman Butterfield, Colin McCleod, Rev. William Granger, Howard K. Smith, Charles Turck, Norton Nelson, and Laurence Winship. John Kenneth Galbraith, who, with James B. Conant, was at that very time sponsoring President John F. Kennedy for membership in the club, also resigned, thereby automatically withdrawing the president's nomination.[16] Demands for reconsideration poured in on every member of the Admissions Committee but, despite the opinion of Judge Henry Edgerton and other distinguished lawyers that a motion for reconsideration could be made at the next meeting of the Admissions Committee, the Board of Management ruled that reconsideration was not permissible, a strange attitude in view of the president's earlier statement that the Admissions Committee was the sole judge of eligibility.

Meantime rumors circulated that the whole chain of events had been engineered by the Kennedy administration to prove that it favored desegregation not only of public schools but of private clubs. Because this story averring that the nomination of Carl Rowan had been planned by "New Frontiersmen" was both untrue and malicious, and because I happen to know how it all started, I feel duty bound to state the actual facts. One day in early 1961, my Hopkins colleague William C. Johnstone and I had luncheon at the club with Edwin Kretzman, whom I had known in

[16] For Galbraith's reasons for this action, see his *Ambassador's Journal: A Personal Account of the Kennedy Years* (Boston: Houghton Mifflin, 1969), pp. 297–299.

307

Yugoslavia when he served as a political officer in our embassy. In the course of our conversation Ralph Bunche was mentioned and I asked Johnstone, who had been a club member much longer than I, whether Bunche belonged to the Cosmos Club. When Johnstone said no, I asked if there were any Negro members and again the answer was negative. "Well there soon will be," said Kretzman, "because I'm going to nominate Carl Rowan who is one of the brightest government officials I have ever met." Kretzman asked Raymond Gram Swing to serve as co-sponsor and he, in turn, realizing that convincing evidence of eligibility would be necessary, solicited letters from the leading journalists of the country. In the opinion of his sponsors Rowan was eligible under all three categories stipulated in the club bylaws. His five books constituted "meritorious original work," his impressive list of honors and awards testified that he was "well known to be cultivated" in the art of writing and surely proved he was "distinguished in journalism," while his selection to represent the United States abroad and his government position might even qualify him as "distinguished in the public service."

Yet although Carl Rowan never became a member of the Cosmos Club, bearing his rejection with exemplary dignity, he nevertheless served as a bellwether for the several distinguished Negro members the club now has. What happened was this. Rowan's rejection precipitated an insistent demand for a special meeting of the Cosmos Club members at which the question of eligibility was very clearly established. A resolution stating that it was henceforth the policy of the club to admit any properly qualified nominee, "regardless of race, color or national origin," was adopted by a clear and convincing majority. Almost immediately thereafter my esteemed Hopkins colleague Professor Frederic C. Lane asked John Hope Franklin if he would be willing to be nominated for membership. Admittedly this would be a test case to see whether the Admissions Committee would apply the new policy. Like Rowan, Franklin had unimpeachable eligibility. A distinguished historian, he had just returned from England, where he had served as Pitt Professor at Cambridge University, to become professor of history at the University of Chicago. Franklin was elected, and Mrs. Johnson and I were proud to sit with Mr. and Mrs. Franklin and Mr. and Mrs. Lane on the occasion when new members were received into the Cosmos Club. The principles of fairness and toleration had been vindicated and, one by one, other distinguished black men have become Cosmos Club members.

Even so the mutterings of the antagonistic and unconsenting minority are still heard, and this leads me to renewed doubts about the American capacity to deal with problems in countries peopled by "black, brown, or yellow men," whatever validity these pejorative adjectives may have. If, as the Rowan case demonstrated, there is among presumably learned men such fractional toleration for people of another color or culture, what can one expect from the rank and file of less-tutored people? If there are among those who pretend to belong to the universal fellowship of scholars men who cannot endure a Negro in their midst, even though he has proved beyond any doubt his capacity to perform as well as or better than a white man, how can such men represent us abroad when the great majority of people on this planet are black, brown, yellow, or some admixture thereof? If many of our intellectually elite have these Gyntian weaknesses, how will we ever earn the respect, friendship, and confidence of the more than two and a half billion people who are not pale in pigmentation? Consider how other imperialistic nations have dealt with the color problem. Despite their haughty disdain of "lesser breeds," the British admitted upper caste "natives" to their clubs, while the French, wherever they expanded overseas, accepted their political subjects as suitable cultural protégés.

Our failure to resolve racial problems at home has seriously weakened our ability to win the respect of the "third world" countries, thus adding another handicap to our capacity to assume and fulfill properly the responsibilities of a great power. By reason of our amateur tactics, our inability to understand the nature of our almost accidental "imperialistic" ventures, and the lack of any considered long-range policy to guide our foreign relations, we have lost not only the confidence but, after the Cambodian blunder, the respect of the world community. It is time we abandoned the adolescent hope that we can buy gratitude for our fumbling generosity. We have acted like Peer Gynt who, after having profited richly from his African plantations, built schools for his helots in order

> That my mistakes will fade from sight,
> And, more than most, I'll find a rinse
> Of virtue will dissolve my sins.[17]

But there is, I fear, no magic remedy for our sins; they have been less the result of malice than of hubris, that overweening pride that is mostly a result of cultural ignorance.

[17] Henrik Ibsen, *Peer Gynt: A Dramatic Poem*, a new translation with a foreword by Rolf Fjelde (New York: Signet Classics, New American Library, 1964), p. 129.

19

THE SHAMELESSLY
RICH AND
THE WRETCHEDLY POOR

★★★★★★★★★★★★★★★★★★★★★★★★★

NO ONE who has read Plato's *Republic* carefully and contemplatively can forget the opening pages of Book IV where Socrates is asked whether the guardians of his ideal state will be happy. He answers that "our aim in founding the State was not the disproportionate happiness of any one class, but the greatest happiness of the whole." The guardians will draw satisfaction from exercising their responsibility, which should be to ensure functional harmony, the likeliest recipe for justice. The guardians must therefore be alert so that certain "evils" will not infect the State. "What evils?" Adeimantus asks; to which Socrates replies, "Wealth and poverty; the one is the parent of luxury and indolence, the other of meanness and viciousness, and both of discontent."[1] Because I had long wanted to see the dimensions of an extreme rich-poor syndrome, I welcomed an invitation to spend the better part of a year in India, a country characterized by princely splendor and extravagance at one extreme, by abject poverty at the other. I wondered whether this unhappy economic dichotomy had its basis in the cruelty and indifference of the rich and in the supine resignation of the poor and ill-born, or whether it really stemmed less from malice or submissiveness than from the sheer inefficiency of an improperly planned economy, thus tempting the ambitious to exploit their fellow countrymen because this seemed the easiest way to wealth and power.[2] Once a system

[1] *The Republic of Plato: An Ideal Commonwealth*, translated by Benjamin Jowett, Renaissance Edition (New York: Colonial Press, 1901), pp. 106–108.

[2] In a very thoughtful essay Evsey D. Domar has raised anew the troublesome question of the origins of serfdom. Following a thesis first advanced by J. Kliuchevsky, Domar suggests that when the ruling classes (of Russia in this instance) could not derive enough revenue from their monopolized land, because peasants could move out on the frontier of newly conquered land, they persuaded the government

of castes has come into being wherein each "community" has traditionally prescribed functions, and, consequently, where contrasting ways of life, ranging from luxury to squalor, have general approval, how can development be set in motion? Will not every effort of lower castes to improve their status be regarded as sociological and political heresy? More importantly, how then can the mass of people save, invest, or earn more?

I find in my files a letter from the State Department, dated March 20, 1959, inviting me to spend three months in India under the United States cultural exchange program beginning in January 1960. Since I had agreed to leave Bologna to begin my duties at SAIS during the academic year 1959–60, with deep regret I had to decline this invitation. But another came four years later from the Institute of International Education. The institute had been asked to recruit an economist willing to serve for at least eight months with the (Indian) National Council of Applied Economic Research. Very eagerly I accepted this invitation even though it conflicted with a previous arrangement I had made to spend a semester lecturing at University College, Dublin. But an opportunity to spend a sizable block of time in India took precedence. The council asked me to come to New Delhi immediately after the close of the 1963–64 school year, and my wife and I decided to go in early June despite the very strong warnings of an old Asia hand, Victor Purcell,[3] that no one in his right senses would go to India in June. We decided to condition ourselves climatologically by stopping en route in Egypt, Iraq, Iran, and Pakistan. It proved to be a good idea; after experiencing a temperature of 120 degrees at Luxor, the 109 degrees we encountered when we arrived in Delhi seemed bearable.

I had been in the Middle East before, not only in Greece and Turkey, but in Lebanon and Syria. But this time Egypt was to be a main diversion, and our few days there proved wonderfully instructive. We had been advised to start our touristic explorations not at the fabulous Cairo National Museum but in Luxor, so that we might understand the necrology that occasioned the gorgeous artifacts which the Egyptian genius produced. After a single late afternoon and night in Cairo, where from our hotel room we could not only look down on the Nile but see the pyramids silhouetted in the sunset, we flew the four hundred miles to Luxor. The Nile valley, that amazingly narrow ribbon of green, bordered by desert, can only be appreciated from a high enough perspective; only when one sees this lush, allu-

to restrict the mobility of peasants and thereby began an exploitation of people rather than of land. Free land, free peasants, and nonworking landowners, he argues, cannot exist simultaneously. For an explanation of this thesis and for a description of models that show why serfdom came so late to Russia, see Domar, "The Causes of Slavery or Serfdom: A Hypothesis," *Journal of Economic History*, vol. XXX, no. 1 (March 1970), pp. 18–32.

[3] I have sketched Purcell's career in Asia in chapter 1.

vial stripe, meandering through seemingly endless sand, can one sense the essentially parasitic nature of this riverine economy which has lived for thousands of years on the top soil leeched away from the upper reaches of the White and the Blue Nile. When our plane landed at Luxor the crushing, debilitating mid-morning heat made it almost impossible for us to walk a couple hundred yards to a waiting taxi. We went directly to the Winter Palace, where we were shuttered against the burning rays of the sun, and here we engaged a guide who told us we should make our visit to the great temple of Karnak in the evening and cross the Nile very early the next morning for our expedition to the Valley of the Kings.

In this necessarily brief account of our "passage to India" it would be quite impossible for me to describe the majesty of Luxor or the weird beauty of the royal underground tombs. But when we flew back to the relatively cool 102 degrees of Cairo from the furnacelike heat of Luxor, we knew what we wanted to see at the National Museum. We knew how these beautiful things had been stored in the gorgeous subterranean tombs; we understood the contrast between the "city of the living" at Karnak and the "city of the dead" deep in the barren hills across the river.

After the exciting archaeological richness of Egypt the drabness of Bagdad was depressing although I realized from a visit I made to Damascus in 1949 that lovely perfumed courts may lie behind austere mid-Eastern façades. Even so, I must agree with a description of Bagdad which is honest enough to point out that "the streets are crooked, narrow and filthy, houses are low, and the absence of windows in the front renders them exceedingly somber and uninviting."[4] The father of one of my SAIS students, a Harvard doctor of medicine and a master of public health, who graciously drove us around the city and entertained us lavishly on an island in the Tigris River, gave us an even worse impression of Iraq's capital by showing the mud-walled slums where thousands upon thousands of displaced peasants lived with their water buffaloes along the whole city perimeter. "How can one begin to deal with these public-health problems?" asked the discouraged American-trained doctor.

Teheran, the capital of Iran, presented a pleasant contrast. Cool air flows down from the mountains that rise up south of the Caspian Sea, making it pleasant to walk the wide, well-swept streets lined with tempting rug shops. A fine museum allows one to sense the importance of the Zoroastrians and to appreciate the charming, delicate artistic achievements of Persia. We drove to the nearby village of Re where rug makers from a wide area come to wash their "carpets," as rugs are always called in Persia. For rug collectors such as we are this was a high point in our visit to

[4] *The New Funk and Wagnalls Encyclopedia* (New York: Unicorn, 1949), vol. 3, p. 904.

Teheran. To our amazement the lovely Feraghans, Gorevans, Khorassans, and other rugs of the region were carelessly spread out on the red clay hillocks bordering the springs which supply the soft water so eagerly sought. Even more astonishing was the way the dripping wet rugs were "napped" with common hoes before they were tossed on the ground to dry. Unfortunately we could not stay in Iran as long as we would have liked, and soon we were flying over the wide, forbidding deserts on our way to Pakistan. Friends met us at the Karachi airport, and took us to see the few points of interest in this relatively modern city; only some unique small Mughal sarcophagi gave any real flavor of antiquity. For the rest, the excellent port facilities and warehouses, the "bungalows," and the surviving club atmosphere all reflect rather late phases of British imperialism.

We arrived in New Delhi on June 15 and taxied to Claridges Hotel where we had booked our accommodations weeks in advance. On this trip we first saw the great, stately distances in New Delhi, that imperial city of wide avenues and impressive pleasances so majestically conceived for the British raj by Sir Edwin Lutyens. Aside from a few concessions to Mughal architectural ornamentation, the whole spirit of the new-built city of New Delhi is essentially British, a trend noted with some bitterness by Indians as early as 1913. "Why should the style of our Capital," asked an Indian architect, "be such as to express most strongly those alien characteristics in the administration which every year tend more and more to disappear?"[5] By the time New Delhi had been completed and the government moved from Calcutta into the new palatial structures, the British raj had but two more decades to rule the Indian subcontinent. Independence therefore gave the federal government of India a stately, imposing, august capital city, but one that displayed such an essentially European provenance that it "stands vast, incongruous, and wholly alien to northern India. Its huge range of offices are . . . unsuited to the climate. . . . In front there are miles of bungalows and hostels, a hybrid collection. New Delhi is in many ways a fitting monument to [British] rule, but it will remain as a *damnosa hereditas* for the new Federation."[6]

Next day a long drive in a decrepit taxi, driven by a Sikh, took me to the National Council. Down long, wide boulevards I rode; past India Gate with its red-stone arch, past the statue of George V high on a plinth under a Mughal canopy, along another majestic avenue flanked by elegant structures once the embassies of the Princely States, under the Harding railway bridge into a new part of Old Delhi where swarms of white-clad government workers thronged the streets on their way to their bureaucratic duties.

[5] *Report on Modern Indian Architecture*, quoted in *The Legacy of India*, ed. C. T. Garratt (Oxford: Clarendon Press, 1937), p. 406.
[6] *Legacy of India*, p. 407.

Right in the center of a huge cluster of new government and institute buildings a cantonment of miserable huts had grown up, properly labeled as reserved for "backward people." At the public water faucet stood a long queue of seminaked men eagerly waiting their turn for morning ablutions. A few wandering cows further complicated our progress but presently we reached our destination, the National Council's new but already tarnished building, the place where I was to do my research and write my *Market Towns and Spatial Development in India.* But at that moment, I had only the vaguest idea of what would be expected of me.

The very talented director-general of the National Council of Applied Economic Research (NCAER), P. S. Lokanathan[7] graciously assured me that I could choose whatever area of research I wanted to pursue provided it appertained to India; he hoped it might be mainly concerned with the country's Fourth Five-Year Plan which was at the time being drafted. He would, he said, from time to time call upon me to criticize other research activities of my council associates. Such latitude I had scarcely dared hope for, and it was with eager contentment that I settled into my simple workroom and explored the library resources of the council. Staffed with about a score of economists and engineers, working under the supervision of four "directors," the NCAER represented a group of very capable and experienced research workers. A typing pool of about forty men, a number of research and administrative assistants, together with quite a swarm of servants, brought the council's population up to nearly a hundred and fifty people. Four overseas consultants, besides myself, were in residence, two from Canada (an economist and an engineer), one from Australia (a metallurgist), and one from the United States (another economist). During the first few weeks while I was blocking out my research plans, Dr. Lokanathan asked for my critical comments on debt management, proposals for the control of monopolies, the Indian management-agent system and its oligopolistic effects, and a number of other current research projects. But once my own plans had been formulated he left me almost entirely free to concentrate on my own explorations. He approved my over-all research plan and took the time from his very pressing and manifold tasks to read each of my chapters seriatim.

A few days' careful examination of Indian census data confirmed what I already knew in a general way: that almost 80 percent of India's work force was engaged in rural economic activities and that the prospects of

[7] Educated at the University of Madras and the London School of Economics (D.Sc.Econ.), Lokanathan had served as executive secretary of the United Nations Economic Commission for Asia and the Far East (1947–56). Before that appointment he was a member of the Labour Advisory Board of the government of Madras, had been a professor of economics, University of Madras, and editor of the *Eastern Economist.*

development and transformation of the country depended therefore upon finding solutions for something I styled "the village problem," a pattern of economic settlement "where markets are small, where the scale of operations in both agriculture and auxiliary crafts is inadequate and hence largely inefficient; where a good part of the economy is not monetized, and, for that reason, where demand is ineffective as an energizer of industry."[8] There is, to be sure, nothing exceptional about this dispersion of the Indian population; all underdeveloped countries have bloated, slum-cursed, primate cities, on the one hand, and landscapes polka-dotted with simple villages, on the other. The Indian situation merely reflected a greater proliferation of this familiar syndrome, for although the 1961 census revealed that India had 564,718 villages,[9] no corresponding hierarchy of towns and cities existed to link these half-million and more villages to urban areas, to industrial sectors, or to the world economy. With only 2690 towns and cities of every description, the village-town or city ratio factored out at almost 210 to 1. But since, on the average, not more than 35 or 40 villages lay within bullock-cart travel range of any town or city, perhaps 80 percent of the villages had no real reciprocal relations with the Indian urban economy. Because I was convinced that a far more complete integration of agriculture and industry, of town and country, would be necessary if growth, development, and transformation were to be set in motion, I addressed myself to a critical examination of certain institutions that might be utilized for a nationwide "town-centering"[10] program.

As contrasted with all mature or "developed" countries where market towns, spatially dispersed and adequately linked by road networks with hinterland villages, have progressively emerged,[11] in India for centuries the great rural areas have remained almost static in organization. The crying need is for intermediate urbanization, and my rough calculations indicated that if the 564,718 villages were to be linked with the urban-industrial economy in any tolerably satisfactory way, India would need from 14,000 to 16,000 more market towns. Because the architects of the First, Second, and Third Five-Year Plans had almost entirely ignored this prob-

[8] *Market Towns and Spatial Development in India* (New Delhi: National Council of Applied Economic Research, 1965), p. 1.

[9] *Census of India, 1961, Final Population Totals* (New Delhi, 1961), pp. LXI–LXII.

[10] This very useful term has been imaginatively defined and well described by John P. Lewis in his closely reasoned and most provocative book *Quiet Crisis in India: Economic Development and American Policy* (Washington, D.C.: Brookings Institution, 1962), chapter 7.

[11] For historical details for Britain, Belgium, Japan, and the United States, see chapter 2 of my *Organization of Space in Developing Countries* (Cambridge, Mass.: Harvard University Press, 1970).

lem,[12] it would be my argument that the designers of a Fourth Plan ought to face this structural shortcoming of the Indian economy forthrightly and imaginatively by devising programs for coordinating investment activities in such ways that a planned increase in the number of market towns could be achieved. As my research went forward I found striking regional differences in urbanization and market facilities. Thus in northern Mysore, western Maharashtra, southern Gujarat, and the Punjab tolerably satisfactory market-town dispersion had occurred, since these four areas, in 1964, had 70 percent of India's "regulated markets" although they accounted for only 24 percent of the nation's population.[13] But in contrast with these relatively advanced areas, where most villages had some reciprocal relations with market towns, and therefore were parts of "agro-urban" communities, there lay vast stretches of territory where subsistence agriculture was typical and where not thousands but hundreds of thousands of villages had virtually no functional linkage with the national economy. I defined the problem succinctly in a later study[14] as one of finding ways and means for integrating agriculture and industry. As I saw things, promising "growth points" could be found, where development might be quickened by the judicious encouragement of "investment clusters," by the establishment of "regulated markets," and by governmental provision of basic infrastructure — roads, electric power, and warehouses. This is what my book on *Market Towns and Spatial Development* is about, and I am happy that my study has been cordially received not only in academic circles but by government agencies in India, the United States, and elsewhere. Yet my India investigation proved to be merely a pilot study, one that opened up a whole new territory for exploration, and showed the need for a general spatial theory of development. This is what I have tried to articulate and document in my *Organization of Space in Developing Countries*, a book I wrote in 1968–69 when I had the privilege of being a "senior specialist" at the East-West Center in Honolulu.

I worked very, very hard in India and in seven months my market-town study had been completed. My dutiful, quick-witted Indian assistant, P. C.

[12] "Anyone who has lingered in those New Delhi offices where the Third Five Year Plan outlines were being fitted together . . . could only judge that most of the key planners were relatively unexcited about the average geographical scale of developmental activities. They acted as though they thought either that they had other more important things to worry about, or that there was comparatively little . . . they could do . . . to control this aspect of the development pattern." Lewis, *Quiet Crisis in India*, p. 168.

[13] For the figures, and for an explanation of the nature of "regulated markets," see my *Market Towns and Spatial Development in India*, pp. 44–62.

[14] See my chapter on "The Integration of Industrial and Agrarian Development in Regional Planning," in *Regional Perspective of Industrial and Urban Growth: The Case of Kanpur*, ed. P. B. Desai, I. M. Grossack, and K. N. Sharma (Bombay: Macmillan, 1969), pp. 171–190.

Nair, had a wonderful knack of persuading Indian government agencies to release relevant figures and documents. I am also particularly grateful to G. L. Hiranandani of the Directorate of Marketing and Inspection who not only provided me with data on the progress being made by the Indian states in increasing the number and the dispersion of regulated markets but planned a trip for me through Maharashtra and Mysore so that I could visit well-developed market towns and confer with market committees. My wife accompanied me on this journey and very courageously put up with quite a number of unforeseen inconveniences. In our innocence we did not know that travelers on Indian sleeping cars must bring their own bedding, and our first night's trip, from Nagpur to Jalgaon, persuaded us to make hasty arrangements the next day for sheets, blankets, and pillows. We stayed at government "guest houses" where our washing and bathing facilities usually consisted of a faucet and a pail. Many things were unexpected. We had not realized, for example, that on the main rail line from Bombay to Bangalore a first-class sleeping car ticket only gave us each a berth, and we had little privacy in a compartment for twelve men and women. We did, however, make part of our trip by car, so that we could visit the fabulous rock-cave temples of Ajanta and Ellora. We learned a great deal on this trip, however rugged it proved to be. But this journey had not been planned as a pleasure trip; I needed to know very precisely how the very best part of India's rural market system operated. The poorer parts were all too evident.

The contrasts between wealth and poverty, between Plato's "evils" in a commonwealth, literally shriek at you in India. The large homes and the lavish gardens of successful businessmen and the imposing splendor of the maharajas' palaces tend to make the poverty of the millions of pavement dwellers all the more pathetic. I came to understand this gypsylike life of the homeless when, in 1966–67, I participated for several weeks in an international evaluation of the growth, development, and transformation prospects of Kanpur, the largest city (over one million) of Uttar Pradesh, India's most populous state (over 82,000,000). More than 70,000 people live on the Kanpur streets, cooking over open fires, using the fields for toilet facilities, huddling for shelter wherever it can be found when the monsoonal rains deluge the Gangetic plain. Yet the pavement dwellers are only a little worse off than those who have shelter. More than two-thirds of Kanpur's population under roofs live in single-room tenements, where seven to ten persons per room is typical. Only 9.3 percent of the city's tenements have water taps, less than 24 percent have latrines, and only 5.3 percent are equipped with electric lights.[15] To live in India, it has been

[15] For these and other grim features of Indian urban life, see Jal Feerose Bulsara, *Problems of Rapid Industrialization in India* (Bombay: Popular Prakashan, 1964).

said, one must have a very big heart or no heart at all. While we lived at the India International Centre, a well-planned dormitory, library, and dining complex that had been built for visiting scholars by an American foundation, we saw almost every week the striking contrast between the rich and the poor. The rich rented the center facilities to give elaborate parties for their friends and relatives. Groups of a hundred, of two hundred, often even more, were entertained. I asked the center's manager how much per person these parties cost on the average. "They vary widely," he replied, "but five or six dollars per person is about the average cost." The poor, of course, could only stand outside the gates of the center and watch the rich arrive. Still another example will indicate the priorities of the rich in a country whose leaders are very earnestly trying to reduce the spread between luxury and poverty. Each week for the entire eight months we were in India I tried to obtain air tickets so we could visit Kashmir but all to no avail. No travel agency, and not even the NCAER, could help us. Wealthy Indians had booked tickets so far in advance that without using methods I preferred not to employ no tickets could be obtained.

In India, as in most underdeveloped countries, the great cities are steadily leeching talented young people from their ancestral villages. Understandably the young are trying to escape from the hopelessness, the drabness, and the stratification of the villages which are, almost without exception, still controlled by the local landlords and money lenders.[16] The tragedy is the inability of the already overcrowded cities to utilize this incoming stream of young manpower. Careful studies have shown that the "freshers," as the new arrivals are called, have grave difficulty in finding employment[17] even though they are at the very prime of their productive power. Adequate employment that millions of young Indians need can never be found in the burgeoning, slum-cursed cities. Most of it must ultimately be provided in smaller cities and in market towns within con-

See also Ved Mehta, *Portrait of India* (New York: Farrar, Straus and Giroux, 1967), especially pp. 362–363.

[16] The British must bear some responsibility for strengthening the power of this "ruling class" in the villages. In order to assure systematic collection of taxes, the India Company and the British imperial authorities aided and abetted the consolidation of a semifeudal landlordism, widening and normalizing the *Jagirdari* system already in use in the Princely States whereby the *thakurs*, or nobles, collected revenues and exercised feudal authority over tenants and cultivators. This British-favored system steadily encroached on the *ryotwari* system of peasant proprietorship as the larger landholders, by leasing or buying parcels of land, hastened a process of land fragmentization that was making Indian agriculture woefully inefficient.

[17] Bulsara's research group found that "freshers" had unemployment rates that ranged from 33.4 percent (Surat) to 52.8 percent (Gorakhpur). *Problems of Rapid Industrialization in India*, p. 57. I have analyzed in considerable detail the consequences of this planless townward drift in my *Organization of Space in Developing Countries*. See chapter 5 on "Great Cities and the Macro-Economic Consequences of Dual Economies."

venient reach of villages where the workers can continue to live. Agro-urban communities must therefore be planned with complements of industries and trades that will give range and scope to the latent talents and creativity of young people. Yugoslavia has demonstrated how commuting zones can be developed, once the proper kind of investment is made in market towns. In India such market and manufacturing centers not merely could provide employment to men and women in outlying villages, but could be the means whereby the young village population might escape from the debt peonage of village money lenders. Thanks to the emphasis laid on this spatial problem by John P. Lewis, the director of the United States aid program in India from 1965 to 1969, and to the publicity given to my *Market Towns and Spatial Development in India*, recognition of the need for commercial-industrial urban countermagnets is growing. Already by the winter of 1966–67 it was possible to assemble Indian geographers, economists, demographers, town planners, and sociologists to work with a cadre of scholars from the United States and Britain on this spatial development problem in the Kanpur area.[18]

It will not be enough, however, to convince the leaders of underdeveloped countries of the importance of structural reorganization of economic landscapes. If United States aid is to help speed this truly important program, there must be a greater awareness among Washington bureaucrats of the role of spatial factors in development. I was shocked to learn that in the Argentine, where more than a third of the nation's population live in Buenos Aires which is a typical primate city already "strangled for lack of housing,"[19] the United States Agency for International Development (AID) instead of attempting to develop smaller urban countermagnets could think of nothing better to do than to allocate $42,300,000 [20] for cheap housing in Buenos Aires, which will undoubtedly lure still more people to a city now so large that it cannot provide minimally tolerable municipal utilities. Surely this kind of blundering activity on the part of a presumed guiding agency does little honor to the executors of our unplanned imperialism. My experiences in India and my extensive research on this subject have convinced me that the poverty of most underdeveloped countries stems primarily from faulty spatial organization, and that only when agriculture and industry are integrated within "functional economic areas"[21] will the economy be capable of utilizing the economics of scale

[18] The papers produced by the "workshop" that spent several weeks in topical and methodological research before the formal "seminar" was held (January 29 to February 4, 1967) have been published in *Regional Perspective of Industrial and Urban Growth*.

[19] *New York Times*, April 10, 1970.

[20] Ibid.

[21] A term popularized by Brian J. L. Berry, but probably first formulated by Karl A. Fox.

319

and, concurrently, of increasing productivity by intensifying incentives and releasing creative aptitudes so often wasted in occupationally undifferentiated economics.

Since I worked in an Indian research agency, I saw comparatively little of my fellow countrymen in India. I did receive help from some of the AID officials, particularly from John P. Lewis, Laurence Hewes, Jr., Edward Lindblom, Kenneth Kaufman, and Howard Hyde. I met no one from the Ford Foundation even though my salary came from that source. The ambassador, Chester Bowles, probably did not know that I existed. Since I met so few of the people who formally represented the United States, I cannot, from my personal experience, evaluate how successfully they played their several roles. Most of them, including the ambassador, lived modestly, although one at least, aping the customs of imperial nabobs, made an unseemly display of affluence by such archaic symbols as a richly caparisoned coach drawn by four spirited horses. Such aristocratic reversions to nineteenth-century imperialism contrasted with the ambassador's insistence on bush shirts as proper diplomatic attire, presumably as a badge of democracy, or Mrs. Bowles's unfailing choice of a sari rather than a dress. This studied informality of the Bowles family, I was told, offended many Indians, and created most awkward problems of protocol for other diplomats and for Americans with long experience in the foreign service. It is interesting to learn that our present ambassador, Kenneth Keating, and his staff have returned to more formal and traditional attire.

More important than the way our American representatives dressed, the type of households they maintained, or the number of servants they hired, were the policies they recommended to Washington and the evaluation they made of the Indian political and economic situation. I would not presume to appraise the political portion of this policy package, but I did have many reservations about the economic program, which I considered both extravagant and myopic. To provide free food for India's ever-growing population so that at times almost 10 percent of bread grains comes from our largesse does not take very much imagination on the part of program designers, nor does it have any very beneficial effect on investment or productivity.[22] The fertilizer program and the provision of improved seed have had some rather dramatic results, but whether initial soil responses to better seeds and fertilizers can be sustained is by no means clear.[23] Meantime far too much encouragement, in my judgment, has been given to "com-

[22] It has some investment effects, since if the bread grains are sold for local currency, counterpart funds (in this case rupees) will accumulate which, by assumption, can be spent on capital projects without any serious inflationary effects.

[23] For a succinct and skeptical analysis of this problem, see Clifton R. Wharton, Jr., "The Green Revolution: Cornucopia or Pandora's Box?" *Foreign Affairs*, vol. XLVII, no. 3 (April 1969), pp. 464–476.

munity development," a very doubtful recipe for economic progress based on a rather naive assumption that "grass-roots" democracy can be promoted in the unchanged and unreconstructed village communities where local landlords and money lenders have solidified their control over lower castes by pretending to favor cooperatives and village *panchayats*.

I lectured at Andhra and Mysore universities and found in both places an immediate interest in my ideas about spatial development. But I learned more from the very practical farmers and merchants whom I met when I talked to committees that administer "regulated markets" than I did from Indian professors. For these were the men who were actually planning the expansion of market facilities, investing in "industrial estates" to attract light manufacturing, or expanding the mercantile and warehouse facilities of market towns. Strangely enough this whole movement, which has partially modernized large sections of western India, had its origins in British imperialistic ambitions. Ever since the "cotton famine," which caused such serious unemployment in the Lancashire cotton textile towns during the American Civil War, the British tried to promote cotton growing in India. But peasant proprietors or tenant farmers were fearful that specialized agriculture would only deepen their debt peonage to local money lenders. To allay these fears, the British established "regulated markets" for cotton, where growers and traders would control the market operations, and where every cartload of cotton would be sold at open auction by licensed commission agents who would be required to make immediate cash payments for their purchases. By this means a network of regulated markets developed, mostly after the 1890's, to which not only cotton but many other designated farm products were brought. Gradually farmers were able to bypass the local traders and local money lenders, finding their needed market and financial facilities in the far more impersonal, but much more competitive, market towns. But unfortunately in some of the best agronomical areas of India, skinflint usurers and traders have been able, up to the present, to prevent the spread of regulated markets into their monopolized preserves.[24]

We returned from India by way of Karachi, Beirut, Jerusalem, Istanbul, Belgrade, and Geneva. My friend Ernest Teilhac, now a professor at St. Joseph's University in Beirut, met us at the airport there, a delightful reunion after thirty-six years. A former SAIS colleague, Eli Salem, dean of American University, Beirut, also entertained us and we shall long remember the cordial reception we received in Lebanon. Although our stopover in Istanbul was my third visit to that city of slender minarets, the mosques, the early churches, the grand bazaar, and the Seraglio were as

[24] I have explained this monopoloid situation in some detail in chapter 6 of my *Organization of Space in Developing Countries.*

fascinating as ever. In Belgrade dear friends awaited us and it was like old times to visit our former home, to see a faultless reading of *Swan Lake* by the superb Belgrade ballet, and to taste some of our favorite Serbian food again. In Geneva we saw our lovely granddaughter who had been born soon after we arrived in India. All too quickly our long journey was over when, on a bleak cold January night, we arrived at Dulles airport, some twenty miles from Washington, completing my forty-eighth ocean crossing. A year later another trip to India brought the total to an even fifty, thirty-five by air, fifteen by sea. What had all these wanderings, exciting to be sure but often annoying,[25] taught me? I shall try to answer that in my final chapter.

[25] Not only was our house and my office burglarized in Korea, but over a thousand dollars' worth of personal effects were stolen from us in Germany, while in India mail clerks intercepted a letter I had sent to my son and cashed an enclosed check for $250. It takes considerable compassion to forgive and forget all these plus dozens of smaller troubles. Yet in a world where great differences in wealth and income exist, it is entirely possible that we invite predaceous acts by our conscious or unwitting display of affluence.

20

REFLECTIONS ON
A DROP OF DEW

★★★★★★★★★★★★★★★★★

In June 1969 I retired from active teaching at Johns Hopkins and was appointed professor emeritus of economic history. My colleagues arranged a dinner for Mrs. Johnson and myself and I was flattered by the kind things said about me. I particularly appreciated the compliment paid me by the dean of the Faculty of Philosophy of the Johns Hopkins University, G. Heberton Evans, who said that I deserved more credit for making economic history a scientific discipline than anyone else he knew. This, of course, was an overstatement, although it is true that I did start the *Journal of Economic History* and, as Sir William Petty once said, even the blackest crows like to think their offspring are the fairest. My SAIS colleagues also had gracious words, and to all the charitable remarks it became my duty to reply. I began, stealing a phrase from E. B. White, who once pretended to retire, by saying that I thought an emeritus professor, like an apprehended criminal, should just "go quietly," for surely his retirement was no earth-shaking event; all that had happened was that a superannuated old scholar had finally given his last lecture and turned in his last grade sheet. Someone else, very likely someone far more alert to current ideas and modern methodology, would replace him. Quite probably the old man had been out of step with his discipline for quite some time even though his colleagues had listened politely to his outmoded ideas in faculty meetings, and his students, with corresponding charity, had laughed at his oft-repeated archaic jokes. Yet, for all that, should not an oldster, flattered by his designation as professor emeritus, be allowed one more opportunity to voice his views? We all remember in Richard Strauss's tone poem *Till Eulenspiegel* how, even after he was hanged, Till would not yet be quiet; and in the lovely coda his leitmotiv feebly but clearly is heard. There is an extraordinary tenderness in this closing passage because, despite his many mischievous acts, Till was not really despised, and his neighbors were secretly sorry that they had hanged the devilish, lovable rascal. In a sense, I said, I shared this fanciful ambivalence; in this moment of academic immolation might I not, like Till, be allowed one final word?

So I thought that at my symbolic hanging, much in the spirit of another remembered rascal, François Villon, I should offer a garland made of some "flowers of hemp," a chaplet from a few strands of my academic and nonacademic memories. For oddly enough as one grows older, memories assert themselves with amazing vitality, distorted no doubt, but perhaps in an ugly world this might be fortunate. Just fifty years before my retirement from Johns Hopkins, I had been graduated from high school,[1] years that had passed so fast that I was reminded of two precious lines from Housman:

> And since to look at things in bloom
> Fifty springs are little room.[2]

Most of these years had been spent in universities as a student and as a teacher. And what rich opportunity I had to appraise the virtues of almost all varieties of our American higher education — our public universities (Illinois where I was an undergraduate, Oklahoma where I first taught, Maryland and California where I gave seminars); urban universities (George Washington and New York universities — I taught briefly in the former and six years in the latter); and Ivy League universities (Harvard where I taught while taking my doctorate, Cornell where I was an assistant professor for six years, and Pennsylvania where I was briefly a visiting professor). Nor should I fail to mention Johns Hopkins, that citadel of scholarship and academic freedom which had now honored me by an appointment as professor emeritus. Here I spent perhaps the ten happiest years of my life.

But these fifty years were not wholly quiet years for study, writing, and teaching. How can anyone of my generation forget Georges Clemenceau's bittersweet words, "The glory of our civilization is that it enables us occasionally to live an almost normal life"? Yes, but only occasionally. From high school I went into the army even as I did again in 1943. Seven years

---

[1] When on the fiftieth anniversary of my graduation from high school I endowed an annual prize and gave the commencement address, I recalled Samuel Johnson's remark to Sir Joshua Reynolds. "Everyone," said the crusty lexicographer, "has a lurking wish to appear considerable in his native place."

[2] From "Loveliest of Trees," from *A Shropshire Lad* (authorized edition), from *The Collected Poems of A. E. Housman*. Copyright 1939, 1940, © 1959 by Holt, Rinehart and Winston, Inc. Copyright © 1967, 1968 by Robert E. Symons. Reprinted by permission of Holt, Rinehart and Winston, Inc., and The Society of Authors as the literary representative of the Estate of A. E. Housman.

later a third war involved me, that cruel war in Korea which destroyed almost everything that five years of dedication, unbelievable dedication by Koreans and Americans, had created. Yet despite these military and governmental interludes that brought me to the trial of Vidkun Quisling and the inauguration, for better and for worse, of Syngman Rhee, it had been in the university world that I had mostly lived.

I was only twenty-two years old when I began my university career as an instructor at the University of Oklahoma. By odd circumstance an amateurish poem by an Oklahoma undergraduate may have had a rather important influence in shaping my academic style. In a small book of verses, the *University Anthology*, published in 1922, there was a short poem I have never forgotten. It was called "The Professor" and went as follows:

> Here he sits droning
> Of some forgotten truth
> Heedless of springtime
> Intolerant of youth.
>
> Here he sits dryly
> Day after day
> Woodenly sober and
> Slim as his pay.

For me there was a razorlike edge to this student reaction to professorial remoteness, and I resolved the instant I read it that I would never be pedantic, I would never be dull, and I would not be poor. This did not mean, however, that I would try to ingratiate myself with students, ape their ways, or become familiar or informal. To the best of my knowledge I have never called a student, undergraduate or graduate, by his first name while he was my student. Some may call this snobbishness; I call it respect. If there has been any one thing I have tried to do as a teacher it has been to maintain in my small way those rich traditions of the great medieval universities wherein a scholar was treated like a prince because his kingdom was the domain he had chosen in the *oikoumenikos* of scholarship.

There are a few things that I have absorbed not from books or from learned colleagues but from the harsh world of war and difficult reconstruction tasks after war. I have thought a great deal about my experiences in Britain, Norway, Germany, Korea, Japan, Greece, Yugoslavia, and Italy. What did I really learn in these days of frightening responsibility? Actually only three things. The first is easiest to explain; indeed it needs no explanation because the post-World War II period has made it so patently clear. It is just this: as a nation we are seldom as moral as we would like to believe we are!

The second thing I learned calls for a little explanation, as does the third. It was in Norway in 1945 that a second truth was revealed. During the winter of 1944 the Germans had withdrawn from north Norway under terrific Russian pressure. After destroying virtually every house, haystack, barn, and boat in the northern Norwegian provinces, they built, in the dead of winter, what they thought would be impregnable defenses at the narrowest point between the mountains and the sea. Here a German army holed up for the winter with some 30,000 horses. In April of 1945, when the Allied Land Forces liberated Norway, the feeding of these 30,000 horses became our problem. After fruitless efforts to find oats and hay, and ships to move animal food almost a thousand miles, I had to make a decision about these German horses. In consort with G-4, the air force, and the Norwegian Department of Agriculture, the decision was made: we would fly every available veterinarian to the German camp and these experts would examine the horses to determine how many could begin the long trek south through fields still covered with snow. The rest would be slaughtered. It was a very easy decision to make, and everything went according to plan. The Norwegians had a fine supply of good, nutritious (nature-frozen) horse meat which they desperately needed, plus some 21,000 green hides, which they needed fully as much; meantime we were saved the trouble and expense of finding food for thousands of hungry horses, nor did we need to mortgage scarce shipping space for moving animal fodder and feed. By this strange event I learned that it is really much easier to make large decisions than to make small ones. But whereas this decision proved to be a wise one, not all easily made big decisions are necessarily the most judicious.

The third thing I learned in ten years and more of decision-making was by no means as agreeable. When, because I had had considerable experience in Norway, France, and Germany in civil-affairs operations, I was made civil administrator two months after I arrived in Korea in 1946, I was understandably flattered by that appointment but my vanity lasted less than one calendar week. I think it was the fourth or fifth day after I took office that I received from the Justice Department of our government in Korea a "writ of execution" to be signed by the military governor. It was sent to me for my approval. Not knowing what to do I wrote on a "buck slip" addressed to General Archer Lerch, the military governor, "any commutation of this [death] sentence is discretionary with the Military Governor." A half hour later General Lerch came into my palatial office and told me in no uncertain terms that he expected a recommendation on every single piece of paper I sent to him. I had not expected to have responsibility over the life or death of Koreans, and the weight of this responsibility was overwhelming. I spent hours reviewing death sentences before I made my recommendations. But I came to an agreement with

General Lerch: he promised never to tell me what decision he reached; and from this I derived a little peace of mind because when I made my recommendation I had squared things as best as I could with my conscience. What did I learn from this painful experience? Brooding about it I concluded that most of the achievements that are commonly called "success" are really not worth seeking; and this conclusion has profoundly tempered my ambition, leaving me sadder and older, but, I hope, perhaps just a little wiser.

With these three important lessons that I had learned in a troubled decade when one's work was seldom noticed or appreciated except by a few, I came back to the university world, years behind my stay-at-home colleagues, with a vast backlog of unread new books and articles to study. How fortunate I was to come to Johns Hopkins, particularly to the School of Advanced International Studies where some of my overseas experiences could partially compensate for my deficiencies. But back in the classroom after so long an absence, once again I was faced with an intellectual problem that had haunted me before the war: the question of what one can teach or should try to teach. This issue is no longer an academic one; year by year the revolt of young people throughout the world has made it a question of the greatest urgency. Perhaps we university teachers are largely responsible for this endemic dissatisfaction, this wave of scorn. Hear what Yevtushenko says:

> How do they dare teach anyone
> While they themselves are not quite normal?
> They give prescriptions but cannot, even
> Take the country's temperature.[3]

Perhaps we have worshiped false gods. Perhaps scholarship is not enough. I wonder how many thousand times I have thought about Santayana's admonition:

> It is not wisdom to be only wise,
> And on the inward vision close the eyes,
> But it is wisdom to believe the heart.[4]

Perhaps the revolt that distresses so many — I cannot quite decide whether to applaud or censure — has arisen because we have tried to be too wise, offering only what we thought was wisdom to hungry souls. I have long been puzzled and worried about what Havelock Ellis expressed so succinctly when he said that we have but two choices; we may seek truth or we may seek beauty. Either is a meritorious goal, but there is this fundamental difference: if a man seeks truth he can find it only relatively, where-

[3] "Monologue of Dr. Spock," printed in the *Washington Post*, June 18, 1968.
[4] "Sonnet III," from *Poems* by George Santayana (New York: Scribner's, 1923), p. 5.

as if he seeks beauty he can find it absolutely. Perhaps the sin for which we are expiating is that we forgot to give the young men and women entrusted to our care any vision of beauty. "The prophet and the poet may regenerate the world without the economist," said Philip Wicksteed, "but the economist cannot regenerate it without them."

There is a hunger for something better than the fare our generation has given the young. We have been vainglorious, wanting to bask in the reflected glory that would come from our scholarly students. We have trained them to be like ourselves not realizing that the whole pattern of values was changing. All too many of us, I fear, may have forgotten Kierkegaard's observation that although life can be understood backward "it must be lived forward." And yet before we despair and conclude ruefully that all our striving has been in vain — those endless hours of study and research, those thousands of lectures, seminars, and conferences, those meticulously handwritten pages of manuscripts — perhaps we need to ask ourselves what we have a right to expect. What makes us so vain as to suppose that any one of us can make a noticeable permanent impression on this vast, everchanging world? The answer, of course, is that we can never know what imprint we may have made. Perhaps we should think about those lovely last lines of the poem Yeats called "Gratitude to the Unknown Instructors":

> What they undertook to do
> They brought to pass;
> All things hang like a drop of dew
> Upon a blade of grass.[5]

And there I suspect I had best leave this mystery. For myself I am wholly content with a drop of dew. For I recognize that we live in an infinity of space and, like Whitman, "I know the amplitude of time." What I have tried to do, and others must decide whether I have succeeded, is to impart, to those who cared, some small measure of truth linked in some hidden way with an intimation of beauty.

What could I then say as a final word to my beloved colleagues? What wish could I make for them and for our wonderfully useful institution? If an agnostic may invoke the deity without blasphemy, I said, perhaps I could do no better than to repeat the words of Miguel de Unamuno, "May God deny you peace but give you glory," with only this one addendum. May that glory be something more than scholarship, however correct and felicitous; may it be a glory that will flame like a roseate Grecian sunrise because it stems from a deeper understanding of the intellectual and artistic hunger of creative young minds, from a more honest effort to discover their needs, their aspirations, and their dreams.

[5] *The Collected Poems of W. B. Yeats* (New York: Macmillan, 1934), p. 292. Permission to reprint these lines was granted by Macmillan and A. P. Watt and Son.

PUBLISHED WRITINGS OF E. A. J. JOHNSON

PUBLISHED WRITINGS OF
E. A. J. JOHNSON, 1928-1971
★★★★★★★★★★★★★★★★★★★★★★★★★★★

BOOKS

1. *American Economic Thought in the Seventeenth Century*. London: P. S. King, 1932. Reprinted, New York: Russell and Russell, 1961.
2. *Some Origins of the Modern Economic World*. New York: Macmillan, 1936.
3. *Predecessors of Adam Smith: The Growth of British Economic Thought*. New York: Prentice-Hall, 1937; London: P. S. King, 1937. Reprinted, New York: Augustus M. Kelley, 1960 and 1965.
4. *An Economic History of Modern England*. New York: Nelson, 1939.
5. *The Origins and Development of the American Economy* (with Herman Krooss). New York: Prentice-Hall, 1953. Serbo-Croatian translation, Zagreb, 1958.
6. *The American Economy: Its Origins, Development and Transformation* (with Herman Krooss). New York: Prentice-Hall, 1960.
7. *Market Towns and Spatial Development in India*. New Delhi: National Council of Applied Economic Research, 1965.
8. *The Organization of Space in Developing Countries*. Cambridge, Mass.: Harvard University Press, 1970.
9. *American Imperialism in the Image of Peer Gynt: Memoirs of a Professor-Bureaucrat*. Minneapolis: University of Minnesota Press, 1971.
10. Translator, *Pioneers of American Economic Thought in the Nineteenth Century*, by Ernest Teilhac. New York: Macmillan, 1936. Reissued, New York: Russell and Russell, 1967.
11. Editor, *The Dimensions of Diplomacy*, by McGeorge Bundy, Henry A. Kissinger, W. W. Rostow, James R. Killian, Jr., Adolf A. Berle, and Livingston Merchant. Baltimore: The Johns Hopkins Press, 1964. Reprinted, 1967.

CHAPTERS IN BOOKS

12. "The Age of Mercantilism." In *Planned Society, Yesterday, Today and Tomorrow*, ed. Findlay Mackenzie. New York: Prentice-Hall, 1937. Pp. 79–107.
13. "Cambiamenti Nell'Orientamento E Nella Composizione Del Commercio Estero Dal 1918 in Poi." In *Lezioni Sul Commercio Estero*. Padua: Cedam, 1958. Pp. 205–219.
14. "Problems of 'Forced-Draft' Industrialization: Some Observations Based on the Yugoslav Experience." In *Contributions and Communications, First Inter-*

national Conference of Economic History. Paris and The Hague: Mouton, 1960. Pp. 479–488.

15. "Economic Ideas of John Winthrop." In *Issues in American Economic History*, ed. Gerald D. Nash. Boston: Heath, 1964. Pp. 8–12.

16. "New Tools for the Economic Historian." In *Readings in United States Economic and Business History*, ed. Ross M. Robertson and James L. Pate. Boston: Houghton Mifflin, 1966. Pp. 12–18.

17. "The Place of Learning, Science, Vocational Training and 'Art' in Pre-Smithian Economic Thought." In *Readings in the Economics of Education*, ed. Mary Jean Bowman, Michel Debeauvais, V. E. Komarov, and John Vaizey. Paris: UNESCO, 1968. Pp. 25–37.

18. "The Nature and Significance of Creativity." In *Contributions to Psychology*, ed. A. K. P. Sinha. New Delhi: Institute for Social and Psychological Research, 1968. Pp. 60–72.

19. "The Integration of Industrial and Agrarian Development in Regional Planning." In *Regional Perspective of Industrial and Urban Growth: The Case of Kanpur*, ed. P. B. Desai, I. M. Grossack, and K. N. Sharma. Bombay: Macmillan, 1969. Pp. 171–190.

DICTIONARY AND ENCYCLOPEDIA ARTICLES

20. "Jonathan Amory." *Dictionary of American Biography*, vol. I, pp. 260–261.
21. "Elisha Cooke." *Dictionary of American Biography*, vol. IV, pp. 381–382.
22. "Thomas Cushing." *Dictionary of American Biography*, vol. IV, pp. 632–633.
23. "Gerard de Malynes." *Encyclopaedia of the Social Sciences*, vol. X, pp. 69–70.
24. "Edward Misselden." *Encyclopaedia of the Social Sciences*, vol. X, pp. 535–536.
25. "John Rae." *Encyclopaedia of the Social Sciences*, vol. XIII, p. 68.

JOURNAL ARTICLES

26. "Some Evidence of Mercantilism in the Massachusetts Bay," *New England Quarterly*, vol. I (July 1928), pp. 371–375.

27. "Economic Ideas of John Winthrop," *New England Quarterly*, vol. II (April 1930), pp. 235–250.

28. "Sir William Petty's Views on London," *Sociological Review*, vol. XXII (July 1930), pp. 219–223.

29. "The Mercantilist Concept of 'Art' and 'Ingenious Labour,' " *Economic History*, vol. II (January 1931), pp. 234–253.

30. "Nehemiah Grew, Forgotten Mercantilist," *American Economic Review*, vol. XXI (September 1931), pp. 463–480.

31. "L'économie synthetique de Hume," *Revue d'histoire économique et sociale*, vol. XIX, No. 3 (1931), pp. 225–243.

32. "Unemployment and Consumption; the Mercantilist View," *Quarterly Journal of Economics*, vol. XLVI (August 1932), pp. 698–719.

33. "British Mercantilist Doctrines Concerning the 'Export of Work' and 'Foreign-Paid Incomes,' " *Journal of Political Economy*, vol. XL (December 1932), pp. 750–770.

34. "Early American Economic Thought," *Papers and Proceedings of the Forty-Fifth Annual Meeting of the American Economic Association* (Supplement to vol. XXIII of the *American Economic Review*), March 1933, pp. 85–87.

35. "Gerard de Malynes and the Theory of the Foreign Exchanges," *American Economic Review*, vol. XXIII (September 1933), pp. 441–455.

36. "The Encyclopaedia of the Social Sciences," *Quarterly Journal of Economics*, vol. L (February 1936), pp. 355–366.

37. "Just Price in an Unjust World," *International Journal of Ethics*, vol. XLVIII (January 1938), pp. 165–181.
38. "New Tools for the Economic Historian," *Tasks of Economic History* (Supplemental Issue of *Journal of Economic History*), vol. I (December 1941), pp. 30–38.
39. "Riflessioni Sull'Esperienza Americana in Materia di Monopoli," *Rivista Della Società*, vol. II (July–August 1957), pp. 878–895.
40. "Federalism, Pluralism and Public Policy," *Journal of Economic History*, vol. XXII (December 1962), pp. 427–444.
41. "The Place of Learning, Science, Vocational Training and 'Art' in Pre-Smithian Economic Thought," *Journal of Economic History*, vol. XXIV (June 1964), pp. 129–144.
42. "Capitalism and Communism: Problems of Coexistence," *Conspectus* (Quarterly Journal of the India International Centre), First Quarter, 1965, pp. 28–46.
43. "Istota i znaczenie twórczósci," *Zagadnienia Naukoznawstwa*, vol. IV, no. 8 (1966), pp. 164–173.
44. "Industrialization and Economic Growth: Problems of Methodology," *Journal of Economic Issues*, vol. I (September 1967), pp. 221–230.

OTHER ARTICLES

45. "Echoes of Hellas in Tompkins County," *The Jeffersonian*, December 1934, pp. 10–11.
46. "The Kress Library of Business and Economics," *Harvard Alumni Bulletin*, November 11, 1938, pp. 219–223.
47. "The Nature and the Price of Economic Progress," *SAIS Review*, Summer 1962, pp. 3–18.
48. "The Meaning of History, Change and Progress," *India International Centre Pamphlet*, August 1964, pp. 1–17.

BOOK REVIEWS

49. *L'Amérique a la conquête de l'Europe*, by Charles Pomaret. *Books Abroad*, October 1931, pp. 368–370.
50. *Readings in the History of Economic Thought*, by S. H. Patterson. *American Economic Review*, vol. XXII (September 1932), pp. 479–480.
51. *Property in the Eighteenth Century with Special Reference to England and Locke*, by Paschal Larkin. *Journal of Political Economy*, vol. XLI (June 1933), pp. 427–428.
52. *English Public Finance, 1558–1641*, by Frederick C. Dietz. *American Economic Review*, vol. XXIII (June 1933), pp. 345–347.
53. *Studies in English Trade in the Fifteenth Century*, by Eileen Power and M. M. Postan. *American Economic Review*, vol. XXIII (December 1933), pp. 704–705.
54. *Tracts on Political Economy*, by W. Spence. *American Economic Review*, vol. XXIV (June 1934), pp. 290–291.
55. *The Money Supply of the American Colonies before 1720*, by Curtis P. Nettels. *Annals of the American Academy of Political and Social Science*, July 1955, p. 221.
56. *The Estates of Crowland Abbey, a Study in Manorial Organization*, by Frances M. Page. *Journal of Political Economy*, vol. XLIII (August 1935), pp. 562–564.
57. *Financial and Commercial Policy under the Cromwellian Protectorate*, by M. P. Ashley. *American Economic Review*, vol. XXV (September 1935), pp. 525–527.

58. *Ottoman Statecraft*, by W. L. Wright, Jr. *American Economic Review*, vol. XXV (September 1935), pp. 535–536.
59. *Le Livre de Comptes de Guillaume Ruyelle, changeur à Bruges*, by Raymond De Roover. *American Economic Review*, vol. XXV (December 1935), pp. 769–770.
60. *Myself*, by John R. Commons. *Philosophical Review*, vol. XLV (May 1936), p. 326.
61. *Mercantilism*, by Eli Hechscher. *American Economic Review*, vol. XXVI (June 1936), pp. 306–307.
62. *Boisguilbert, Economist of the Reign of Louis XIV*, by Hasel Van Dyke Roberts. *American Economic Review*, vol. XXVI (September 1936), pp. 720–721.
63. *An Economic History of the Western World*, by Harry Elmer Barnes. *Annals of the American Academy of Political and Social Science*, September 1937, pp. 192–193.
64. *Paradoxes inedits de Malestroit*, by Luigi Einaudi. *American Historical Review*, vol. XLIII (January 1938), pp. 370–371.
65. *Les relations politiques et les échanges commerciaux entre le Duche de Brabant et l'Angleterre au moyen âge*, by J. de Sturler. *American Economic Review*, vol. XXVIII (March 1938), pp. 135–136.
66. *The Economic Library of Jacob H. Hollander*, compiled by Elsie A. G. Marsh. *Journal of the American Statistical Association*, vol. XXXIII (September 1938), pp. 608–609.
67. *Authority and the Individual; Independence, Convergence and Borrowing in Institutions*, Harvard Tercentenary Lectures. *Philosophical Review*, vol. XLVII (July 1938), pp. 442–445.
68. *Economic History of Modern Britain*, Vol. III, by J. H. Chapham. *Annals of the American Academy of Political and Social Science*, January 1939, pp. 270–271.
69. *Christianity, Capitalism and Communism*, by Albert Hyma. *Journal of Modern History*, vol. XI (January 1939), pp. 70–71.
70. *Nassau Senior and Classical Economics*, by Marian Bowley. *Annals of the American Academy of Political and Social Science*, May 1939, pp. 233–234.
71. *The English Business Company after the Bubble Act, 1720–1800*, by Armand B. DuBois. *Annals of the American Academy of Political and Social Science*, May 1939, pp. 245–246.
72. *Adam Smith as Student and Professor*, by William R. Scott. *Annals of the American Academy of Political and Social Science*, May 1939, pp. 232–233.
73. *On the Economic Theory of Socialism*, by Oskar Lange and Fred M. Taylor. *Philosophical Review*, vol. XLVIII (July 1939), pp. 445–446.
74. *Early British Economics from the XIIIth to the Middle of the XVIIIth Century*, by M. Beer. *American Economic Review*, vol. XXIX (September 1939), pp. 560–561.
75. *The Zollverein*, by W. O. Henderson. *Annals of the American Academy of Political and Social Science*, November 1939, pp. 206–207.
76. *Henry George*, by Albert Jay Nock. *Annals of the American Academy of Political and Social Science*, January 1940, pp. 234–235.
77. *La Guerre dans la pensée économique du XVIe au XVIIe siècle*, by Edmond Silberner. *Journal of Modern History*, vol. XII (September 1940), pp. 391–392.
78. *Colbert and a Century of French Mercantilism*, by Charles W. Cole. *American Economic Review*, vol. XXX (June 1940), pp. 376–378.
79. *A Hundred Years of Economic Development*, by G. P. Jones and A. G. Pool. *Annals of the American Academy of Political and Social Science*, January 1941, pp. 217–218.
80. *Industry and Government in France and England, 1540–1640*, by John U. Nef.

Annals of the American Academy of Political and Social Science, January 1941, pp. 219–220.

81. *A History of Economic Ideas,* by Edmund Whittaker. *Philosophical Review,* vol. LI (January 1942), pp. 80–81.

82. *The Immigrant in American History,* by Marcus Lee Hansen. *Annals of the American Academy of Political and Social Science,* March 1941, pp. 236–237.

83. *The Triumph of American Capitalism,* by Louis M. Hacker. *Annals of the American Academy of Political and Social Science,* March 1941, pp. 252–253.

84. *English Economic History Mainly since 1700,* by C. R. Fay. *Journal of Economic History,* vol. II (March 1942), pp. 89–90.

85. *The Politics of Mercantilism,* by Philip W. Buck. *American Economic Review,* vol. XXXII (September 1942), pp. 564–566.

86. *The Economic Mind in American Civilization,* vols. 4 and 5, 1918–33, by Joseph Dorfman. *Economic History Review,* vol. XII (April 1959), pp. 489–490.

87. *Etudes d'économie humaniste: introduction, l'économie humaniste et le capitalisme mercantiliste,* by E. Antonelli. *Journal of Political Economy,* vol. LXIX (February 1961), p. 84.

88. *Nouvelles études d'économie humaniste: le capitalisme du XIXeme siècle, de 1814 à 1914 et le monde économique present de 1914 à 1957,* by E. Antonelli. *Journal of Political Economy,* vol. LXIX (February 1961), pp. 84–85.

89. *Alexander Hamilton, The National Adventure, 1788–1804,* by Broadus Mitchell. *Journal of Economic History,* vol. XXIII (March 1963), pp. 122–124.

90. *New Korea: New Land of the Morning Calm,* by Kyung Cho Chung. *American Historical Review,* vol. LXVIII (April 1963), pp. 816–817.

91. *The Great Hunger,* by Cecil Woodham-Smith. *Journal of Economic History,* vol. XXIV (March 1964), pp. 120–121.

92. *The Common Aid Effort,* by Milton J. Esman and Daniel S. Cheever. *Journal of Economic Issues,* vol. II (December 1968), pp. 238–239.

93. *The Agrarian History of England and Wales,* vol. IV, 1500–1640, ed. Joan Thirsk. *Journal of Economic History,* vol. XVIII (December 1968), pp. 742–745.

94. *The Cambridge Economic History of Europe,* vol. IV: *The Economy of Expanding Europe in the Sixteenth and Seventeenth Centuries,* ed. E. E. Rich and C. H. Wilson. *Journal of Economic History,* vol. XXIX (June 1969), pp. 389–391.

EDITED BOOKS IN THE PRENTICE-HALL ECONOMICS SERIES

95. *Planned Society, Yesterday, Today and Tomorrow,* ed. Findlay Mackenzie. 1937.

96. *Elements of Modern Economics,* by Albert L. Meyers. 1937; second edition, 1941; third edition, 1948; fourth edition, 1956.

97. *Modern Banking,* by Rollin G. Thomas. 1937.

98. *The Theory of Prices,* by Arthur Marget. 2 vols. 1938.

99. *Labor Problems and Labor Law,* by Albion G. Taylor. 1939; second edition, 1950.

100. *History of Economic Thought,* by Eric Roll. 1940; second edition, 1942; third edition, 1956.

101. *Modern Economic Problems,* by Albert L. Meyers. 1940; second edition, 1948.

102. *Business Cycles,* by James A. Estey. 1941; second edition, 1950; third edition, 1956.

103. *The Economics of War,* by Horst Mendershausen. 1941; second edition, 1943.

104. *Modern Economics: Elements and Problems,* by Albert L. Meyers. 1941.

105. *Our Modern Banking and Monetary System,* by Rollin G. Thomas. 1942; second edition, 1950.

106. *Economic Analysis and Public Policy*, by Mary Jean Bowman and Lee Bach. 1943, second edition, 1949.
107. *Corporate Concentration and Public Policy*, by Harry S. Purdy, William Carter, and Martin Lindahl. 1943; second edition, 1950; third edition, 1959.
108. *The Growth of the American Economy*, by Harold Williamson. 1944; second edition, 1951.
109. *Modern Economic Thought*, by Allan Gruchy. 1948.
110. *Income and Employment*, by Theodore Morgan. 1948.
111. *The Economics of John Maynard Keynes*, by Dudley Dillard. 1949.
112. *Introduction to Economics*, by Theodore Morgan. 1950; second edition, 1957.
113. *Intermediate Economic Theory*, by Stephen Enke. 1950.
114. *Elementary Economics*, by J. A. Norden and Virgil Salera. 1950.
115. *Economic Ideas*, by Ferdinand Zweig. 1950.
116. *Elements of Economic Analysis*, by Archibald McIsaac. 1951.
117. *Russia's Soviet Economy*, by Harry Schwartz. 1951; second edition, 1955.
118. *Fiscal Policy and the American Economy*, by Kenneth Poole. 1951.
119. *Industrial Pricing and Market Practices*, by Alfred R. Oxenfeldt. 1951.
120. *Economics, Basic Problems and Analysis*, by Clifford James. 1951.
121. *Managerial Economics*, by Joel Dean. 1951.
122. *Taxation and the American Economy*, by William Anderson. 1952.
123. *Development of Economic Thought*, by Philip Newman. 1952.
124. *An Economic History of Europe*, by Heinrich Friedlaender and Jacob Oser. 1952.
125. *Economic Warfare*, by L. Wu. 1953.
126. *American Economic Development*, by Herman Krooss. 1956.
127. *Economic Development of the North Atlantic Community*, by Dudley Dillard. 1967.

FORTHCOMING PAPERS

128. "Sources and Methods of Study of Land Transport." In *Contributions and Communications, Fifth International Congress of Economic History* (Leningrad).
129. "Spatial Reconstruction as a Condition of Economic Growth." In *Contributions and Communications, Fifth International Congress of Economic History* (Leningrad).
130. "The Responsibility of the International Fraternity of Scientists for Economic Development." In *Proceedings of the Fourth International Conference on Science and Society* (Herceg-Novi, Yugoslavia).

INDEX

INDEX

★★★★★★